THE BEL CANTO OPERAS

Other Books by
Charles Osborne

The Complete Operas of Mozart
The Complete Operas of Puccini
The Complete Operas of Strauss
The Complete Operas of Verdi
The Complete Operas of Wagner

The
BEL CANTO
Operas

of Rossini, Donizetti and Bellini

CHARLES OSBORNE

METHUEN

First published in Great Britain in 1994
by Methuen London
an imprint of Reed Consumer Books Ltd
Michelin House, 81 Fulham Road, London SW3 6RB
and Auckland, Melbourne, Singapore and Toronto

A CIP catalogue record for this book
is available at the British Library

ISBN 0 413 68410 5 hardback
ISBN 0 413 68650 7 paperback

Typeset by
Wilmaset Ltd, Birkenhead, Wirral
Printed and bound in Great Britain
by Mackays of Chatham, plc

CONTENTS

Introduction   1

I. Gioachino Rossini (1792–1868)   3
1. From *Demetrio e Polibio* to *Il Signor Bruschino*   5
2. From *Tancredi* to *Sigismondo*   29
3. From *Elisabetta, regina d'Inghilterra* to *Otello*   46
4. From *La Cenerentola* to *Mosè in Egitto*   69
5. From *Adina* to *La Donna del lago*   85
6. From *Bianca e Falliero* to *Semiramide*   98
7. From *Il Viaggio a Reims* to *Guillaume Tell*   115

II. Gaetano Donizetti (1797–1848)   137
8. From *Il Pigmalione* to *Il Fortunato inganno*   139
9. From *L'Ajo nell'imbarazzo* to *Il Giovedì grasso*   155
10. From *Il Paria* to *Ugo, Conte di Parigi*   183
11. From *L'Elisir d'amore* to *Marino Faliero*   209
12. From *Lucia di Lammermoor* to *Les Martyrs*   240
13. From *Le Duc d'Albe* to *Ne m'oubliez pas*   270

III. Vincenzo Bellini (1801–1835)   307
14. From *Adelson e Salvini* to *I Capuleti e i Montecchi*   309
15. From *La Sonnambula* to *I Puritani*   332

Bibliography   355
Discography   356
Appendix   367
Index   369

For

JOAN SUTHERLAND

and

RICHARD BONYNGE,

beloved twentieth-century keepers

of the bel canto flame

INTRODUCTION

The Italian term 'bel canto' can have a number of meanings. Literally 'beautiful song' or 'beautiful singing', it is applied to a method of singing taught by the Italian masters of the seventeenth and eighteenth centuries in which smooth emission of tone, beauty of timbre and elegance of phrasing are among the most important elements. Although Rossini is said to have exclaimed, in a conversation which took place in Paris in 1858, 'Alas for us, we have lost our bel canto', the expression did not begin to be generally used in this sense until the late nineteenth century, at a time when the kind of opera to which the bel canto style of performance was most suited had been superseded by the music dramas of Wagner and the operas of the Italian school of *verismo* or realism.

Today, the term is used mainly to describe the predominant style of Italian opera in the first half of the nineteenth century, from Paisiello, for example, to middle-period Verdi. The composers of this era include Cherubini, Mayr, Spontini, Federico Ricci, Luigi Ricci, Pacini, Mercadante, and a host of lesser names such as Federici, Generali, Carafa, Coppola, Fioravanti, Paer and Morlacchi.

However, the three great composers of the bel canto era were Rossini, Donizetti and Bellini, and it is the *oeuvre* of these giants of Italian opera in the first half of the nineteenth century that I examine and describe in this volume. Somewhat, though never completely, out of favour in the earlier years of the twentieth century, the operas of these three composers began to be performed again in the 1950s and subsequently, to a large extent because of the emergence of several sopranos and mezzo-sopranos with the style, technique, range and beauty of voice to perform their leading roles in the manner in which they were meant to be heard. Pre-eminent among these artists were Joan Sutherland, Maria Callas, Leyla Gencer, Beverly Sills, Montserrat Caballé, Giulietta Simionato and Marilyn Horne. They have fortunately been succeeded by a number of exciting younger singers, just as Nicolai Gedda and Alfredo Kraus have been followed by several younger tenors, most of them American, able to cope with the high-lying tessitura frequently required of the bel canto tenor.

To the average opera-goer in the first half of the twentieth century, Rossini meant *Il Barbiere di Siviglia*, Donizetti *Lucia di Lammermoor* and Bellini *Norma*. But now, at least a dozen other operas by Rossini are quite frequently to be encountered, along with many more by Donizetti, and even four or five by the less prolific, shorter-lived Bellini. And more are being offered from year to year. I hope this volume may prove a useful guide to these composers' operas, some of them more imposing works than others, but all of them springing from a genre whose intention was to move, to delight, but never to depress its audience. I have included not merely the major operas of these three composers, but all of their operas: Bellini's ten, Rossini's thirty-nine, and Donizetti's sixty-five.

My thanks are due to Mr John Carter for his help in compiling the Discography.

C.O.

I

Gioachino Rossini

1792–1868

I

From *Demetrio e Polibio* to *Il Signor Bruschino*

Demetrio e Polibio

opera seria in two acts

Principal characters:
Demetrio, King of Syria   (tenor)
Polibio, King of Parthia   (bass)
Lisinga, daughter of Polibio   (soprano)
Siveno, son of Demetrio   (contralto)

LIBRETTO by Vincenza Viganò Mombelli

TIME: The second century B.C.
PLACE: Parthia

FIRST PERFORMED at the Teatro Valle, Rome, 18 May 1812, with
Domenico Mombelli (Demetrio); Lodovico Olivieri (Polibio);
Ester Mombelli (Lisinga); Marianna Mombelli (Siveno)

Giuseppe Antonio Rossini, the thirty-two-year-old municipal
trumpeter of the small Adriatic seaside town of Pesaro, lodged in the
house of the Guidarini family, one of whose three daughters was a
local prostitute. The eldest daughter, Anna, was nineteen, a
beautiful young seamstress whose fine natural soprano voice was
later to earn her engagements at provincial opera houses despite her
lack of musical knowledge or training. Giuseppe Rossini and Anna
Guidarini became lovers. When it was discovered that Anna was
pregnant, they were married, and five months later, on 29 February

1792, their first child, Gioachino Antonio was born. (Though the customary modern spelling is 'Gioacchino', Rossini himself usually spelled his name with one c.)

Gioachino Rossini began to reveal his musical ability at a very early age: by the age of thirteen he was proficient not only on the piano but also on viola and horn. In addition, he was much in demand locally as a boy soprano, and soon began to compose music, including a number of arias, and five duets for horns which he wrote for his father and himself to play. When Rossini senior was dismissed from his ill-paid municipal post because of his political opinions, he and his wife Anna accepted engagements in a number of theatres in the vicinity, he as instrumentalist, she as soprano.

While they were touring, Gioachino was left in Pesaro in the care of his aunt and his grandmother. Eventually his parents settled in Bologna, and young Rossini, now aged fourteen, joined them there. In Bologna he was able to obtain at the Liceo Musicale the kind of musical tuition which had been lacking in Pesaro. His teacher, Padre Stanislao Mattei, had been a pupil of the famous Padre Martini (with whom, thirty-five years earlier, the fourteen-year-old Mozart had studied briefly in Bologna).

Mattei gave Rossini the basic grounding in strict counterpoint which was to stand him in good stead in later years. The young composer was eighteen when he left the Liceo, by which time he had won a prize for counterpoint and had written a great deal of music. The six delightful *sonate a quattro* for two violins, cello and double-bass which he composed in 1804 are by no means mere juvenilia. But by 1806, when he was fifteen, Rossini had also written his first opera, although it was not to reach the stage until 1812. This was *Demetrio e Polibio*.

In 1805, the tenor Domenico Mombelli and his family arrived in Bologna. Mombelli, his two daughters Ester and Marianna, and a bass, Lodovico Olivieri, comprised a small touring opera group, and it was during their sojourn in Bologna that the tenor gave Rossini, piece by piece, the libretto of an *opera seria*, *Demetrio e Polibio*, written by his wife Vincenza Viganò Mombelli, and asked the young composer to write several numbers for it. Signora Mombelli's libretto, derived from Metastasio's *Demetrio*, which in turn may have taken some of its situations from Corneille's *Don Sanche d'Aragon*, tells the story of two lovers, Lisinga, daughter of Polibio, King of Parthia, and Siveno, estranged son of Demetrio, King of Syria. Siveno is living in the Parthian court under the patronage of Polibio. When his father, Demetrio, arrives and demands his return to Syria, Siveno refuses to go, at which Demetrio has Lisinga seized. Her father, Polibio, in turn arrests Siveno, and the plot develops along easily predictable lines.

Though he can hardly have been inspired by Vincenza Mombelli's stiffly conventional libretto, and indeed composed most of the numbers without knowing the entire plot, Rossini produced a score which was perfectly stageworthy, and in parts rather more than that. In later life he was to tell the German conductor-composer Ferdinand Hiller, 'Originally I composed it for the Mombelli family without knowing that it would turn into an opera.' Presumably it cost Domenico Mombelli less to buy a number of separate pieces from the child-composer than to commission an opera from him. By the time Mombelli staged the work in Rome in 1812, the young Rossini's name had become known because of the five other operas which he had written subsequently and which had been successfully produced in Venice, Bologna and Ferrara. It is possible that two arias, Demetrio's 'Presenta in questi doni', and Siveno's 'Perdon ti chiedo, o padre', as well as all the recitative, were composed by Mombelli.

The overture and the majority of the solo numbers are undistinguished, and the score exhibits a distinct lack of dramatic movement except in the vigorous Act I finale, and the Act II quartet, 'Donami ormai, Siveno', with its lively opening and the delicate charm of its *andante*, 'Padre, qual gioia prova', launched by the soprano. By far the most attractive number in the entire opera is the lovers' Act I duet, 'Questo cor ti giura amore', in which the mature Rossini's authentic voice (or one of them) makes its first appearance. Typically Rossinian in its mood of idyllic rapture, the melody sung in thirds by Siveno and Lisinga is one which the composer was to make use of on several future occasions. It is this kind of melody, concealing ecstatic feeling under a serenity of expression, which is at the heart of bel canto. In his *Life of Rossini* (published during the composer's lifetime, in 1824), the French novelist and critic Stendhal wrote of this duet that 'it is impossible to convey the mystic sweetness of love with greater delicacy, or with less poignant sadness'.

After its première in Rome in 1812, *Demetrio e Polibio* was performed in a few other Italian towns, and by 1820 had also been staged abroad in Vienna, Dresden and Munich, after which it seems not to have been heard of again until 1979 when it was revived in the small Italian town of Barga, in the province of Lucca. A concert performance was given in Martina Franca in 1992, but the work is unlikely ever to make its way into the general operatic repertory.

Stendhal, who saw *Demetrio e Polibio* in Como only two years after its Rome première, thought ludicrously highly of it:

> We were *transported* – there is no other word for it. Each successive item was a positive banquet, a miracle of singing at its purest, of melody at its most enchanting. In a moment we seemed to be spirited away among the shady walks of some enchanted parks – it might have been Windsor – where each new vista seemed fairer than all that had gone before, until at last, reflecting upon one's own wondering astonishment, one realised with something of a shock that one had bestowed the supreme award for beauty upon twenty different objects.

Stendhal reserved his greatest praise for the quartet, 'Donami omai, Siveno':

> ... I do not hesitate to assert that this quartet must number among Rossini's most masterly inventions. I know nothing anywhere which can surpass it. If Rossini had composed nothing but this one quartet, Mozart and Cimarosa would still have recognised in him a man who was their equal as an artist.

La Cambiale di matrimonio
(The Bill of Marriage)

farsa giocosa in one act

Principal characters:

Tobia Mill, an English merchant	(bass)
Fanny, his daughter	(soprano)
Slook, a Canadian merchant	(bass)
Edoardo Milfort, in love with Fanny	(tenor)
Norton, Mill's cashier	(bass)
Clarina, Fanny's chambermaid	(mezzo-soprano)

LIBRETTO by Gaetano Rossi

TIME: The eighteenth century

PLACE: London

FIRST PERFORMED at the Teatro San Moisè, Venice, 3 November 1810, with Rosa Morandi (Fanny); Tommaso Ricci (Edoardo Milfort); Luigi Raffanelli (Tobia Mill); Nicola de Grecis (Slook); Domenico Remolini (Norton); Clementina Lanari (Clarina)

In 1810, shortly after leaving the Bologna Liceo, Rossini met the composer-conductor Giovanni Morandi and his soprano wife Rosa. The Morandis, friends of Rossini's parents, were on their way to Venice to join the Marchese Cavalli's company at the Teatro San Moisè, a small theatre specialising in one-act comic operas which were known as *farse* (farces). When a German composer failed to deliver the opera he had been contracted to write, the Morandis persuaded Cavalli to take a chance on the eighteen-year-old Rossini who, although he had already written his first opera, *Demetrio e Polibio*, had not yet seen it staged. The young composer left at once for Venice, where Cavalli handed him a one-act farce libretto, *La Cambiale di matrimonio* written by Gaetano Rossi and based on a 1790 comedy, *Matrimonio per lettere di cambio*, by Camillo Federici. Within a few days Rossini had completed the composition of his first comic opera.

At the first rehearsal, some members of the cast complained that Rossini's music was difficult to sing, and that his orchestration was too heavy. The young composer retired to his lodgings and wept, but then made a few adjustments to his score. Coupled with another one-act piece, Farinelli's *Non precipitare i giudizi*, Rossini's farce in one act of approximately eighty minutes opened at the Teatro San Moisè on 3 November 1810, and was given at least twelve performances during the month. It was reasonably successful in Venice, was staged the following year in Trieste and Padua, and was first performed abroad in Barcelona in 1816. It was produced in Vienna, first in 1834 as *Der Bräutigam aus Canada*, and then three years later in its original Italian. Years of neglect followed, but the opera was revived in its centenary year, 1910, at the Teatro La Fenice, Venice, since when it has managed to hold the stage reasonably well. Its first American performance was in New York in 1937, and the work reached Britain in 1954 when a company from Rome performed it in London at Sadler's Wells Theatre.

The opera's very busy plot concerns the attempts of Tobia Mill, an English businessman, to force his daughter Fanny into marriage with Slook, a rich Canadian merchant who has offered him a large sum of money for a beautiful young wife. Fanny, who is in love with young Edoardo Milfort, learns of the scheme from Clarina, her chambermaid, and Norton, her father's cashier. When Slook arrives, Fanny immediately makes it clear to him that his attentions are unwelcome, at which the understanding and magnanimous Slook signs the marriage contract over to Edoardo and makes him his heir. Slook's announcement to Tobia that he will not marry Fanny leads to his being challenged to a duel, but when Tobia learns that his daughter is in love with Slook's heir, he professes himself satisfied. Slook prepares to return to Canada, and the opera ends in general rejoicing. (Some synopses of the plot refer to 'Sir Tobia Mill', but both Tobia and Edoardo are once or twice addressed by other characters as though they were knights only because the Italian librettist failed to distinguish between 'Sir' and 'Esquire'.)

Rossi's libretto is neither better nor worse than the average *opera buffa* which Italian librettists were churning out in the early nineteenth century, but it is greatly enhanced by Rossini's sparkling score. The eighteen-year-old composer, whose only previous writing for the stage had been in the high romantic vein of *opera seria*, proved to have a distinct gift for comedy.

La Cambiale di matrimonio consists of an overture and eleven numbers, mostly separated, as was customary, by dialogue delivered in *recitativo secco*, or recitative accompanied not by the orchestra but by a keyboard instrument. The overture to an opera, in the pre-Verdian era of Italian opera, did not usually include themes from the work itself. It was a free-standing orchestral piece which was expected to anticipate the mood of the opera it preceded. With only a few days in which to compose *La Cambiale di matrimonio*, Rossini merely revised an Overture in E flat which he had written the previous year, one of four which he had composed as a student in Bologna. A charming, if conventional piece, it happens to end in exactly the same way, with the same chords and rhythm, as the overture to Rossini's final opera, *Guillaume Tell*, composed twenty years later.

The opening duettino, 'Non c'è il vecchio sussurone', for Clarina and Norton, gets the comedy off to a lively start, and it is swiftly followed by Tobia Mill's engaging cavatina, 'Chi mai trovo il dritto, il fondo'. The duet for Fanny and Edoardo, 'Tornami a dir che m'ami', is delightful, Slook's entrance music is wittily scored, and his cavatina ('Grazie, grazie') is attractive, as is his duet with Fanny, 'Darei per si bel fondo'. The beginning of the trio which ensues when Edoardo enters ('Quell' amabile visino') adds a certain elegance to the general vivacity, and there is some fluent *buffo* writing for the two basses, Tobia Mill and Slook, in their *allegro vivace* duet, 'Dite, presto', Mill's frenzy contrasting nicely with Slook's calmer *legato*. Their second duet, 'Porterò così il cappello', when Mill challenges Slook to a duel, makes a somewhat tame beginning to the finale which, however, eventually makes up in high spirits for what it lacks in invention. The chambermaid Clarina's aria, 'Anch'io son giovane', is a charming little piece, but by far the most enjoyable number in the score is Fanny's *allegro agitato* aria, 'Vorrei spiegarvi', whose lively yet graceful opening is followed by a melody of gentle charm and an agile concluding section which its parsimonious composer was to put to good use again six years later in the Rosina–Figaro duet, 'Dunque io son la fortunata', in *Il Barbiere di Siviglia*.

In its blend of gaiety and sentiment, *La Cambiale di matrimonio* engagingly initiates the individual style which Rossini was to display in his later and better-known *opere buffe*. Though perhaps a trifle long (about eighty minutes) for a one-act comic opera, it would make a delightful companion-piece to a more dramatic curtain-raiser in any double bill.

L'Equivoco stravagante
(The Absurd Misunderstanding)

dramma giocoso in two acts

Principal characters:

Ernestina, daughter of Gamberotto   (soprano)
Rosalia, her maid   (mezzo-soprano)
Gamberotto, a farmer   (bass)
Buralicchio   (bass)
Ermanno, Ernestina's tutor   (tenor)

LIBRETTO by Gaetano Gasparri

TIME: The early-nineteenth century
PLACE: Italy

FIRST PERFORMED at the Teatro del Corso, Bologna, 26 October
1811, with Marietta Marcolini (Ernestina); Angiola Chies
(Rosalia); Domenico Vaccani (Gamberotto); Paolo Rosich
(Buralicchio); Tommaso Berti (Ermanno)

After the success of *La Cambiale di matrimonio* in Venice, Rossini
returned to Bologna fairly confident that he would soon receive
another commission. New operas in the early nineteenth century
were staged as frequently as new plays are today, and any composer
of reasonable competence could expect to make a decent living by
accepting invitations from theatres and impresarios who needed a
fresh supply of operas each season. In Bologna, Rossini took up a
position as coach with the Accademia dei Concordi, for whom he
conducted a performance of Haydn's oratorio, *The Seasons*, shortly
after his return from Venice. It was some months later, in the
summer of 1811, that he received a commission from an impresario
who was mounting a season of operas in Bologna at the Teatro del
Corso. Rossini was engaged to conduct, from the cembalo, performances of two operas by other composers, Portogallo's *L'Oro non
compra amore* and Pavesi's *Ser Marcantonio*, and to compose a new
opera.

The libretto he was given was *L'Equivoco stravagante*, a comedy in
two acts by Gaetano Gasparri, who is described by a twentieth-
century biographer of Rossini as 'a very mediocre bungler of
librettos living in Florence'. Gasparri's absurd plot involves a young
woman's impecunious lover, Ermanno, tricking his rich rival,
Buralicchio, into believing that Ernestina, the object of their
affections and the daughter of a *nouveau riche* farmer, is really a
eunuch disguised as a woman, who has deserted from the army.
Ernestina is arrested by a troop of soldiers, but is freed by Ermanno,
and all eventually ends well, at least for her and Ermanno whom she
realises she really loves.

Gasparri's libretto (which Stendhal thought was 'of surpassing
badness') was set to music by Rossini very swiftly, as was his wont,
and the opera was staged at the Teatro del Corso on 26 October
1811. A newspaper report published a few days later stated that the
music was greeted with applause, and that an aria and a quintet

were encored. 'However,' it continued, 'that the libretto is vicious is demonstrated by the resolution taken by the extremely vigilant prefecture which has forbidden any further performance.' In other words, after three performances Rossini's opera was suppressed by the police on grounds of obscenity. Adapted to another libretto, *L'Equivoco stravagante* was staged in Trieste in 1825, after which it fell into complete neglect until it was revived in Siena in September 1965 in a version edited by Vito Frazzi which was subsequently staged in Ireland at the Wexford Festival in 1968.

A vocal score of the opera published by Ricordi in the mid-nineteenth century begins with the orchestral piece we know today as the Overture to *Il Barbiere di Siviglia*. When Rossini used it for that opera in 1816, he had already made use of it on at least two earlier occasions, as the overture to both *Aureliano in Palmira* (1813) and *Elisabetta, regina d'Inghilterra* (1815). Whether he composed it first for *L'Equivoco stravagante* is not certain. It is possible that the original overture to *L'Equivoco stravagante* may have been used again later by Rossini for another opera, and that his publisher made the choice of overture for publication.

The opera contains highly delightful arias for Ernestina and Ermanno, less interesting ones for Gamberotto and Buralicchio, and some lively ensembles. The finest number in the score is a quintet in Act II which is taken in part from the quartet in *Demetrio e Polibio* and was to be used again the following year in *La Pietra del paragone*. Much is made by writers on Rossini of his self-borrowings; but many great composers, Bach and Handel among them, recycled their works in this manner, and it would have been ridiculously profligate for an Italian composer of the first half of the nineteenth century not to re-use arias or ensembles buried in operas which he had no reason to expect would ever be revived.

L'Inganno felice
(The Happy Stratagem)

farsa in one act

Principal characters:
Isabella　　　　　　　(soprano)

Duke Bertrando   (tenor)
Tarabotto, a miner   (bass)
Batone   (bass)

LIBRETTO by Giuseppe Maria Foppa

TIME: The distant past
PLACE: A seaside mining village in Italy.

FIRST PERFORMED at the Teatro San Moisè, Venice, 8 January 1812, with Teresa Giorgi-Belloc (Isabella); Raffaele Monelli (Bertrando); Filippo Galli (Tarabotto); Luigi Raffanelli (Batone)

A few weeks after the ban on further performances of *L'Equivoco stravagante*, its doubtless somewhat depressed composer was delighted to be offered another commission by the Teatro San Moisè in Venice, where *La Cambiale di matrimonio* had been successful the previous year. In December 1811 Rossini left Bologna again for Venice, and set to work composing *L'Inganno felice* to a libretto by the Venetian Giuseppe Maria Foppa (based on Giuseppe Palomba's libretto for an opera of the same title by Paisiello which had been staged in Naples in 1798). At its première in January 1812, Rossini's *L'Inganno felice* was greeted enthusiastically, and proved to be even more successful than *La Cambiale di matrimonio*. It played until the last night of the season, when portraits of its prima donna, Teresa Giorgi-Belloc, were sold in the theatre, and her fans let loose doves, canaries and guinea-fowl from the boxes. Within the next few years the opera was performed in Barcelona, Munich, Vienna, Lisbon, Dresden, Berlin, London (on 1 July 1819), Madrid, Warsaw and Paris. On 11 May 1833 it was given its American première in New York. It has been revived occasionally in the present century, most notably in Rome in 1952, at the Wexford Festival in 1970, and at the Rossini Festival in Pesaro in 1980.

Though classified as a farce, *L'Inganno felice* is really a romantic comedy, if indeed it can be described as a comedy at all. Banished and abandoned at sea years previously by her husband, Duke Bertrando, at the instigation of Ormondo, his villainous confidant, the Duchess Isabella has been living in a seaside mining village as Nisa, the niece of Tarabotto, the miners' leader who had rescued her. The arrival of the Duke with Ormondo and his henchman, Batone, leads eventually to Bertrando and Isabella being reunited.

The opera's serious aspect is introduced at the beginning of its graceful overture in which Rossini later offers his first and somewhat tentative attempt at the orchestral *crescendo* for which he was to become famous. The nine tuneful and attractively scored numbers include two arias for Isabella, a wistful cavatina, 'Perchè dal tuo seno', and the affecting 'Al più dolce e caro oggetto' with its forceful cabaletta. Even the villainous Batone is allowed a graceful aria ('Una voce m'ha colpito') with cabaletta. A splendid *buffo* duet, 'Va taluno mormorando', for Tarabotto and Batone, reveals the young Rossini's skill in writing effervescent and light-hearted music. Duke Bertrando's aria, 'Qual tenero diletto', is rather bland, but an extended trio, 'Quel sembiante, quello sguardo' (which borrows from *L'Equivoco stravagante*), is notable for Isabella's affecting contribution to it. The opera's cleverly constructed finale is lively, inventive and colourfully scored.

Lasting no more than seventy-five minutes, *L'Inganno felice* is among the most interesting and attractive of early Rossini operas. Writers have noted traces of Paisiello, Cimarosa, and even Mozart in its score, but what is surely more notable is the apparent ease with which so youthful and inexperienced a composer assumed his own voice. As the Italian musicologist Guido Pannain put it, 'Non ebbe infanzia artistica, e fu subito lui' (He did did not have an artistic infancy: he was suddenly himself).

Ciro in Babilonia
(Cyrus in Babylon)

opera in two acts

Principal characters:

Baldasarre (Belshazzar), King of Babylon	(tenor)
Ciro (Cyrus), King of Persia	(contralto)
Amira, his wife	(soprano)
Argene, her confidante	(soprano)
Zambri, adviser to Baldasarre	(bass)
Arbace, Captain of the Babylonian army	(tenor)
Danielo (Daniel), a Hebrew prophet	(bass)

LIBRETTO by Conte Francesco Aventi

TIME: 539 B.C.
PLACE: Babylon

FIRST PERFORMED at the Teatro Comunale, Ferrara, 14 March 1812, with Marietta Marcolini (Ciro); Elisabetta Manfredini (Amira); Anna Savinelli (Argene); Eliodoro Bianchi (Baldasarre); Giovanni Layner (Zambri); Francesco Savinelli (Arbace); Giovanni Fraschi (Danielo)

After the success of *L'Inganno felice* in Venice in January 1812, its twenty-year-old composer was much in demand. For the Teatro Comunale in Ferrara he wrote his next opera within two or three weeks, and it was given its première in Ferrara on 14 March. *Ciro in Babilonia*, if one discounts *Demetrio e Polibio*, was Rossini's first real attempt at full-scale *opera seria*, though it was deliberately announced as a 'dramma con cori' (drama with choruses) or oratorio, in order to allow it to be staged during Lent when secular theatrical performances were forbidden. Drama was promised in the opera's subtitle, 'La Caduta di Baldasarre' (The Fall of Belshazzar), but its libretto by a Ferrara literary dilettante, Count Francesco Aventi, emphasised the choral element and was written in a stiff, essentially undramatic style.

Years later, Rossini told Ferdinand Hiller that *Ciro in Babilonia* had been a fiasco: 'When I returned to Bologna after its unfortunate performance, I found an invitation to a meal. I went to the confectioner's and ordered a ship made of marzipan. On its pennant it bore the name "Ciro". Its mast was broken, its sails were in tatters, and it lay on its side, shipwrecked in an ocean of cream. Amid great hilarity, the happy company devoured my wrecked vessel.' But *Ciro* was by no means a complete failure. It was produced in a number of Italian towns during the fifteen years following its première, as well as being staged abroad in Munich, Vienna and Weimar. In London it was given a concert performance at the Theatre Royal, Drury Lane, on 30 January 1823. The opera seems not to have been performed subsequently until it was revived in Savona in 1988.

Aventi's libretto is derived largely from the *Cyropedia*, the Athenian writer Xenophon's biography of Cyrus; from Book 1 of the Greek historian Herodotus; and from Chapter 5 of the Old Testament Book of Daniel. Belshazzar (Baldassare in Italian), King of Babylon, lusts after his prisoner Amira, whose husband Cyrus (Ciro), King of Persia, he has defeated in battle. In an attempt to rescue her, Cyrus too is captured and imprisoned. Belshazzar's feast is interrupted by thunder, lightning, and a mysterious hand which writes on the palace wall an obscure message: 'Mene, Mene, Tekel, Upharsin'. The prophet Daniel (Danielo) interprets the words as a sign of the wrath of God, and Belshazzar's astrologers advise him to sacrifice Cyrus, Amira and their child. However, before sentence of death can be carried out, news is received of the defeat of Babylon by Persian forces. Cyrus now becomes King of Babylon and is acclaimed by his people.

As the town of Ferrara had not heard a note of *L'Inganno felice*, Rossini clearly saw no reason why he should not use its overture again for *Ciro in Babilonia*, and did so. The Babylonians' opening chorus of celebration is appropriately jolly, and the bass cavatina, 'Ed a Ciro oppresso e vinto', with its cabaletta or concluding section in a somewhat faster tempo, contains some enjoyable florid writing for the voice. The duet which follows for Baldasarre and Amira, 'T'arrendi', is equally lively, and Ciro's first aria, 'Ahi! come il mio dolore, come calmar potrò'', has a delicate and affecting vocal line. The arias for Arbace and Danielo are disappointingly lifeless, but the choral writing throughout the opera is confident.

The most attractive numbers are Amira's two plaintive arias – although in the second, 'Deh, per me non v'affligete', her vocal line is upstaged by a sensuous violin obbligato – and the Act II finale in which Rossini really gets into his stride, even though he has recourse to some material from *Demetrio e Polibio*. (Amira's first aria, 'Vorrei veder lo sposo', was to be pressed into service again six years later in *Mosè in Egitto*.)

Argene's 'Chi disprezza gli infelici', an *aria di sorbetto*, or short aria sung by a subsidiary character while the gentry in the boxes took refreshments, has an amusing provenance. As Rossini told Hiller, Anna Savinelli, Ferrara's *seconda donna* who sang the role of Argene, was

> ugly beyond all description, and with a voice to match. After the most careful testing, I found that she had a single note, the middle B flat, which didn't sound too bad. I therefore wrote an aria in which she had to sing only that one note. I gave all the melody to the orchestra and, as the piece was liked and applauded, my singer-on-one-note was delighted with her triumph.

Ciro in Babilonia is undoubtedly an uneven work. However, although it lacks the feeling for pace and dramatic structure which Rossini was already exhibiting in his *farse*, it nevertheless contains some charming and, in places, powerful music. Its neglect is undeserved: it certainly merits an occasional revival.

La Scala di seta
(The Silken Ladder)

farsa in one act

Principal characters:

Giulia	(soprano)
Lucilla, her cousin	(mezzo-soprano)
Dorvil, Giulia's husband	(tenor)
Germano, a servant	(bass)
Blansac	(bass)
Dormont, Giulia's father	(tenor)

LIBRETTO by Giuseppe Maria Foppa

TIME: The eighteenth century
PLACE: Paris

FIRST PERFORMED at the Teatro San Moisè, Venice, 9 May 1812, with Maria Cantarelli (Giulia); Carolina Nagher (Lucilla); Rafaele Monelli (Dorvil); Gaetano Del Monte (Dormont); Nicola De Grecis (Blansac); Nicola Tacci (Germano)

Even before the première of *Ciro in Babilonia*, it was announced in the press that the young Rossini had agreed to write a new farce for the spring season at the Teatro San Moisè, Venice, where two of his operas, *La Cambiale di matrimonio* and *L'Inganno felice* had already been successfully launched. The libretto of the new piece, *La Scala di seta*, was by Giuseppe Maria Foppa, the librettist of *L'Inganno felice*, and was based on the play *L'Échelle de soie* by François-Antoine-Eugène de Planard, or more probably on the libretto (derived from the same play) of the French composer Pierre Gaveaux's *L'Échelle de soie*, which had been staged in Paris in 1808.

On 9 May 1812, less than two months after the première of *Ciro in*

Babilonia, the new opera was staged at the Teatro San Moisè, sharing a triple bill with a ballet and one act of Pavesi's *Ser Marcantonio*, an opera which had scored an enormous success at its première in Milan eighteen months earlier. (*Ser Marcantonio* held the stage until 1843 when Donizetti's *Don Pasquale*, a setting of the same subject, displaced it.)

Although it continued to be played in repertoire for several weeks, *La Scala di seta* was criticised, principally for the staleness of its libretto whose plot was considered to have plagiarised that of Cimarosa's opera, *Il Matrimonio segreto* (1792), which at the time of its première had been thought to lean heavily on the play, *The Clandestine Marriage* by George Colman and David Garrick (1766).

After being performed in Sinigaglia in 1813, revived at the San Moisè, the theatre of its première, in 1818, and produced abroad, in Barcelona in 1823 and Lisbon in 1825, *La Scala di seta* seems to have disappeared from the stage for more than a century, although its overture became a popular concert piece. The opera was revived in Florence in 1952, and in Rome in 1953. The Rome ensemble, the Piccolo Teatro dell' Opera Comica, brought their production to London, where *La Scala di seta* was seen for the first time on 26 April 1954, at Sadler's Wells Theatre. It is now quite frequently performed: in 1992 it surfaced in several towns in Italy, Germany and Poland.

The silken ladder of the title is used nightly by Dorvil to join Giulia whom he has secretly married, but who is still living in the house of her father, Dormont, who wishes to marry her to Blansac (who is loved by Giulia's cousin, Lucilla). An occasion on which the ladder is used in turn by Dorvil, Blansac and Dormont leads to the opera's denouement in which Dorvil reveals to all that he is Giulia's husband, Dormont accepts the situation, and Lucilla and Blansac are paired off happily.

After the bubbling and justly popular overture with its fresh, bright orchestral colours and delightful writing for the woodwind, a piece which a critic once happily described as being like 'a brightly coloured puppy chasing its tail', the opera begins with a prolifically tuneful duet for Giulia and the servant Germano, which becomes a trio with the entrance of Lucilla. Of *La Scala di seta*'s eight separate numbers, only four are arias, the plot being for the most part carried forward swiftly by its ensembles. Even so, the opera contrives to last for a good hour and a half, just a little too long for its content, delightful though most of that is. The copious *recitativo secco* between numbers could, with impunity, be shortened for performance.

A duet for Giulia and Germano, 'Io so ch'ai buon core', begins delicately and ends in vivacious *fioriture*. Dorvil's aria, 'Vedrò qual sommo incanto', a gift to any bel canto tenor with its languorous opening section and robust cabaletta, is followed by one of the finest numbers in the score, the quartet, 'Si che unito a cara sposa', an ensemble which anticipates Verdi in its intensity and rhythmic energy in which the four characters, Giulia, Dorvil, Blansac and Germano, express their differing emotions of astonishment, jealousy, annoyance and embarrassment. In the quartet's concluding *allegro*, Rossini's *crescendo* trademark makes an effective appearance.

Lucilla's scintillating 'Sento talor nell' anima' (which Rossini later turned into a chorus in *Il Turco in Italia*) is followed by Giulia's beautiful three-part aria, 'Il mio ben sospiro e chiamo', with its delicate writing for woodwind and its air of what Stendhal calls Rossini's 'candeur virginale'. Germano's 'Amore dolcemente', in the course of which he sings himself to sleep, is attractive, and the elaborate finale, involving all the characters, reveals the composer at his most elegantly inventive.

Many years after Rossini's death, a letter was published which was supposed to have been written by the young composer to Cera, the Venice impresario, immediately after the première of *La Scala di seta*, denouncing Cera for having provided him with an awful libretto, and boasting that, 'in causing you to have a fiasco, I have repaid you with interest.' The letter (no autograph of which has ever surfaced) was almost certainly a fake, not only because it is highly unlikely that the young Rossini would have behaved in so professionally suicidal a manner, but also because the *opera buffa* he composed for Cera is a perfectly delightful piece of its kind.

La Pietra del paragone
(The Touchstone)

melodramma giocoso in two acts

Principal characters:
Donna Fulvia   (mezzo-soprano)

La Baronessa Aspasia	(soprano)
La Marchesina Clarice	(contralto)
Giocondo	(tenor)
Il Conte Asdrubale	(bass)
Pacuvio	(bass)
Il Conte Macrobio	(bass)
Fabrizio	(bass)

LIBRETTO by Luigi Romanelli

TIME: The eighteenth century
PLACE: An Italian country villa

FIRST PERFORMED at the Teatro alla Scala, Milan, 26 September 1812, with Marietta Marcolini (Clarice); Carolina Zerbini (Aspasia); Orsola Fei (Fulvia); Filippo Galli (Asdrubale); Claudio Bonoldi (Giocondo); Antonio Parlamagni (Macrobio); Pietro Vasoli (Pacuvio); Paolo Rossignoli (Fabrizio)

On 18 May 1812, nine days after the Venice première of *La Scala di seta*, Rossini's very first opera, *Demetrio e Polibio*, reached the stage in Rome (see pp 5–8). Rossini had returned from Venice to Bologna, where he received a commission (probably on the recommendation of the contralto Marietta Marcolini with whom he had become intimate) to compose an opera for the Teatro alla Scala, Milan, which was then, as now, the leading opera house in Italy. Making his way to Milan, he began work immediately on *La Pietra del paragone*, a two-act *opera buffa* with a libretto by Luigi Romanelli, who had been writing libretti for La Scala for several years. When *La Pietra del paragone* was given its première at La Scala on 26 September 1812 with Marietta Marcolini as Clarice, it was an instantaneous success and was performed fifty-three times during the season.

Rossini was now without a doubt Italy's leading young composer. Within the following ten years his new opera was staged abroad in Munich, Oporto, Paris, Lisbon and Barcelona. It reached Vienna in 1821, in German translation as *Weiberproben*. The opera's first American performance did not take place until 1955, at the Hartford College of Music. Its British première followed in 1963 at the St Pancras Town Hall, London. During the 1950s and 1960s there were Italian productions in Florence, Milan, Naples, Venice and

Pesaro. A German adaptation by Günther Rennert, entitled *Die Liebesprobe* (The Love Test), was produced in Hamburg in 1962, and soon became popular in other German opera houses. (It was this version, translated back into Italian from Rennert's German, which Glyndebourne in 1964 oddly chose to stage.) A successful Piccola Scala production of 1982 was revived in Modena as recently as 1992.

Romanelli's plot can briefly be summarised as follows: in order to test the sincerity of three women, Clarice, Aspasia and Fulvia, all of whom hope to marry him, the wealthy Count Asdrubale pretends to have been dispossessed of his fortune. Clarice, the only one to survive the test, then turns the tables on Asdrubale by impersonating her twin brother who objects to their union. Of course all ends happily, except for Aspasia and Fulvia who are forced to seek other lovers.

Act I contains some dull patches, but also several lively ensembles: the opening number sung by Asdrubale's guests, the cheerful gardeners' chorus ('Il Conte Asdrubale'), a gently flowing trio ('Su queste piante incisi') and the energetic finale which Stendhal thought 'the most perfect *buffo* finale that [Rossini] ever composed'. (But Stendhal's chapter on *La Pietra del paragone*, which he considered 'Rossini's masterpiece of unadulterated *opera buffa*', ranking it above *Il Barbiere di Siviglia*, abounds in extravagant judgements.) It is in a sextet in this finale that Count Asdrubale, disguised as a Turk intent on sequestering Asdrubale's estate, keeps repeating the word 'Sigillara' (let the seals be affixed) to great comic effect – or at least Rossini's Milanese audiences thought so. A duet for Clarice and Asdrubale ('Conte mio') in Act I with romantic horn accompaniment is quite charming, but Pacuvio's ostensibly comic aria, 'Ombretta sdegnosa del Missipipi' (*sic*), is more than somewhat laboured.

The *allegro giusto* ensemble which begins Act II is irresistible, and so, too, is the hunting chorus which follows it. Rossini must have been pleased with the music with which he depicts a storm, for he was to use it in two later operas. It gives way to an atmosphere of peacefulness into which Giocondo's *andante* aria, 'Quell' alme pupille', with its attractive writing for the clarinet, is gently inserted. A dull, lengthy quintet, 'Spera se vuoi', is followed by Fulvia's brilliant aria, 'Pubblico fu l'oltraggio', and a fine trio, 'Prima fra voi coll' armi' which Rossini used again four years later in *La Gazzetta*.

Clarice's double aria, 'Se per voi le care io torno', leads into the opera's energetic finale.

Although in his later comedies Rossini's musical characterisation was to become more assured, and certainly more precise, *La Pietra del paragone* is valuable for the wealth of melodic invention and rich orchestration its composer brought to it, as well as for its, at times, almost Mozartian tenderness of mood.

L'Occasione fa il ladro
(Opportunity Makes the Thief)

burletta per musica in one act

Principal characters:

Berenice	(soprano)
Ernestina, her servant	(soprano)
Conte Alberto	(tenor)
Don Eusebio, Berenice's uncle	(tenor)
Don Parmenione	(bass)
Martino, his servant	(bass)

LIBRETTO by Luigi Prividalli

TIME: The eighteenth century
PLACE: In and near Naples

FIRST PERFORMED at the Teatro San Moisè, Venice, 24 November 1812, with Giacinta Canonici (Berenice); Carolina Nagher (Ernestina); Gaetano Del Monte (Don Eusebio); Tommaso Berti (Conte Alberto); Luigi Pacini (Don Parmenione); Luigi Spada (Martino)

After the huge success of *La Pietra del paragone* at La Scala, Rossini, though still not twenty-one years of age, could have had his next opera produced at any theatre he chose. What he chose was to accept another commission – actually two commissions – from the not especially prestigious Teatro San Moisè in Venice, which had been the first to stage an opera by Rossini two years earlier. (Another consequence of the success of *La Pietra del paragone* was that its composer, who would have been liable to be called up for military service on reaching his twenty-first birthday, was granted exemption.)

Of the two one-act farces Rossini now agreed to write for the Teatro San Moisè, the first was *L'Occasione fa il ladro, ossia Il Cambio della valigia* (Opportunity Makes the Thief, or A Suitcase Exchanged). The libretto which the impresario Cera gave Rossini had been written by a Venetian hack, Luigi Prividalli. Rossini composed his score in eleven days, and the opera was performed on 24 November 1812 to an audience which received it with indifference. It was given four further performances before being dropped from the repertoire of the San Moisè.

Rossini's great international fame a few years later led to *L'Occasione fa il ladro* being staged in Barcelona in 1822, Lisbon (1826), St Petersburg (1830) and Vienna (1834), but it has never succeeded in achieving popularity. It was revived in Pesaro, its composer's home town, in 1892 on the occasion of the hundredth anniversary of his birth, but otherwise there were only isolated performances in Turin (1913) and Trieste (1924) until the second half of the twentieth century when the revival of interest in the bel canto repertoire led to several productions in Italy and elsewhere. British audiences first heard the opera given with Italian marionettes at the Little Theatre, London, on 14 January 1929, but had to wait until 8 August 1987 to see it performed by live singers at the Opera House, Buxton, during the Buxton Festival, when it shared the evening with Donizetti's *Il Pigmalione* (see p 139). In 1992 it was successfully revived in Macerata, Paris, Cologne and Schwetzingen.

Don Parmenione and Count Alberto meet in an inn while taking shelter from a storm. When Alberto's servant carries off the wrong suitcase, Parmenione and his servant Martino examine the one left behind. Finding not only money but a portrait of the beautiful Berenice whom Alberto is travelling to Naples to marry, Parmenione decides to make his way to Naples, pass himself off as Count Alberto, whom Berenice has never met, and marry her. But Berenice is clever enough to test the sincerity of her husband-to-be by exchanging identities with her servant, Ernestina. Predictable complications ensue before the obligatory happy ending.

In place of a full-scale overture, there is a brief orchestral *andante* prelude leading into the *allegro* storm music which, familiar from *La Pietra del paragone*, will turn up again three years later in *Il Barbiere di*

Siviglia. Throughout the opera, Rossini's score displays his usual virtues of high spirits, an easy tunefulness, and imaginative scoring. The *andante* cavatinas for Alberto ('Il tuo rigore insano') and Berenice ('Vicino è il momento') are both elegant pieces, Alberto's developing into an *allegro* drinking trio with Parmenione and Martino, and Berenice's luxuriating in some florid vocal writing. Parmenione's first solo ('Che sorte, che accidente') seems hastily put together, but his duet ('Quel gentil, quel vago oggetto') with Ernestina, whom he takes to be Berenice, is amusing, and Count Alberto's *andantino* duet with the real Berenice ('Se non m'inganna il core') is properly romantic. The central number in the score is an ensemble ('Che strana sorpresa') in which the various characters' identities are called into question, ending in a gloriously hectic stretta ('Di tanto equivoco').

The second half of the opera contains a delightful aria for Alberto ('D'ogni più sacro impegno'), its smoothly flowing *andante* opening section giving way to a lively cabaletta ('Amor da voi non chiede'), and an amusing duet ('Voi la sposa') in which Berenice cross-examines the rascally Parmenione. After Martino's sprightly *allegro* aria, 'Il mio padrone', in which he offers an engagingly frank description of his master, Berenice dominates the proceedings with her *maestoso* 'Voi la sposa pretendete' which progresses through an affecting *andante* ('Deh, non tradirmi, amore') to culminate in a brilliant *allegro* cabaletta ('Io non soffro quest' oltraggio'). An *allegro* trio ('Quello che fui ritorno') for the subsidiary pair of lovers and Eusebio, and a more romantic *andantino* duet ('Oh, quanto son grate le pene in amore') for Berenice and Alberto, lead to the final *allegro* ensemble with which, as Eusebio remarks, 'un doppio matrimonio la burletta finirà' (a double marriage will bring the farce to an end).

Il Signor Bruschino
(Mr Bruschino)

farsa giocosa in one act

Principal characters:
Gaudenzio, a rich tutor   (bass)

Sofia, his pupil	(soprano)
Bruschino Senior, a rich citizen	(bass)
Bruschino Junior, his son	(tenor)
Florville, Sofia's lover	(tenor)
Filiberto, an innkeeper	(baritone)
Marianna, Sofia's chambermaid	(mezzo-soprano)

LIBRETTO by Giuseppe Foppa

TIME: The eighteenth century
PLACE: A castle in France

FIRST PERFORMED at the Teatro San Moisè, Venice, late January 1813, with Teodolinda Pontiggia (Sofia); Carolina Nagher (Marianna); Luigi Raffanelli (Bruschino Senior); Gaetano Del Monte (Bruschino Junior); Nicola De Grecis (Gaudenzio); Tommaso Berti (Florville); Nicola Tacci (Filiberto)

As soon as *L'Occasione fa il ladro* had been staged at the Teatro San Moisè, Rossini began to compose his next opera for that theatre, another one-act farce with a libretto by Giuseppe Foppa who had been his collaborator on two earlier comic operas for the San Moisè, *L'Inganno felice* and *La Scala di seta*. *Il Signor Bruschino*, whose alternative title was *Il Figlio per azzardo* (A Son by Chance), was based by Foppa on a French comedy, *Le Fils par hazard* by Alisan de Chazet and E.-T. Maurice Ourry, staged in Paris in 1809. Rossini composed his new comic opera even more quickly than usual, for he had already received a more important commission. He had been invited by that most prestigious of Venetian theatres, the Fenice, to write a serious opera, *Tancredi*, and he was impatient to begin.

Il Signor Bruschino was a failure at its first performances in Venice, due partly to the fact that, within a few days of its première, Rossini's *Tancredi* (see pp 29–34) opened at the Teatro Fenice to tumultuous acclaim. A one-act farce in a secondary theatre could hardly compete with the triumph of a full-length serious opera which, it was immediately clear, was going to be taken up by opera houses throughout Italy and abroad. It was not until several decades later that *Il Signor Bruschino* was revived, in Milan in 1844, Madrid (1858), Berlin (1858) and Brussels (1859). When Offenbach staged it in Paris in 1857 in his own French adaptation, Rossini, then living in Paris, refused to be involved. 'I have let you do what you wanted to do,' he replied upon being invited to attend a rehearsal, 'but I certainly have no intention of being your accomplice.'

Il Signor Bruschino did not reach English-speaking audiences until the twentieth century. Its first performance in the United States was given at the Metropolitan Opera, New York, on 9 December 1932, as a curtain-raiser to Strauss's *Elektra*. Tullio Serafin conducted, and the cast included Armand Tokatyan, Giuseppe de Luca and Ezio Pinza. The (amateur) Kentish Opera Group staged *Il Signor Bruschino* in Great Britain, at Orpington, on 14 July 1960. Since then it has been produced in a number of cities in Italy and elsewhere in Europe, as well as in Buenos Aires. In 1992 it was staged in Paris and Macerata.

Like *La Scala di seta*, *Il Signor Bruschino* suffered for a time from the absurd claim (which first appeared in print in a biography of Rossini by Alexis-Jacob Azevedo, published in 1864) that when Cera, the San Moisè impresario, voiced his objection to Rossini's acceptance of a commission from the Teatro La Fenice, the young composer took his revenge by deliberately filling his score with all kinds of absurd extravagances, writing angry music for tender scenes, gentle melodies for outbursts of fury, ludicrously high notes for the bass voice, impossibly low ones for the soprano, and inserting a protracted funeral march into what was ostensibly a farce. The unusual effect produced by the second violins tapping their desks with their bows during the overture was also cited as evidence of Rossini's determination to wreck his own opera. It is difficult to accept, however, that anyone who had either seen the opera performed or examined its score could possibly give credence to Azevedo's story.

The plot of *Il Signor Bruschino* is typical of Rossinian *opera buffa* both in its complexity and its inconsequentiality. The young lovers Florville and Sofia wish to marry, but Sofia's guardian, Gaudenzio, has promised her to young Bruschino whom neither he nor she has ever met. Florville, posing as Bruschino, presents himself to Gaudenzio, and by the time Bruschino's father arrives all are convinced that Florville is his son, to the apoplectic fury of Bruschino senior whose protestations no one believes. Florville and Sofia are safely married before the confusion is cleared up.

A brisk gaiety pervades the overture with its comic device of the wooden parts of violin bows tapping against music stands. (At the

Teatro San Moisè the violinists would have tapped their bows against the tin covers of their candle stands.) Florville's G major aria, 'Deh, tu m'assisti, Amore', is a graceful *andantino* with a cadenza taking the tenor to a high C (or an optional A for the less adventurous). His love duet with Sofia, 'Quanto è dolce a un alma amante', a little self-plagiarism on Rossini's part (from *Demetrio e Polibio*), is delicately sentimental. Florville's *buffo* duet with Fili-berto, 'Io danari vi darò', is admittedly eccentric.

Gaudenzio's cavatina, 'Nel teatro del gran mondo', offers fine opportunities for a flexible comic bass, and the central trio, 'Per un figlio già pentito', for Gaudenzio, Florville and old Bruschino, shows Rossini at his most inventive and original. Sofia's recitative and aria ('Ah donate il caro sposo') with cabaletta is equally original, an obbligato part for cor anglais contributing a distinctly plaintive feeling. The aria ('Ho la testa') and ensemble in which Bruschino is sorely put upon nevertheless allow the old man his few moments of pathos, as well as one of anguish when he, a mere bass, is driven up to the baritone's high G. A duet for Sofia and Gaudenzio ('È un bel nodo') is rather dull, and the opera's finale is a fairly perfunctory affair, although enlivened for sixteen bars by young Bruschino's minor key mock-funeral march and his expression of repentance, 'Son pentito-tito-tito'. But *Signor Bruschino*, for most of its length, is a vivacious and fast-moving musical comedy, whose graceful score reveals traces still of Cimarosa and even Mozart.

2

From *Tancredi* to *Sigismondo*

Tancredi

melodramma eroico in two acts

Principal characters:

Tancredi	(contralto)
Amenaide	(soprano)
Argirio, her father	(tenor)
Orbazzano	(bass)
Isaura, Amenaide's friend	(soprano)
Roggiero	(soprano)

LIBRETTO by Gaetano Rossi

TIME: 1005 A.D.
PLACE: Syracuse, Sicily

FIRST PERFORMED at the Teatro La Fenice, Venice, 6 February 1813, with Adelaide Malanotte-Montresor (Tancredi); Elisabetta Manfredini-Guarmani (Amenaide); Teresa Marchesi (Isaura); Carolina Sivelli (Roggiero); Pietro Todràn (Argirio); Luciano Bianchi (Orbazzano)

It was while he was in Venice in November 1812, preparing for the première of *L'Occasione fa il ladro*, that Rossini was invited by the Teatro La Fenice to compose an *opera seria* for the following season. The subject and the librettist had already been chosen: Gaetano

Rossi, who had written *La Cambiale di matrimonio* for Rossini, based his *Tancredi* on Voltaire's five-act tragedy, *Tancrède* (1760).

A number of earlier writers on Rossini – even the usually dependable *Annals of Opera* by Alfred Loewenberg, and the fifth edition of Grove's Dictionary (1954) – state that Rossi's libretto also derives from episodes in the poem *Gerusalemme liberata* by the sixteenth-century poet, Torquato Tasso. This, however, is incorrect. Voltaire's *Tancrède* and Rossini's *Tancredi* are set in Sicily in the year 1005. *Gerusalemme liberata* (Jerusalem Liberated) takes place, of course, in the Middle East at the time of the Crusades, which did not begin until 1096. 'Il prence Tancredi' of Tasso's poem is Tancred of Lecce, a Norman soldier who took part in the siege of Jerusalem during the First Crusade, and who died in 1112. He is a character in Monteverdi's music drama, *Il Combattimento di Tancredi e Clorinda* (1624), but not Rossini's *Tancredi*. Voltaire's and Rossini's hero is based on another historical character, Tancred of Hauteville, also a Norman. There is not the slightest similarity between the events depicted in Tasso's poem and those of Rossini's *Tancredi*.

Rossini, as usual, composed his opera in a remarkably short time, and it was given its première at the Fenice on 6 February 1813. However, at that performance and the following one, both leading ladies were indisposed and the opera had to be abandoned in the middle of Act II. It was not until 12 February that a Venetian audience heard the whole of *Tancredi*.

The work was favourably received, and performed about fifteen times during the season. For its second staging, in Ferrara several weeks later, Rossi's libretto was altered to accord more closely to Voltaire, and the opera ended with the death of Tancredi, who had been wounded in battle. Rossini composed some new music for this version, but audiences disliked the tragic ending, and the original version was used for subsequent performances.

Tancredi soon began to be staged in other Italian towns, always to great acclaim. Within the next few years it was translated into twelve languages and performed in most of the major European cities as well as in the Americas. The opera was first seen in London on 4 May 1820 and in New York on 31 December 1825. It was after a revival of *Tancredi* in Venice in the autumn of 1815 that the sprightly tune of one of its arias, Tancredi's 'Di tanti palpiti', began to achieve its phenomenal popularity. The hyperbolic Stendhal declared that it 'has enjoyed a wider and more universal popularity than perhaps any other aria in the world'. In Venice it was sung by gondoliers and by the gentry, just as, thirty years later, another catchy tune, Verdi's 'La donna è mobile', would be. (Today almost everyone is familiar with Verdi's tune, but only Rossini enthusiasts know 'Di tanti palpiti'.)

For many years, *Tancredi* retained its international popularity until, along with the bel canto era in general, it began to be forgotten towards the end of the nineteenth century. It reappeared with the mid-twentieth century's revival of interest in bel canto, and was staged very successfully at the Florence Maggio Musicale in 1952, with Giulietta Simionato (Tancredi) and Teresa Stich-Randall (Amenaide), conducted by Tullio Serafin. Since then, there have been numerous productions in Europe and the United States. Those in Houston (1977), Rome (1977), San Francisco (1979), Aix-en-Provence (1981), Venice (1982), Barcelona (1989), Chicago (1989) and Los Angeles (1989) benefited from the participation of the prodigious Marilyn Horne as Tancredi. During Rossini's bi-centennial year, 1992, it was staged in Bologna and given two concert performances at the Salzburg Festival.

The action of Rossini's *Tancredi* takes place in the Sicilian city of Syracuse in a year which the libretto insists is 1005. Argirio, ruler of the city, has promised his daughter Amenaide in marriage to Orbazzano, leader of a rival family, in an attempt to unite all factions against their common enemy, the Saracens. But Amenaide is in love with Tancredi, son of the deposed King of Syracuse. Tancredi returns from his exile in time to prevent Amenaide's marriage, but reproaches her for what he considers to be her disloyalty to him. Orbazzano has Amenaide arrested on a false charge of treason, for which she is to be executed unless a champion appears to defend her honour. Though he believes her guilty, Tancredi offers himself as her defender, and kills Orbazzano in combat. After he has led a successful expedition against the Saracens, the truth regarding Amenaide's supposed treason is revealed, and she and Tancredi are united.

Tancredi's plot is considerably more complicated than that, but as with so much *opera seria*, the details of a sometimes quite ludicrous plot are less important than the central situations which give rise to the arias, duets and ensembles. What Rossini sought in the libretti he set to music was not dramatic credibility but characters whose emotions he could clothe in appropriate melody; although, disconcertingly, he could sometimes make the same music serve to express widely differing emotions.

As Venice had not heard *La Pietra del paragone* which had been given its première in Milan the previous September, Rossini saw no reason not to re-use the overture of that comedy for his serious opera, *Tancredi*. And indeed his overture introduces one opera as effectively as it does the other. After an opening chorus, a duet ('Se amistà verace e pura') for Argirio and Orbazzano in which Argirio's tenor vocal line is highly decorated, and an even more florid cavatina ('Come è dolce all' alma mia') for Amenaide, Tancredi makes his first entrance. Rossini wrote the role of the warrier Tancredi for a female contralto, since the old, dying tradition of the hero being sung by a male castrato had led audiences still to expect, or at least to accept, an alto timbre in a male heroic role. In *Tancredi* the tenor is not the romantic hero, but the heroine's father.

Preceded by a portentous orchestral introduction, Tancredi's accompanied recitative gives him an air of gravity. His cavatina ('Tu che accendi questo'), though brief, is highly effective. It gives way quickly to its famous cabaletta, 'Di tanti palpiti', with its fresh, insouciant tune and its suave, oddly moving cadences. Apparently 'Di tanti palpiti' was composed by Rossini the night before the première for Signora Malanotte-Montresor who was dissatisfied with her cavatina. It was known as 'the rice aria' because Rossini remarked that he took no longer to compose it than it takes to boil rice (a claim which should probably be taken with a grain of rice), and became such a favourite with the Venetians that it was continually being whistled in the streets. Many years later, Wagner was sufficiently annoyed by the continuing popularity of Rossini's catchy tune to parody it in the Tailors' Song in Act III of *Die Meistersinger*.

After Argirio has been given a chance to display his tenorial virtuosity in the aria, 'Pensa che sei mia figlia', Tancredi and Amenaide combine in the first of their two great love duets. The tenderness with which Rossini tempers the vocal fireworks in these duets is remarkable. The Act I duet, 'L'aura che intorno spiri', moves from an *allegro* opening, through a lyrical section with the two voices combining in thirds and sixths, to a lively cabaletta. A chorus ('Amori scendete') and march lead to the Act I finale which begins with the accompanied recitative in which Orbazzano denounces Amenaide, after which a great ensemble for sextet and chorus builds up, its *andante* opening ('Ciel! che feci!') and affecting central section of dramatic confrontation and reflection followed by an exciting *allegro* conclusion, though it must be admitted that one could imagine the same music being used by Rossini for the Act I finale of a comic opera: *Il Barbiere di Siviglia* comes to mind quite easily.

Argirio's aria ('Ah! segnar invano io tento') with cabaletta, after he has unwillingly condemned his daughter to death, is even finer – and more highly decorated – than his Act I aria, but Isaura's 'Tu che i miseri conforti' which follows it seems lacking in individuality. The rather stately but impressive orchestral introduction to Amenaide's prison scene, with its cor anglais solo, would not sound out of place in Gluck's *Orfeo ed Euridice*, and Amenaide's recitative and *andante giusto* aria, 'Ah, che il morir non è', are both dignified and moving.

Equally fine is the two-part duet, 'Ah se de' mali miei', for Argirio and Tancredi. Amenaide's aria, 'Giusto Dio, che umile adoro', is quite beautiful, and its cabaletta, when she learns that she has been saved by Tancredi, displays an exhilarating lightness of spirit. Tancredi's victory is celebrated in a joyful chorus, 'Plaudite, o populi', whose mood momentarily becomes more reflective with the entrance of Tancredi ('Dolce è di gloria'). The duet, 'Lasciami: non t'ascolto', for Tancredi and Amenaide, is one of the opera's highlights and a splendid example of the bel canto style, with virtuosity and expressiveness blending into one mood as smoothly and perfectly as do the contralto and soprano voices of Tancredi and Amenaide.

Tancredi's friend, Roggiero, a minor character, has to be given an aria, and his 'Torni alfin' is an attractive, brief *allegro*. The love-sick anguish of Tancredi's cavatina, 'Ah! che scordar non so', sung as he wanders restlessly in the vicinity of Mount Etna, is banished by a rather muted chorus of Saracens ('Regna il terror'), and his 'Perchè turbar la calma', addressed to Amenaide, is expressive in its simplicity. After Tancredi's cabaletta, the opera's finale is brisk and somewhat perfunctory.

The alternative Ferrara ending, in which a mortally wounded Tancredi dies on stage, has been used in recent stagings of the opera, but is stylistically inappropriate. (The chorus, 'Muore il prode', composed for Ferrara, seemed too good to waste, so Rossini used it again later in the year in *Aureliano in Palmira*.)

Tancredi is Rossini's earliest great *opera seria*, a work which, given singers able to cope with its demands on their virtuosity, can hold the stage today as effectively as when it was first performed, 'a genuine thunderbolt out of a clear, blue sky for the Italian lyric theatre', as Stendhal described it. Though perhaps it was not so much a thunderbolt in a blue sky as a precursor, during the last years of *opera seria*, heralding the dawning of a new era, that of romanticism. Its inspiration may be uneven, but its freshness and vigour are never in question. The opera's finest passages are quite simply superb, and if Rossini ever wrote a more delectable tune than 'Di tanti palpiti' it has certainly never come to light.

L'Italiana in Algeri
(The Italian Girl in Algiers)

dramma giocoso in two acts

Principal characters:

Isabella, a young Italian woman   (contralto)
Mustafà, Bey of Algiers   (bass)
Elvira, his wife   (soprano)
Lindoro, an Italian   (tenor)
Zulma, Elvira's confidante   (mezzo-soprano)
Taddeo, Isabella's companion   (bass)
Haly, in the Bey's service   (bass)

LIBRETTO by Angelo Anelli

TIME: The past
PLACE: Algiers

FIRST PERFORMED at the Teatro San Benedetto, Venice, 22 May 1813, with Marietta Marcolini (Isabella); Luttgard Annibaldi (Elvira); Annunziata Berni Chelli (Zulma); Filippo Galli (Mustafà); Serafino Gentili (Lindoro); Paolo Rosich (Taddeo)

After the final performance of *Tancredi* in Venice on 7 March 1813, Rossini travelled to Ferrara to supervise its production there, and to compose the new ending already mentioned. But he had also agreed to write a comic opera for another theatre in Venice, the San Benedetto, for performance in May. By mid-April, therefore, he was back in Venice and at work setting to music the libretto which had been given to him. This was *L'Italiana in Algeri* which Angelo Anelli, a prolific librettist of the day, had based on the legend of Roxelane, the beautiful slave of the famous sixteenth-century Turkish ruler, Suleiman the Magnificent. The librettist may also have had in mind the story of Antonietta Suini, a young, aristocratic Milanese woman whom Algerian pirates abducted from a ship in 1805. After being confined to several harems, she was returned to Italy a few years later on board a Venetian ship. Anelli's libretto was not new: it had been written for Luigi Mosca, whose *L'Italiana in Algeri* was staged in Milan in 1808.

According to the Venetian *Giornale dipartimentale dell' Adriatico*, Rossini composed *L'Italiana in Algeri* in twenty-seven days, although the composer told the Venice correspondent of a German newspaper that it took him only eighteen days. He was, it seems, proud of his speed in composition. At its première the opera aroused great enthusiasm, and at a later performance verses in praise of Rossini floated down from the higher reaches of the theatre into the pit. Delighted with the work's reception, Rossini is said to have exclaimed, 'I thought that, when they heard my opera, the Venetians would decide I was crazy. But they have shown themselves to be crazier than I am.' The *Giornale* wrote that *L'Italiana in Algeri* would 'find a place among the finest works of genius and art'.

The new opera soon became immensely popular throughout Italy and abroad. In 1816, in Munich, it was the first of Rossini's operas to be staged in Germany, and in the following year the first to reach Paris. London heard it, at His Majesty's Theatre, on 26 January 1819, and New York on 5 November 1832.

Though it disappeared from opera houses for a time at the beginning of the twentieth century, *L'Italiana in Algeri* began to be staged again well before the post-Second World War revival of interest in bel canto. Highly successful performances with the Spanish coloratura mezzo-soprano Conchita Supervia in the title-role were given in Turin (1925), Rome (1927) and London (1935). Vittorio Gui, who conducted the Turin performances, told a writer on Rossini that 'Richard Strauss, who did not know this opera, seemed mad with enthusiasm after becoming acquainted with it here in Turin'. In the years immediately following the Second World War, Giulietta Simionato was a popular Isabella, and later Marilyn Horne was greatly successful in the role.

Anelli's libretto is one of the finest of its kind. Though fast-moving, it allows its characters, farcical caricatures though they may be, time to establish themselves clearly. Isabella, accompanied by her elderly admirer Taddeo, has been sailing the Mediterranean in search of her lover Lindoro. When their ship is wrecked off the coast of Algiers, she is taken to Mustafà, the Bey, who plans to add her to his harem. Isabella discovers that Lindoro is a slave in the Bey's service, and in imminent danger of being married off to Elvira, the neglected wife of Mustafà. With Elvira's aid, Isabella and Lindoro finally escape together with Taddeo, and Mustafà returns to Elvira.

The brilliantly scored overture, one of his most suave and engaging, contains such typical Rossini touches as sprightly tunes for the woodwind and, of course, the by now inevitable *crescendo*. It remained a favourite in the concert hall even during the opera's years of neglect. The opening *allegro* ensemble, 'Serenate il mesto ciglio', establishes tunefully the suffering of the neglected Elvira, as well as the comical blustering tyranny of the Bey, caricatured in his excessively florid vocal line. The unhappy Lindoro, pining for his Isabella, is introduced by a romantic French horn solo. His cavatina, 'Languir per una bella', a graceful *andantino*, and its optimistic cabaletta, 'Contento quest' alma', are followed by Lindoro's duet with the Bey, 'Se inclinassi a prender moglie', one of the highlights of the opera, a comical and tunefully effervescent piece in which Mustafà attempts to coerce the young Italian into taking the unwanted Elvira off his hands.

In the scene by the rocky sea-shore, Isabella makes a formidable first impression with her aria ('Cruda sorte') and cabaletta ('Già so per pratica'). Her music throughout the opera combines tenderness and determination in equal amounts, the first quality expressed through Rossini's gift for languishing melody, the second in comically fierce coloratura. The *allegro* duet, 'Ai capricci della sorte', in which Isabella and Taddeo quarrel and make up, is both witty and tuneful. In the next scene, Mustafà's aria, 'Già d'insolito ardore', is pompously in character, while the wittily scored Act I finale is one of Rossini's masterpieces. 'Viva, viva, il flagel delle donne' (Long live the flogging of women), the eunuchs of the harem (though some of them have bass voices) sing in their innocent pre-feminist glee, before Isabella launches a marvellous duet with the barely suppressed laughter of her 'Oh! che muso, che figura!' at the sight of the Bey whose contribution to their duet is one of amazed admiration.

When Lindoro and Isabella meet, a mood of genuine feeling steals into the music, and a septet ('Confusi e stupidi') ensues in which all the characters muse on the strange atmosphere which has developed. Its *allegro vivace* conclusion has them making onomatopoeic noises to express their confusion which is like the cawing of crows (Taddeo), the sound of hammering (Lindoro and Haly, a servant of the Bey), cannon-fire (Mustafà) or the ringing of bells (Elvira, Zulma and Isabella). Rossini welds this cacophony into a harmonious but hilariously hectic climax.

Nothing in Act II quite equals this, but Lindoro's ardent cabaletta-like *allegro* with oboe obbligato, 'Ah, come il cor di giubilo', is attractive, and the scene in which Taddeo is invested with the order of 'Grande Kaimakan', and responds in a *buffo* aria, 'Ho un gran peso sulla testa', can be very funny in performance. There is deep feeling in Isabella's sensuous *andante grazioso* cavatina, 'Per lui che adoro', although – or perhaps because – she sings it knowing that she is being overheard by her three admirers.

The sneezing quintet ('Ti presento'), Haly's aria, 'Le femmine d'Italia', and especially the Trio in which Mustafà is tricked into accepting membership of the order of 'Pappataci', are all delightful. Isabella's recitative and splendidly inflammatory rondo, 'Pensa alla patria' (Think of your country), bring a realistic note of Risorgimento propaganda into the farcical proceedings. At least, various Italian censorship authorities thought so, and in Naples 'Pensa alla patria' was banned, while in Rome the word 'patria' had to be replaced by 'sposa' (wife). The opera's finale is somewhat anticlimactic.

The earliest of Rossini's great full-length comedies, *L'Italiana in Algeri* is also one of the most ebullient; an opera rich in youthful high spirits and graceful melody. Rossini's twentieth-century biographer Radiciotti was of the opinion that, in it, the composer had not yet completely acquired his own personality. But surely he had. If there are slight traces of Mozart or Cimarosa to be found in *L'Italiana in Algeri*, there are as many also to be found in Rossini's final opera, *Guillaume Tell*. To the end of his short operatic career, Rossini retained at least one characteristic of the bird he was to write about in 1817 in *La Gazza ladra* (see p 73).

Aureliano in Palmira
(Aurelianus in Palmyra)

dramma serio in two acts

Principal characters:

Aureliano, Roman Emperor	(tenor)
Zenobia, Queen of Palmyra	(soprano)
Arsace, Prince of Persia	(male soprano)
Publia, daughter of Valerian	(soprano)
Gran Sacerdote (High Priest)	(bass)

LIBRETTO by Gian Francesco Romanelli

TIME: 271-272 A.D.
PLACE: Syria

FIRST PERFORMED at the Teatro alla Scala, Milan, 26 December 1813, with Luigi Mari (Aureliano); Lorenza Correa (Zenobia); Luigia Sorrentini (Publia); Giovanni Battista Velluti (Arsace); Vincenzo Botticelli (Gran Sacerdote)

Some months after the première of *L'Italiana in Algeri*, Rossini agreed to compose a new *opera seria*, *Aureliano in Palmira*, to open the winter or carnival season on 26 December at the Teatro alla Scala, Milan, where *La Pietra del paragone* had done so well the previous year. The libretto of the new opera, attributed on its frontispiece to 'G.F.R.', was for some time attributed to Felice Romani (1788–1865), the leading Italian librettist of his day, but is almost certainly the work of a lesser writer, Gian Francesco Romanelli.

The Aureliano of the title is the Roman Emperor, Lucius Domitius Aurelianus (*c*.A.D. 214–275), who, in A.D. 271–272, defeated and captured the Syrian Queen Zenobia, and laid waste her country of Palmyra in the Syrian desert. A third character in the opera is Arsace, Prince of Persia, who is in love with Zenobia. Rossini's opera ends with Aureliano magnanimously freeing Zenobia and Arsace who in turn proclaim their loyalty to Rome.

Aureliano in Palmira was unenthusiastically received by its audiences in Milan, and pronounced boring by the *Corriere Milanese*. Nevertheless, it was performed fourteen times during the season, and later given in Vicenza, Venice, Barcelona, Lisbon and Corfu.

Its first London performance was on 22 June 1826. It was staged in Buenos Aires in 1829, but has yet to be seen in the United States, and its revival in Genoa in 1980 has not led to productions elsewhere. It has not been staged in London since 1826.

Rossini wrote the role of Arsace for the famous male soprano, Giovanni Battista Velluti (1781–1861), who had made his debut in 1801, had sung in operas by Cimarosa and other composers in Naples, Rome and Milan, and had caused a sensation with his appearances in Vienna in 1812. Velluti was in the habit of overdecorating and embellishing his arias and, according to Stendhal, his doing so at the première of *Aureliano in Palmira* led Rossini to decide that, in future, he would write out in full the ornaments he was prepared to allow, rather than leave them to his singers as had been the general custom. There is no evidence in Rossini's scores to support this unlikely story; nevertheless, *Aureliano in Palmira* remains the first and only opera in which Rossini wrote a castrato role. Velluti, the last of the great castrati, continued to appear on stage until he was in his late forties. In 1826 he sang the role of Arsace in *Aureliano in Palmira* in London.

Though it is not difficult to comprehend the lack of enthusiasm with which audiences in the early nineteenth century may have greeted *Aureliano in Palmira*, especially after they had experienced the greater delights of *Tancredi* and *L'Italiana in Algeri*, contemporary ears would surely respond gratefully to its stately alternation of tuneful, elegiac arias and florid cabalettas with mellifluous duets and attractive choruses. An occasional dullness is, after all, to be preferred to the mindless cacophony offered by too many – not all – of the new operas produced in the late twentieth century.

The overture to *Aureliano in Palmira* may sound rather too light-hearted for the opera that is to follow. It will almost certainly sound familiar to anyone hearing it now, for Rossini recycled it not only for *Elisabetta, regina d'Inghilterra* in 1815 but also for *Il Barbiere di Siviglia* in 1816. Equally familiar is the beginning of the opera's opening chorus, 'Sposa del grande Osiride', for it was to become Almaviva's serenade, 'Ecco ridente in cielo', in the opening scene of *Il Barbiere*.

In Act I of *Aureliano in Palmira*, the duet, 'Se tu m'ami, o mia regina', for Arsace and Zenobia, is gently decorative, and the High Priest's somewhat jaunty prayer oddly attractive. Aureliano's aria, 'Cara patria', puts one in mind of Mozart's Titus, and his duet with Arsace, 'Pensa che festi a Roma', contains some accomplished writing for the voices. Zenobia's aria ('Là pugnai') and cabaletta ('Non piangete, o sventurati') are lively, and the trio ('Serena i bei rai') which leads into the Act I finale displays Rossini's youthful charm at its most engaging.

Among the most effective numbers in Act II are the duet, 'Se libertà t'è cara', for Aureliano and Zenobia; a chorus of shepherds and shepherdesses which contains a delightful violin obbligato; Arsace's 'Perchè mai le luci aprimmo', whose orchestral introduction utilises music from the overture; Arsace's coloratura rondo, 'Non lasciarmi in tal momento', whose first eight bars were to turn up again in *Il Barbiere* in Rosina's 'Una voce poco fa'; and Aureliano's virtuoso aria and cabaletta, 'Più non vedrà quel perfido'. Though not one of Rossini's more imposing creations, *Aureliano in Palmira* certainly deserves an occasional hearing.

Il Turco in Italia
(The Turk in Italy)

dramma buffo in two acts

Principal characters:

Selim, Turkish Prince	(bass)
Donna Fiorilla, wife of Don Geronio	(soprano)
Don Geronio	(bass)
Don Narciso	(tenor)
Prosdocimo, a poet	(bass)
Zaida, a slave	(mezzo-soprano)
Albazar, confidant of Selim	(tenor)

LIBRETTO by Felice Romani

TIME: The eighteenth century
PLACE: In and around Naples

FIRST PERFORMED at the Teatro all Scala, Milan, 14 August 1814, with Francesca Maffei-Festa (Fiorilla); Adelaide Carpano (Zaida); Giovanni David (Narciso); Filippo Galli (Selim); Luigi Pacini (Geronio); Pietro Vasoli (Prosdocimo); Gaetano Pozzi (Albazar)

Despite the coolness with which the Milanese had received *Aureliano in Palmira*, only a few months passed before the management of La Scala offered Rossini another contract, to write a two-act *opera buffa* (or *drama buffo*, as the libretto describes itself), *Il Turco in Italia*. The libretto this time was by Felice Romani (1788–1865), who was then at the beginning of his career, but who would in time become the most famous librettist of his day and a considerably more accomplished poet and dramatist than any of his rivals. He collaborated with Rossini, Donizetti and Bellini on twenty operas, and wrote at least a hundred libretti for other composers.

Unfortunately, Rossini for the second time failed to please the Milanese public. The audience on the first night of *Il Turco in Italia* was misled by the fact that the opera's title sounded like a riposte to *L'Italiana in Algeri* into thinking that the composer was merely repeating himself. According to the *Corriere Milanese*, a man in the stalls shouted 'Potpourri, potpourri'.

Il Turco in Italia was produced in several other Italian theatres, and abroad, usually with success and occasionally under other names: in Vicenza in 1816 it was given as *Il Tutore deluso*, and in Rome in 1819 as *La Capricciosa corretta*. It was first performed in London at His Majesty's Theatre on 19 May 1821 (in Italian) and at the Theatre Royal, Drury Lane, on 1 May 1827 in an English adaptation as *The Turkish Lovers*. Its first New York performance was on 14 March 1826. After the middle of the century, however, *Il Turco in Italia* virtually disappeared from the repertoire until a 1950 revival in Rome with Maria Callas as Fiorilla, since when it has come to be recognised as one of Rossini's most delightful comic operas.

Romani's highly artificial, quasi-Pirandellian text is based on a libretto written by Caterino Mazzolà for Franz Seydelmann, a German contemporary of Mozart. Seydelmann's *Il Turco in Italia* was successfully staged in Dresden in 1788, and in Vienna the following year. Though much of Romani's dialogue is new, some of his verses are lifted verbatim from Mazzolà.

The poet, Prosdocimo, is in search of ideas for his next play. He finds them in a gypsy encampment on a beach not far from Naples where he encounters several characters. Among them are Zaida, who has fled from the harem of the Turkish Prince Selim since he, in the mistaken belief that she was unfaithful to him, had condemned her to death; Don Geronio, a Neapolitan whose capricious and temperamental wife, Fiorilla, has a young admirer, Narciso; and

Selim, whose ship arrives in the harbour from Turkey. Prosdocimo manipulates an intrigue between Fiorilla and Selim, but finally Fiorilla and Geronio are reconciled, Narciso promises to mend his philandering ways, and Selim, realising that he has misjudged Zaida, sails back to Turkey with her. Prosdocimo now has the plot for his play, and hopes his public will like it.

The ebullient overture is one which Rossini was to plunder on two later occasions, for *Sigismondo* and *Otello*. Though the opera takes its time to get under way, and though its score is uneven – and some of it not by Rossini – the best numbers in *Il Turco in Italia* are sheer delight. The first to be heard is an enchanting trio ('Un marito – scimunito!') in which the poet plans his comedy to the annoyance of two of its characters, Geronio and Narciso. The trio grows from a broad theme in semibreves in the orchestra – some writers have found significance in a resemblance to the finale of Mozart's 'Jupiter' Symphony – which persists beneath the jauntier phrase punctuating the initial utterances of the three men.

A delightful quartet ('Siete Turchi') ensues when Fiorilla's assignation with Selim is interrupted by both her husband and her lover. The ambivalent mood of the duet, 'Per piacere alla Signora', for Fiorilla and Geronio is fascinating. The duet begins as sparkling comedy, its theme borrowed from a duet in *Il Signor Bruschino*, assumes a mock-serious tone in its central *andante* when Fiorilla pretends to be in tears, and then returns to high spirits in its concluding section. The Act I finale finds time for graceful ariettas for Narciso ('Perchè mai se son tradito'), in which he begs the god of love to return Fiorilla to him, and for Fiorilla ('Chi servir non brama Amor') who is lost in romantic reverie.

The first number in Act II, 'D'un bell'uso di Turchia', is a superb *buffo* duet for the two basses, Selim and Geronio, when Fiorilla's outraged husband refuses to sell his wife to her Turkish admirer. It works itself up into a brilliant concluding section, in which great use is made of Rossini's favourite *crescendo* effect. Fiorilla's 'Se il zefiro si posa' has a simple, oddly un-Rossinian, folkish charm, but Act II in general is less enjoyable than Act I. It seems swamped with *recitativo secco*, none of which is by Rossini, and its action is held up by two disappointing tenor arias, Narciso's 'Tu seconda il mio disegno' and Albazar's 'Ah, sarebbe troppo dolce', the latter not by Rossini. The duet, 'Credete alle femmine', for Fiorilla and Selim is surprisingly nondescript, but the quintet, 'Oh, guardate che accidente', is masterly in its dramatic complexity and musical audacity. The opera's finale, another non-Rossini number, is anti-climactic.

It was no doubt because he was short of time that Rossini farmed out the arias for Geronio and Albazar, the Act II finale and all the unaccompanied recitative to another composer, who may have been Vincenzo Lavigna, a conductor at La Scala who seventeen years later was to teach composition to the eighteen-year-old Verdi. The rest of *Il Turco in Italia* shows no signs of haste or carelessness, and the opera's best numbers are vintage Rossini. But its leading characters, none of them wholly sympathetic, fail to come completely to life. Though it is not the piece of self-plagiarism which the Milanese audiences evidently thought it to be, it is by no means as enjoyable an opera as *L'Italiana in Algeri*.

Sigismondo

dramma in two acts

Principal characters:

Sigismondo, King of Poland	(contralto)
Aldimira, his wife	(soprano)
Anagilda	(soprano)
Ladislao, Chief Minister to the King	(tenor)
Ulderico, King of Bohemia	(bass)
Radoski	(tenor)

LIBRETTO by Giuseppe Foppa

TIME: The sixteenth century
PLACE: Poland

FIRST PERFORMED at the Teatro La Fenice, Venice, 26 December 1814, with Marietta Marcolini (Sigismondo); Elisabetta Manfredini-Guarmani (Aldimira); Marianna Rossi (Anagilda); Claudio Bonoldi (Ladislao); Luciano Bianchi (Ulderico); Domenico Bartoli (Radoski)

Three months after the Milan première of *Il Turco in Italia*, Rossini was in Venice, having been commissioned again by the Teatro La Fenice, this time to compose a two-act *opera seria*, *Sigismondo*, to a libretto by Giuseppe Foppa who had previously collaborated with him on three of his comic operas. At its première on the first night of the carnival season on 26 December 1814, *Sigismondo* was politely received, but it was clear that the opera was a failure. (Writing to his mother about it, Rossini drew a flask or *fiasco* on the letter.) Though it was staged occasionally in other Italian towns up until 1827, *Sigismondo* was not seen or heard of again until the autumn of 1992 when the Teatro Comunale Chiabrera mounted a production which, conducted by Richard Bonynge, was performed in Rovigo, Treviso and Savona. On the day after the opera's première in 1814, a Venetian critic wrote that 'the libretto is the unhappy child of a writer who now submits the hundredth proof of his ineptitude'. Rossini's score was generally considered boring, even though at rehearsals the musicians of the Fenice orchestra had applauded it warmly.

The Rossini biographer Azevedo, referring to the ennui with which the opera was greeted, wrote that the composer, 'leading the performance, was himself seized by this boredom. Never, he said afterwards, had he suffered so much at a first performance as at that of *Sigismondo*.' Many years later Rossini told Hiller: 'One evening, I was really touched by the Venetians. That was at the première of *Sigismondo*, an opera that bored them dreadfully. I could see how gladly they would have given vent to their annoyance, but they restrained themselves, kept quiet, and let the music pass over them without disturbance. That kindness made me go quite soft!'

Sigismondo, King of Poland, has banished his wife, Aldimira, from court on the advice of his chief minister, Ladislao, an action which leads Aldimira's father, Ulderico, King of Bohemia, to declare war on Poland. In due course, Aldimira regains her rightful position. Rossini's score looks unpromising, except perhaps for Anagilda's aria, 'Sognava contenti', and a few bars here and there in other pieces. The composer made use of some of the score's better pages in subsequent operas: parts of two numbers were to turn up two years after the failure of *Sigismondo*, in that most popular of all Rossini operas, *Il Barbiere di Siviglia*. A theme from the opening chorus of *Sigismondo*'s Act II, 'In segreto a che ci chiama', is used as the theme of the opening number ('Piano, pianissimo') of *Il Barbiere*, while a *crescendo* from the Ladislao–Aldimira Act I duet, 'Perchè obbedir disdegni', was to become the famous *crescendo* in Don Basilio's aria, 'La calunnia'.

Opera composers of the eighteenth and early nineteenth centuries thought they were quite safe in recycling music from unsuccessful operas which, it seemed, were unlikely ever to be staged again. When the publication of his complete works was announced by his publishers in the 1850s, Rossini wrote that he was furious, because this would

> bring all my operas together before the eyes of the public. The same pieces will be found several times, for I considered that I had the right to remove from my fiascos those pieces which seemed the best, and to rescue them from shipwreck by placing them in new works. A fiasco appeared to be completely dead, but now, see, they've resuscitated them all!

After attending a performance in Savona of the 1992 revival of *Sigismondo*, Julian Budden wrote in *Opera*: 'Good to hear once, but definitely not for the repertoire.'

3

From *Elisabetta, regina d'Inghilterra* to *Otello*

Elisabetta, regina d'Inghilterra
(Elizabeth, Queen of England)

dramma in two acts

Principal characters:

Elisabetta, Queen of England   (soprano)
Leicester, Commander of the Army   (tenor)
Matilde, Leicester's wife   (soprano)
Enrico, Matilde's brother   (mezzo-soprano)
Norfolk, a Lord of the Realm   (tenor)
Guglielmo, Captain of the Guards   (tenor)

LIBRETTO by Giovanni Federico Schmidt

TIME: The late-sixteenth century
PLACE: London

FIRST PERFORMED at the Teatro San Carlo, Naples, 4 October 1815, with Isabella Colbran (Elisabetta); Girolama Dardanelli (Matilde); Maria Manzi (Enrico); Andrea Nozzari (Leicester); Manuel Garcia (Norfolk); Gaetano Chizzola (Guglielmo)

At the age of twenty-three Rossini was an extremely successful young composer who was perhaps beginning to mark time. *Sigismondo* had certainly not been considered by anyone to be an advance on his earlier operas. He was now, however, about to embark upon a highly fertile creative period, not in Venice, the scene of his previous triumphs, but in the south, in the city of Naples. Summoned there in the spring of 1815 by the colourful and influential impresario, Domenico Barbaja, he signed a contract under the terms of which he became musical director of two of Barbaja's theatres in Naples, the San Carlo and the Fondo, and agreed to compose two operas each year for Naples. He would be allowed, occasionally, to compose operas for other cities. In fact, during the first two years of his association with Naples, Rossini composed five operas for other cities, four of them for Rome. Naples, however, was to be his base for the next eight years, during which period he composed some of his greatest *opere serie*, moving away from the farces and comic operas of his youth.

After his initial meeting with Barbaja in the spring, Rossini returned to Bologna where he began work on his first opera for Naples, *Elisabetta, regina d'Inghilterra*. He was back in Naples in September to complete the opera after making the acquaintance of the singers engaged by Barbaja, among them the famous Spanish dramatic soprano Isabella Colbran, who was reputed to be Barbaja's mistress. It was for Colbran that Rossini composed the opera's title-role of Elizabeth I, Queen of England.

In 1815, only months after the battle of Waterloo, subjects drawn from English history were popular. The libretto of this pseudo-historical drama by Giovanni Federico Schmidt, a forty-year-old Tuscan who had already written a number of libretti for Neapolitan theatres, was based on a play by Carlo Federici which had been staged in Naples the previous year at the Teatro del Fondo. Federici's play was in turn derived from *The Recess, or A Tale of Other Times* by an English eighteenth-century novelist, Sophia Lee.

Queen Elizabeth learns from the Duke of Norfolk that Leicester, whom she loves, is secretly married to Matilde (not to Amy Robsart, as in real life). Elizabeth has Leicester imprisoned; but, when Norfolk's intrigues against her are revealed, she pardons Leicester. (Schmidt's libretto is said by some commentators, among them Herbert Weinstock in his biography of Rossini, to be based on Sir Walter Scott's *Kenilworth*, to whose plot it does indeed bear some similarity. But Scott's novel was not published until six years after the première of Rossini's opera.)

At its première on 4 October 1815, *Elisabetta* was received with immense enthusiasm. It was staged in other Italian towns and abroad, though not always with the success which had attended its Naples première. It was, for instance, a failure in Vienna in 1818. Its first London production was at the King's Theatre on 30 April 1818, but it seems never to have been staged in the United States. After March 1841, when *Elisabetta* was performed in Würzburg, its next appearance on the stage was at the Camden Festival in London in 1968, although Italian Radio had broadcast it in 1953 as a special coronation tribute to Queen Elizabeth II, with Lina Pagliughi as Elisabetta. Since then, the opera has been revived in Palermo in 1971 with Leyla Gencer superb as Elisabetta, at Aix-en-Provence in 1975 with Montserrat Caballé, in Turin in 1985 with Lella Cuberli, and in Naples in 1991 with Anna Caterina Antonacci.

With its orchestration strengthened to suit the immense size of the Teatro San Carlo, the overture Rossini had composed for *Aureliano in Palmira* in Milan two years previously was pressed into service again. The following year it was to be used once again for *Il Barbiere di Siviglia*, in which guise it remains a popular favourite today. That Rossini was perfectly happy to use the same overture for a drama as for a comedy may perhaps be thought cynical of him. He certainly was not someone to let a good piece of music go to waste, but he did not force unsuitable music upon dramatic situations. Music, after all, is remarkably ambiguous in its conveying of emotion. It can distinguish languid from martial, of course, but often has more difficulty with anger and merriment. A change of text can turn a vocal expression of fury into one of joy.

Elisabetta, regina d'Inghilterra is unusual in that it contains no roles for the lower male voices: all three male roles are written for tenors, the Naples company being at the time well supplied with splendid tenors. Nor does the opera contain any unaccompanied recitative. Rossini's highly dramatic and expressive recitative is at all times accompanied by the orchestra, with the result that *Elisabetta* appears more cohesive than his earlier *opere serie*.

Rossini's score is full of tuneful and dramatic music. Elisabetta's attractive opening cavatina ('Quant'è grato all' alma mia') is followed by a cabaletta ('Questo cor ben lo comprende') which, with a little alteration, was to turn up again the following year as the concluding section ('Io sono docile') of Rosina's aria, 'Una voce poco fa', in *Il Barbiere di Siviglia*. (Part of it had already been heard, the previous year, in Arsace's rondo, 'Più non vedrà quel perfido', in *Aureliano in Palmira*.) Some of the choruses, especially in Act I, are exhilarating, and the duet, 'Incauta, che festi!', for Leicester and Matilde engagingly combines a forceful dramatic attack with a springing lightness which anticipates Verdi. Matilde's aria, 'Sento un'interna voce', begins in a lyrical mood of almost Bellini-like languor. Its cabaletta, however, is irrepressibly Rossinian.

The eloquence of the accompanied recitative for Elisabetta and Norfolk, and the energy and dramatic force of their duet, 'Perchè mai, destin crudele', anticipate early Verdi, while the Act I finale, with its superb quartet, 'Se mi serbasti il soglio', and its florid, wide-ranging vocal line for Elisabetta, designed to show off Isabella Colbran's coloratura technique, is not only one of Rossini's most tautly constructed ensembles but also one of his most intensely dramatic. For its conclusion it borrows the overture's exciting *crescendo*.

The highlights of Act II include an affecting duet, 'Pensa che sol per poco', for the Queen and Matilde, in whose *andante* section ('Non bastan quelle lagrime') more than one writer on Rossini has heard the germination of Bellini's 'Mira, o Norma', and an equally fine trio ('L'avverso mio destino') which follows with the appearance of Leicester. An effective chorus, 'Qui soffermiamo il piè', in which soldiers and citizens join to mourn Leicester's fate, is followed by Norfolk's comparatively dull recitative and aria ('Deh! Troncate i ceppe suoi'), and by the more interesting dungeon scene, its orchestral prelude borrowed from *Ciro in Babilonia*. In this scene, Leicester's recitative and aria ('Sposa amata') are original and arresting, dramatic plausibility taking precedence over the formal requirements of the aria, in which flute and cor anglais play a prominent part. The duet ('Deh! scusa i trasporti') for the two tenors, Norfolk and Leicester, is lively, and the Act II finale with Elisabetta's beautiful aria ('Bell'alme generose') and highly decor-ated cabaletta ('Fuggi amor da questo seno') brings the opera to an exciting conclusion.

Elisabetta, regina d'Inghilterra, the first of Rossini's operas to dispense entirely with that unaccompanied recitative which tended to reduce dramatic tension, was also the first in which he wrote out in full all the embellishments he expected from his singers, although he had been moving towards this for some time. A key work in its composer's development, *Elisabetta* introduced a heightened dramatic vigour while retaining the mellifluous tunefulness of his earlier operas.

Torvaldo e Dorliska

dramma semiserio in two acts

Principal characters:

Torvaldo	(tenor)
Dorliska, wife of Torvaldo	(soprano)
Il Duca d'Ordow	(bass)
Giorgio, Custodian of the Duke of Ordow's castle	(bass)
Carlotta, sister of Giorgio	(mezzo-soprano)
Ormondo, Captain of the Duke's guard	(bass)

LIBRETTO by Cesare Sterbini

TIME: The middle ages
PLACE: Northern Europe

FIRST PERFORMED at the Teatro Valle, Rome, 26 December 1815, with Domenico Donzelli (Torvaldo); Adelaide Sala (Dorliska); Raniero Remorini (Giorgio); Agnese Loyselet (Carlotta); Filippo Galli (Il Duca d'Ordow); Cristoforo Bastianelli (Ormondo)

In November 1815, a month after the première of *Elisabetta, regina d'Inghilterra*, Rossini arrived in Rome to rehearse a production of *Il Turco in Italia* at the Teatro Valle and to compose a new opera for the same theatre. *Il Turco*, a huge success with its Rome audience, was performed frequently during November and December, during which time Rossini worked on the new opera, *Torvaldo e Dorliska*, whose libretto had been written by a thirty-one-year-old Roman civil servant, Cesare Sterbini.

Unlike many professional librettists of the time, Sterbini was well educated, with a knowledge of the classics and a familiarity with French and German literature. In 1813 he had written the text of a cantata, *Paolo e Virginia*, for a minor composer, Migliorucci, but *Torvaldo e Dorliska* was his first operatic commission. His libretto attracted, then and later, a great deal of abuse. Radiciotti wrote that it added 'to the unfortunately exorbitant number of those abortions which then infested the Italian musical theatre', and it is true that a synopsis of its plot does make *Torvaldo e Dorliska* sound incredibly stupid. But, though its tale of abduction and rescue is highly melodramatic, Sterbini's libretto is literate and reasonably well constructed. Reading it, one is by no means surprised that, only some weeks later, its author was to provide Rossini with the stylish libretto of *Il Barbiere di Siviglia*.

Torvaldo e Dorliska, though by no means a success, was apparently not as great a fiasco as *Sigismondo* had been in Venice twelve months previously. At any rate, according to Geltrude Righetti-Giorgi (the first Rosina in *Il Barbiere*) the *fiasco* or bulb-shaped wine flask which Rossini drew on the envelope of a letter to his mother was this time smaller than the one he had sent her after *Sigismondo*. (Francis Toye in his *Rossini* gets the story wrong, and says the drawing was a larger one. He refers to Sterbini's libretto as 'a clumsily constructed, dreary melodrama'.) The critic of the *Notizie del Giorno* wrote: 'The reception of the *opera semiseria* called *Torvaldo e Dorliska*, with new music by the maestro Rossini, has not justified the hopes that were reasonably conceived for it. It must be said that the subject of the very dismal and uninteresting libretto has not awakened Homer from his sleep.'

Thirty-five years later, Rossini told a French admirer that *Torvaldo e Dorliska* had been 'a good success', and indeed the opera was successful enough to be staged in Venice the following season, and in other Italian theatres during the next quarter of a century. It also reached Barcelona, Munich, Lisbon, Paris, Vienna, Budapest, Graz, Prague, Madrid and Moscow within ten years of its Rome première, but appears never to have been staged in London or New York. After a century and a half of neglect, *Torvaldo e Dorliska* was revived in Vienna in 1987 by the Wiener Kammeroper, and in 1989 in Savona.

The opera is set in and around the castle of the Duke of Ordow, somewhere in Northern Europe. The evil Duke, in love with Dorliska, wife of the knight Torvaldo, has ambushed the couple and fought with Torvaldo, whom he has left for dead. Dorliska makes her way to the castle, unaware that it is the Duke's home. Torvaldo, who had not been killed, arrives in disguise to rescue her, but when Dorliska recognises him and inadvertently reveals his identity, he is taken prisoner. Eventually, with the aid of Giorgio, the Duke's disaffected henchman, and the villagers who have decided to rise against their vile overlord, Torvaldo and Dorliska are rescued, and the Duke is led away to imprisonment and death.

In *Torvaldo e Dorliska*, though Rossini reverts to the unaccompanied recitative which he had abandoned in *Elisabetta, regina d'Inghilterra*, he uses it sparingly. The overture is at least new, and the opera contains some fine solo numbers, among them in Act I the arias for the Duke and for Dorliska, and the opening scene for Giorgio, the only *buffo* character in an otherwise serious opera. The dramatic Act I finale is musically convincing, and in Act II the Duke's aria, 'Ah! qual voce d'intorni ribombi!', is powerful enough for Rossini to have plundered it a year later for a duet in *Otello*. Torvaldo's music is mellifluous – a few bars of it turn up in *Otello* – but fails to bring his character to life. Dorliska is more successfully characterised, especially in Act II. The opera's audience in 1815, in addition to finding Sterbini's libretto unoriginal and uninspiring, may also have been confused by the mood of the work, which is not clearly defined. However, although it may not be one of Rossini's finest creations, *Torvaldo e Dorliska* certainly deserves occasional revival.

Il Barbiere di Siviglia
(The Barber of Seville)

commedia in two acts

Principal characters:

Count Almaviva	(tenor)
Doctor Bartolo	(bass)
Rosina, his ward	(mezzo-soprano)
Don Basilio, a teacher of singing	(bass)
Figaro, a barber	(baritone)
Berta, Rosina's governess	(soprano)
Fiorillo, Almaviva's servant	(bass)

LIBRETTO by Cesare Sterbini

TIME: The eighteenth century
PLACE: Seville, Spain

FIRST PERFORMED at the Teatro Argentina, Rome, 20 February 1816, with Geltrude Righetti-Giorgi (Rosina); Elisabetta Loyselet (Berta); Manuel Garcia (Almaviva); Luigi Zamboni (Figaro);

Bartolomeo Botticelli (Bartolo); Zenobio Vitarelli (Basilio); Paolo Biagelli (Fiorillo)

It was on 26 December 1815, the day of the première of *Torvaldo e Dorliska* at the Teatro Valle in Rome, that Rossini signed a contract with a rival opera house in the same city, the Teatro di Torre Argentina, under the terms of which he undertook to compose a comic opera for the carnival season which was opening that evening. He had no idea what the subject of the opera would be: the contract merely stipulated that 'the said Rossini promises and binds himself to compose, and produce on the stage, the second comic drama to be represented in the said season at the theatre indicated, and to the libretto which shall be given to him by the said manager, whether this libretto be old or new'.

Rossini was required 'to deliver his score in the middle of the month of January, and to adapt it to the voices of the singers; obliging himself, moreover, to make, if necessary, all the changes which may be required as much for the good execution of the music as to suit the capabilities or exigencies of the singers'. The composer was also obliged 'to direct his opera according to the custom, and to assist personally at all the vocal and orchestral rehearsals as many times as it shall be necessary, either at the theatre or elsewhere, at the will of the director; he obliges himself also to assist at the first three representations, to be given consecutively, and to direct the execution at the piano'. All this was standard practice.

In return, Rossini was promised the sum of four hundred Roman *scudi* (equivalent to about £500 today), to be paid immediately after the third performance, and 'lodging, during the term of the agreement, in the same house that is assigned to Signor Luigi Zamboni'. Zamboni was a baritone in the company, and a friend of Rossini. Indeed, Rossini wrote the role of Figaro in the new opera for him, so presumably they lodged amicably enough together in the same house. But, in general, the circumstances seem hardly propitious to the creation of a masterpiece: three weeks in which to agree upon a subject, produce a libretto and compose an opera. A masterpiece, however, is precisely what was created. In 1898, the eighty-five-year-old Verdi said of it, 'I cannot help believing that, for abundance of ideas, comic verve and truth of declamation, *Il Barbiere di Siviglia* is the most beautiful *opera buffa* in existence.'

Rossini himself, who was not given to making exaggerated claims for his own works, thought in later years that the third act of his *Otello*, the second act of *Guillaume Tell*, and the whole of *Il Barbiere* might perhaps live on. He was right about *The Barber*, which has never gone out of fashion thanks to its abundant possession of those qualities so accurately ascribed to it by Verdi: musical ideas, pace, and a vocal line of such character that it often seems as natural as speech.

In choosing a librettist for the opera, the impresario of the Teatro Argentina turned first to Jacopo Ferretti, who was later to write *La Cenerentola* for Rossini and four libretti for Donizetti, but Ferretti's synopsis of a plot revolving around the romantic triangular entanglement of an officer, the hostess of an inn, and a lawyer sounded distinctly unpromising. Time being short, the impresario then turned to Cesare Sterbini, the librettist of *Torvaldo e Dorliska*. Sterbini suggested a reshaping of Giuseppe Petrosellini's *Il Barbiere di Siviglia*, based on the play *Le Barbier de Séville* by Beaumarchais. Petrosellini's libretto had been written for Paisiello, whose opera had been staged in St Petersburg in 1782 and subsequently in many opera houses throughout Europe. It possessed the advantages, for Rossini and Sterbini, of being a known subject and of existing already in libretto form, requiring only a certain amount of adaptation.

For Rossini, however, there was a possible disadvantage in the fact that Paisiello's opera, though it had not been recently revived, was still immensely respected. Might not the admirers of Paisiello take offence at a young composer's presumption in appearing to challenge the older master directly? In order to forestall this, Rossini wrote to the seventy-five-year-old Paisiello, declaring (according to Rossini) that 'I had not wanted to enter into a contest with him, being aware of my inferiority, but had wanted only to treat a subject that delighted me, while avoiding as much as possible the exact situations in his libretto'. Paisiello is supposed to have replied that he had no objection, and that he wished the project well. But Rossini and Sterbini were still somewhat nervous, and decided to call their opera *Almaviva*, retaining Beaumarchais' sub-title, *L'Inutile Precauzione* (The Useless Precaution). In addition, the printed libretto on sale at the first performances contained the following prefatory note:

Beaumarchais' comedy, entitled *The Barber of Seville or The Useless Precaution*, is presented in Rome in the form of a comic drama, under the title of *Almaviva or The Useless Precaution*, in order that the public may be fully convinced of the sentiments of respect and veneration by which the composer of the music of this drama is animated with regard to the celebrated Paisiello, who has already treated the subject under its original title.

Invited to undertake this difficult task, Maestro Gioachino Rossini, in order to avoid the reproach of entering rashly into rivalry with the immortal composer who preceded him, expressly required that *The Barber of Seville* should be entirely versified anew, and also that new situations should be added for musical pieces in the modern theatrical taste, which is so much changed since the time when the renowned Paisiello wrote his work.

Certain other differences between the arrangement of the present drama and that of the above-mentioned French comedy were produced by the necessity of introducing choruses, both for conformity with modern usage, and because they are indispensable for musical effect in a large theatre. The courteous public is informed of this in advance, that it may also excuse the author of the new drama who, unless obliged by these imperious circumstances, would never have ventured to introduce the least change into the French work, already consecrated by the applause of all the theatres in Europe.

Despite these protestations on the part of Rossini and Sterbini, it would appear that the first-night audience contained a number of Paisiello supporters bent on creating a disturbance. As can too easily happen on such occasions, events played into their hands. Laughter, catcalls and whistling broke out even before the opera began, when the young Rossini entered the orchestra pit wearing an elegant, hazel-coloured jacket in Spanish style, with gold buttons. In the first scene, the celebrated Spanish tenor Manuel Garcia, as Almaviva, did not sing 'Ecco ridente in cielo' (which Rossini composed for him the following day, or rather adapted from a chorus he had written for *Aureliano in Palmira* in 1814); at the première, Garcia sang a Spanish melody which he had arranged himself, to his own guitar accompaniment. As he was tuning his guitar under Rosina's window, a string broke, which produced more laughter and hisses. The audience was not impressed by the Spanish song and, according to the Rosina of that evening, 'the pit listened to it just enough to be able to give an ironical imitation of it afterwards.' Not surprisingly, when Figaro entered carrying another guitar, the laughter swelled to a sustained fortissimo, and hardly a note of Figaro's 'Largo al factotum' was heard.

In the next scene the bass Vitarelli, who was singing the role of Basilio, stumbled over a small trap-door which had been left open by mistake, bruised his face badly, and almost broke his nose. He had to sing 'La calunnia' with a handkerchief held to his nose, and the audience, thinking that this was all part of the stage business, decided it did not like it, and hissed anew. At the beginning of the Act I finale, a cat appeared on stage. Figaro chased it in one direction, Bartolo another, and the frightened creature took refuge in Rosina's skirts. The curtain fell on a scene of confusion, and Rossini turned to the noisy audience, shrugged his shoulders and began to applaud. Offended by what they considered a contemptuous gesture, the audience was so noisily rebellious throughout Act II that very little of the music was heard. Rossini remained perfectly calm, and left the theatre immediately after the last chord of the finale. When members of the cast went to his house later to console him, they found the composer fast asleep. On the second night he was tactfully ill, and stayed away from the theatre. The second performance went much better, and an account of what happened at its conclusion exists in Rossini's own words:

> I was sleeping peacefully when I was awakened suddenly by a deafening uproar out in the street, accompanied by a brilliant glow of torches. As soon as I got up, I saw that they were coming in my direction. Still half asleep, and remembering the scene of the preceding night, I thought that they were coming to set fire to the building, and I saved myself by going to a stable at the back of the courtyard. But lo, after a few moments, I heard Garcia calling me at the top of his voice. He finally located me. 'Get a move on, you. Come on, now. Listen to those shouts of "Bravo, bravissimo Figaro." An unprecedented success. The street is full of people. They want to see you.' But still heartbroken over my new jacket gone to the devil, I answered, 'Fuck them and their bravos and all the rest. I'm not coming out of here.' I don't know how poor Garcia phrased my refusal to that turbulent throng. In fact, he was hit in the eye by an orange, which gave him a black eye for several days. Meanwhile, the uproar in the street increased more and more.

After its initial seven performances in Rome, *Il Barbiere di Siviglia* (as it began to be called from the time it was staged in Bologna six months later) went on to establish itself as an undoubted success throughout Italy and in countless cities abroad. Its first London performance was at His Majesty's Theatre on 10 March 1818, and its first New York performance on 3 May 1819. It has never lost its immense popularity: any opera house which has not staged Rossini's *Barber of Seville* must be a very new one.

The French dramatist Pierre-Augustin Caron de Beaumarchais was born in 1732, and died in 1799. His three plays about the barber Figaro and the Almaviva family were not conceived as an integrated trilogy: the first of them, *Le Barbier de Séville*, almost began its life as an *opéra comique*, for Beaumarchais was himself a musician and amateur composer. When the Paris Opéra-Comique refused it, he rewrote it as a play, which was staged in 1775 by the Comédie-Française and has remained in the repertoire of that august company ever since. Seven years after the play's première in Paris, Paisiello's opera based on it was staged for the first time. *Le Mariage de Figaro*, Beaumarchais' play about the same characters a few years later, was performed in 1784, and Mozart's operatic version, *Le Nozze di Figaro*, was first heard in Vienna in 1786. The third play, *La Mère coupable* (The Guilty Mother), first performed in 1797, unlike the others was written not as comedy but as sentimental drama. In it, the Countess Rosina is seen twenty years later. The two children of her marriage, Léon and Florestine, are in love with each other: not incestuously, for they are finally proved to be the illegitimate offspring of the Count and the Countess respectively, with other partners.

Social criticism permeates *The Marriage of Figaro*, but there is no trace of it in *The Barber of Seville*, a sunny comedy whose simple plot of an old guardian with designs on his ward being foiled by the girl and her lover goes back to Molière's *École des femmes*. Beaumarchais' achievement lay in his realistic delineation of the characters, and in particular his creation of the quick-witted Figaro who, though clearly descended from a long line of gaily scheming servants that can be traced back to Plautus, is also an individual, and a modern one. *The Marriage of Figaro* brought Mozart's masterpiece into being, yet in a way *The Barber of Seville* is even better opera material. Mozart and Da Ponte had to take the sting out of *The Marriage of Figaro* in order to turn it into opera. *The Barber of Seville* possesses no sting, and Rossini's effervescent *opera buffa* has little difficulty in remaining faithful to the spirit of the original play.

Rossini liked to boast that it took him only thirteen days to write *Il Barbiere di Siviglia*. (When he heard the story some years later, the even faster-working Donizetti is said to have replied, 'Yes, I know.

Isn't he lazy!') But it is at least possible that Rossini worked on his opera for nearly three weeks, and his score contains quite a lot of music from his earlier operas. The overture was first composed for *Aureliano in Palmira* in 1813, then used with slight modifications of scoring for *Elisabetta, regina d'Inghilterra* in 1815. It came round for the third time with *Il Barbiere*. Other borrowed passages in the opera include the following:

(a) The opening chorus, 'Piano, pianissimo'. This derives from the opening chorus of Act II of *Sigismondo* (1814).

(b) Almaviva's aria, 'Ecco ridente in cielo'. This is based on the first six bars of the chorus of priests, 'Sposa del grande Osiride', in *Aureliano in Palmira*.

(c) Rosina's aria, 'Una voce poco fa'. The second part of the aria, 'Io sono docile', first appeared in Arsace's rondo, 'Non lasciarmi in tal momento', in *Aureliano in Palmira*, and was also used in *Elisabetta, regina d'Inghilterra* in the cabaletta of Elisabetta's opening aria.

(d) Basilio's aria, 'La calunnia'. Its beginning derives from a duet for Arsace and Zenobia in *Aureliano in Palmira*, while the *crescendo* comes from a duet for Ladislao and Aldimira in Act I of *Sigismondo*.

(e) The Rosina–Figaro duet, 'Dunque io son'. The tune sung by Rosina to the words 'Ah, tu solo Amor tu sei' was first heard in Fanny's aria, 'Vorrei spiegarvi il giubilo' in *La Cambiale di matrimonio* (1810).

(f) Bartolo's aria, 'A un dottor della mia sorte'. The orchestral motif, when Bartolo sings 'I confetti alla ragazza, il ricamo sul tamburo', comes from a duet in the one-act opera, *Il Signor Bruschino* (1813).

(g) The Act II trio, 'Ah, qual colpo'. The tune begun by Rosina with the words 'Dolce nodo avventurato' is borrowed from 'Voi che amato, compiangete' in the cantata, *Egle ed Irene* (1814).

(h) The storm music in Act II. This was first heard in *La Pietra del paragone* (1812) and subsequently in *L'Occasione fa il ladro* (also 1812).

Discreet borrowings from other composers include 'Zitti, zitti, piano, piano' in the Act II trio, 'Ah, quel colpo', which is virtually the same tune (though at a quicker tempo) as the opening of Simon's first aria in Haydn's *The Seasons* ('Schon eilet froh der Ackersmann zur Arbeit auf das Feld'); part of the Act I finale ('Mi par d'esser con la testa') which makes use of a tune from the Act II finale of Spontini's *La Vestale*; and Berta's aria, which is said to be taken from a Russian folk song.

The plot of Rossini's opera follows closely that of Beaumarchais' play. Count Almaviva loves Rosina, the ward of Dr Bartolo, a crusty old bachelor who plans to marry her himself. Almaviva persuades the town barber and general factotum, Figaro, to arrange a meeting for him, and gains entrance to Bartolo's house disguised as a soldier seeking a billet. This attempt fails, so he returns disguised as a substitute for Don Basilio, the priest who is Rosina's music master, who Almaviva claims is ill. When the real Don Basilio arrives he is bribed to leave again, and Almaviva makes plans to elope with Rosina.

Bartolo arouses Rosina's jealousy by pretending that Almaviva loves someone else, and she promises to forget him and marry her guardian. When the time for the planned elopement arrives, she reproaches her lover, whom she knows only as Lindoro, but he convinces her of his sincerity and reveals his true identity. Bartolo arrives with officers to arrest Almaviva, only to find that the lovers have, a few moments earlier, been married. He grudgingly accepts the situation.

Although its dramatic energy falters somewhat towards the end of Act II, Rossini's *Barber* is one of the most enjoyable of comic operas, full of delightful and apt melodic invention, and bubbling over with gaiety and high spirits. The underlying air of seriousness to be found in Mozart's *Le Nozze di Figaro* is entirely absent, but this merely reflects the difference between the respective Beaumarchais plays. The French dramatist's Almaviva trilogy becomes more serious as it progresses.

In *Il Barbiere di Siviglia*, Count Almaviva introduces himself in a gracefully flowing two-part C major cavatina, 'Ecco ridente in cielo', whose concluding *allegro* makes it clear that the tenor who sings Almaviva will need to possess great vocal flexibility. Figaro's bustling entrance aria, 'Largo al factotum', is famous for its bullish display of energy, but it too, like virtually every bar of Rossini's score, is graceful as well as hyperactive. One might say that the high baritone voice, which Verdi was to develop so brilliantly, really came into existence with Rossini's Figaro, before whom no real distinction was made between baritone and bass. Rossini's amiable schemer revels in his high G at the end of 'Largo al factotum', flashing it about as a piece of self-advertisement. After 'Se il mio nome', Almaviva's charming serenade to Rosina, the first scene concludes with 'All' idea di quel metallo', a brilliant duet for the Count and Figaro in which Rossini's melodic ideas almost tumble over each other in their profusion. The end of the duet is absolutely exhilarating.

Rosina's cavatina, 'Una voce poco fa', its *andante* first section followed by a faster coloratura conclusion, is remarkable, as is every number in the opera, for the apparent ease with which Rossini creates phrases which are simultaneously both melodic and meaningful. The role of Rosina was written for mezzo-soprano. For many years it was appropriated by coloratura sopranos, necessitating the transposition of 'Una voce poco fa' up a tone as well as alterations elsewhere to the singer's vocal line, but in recent times mezzo-sopranos have won the role back for themselves.

Don Basilio's 'La calunnia' with its famous *crescendo* is a favourite as much with basses as with their audiences. The duet, 'Dunque io son', for Rosina and Figaro, is brilliantly inventive, and the smug Doctor Bartolo's 'A un dottor della mia sorte' is a superb piece of characterisation. A bass in the Florence production of the opera nine months after its première found Bartolo's aria too difficult, so the composer Pietro Romani wrote for him a substitute aria, 'Manca un foglio', which for many years was generally used instead of Rossini's 'A un dottor'. Nowadays, however, no bass worth his salt would admit to finding the tongue-twisting patter of Rossini's aria too difficult to sing, though many make it sound as though it is.

Act II begins with a delightful scene in which Almaviva returns to Bartolo's house in clerical garb ('Pace e gioia') and gives Rosina a singing lesson under the watchful eye of Bartolo who contributes an old-fashioned arietta ('Quando mi sei vicina') in order to demonstrate how much better it used to be done. Later, Don Basilio is seen off the premises to the most suavely lilting of musical phrases ('Buona sera, mio signore') in a quintet. Rossini's storm music makes its third appearance, followed by a trio, 'Ah, qual colpo', which is both amusing and musically enchanting. Just before the brief finale, Almaviva is given a grand recitative and aria ('Cessa di più resistere') in which he formally reveals his identity to all and sundry. The aria with cabaletta is rarely heard in modern performances, for it is long, heavily decorated, and beyond the vocal grasp of most Almavivas. Rossini was to make use of the cabaletta, 'Ah, più lieto, il più felice', a year later for the eponymous heroine's 'Non più mesta' in *La Cenerentola*.

It is in the Act I finale that Rossini is at his magnificent best, its depiction ('Fredda ed immobile') of the stupor in which the characters find themselves leading finally by way of *crescendo* to a riotous climax. Giuseppe Verdi chose a musical phrase (sung to the words 'Signor, giudizia, per carità') from this finale to exemplify

Rossini's genius for truthful dramatic characterisation in music. 'The phrase', Verdi wrote to a friend in 1882, 'is neither melody nor harmony. As declamation it is true and good, and so it is music.' In 1898 Verdi told the French music critic Camille Bellaigue that *Il Barbiere di Siviglia*, 'with its abundance of real musical ideas, its comic verve and its truthful declamation, is the most beautiful *opera buffa* in existence.' It is a verdict with which few would disagree.

La Gazzetta
(The Gazette)

opera buffa in two acts

Principal characters:

Don Pomponio Storione	(bass)
Lisetta, his daughter	(soprano)
Filippo, a young innkeeper in love with Lisetta	(bass)
Doralice, a traveller	(soprano)
Anselmo, her father	(bass)
Alberto, a wealthy young man	(tenor)
Madama La Rose	(mezzo-soprano)
Monsù Traversen	(bass)

LIBRETTO by Giuseppe Palomba and Andrea Leone Tottola

TIME: The eighteenth century
PLACE: Paris

FIRST PERFORMED at the Teatro dei Fiorentini, Naples, 26 September 1816, with Margherita Chabrand (Lisetta); Francesca Cardini (Doralice); Maria Manzi (Madama La Rose); Alberico Curioni (Alberto); Carlo Casaccia (Don Pomponio Storione); Felice Pellegrini (Filippo); Giovanni Pace (Anselmo); Francesco Sparano (Monsù Traversen)

On returning to Naples after the Rome première of *Il Barbiere di Siviglia*, Rossini discovered that, some days previously, the Teatro San Carlo had been destroyed by fire. His next opera for Naples would therefore be staged at the Teatro dei Fiorentini. First, however, he had to compose a cantata to celebrate the marriage of Maria Carolina, daughter of the King of Naples, to the Duc de Berry, second son of the future Charles X of France. Resorting to self-plagiarism for eight of the work's eleven numbers, Rossini plundered the scores of *Il Barbiere* and seven of his earlier operas. The cantata, *Le Nozze di Teti e di Peleo*, was performed for the first and, so far, the only time at the Teatro del Fondo on 24 April 1816. Rossini then turned his attention to the supervision of a production of *Tancredi* in Naples and to the composition of his next opera, *La Gazzetta*, whose première had been scheduled for August.

On this occasion, Rossini failed to complete the opera with his usual celerity. It has been suggested that this may have been because he was being distracted by the charms of Isabella Colbran, the Spanish soprano who was the mistress of the impresario Barbaja, and who had sung the title-role in Rossini's *Elisabetta, regina d'Inghilterra*. At thirty-one, Colbran was the young composer's senior by seven years. She was eventually to become his wife.

Several weeks later than expected, *La Gazzetta* finally reached the stage of the Teatro dei Fiorentini on 26 September 1816. After a few performances it was withdrawn, the general opinion being that its libretto was clumsy and its music undistinguished. The opera was never staged again during Rossini's lifetime, and remained forgotten until an Italian radio performance in 1960 and a stage production by the Vienna Chamber Opera in 1976.

Giuseppe Palomba's libretto (revised at Rossini's request by Andrea Leone Tottola) was based on a play by Carlo Goldoni, *Il Matrimonio per concorso*, which had first been performed in 1763, and which had been the subject of an opera of the same title by Niccolo Jommelli, staged in Ludwigsburg in 1766. Set in a Paris inn, Rossini's opera recounts a complicated story involving a ridiculously pompous old man, Don Pomponio, who has advertised in *The Gazette* for a husband for his daughter, Lisetta, who is in love with Filippo, the young proprietor of the inn. Other guests at the inn include another father, Anselmo, with a daughter, Doralice, to be married off, and Alberto, a wealthy young man in search of a wife. The plot abounds in the usual twists and turns, with mistaken identity, lovers' quarrels and threatened duels well to the fore, but of course all ends happily with the right couples paired off, and the two fathers accepting the situation.

The overture, one of Rossini's jolliest, was rescued from potential oblivion when he used it again some months later in Rome for *La Cenerentola*. The opening chorus of *La Gazzetta* gets the opera off to a lively start, and much of what follows is highly enjoyable, though some of it has been lifted from earlier scores and the *secco* recitative is not only somewhat excessive but also largely in Neapolitan dialect. Several numbers had first been heard in *Il Turco in Italia*, a scene from whose second act, including the chorus, 'Amor la danza mova', and the superb quintet, 'Oh! guardate che accidente', turns up in *La Gazzetta*, as does the Fiorilla–Geronio duet from *Il Turco*. A trio is taken from *La Pietra del paragone*. Even the words of these numbers are largely the same, with some minor alterations to accommodate Don Pomponio's Neapolitan dialect. Other pieces are taken from *Torvaldo e Dorliska*. Lisetta's aria, 'Presto, dico', is 'Presto, amiche', an alternative cavatina which Rossini wrote for Fiorilla in *Il Turco in Italia*.

   Despite all this self-borrowing, *La Gazzetta* is an engaging comic opera, and no less coherent than several others which are still occasionally performed today. Its *buffo* elements are hardly on the level of *Il Barbiere di Siviglia*, but much of its lyrical writing, whether new or borrowed, reveals a typically Rossinian sweetness of utterance. *La Gazzetta* deserves to be revived by some enterprising opera festival.

Otello

dramma in three acts

Principal characters:

Otello	(tenor)
Desdemona	(soprano)
Iago	(tenor)
Rodrigo	(tenor)
Emilia	(soprano)
Elmiro, Desdemona's father	(bass)

LIBRETTO by Francesco Maria Berio di Salsa

TIME: The end of the eighteenth century
PLACE: Venice

FIRST PERFORMED at the Teatro del Fondo, Naples, 4 December 1816, with Andrea Nozzari (Otello); Isabella Colbran (Desdemona); Giuseppe Ciccimarra (Iago); Giovanni David (Rodrigo); Maria Manzi (Emilia); Michele Benedetti (Elmiro)

Rossini's next commission in Naples followed quickly after the failure of *La Gazzetta*, and this time he composed with his habitual speed. *Otello*, its libretto (by the Marchese Francesco Maria Berio di Salsa) a travesty of Shakespeare's *Othello*, was ready for performance at the Teatro del Fondo, the temporary home of the San Carlo company, within a few weeks. At its première on 4 December 1816, *Otello* was greeted with enthusiasm, and before long it was being produced in other Italian cities and abroad. Rival German translations of the opera were staged in Vienna in 1819: in January at the Theater an der Wien, and in April at the Kärntnertor Theater. Four years later it was performed in Vienna in Italian. London first saw *Otello*, in Italian, at His Majesty's Theatre on 16 May 1822. The opera was later staged in English at the Princess's Theatre in 1844. The first New York performance, in Italian, was on 7 February 1826. Rossini's *Otello* continued to be staged in Italy and abroad for the next fifty years or more, but in 1887 the first performance of Verdi's *Otello*, one of the greatest music dramas of all, swept Rossini's opera from the boards.

It is only in recent years that Rossini's *Otello* has begun to re-emerge. A concert performance by the American Opera Society in 1954 at New York's Town Hall was followed in 1961 by the Philopera Circle's stage production in London at the St Pancras Town Hall. A more lavish revival by the Rome Opera in 1964, designed by Giorgio De Chirico, had Agostino Lazzari as Otello and Virginia Zeani as Desdemona. The enterprising Wexford Festival in Ireland staged *Otello* in 1967, and there have been subsequent revivals in Philadelphia (1979), Palermo (1980), Venice (1986) and a much admired production in Pesaro (1988) with the American bel canto specialists, Chris Merritt (Otello), June Anderson (Desdemona) and Rockwell Blake (Rodrigo).

Francesco Maria Berio, Marquis of Salsa (1767–1820), was a Neapolitan aristocratic dilettante whom Stendhal, despite the fact that they were friends, described as an 'unmentionable literary hack'. A more charitable description of him is offered by an English writer, Sydney Morgan (wife of a distinguished physician, Sir

Thomas Charles Morgan), in her *Italy* (1821). 'The Marchese Berio',
Lady Morgan wrote, 'is a nobleman of wealth, high rank, and of
very considerable literary talent and acquirement, which extends
itself to the utmost verge of the philosophy and belles-lettres of
England, France, Germany, and his native country. He has read
everything, and continues to read everything; and I have seen his
sitting-room loaded with a new importation of English novels and
poetry while he was himself employed in writing, *al improvviso*, a
beautiful ode to Lord Byron, in all the first transports of enthusiasm,
on reading (for the first time) that canto of *Childe Harold*, so read and
so admired by all Italy [Canto IV].'

Whether literary hack or nobleman of considerable literary
talent, Berio provided Rossini with an absolutely ludicrous adaptation of Shakespeare's *Othello*, its entire action set in Venice. Otello
interrupts the wedding of Desdemona and Rodrigo (who is a
conflation of Shakespeare's Roderigo and Cassio), challenges Rodrigo to a duel, is exiled, but returns secretly to Venice and kills
Desdemona in a fit of jealous rage. Iago, who has played a
comparatively minor role in these happenings, nevertheless com-
mits suicide in remorse. After seeing a performance in Venice in
1818, Lord Byron wrote:

> They have been crucifying *Othello* into an opera (*Otello* by Rossini).
> Music good but lugubrious – but as for the words! All the real scenes
> with Iago cut out – & the greatest nonsense instead – the handkerchief
> turned into a *billet doux*, and the first Singer [i.e. the Otello] would not
> *black* his face – for some exquisite reasons assigned in the preface.
> Scenery – dresses – & music very good.

It is in the last of its three acts that Berio's libretto strays least from
Shakespeare, and it is in this act that Rossini's music, amiable
enough in the first two acts though not always dramatically apt,
pays its greatest heed to the demands of the drama. But there are
also many passages in the earlier acts which are dramatically
felicitous as well as musically delightful.

The *andante* overture begins as an exact copy of the *Turco in Italia*
overture, and also borrows from that of *Sigismondo*. (Rossini was later
to claim that he wrote it incarcerated in a room against his will 'by
the most bald-headed and frenzied of directors, who left me there
with only a plateful of macaroni and the threat that he would not let
me out until I had written every note of it'.) After an opening chorus
in which the citizens of Venice sing the praises of Otello, and which

certainly gets the opera off to a rousing start, the victorious warrior enters, followed by Iago and Rodrigo, to the accompaniment of a jaunty and busily decorated march. It is as early as this opening scene that one realises what a tenor-heavy opera *Otello* is to be, for the characters participating in it – Otello, Iago, Rodrigo, and even the Doge of Venice – are all tenors. Otello is allowed here his only solo in the entire opera, 'Ah! si, per voi già sento', a three-part aria with a robust opening cavatina, a slower, heartfelt *andantino* in which he thinks of Desdemona while Iago mutters about revenge, and a cabaletta to display Otello's coloratura flexibility.

A duet for Iago and Rodrigo, 'No, non temer', is one of the score's weaker numbers, but the duet for Desdemona and Emilia which follows with the change of scene to a room in the house of Elmiro, Desdemona's father, has both tenderness and charm. Preceded by highly dramatic recitative accompanied, as throughout *Otello*, by full orchestra, the duet itself is exquisite, and its closing section, 'Quanto son fieri i palpiti', where the two female voices, which had earlier been heard alternately, now sing together, reveals a mood of deep feeling. (It also reveals music first heard in *Aureliano in Palmira*.) The Act I finale, launched by the bass voice of Elmiro, the opera's only non-tenor male character, is striking, its varying moods closely matched by Rossini's score. A beautiful and moving central trio, 'Ti parli d'amore', makes use of music first heard in *L'Equivoco strava-gante*, and with the entrance of Otello to prevent Desdemona's imminent marriage to Rodrigo the finale moves to its conclusion with dramatic swiftness.

Rodrigo's aria ('Ah! come mai non senti pietà') with cabaletta at the beginning of Act II, after Desdemona has confused him by saying that she is already Otello's wife, is written for the upper reaches of the tenor voice and replete with hectic coloratura. It is, however, a mundane piece of composition, and those familiar with the song known as Rossini's Comic Duet for Two Cats ('Duetto buffo di due gatti') will be disconcerted to hear the final section of that duet emerging in the cabaletta. (In fact, though it utilises themes from this cabaletta and from the Rodrigo–Iago duet in Act I, the Cat Duet was not assembled by Rossini, but by a certain G. Berthold.)

The scene between Otello and Iago with its duet, 'Non m'in-ganno', in which Iago produces, not a handkerchief, but a letter intended by Desdemona for Otello, and convinces the Moor that it was written to Rodrigo, is in context extremely effective. Rossini's skill in differentiating the two tenor voices and the contrasting emotions they convey is fascinating, even though the duet's final section ('L'ira d'avverso fato') had been composed the previous year for *Torvaldo e Dorliska*. More than one other writer on Rossini has suggested that Verdi, thirty-five years later, may have had the fierce rhythmic thrust of this cabaletta in mind when he composed the Rigoletto–Gilda duet, 'Sì, vendetta, tremenda vendetta', at the end of Act II in *Rigoletto*.

Otello and Rodrigo confront each other in a lively duet ('Ah, vieni'), a battle of the high Cs which becomes, with the arrival of Desdemona, an even livelier trio. A dramatic aria for Desdemona with interjections by Emilia, Elmiro and ensemble, aided by the familiar Rossini *crescendo* when the female chorus announces that Otello is safe, brings Act II to an end on a high pitch of excitement.

After an orchestral prelude which exudes an air of foreboding, Act III begins with a scene between Desdemona and Emilia in accompanied recitative, punctuated by an uneasy figure from the prelude. Emilia's attempts to comfort her mistress are interrupted by the plaintive song of a gondolier heard in the distance. What the gondolier (yet another tenor) sings, somewhat improbably, are the familiar words, 'Nessun maggior dolore/Che ricordarsi del tempo felice/Nella miseria' ([There is] no greater sorrow than to recall past happiness in time of misery), from Canto V of Dante's *Inferno*. The interpolation of Dante into Berio's text was Rossini's idea, and his sensitive setting of the lines, supported by wind and *tremolo* strings, emphasises the atmosphere of foreboding which permeates this entire scene.

Desdemona's strophic Willow Song ('Assisa a piè d'un salice') which she sings to her own accompaniment on the harp, discreetly supported by the orchestra's strings and woodwind, is both exquisite and strangely powerful, its vocal line developing from strophe to strophe from a simple directness to a more florid state of agitation. As in Verdi's *Otello*, the wind's startling interruption is graphically created in the orchestra. The final strophe returns to an undecorated simplicity but remains incomplete as Desdemona, in distress, abandons her song.

After the beautiful and affecting melody of Desdemona's *larghetto* prayer, a jarring note is struck with the oddly jaunty orchestral

accompaniment to the entrance of Otello. Rossini recovers in
Otello's masterly recitative, though the formality and conventional
coloratura at the beginning of the Otello–Desdemona duet ('Non
arrestare il colpo') which follows are somewhat damaging to the
dramatic tension. The conclusion of the duet, in which a raging
orchestra impersonates the tempest outside as Otello stabs (instead
of strangling) Desdemona, is superb, but thereafter the opera moves
to its perfunctory conclusion with an unseemly haste. This third act,
though it shows the composer developing as a musical dramatist, is
not quite the masterpiece some Rossini commentators claim it to be.

Rossini's *Otello* is enjoyable, and still stage-worthy, but it is almost
impossible to listen to it today without Verdi's incontestably greater
work in one's mind and memory.

4

From *La Cenerentola* to *Mosè in Egitto*

La Cenerentola
(Cinderella)

dramma giocoso in two acts

Principal characters:

Angiolina (Cenerentola), step-
  daughter of Don Magnifico   (contralto)
Don Magnifico, Baron of Mountflask (bass)
Don Ramiro, Prince of Salerno   (tenor)
Dandini, his valet   (bass)
Clorinda, daughter of Don Magnifico (soprano)
Tisbe, daughter of Don Magnifico   (mezzo-soprano)
Alidoro, tutor to Don Ramiro   (bass)

LIBRETTO by Jacopo Ferretti

TIME: Mythical
PLACE: A castle and palace in a mythical country

FIRST PERFORMED at the Teatro Valle, Rome, 25 January 1817, with Geltrude Righetti-Giorgi (Angiolina); Caterina Rossi (Clorinda); Teresa Mariani (Tisbe); Giacomo Guglielmi (Don Ramiro); Andrea Verni (Don Magnifico); Giuseppe de Begnis (Dandini); Zenobio Vitarelli (Alidoro)

Before leaving Rome after the first performances of *Il Barbiere di*

Siviglia early in the year, Rossini had agreed to return in the autumn with a new opera to open the carnival season on 26 December 1816. However, he did not arrive in Rome until mid-December and, in any case, a problem had arisen, caused by the papal censor's rejection of the libretto proposed by the Teatro Valle's impresario, Pietro Cartoni. Cartoni then approached Jacopo Ferretti, who had provided a number of libretti for both the Teatro Valle and the Teatro Argentina in Rome, and, according to a memoir left by Ferretti, he, Cartoni and Rossini, two nights before Christmas, spent the evening in a room in the impresario's house, drinking tea and discussing possible subjects for the opera. When Ferretti suggested Cinderella, Rossini, who had already retired to a bed in the room, asked when he could have the libretto and, on being told 'Tomorrow morning, if I stay awake all night', murmured his acceptance and immediately went to sleep.

The libretto that Ferretti produced for Rossini, whether the day before Christmas or somewhat later, was a reworking of the Cinderella story from Charles Perrault's 1697 collection, *Les Contes de ma Mère l'Oye* (Mother Goose Tales), but based largely on the libretto written by Charles-Guillaume Etienne for Nicolas Isouard's *Cendrillon* (Cinderella), which had been produced successfully at the Paris Opéra-Comique in 1810, and subsequently staged in a number of European cities (though nowhere in Italy). Etienne's libretto had also been set by a German composer, Daniel Steibelt, whose *Cendrillon* was performed, also in 1810, in St Petersburg where Steibelt was director of the Imperial Opera. Felice Romani had based his libretto for Stefano Pavesi's *Agatina, o La virtù premiata* (Milan, 1814) on Etienne, and it is this text which Ferretti most probably had before him when he wrote his *Cenerentola* (Cinderella) for Rossini.

As usual Rossini composed swiftly with, as will be seen, the aid of a collaborator and some judicious self-plagiarism. Performed at the Teatro Valle, Rome, on 25 January 1817, with a cast which included two singers – Andrea Verni (Don Magnifico) and Giuseppe de Begnis (Dandini) – who had portrayed the equivalent roles in Pavesi's unsuccessful *Agatina* in Milan three years earlier, Rossini's *La Cenerentola* survived a noisy and somewhat hostile first night to become, in Rome and wherever else it was staged, one of the composer's most popular operas. Although Rossini was disconcerted at the reaction of the first-night audience, he predicted that his opera would be very popular in Rome before the end of the season, throughout Italy by the end of the year, and in France and England within two years.

The composer's prediction turned out to be reasonably accurate. *La Cenerentola* was performed at the Teatro Valle twenty times before the season ended in mid-February, and was soon being staged all over Italy and throughout Europe. Its first London performance was at the King's Theatre in the Haymarket on 8 January 1820, and it reached New York on 27 June 1826 at the Park Theatre. *La Cenerentola* never entirely left the stage, except for those dark years for the bel canto repertoire in the early part of the twentieth century, and today it is second in popularity among Rossini operas to *Il Barbiere*.

The story of Cinderella, probably of Eastern origin, is found in sixteenth-century German literature, but is best known in Charles Perrault's version in his 1697 *Mother Goose Tales*. Rossini's *La Cenerentola* is the Cinderella story with its magic element removed. Angiolina, known as Cenerentola, is ill-treated by her father, Don Magnifico, and her two step-sisters, Clorinda and Tisbe, the 'ugly sisters' of the fairy-tale. Prince Ramiro, posing as his valet Dandini, falls in love with Angiolina, and it is not a fairy godmother with a mice-drawn pumpkin carriage but a purely human agent, the Prince's tutor, Alidoro, who helps Angiolina to attend the ball at the palace.

Since *La Gazzetta* had not been performed in Rome, nor was likely to be, Rossini appropriated its overture, with its ebullient *crescendo*, for *La Cenerentola*. (He also made use of the overture's *crescendo* in his Act I finale.) The opening ensemble, with her two sisters admiring themselves while Cenerentola sings her doleful little quasi-folk song as she works, and Ramiro's male entourage arriving with the Prince's invitation to a ball, contrives to get the opera off to a lively start. The *buffo* patter of Don Magnifico's entrance aria, 'Miei rampolli', in which he recounts his absurd dream to his daughters, characterises him at once as one of Rossini's pompously silly old parents or guardians, ripe for deflation, while the scene and duet ('Un soave non so che') for Cenerentola and the disguised Ramiro, in which mutual love blooms at first sight, charmingly blends tenderness and gaiety as the young couple's delight in each other is followed by Cenerentola's embarrassed confusion and the importunate off-stage demands of her sisters.

Heralded by the male chorus, the valet Dandini makes his entrance impersonating Prince Ramiro with an elegant, highly decorated aria ('Come un' ape ne' giorni d'aprile') which, presumably intended as a parody of elegant formality, gives a remarkably convincing imitation of that quality before leading into a bustling ensemble. The quintet, 'Nel volto estatico', which ensues when Don Magnifico asserts that his third daughter is dead, intrudes into the opera a mood of solemnity which soon gives way to a brilliant stretta. After all except Cenerentola have departed, Alidoro re-enters to take her to the ball as well, pausing only to deliver a not very interesting philosophical discourse on illusion and reality ('Vasto teatro è il mondo'), the work, not of Rossini, but of one Luca Agolini, enlisted by Rossini to compose much of the recitative and some of the less important numbers. (Agolini's other contributions to *La Cenerentola* are a chorus, 'Ah, questa bella incognita', and an aria for Clorinda, 'Sventurata! me credea', both in Act II.)

Cenerentola makes her entrance at the ball in the spacious first act finale, which ends in a fast and furious ensemble making good use of the *crescendo* from the overture. Act II contains an engaging scene for the two *buffo* basses in which Dandini finally reveals his true identity to Don Magnifico; an impassioned recitative and three-part aria ('Sì, ritrovarla io giuro') for Ramiro, prodigal with the tenor's high notes; the almost obligatory Rossinian storm; and a glorious sextet ('Questo è un nodo avviluppato') in which the characters express their stupefaction, making great comical play with the Italian rolled r.

The finale of the opera is a grand scena for Cenerentola and the entire ensemble in which, after she has forgiven her three unpleasant relatives, Cenerentola launches into a joyous rondo, 'Non più mesta', a more highly decorated version of Count Almaviva's cabaletta, 'Ah, il più lieto', in *Il Barbiere di Siviglia*, which Rome audiences had heard less than twelve months previously. It was an odd piece of self-borrowing on Rossini's part, since he usually took care to recycle only pieces from unsuccessful or unfamiliar earlier works, but it makes an exhilarating conclusion to a delightful comic opera.

La Gazza ladra
(The Thieving Magpie)

melodramma in two acts

Principal characters:

Fabrizio Vingradito, a rich farmer	(bass)
Lucia, his wife	(mezzo-soprano)
Giannetto, Fabrizio's son, a soldier	(tenor)
Ninetta, a servant in Fabrizio's house	(soprano)
Fernando Villabella, Ninetta's father, a soldier	(bass)
Gottardo, Mayor of the village	(bass)
Pippo, a young peasant in Fabrizio's service	(contralto)
Isacco, a pedlar	(tenor)
Antonio, a gaoler	(tenor)

LIBRETTO by Giovanni Gherardini

TIME: The past
PLACE: A village near Paris

FIRST PERFORMED at the Teatro alla Scala, Milan, 31 May 1817, with Teresa Giorgi-Belloc (Ninetta); Teresa Gallianis (Pippo); Marietta Castiglioni (Lucia); Savino Monelli (Giannetto); Vincenzo Botticelli (Fabrizio Vingradito); Filippo Galli (Fernando Villabella); Antonio Ambrosi (Gottardo); Francesco Biscottini (Isacco)

Less than three weeks after the première of *La Cenerentola*, Rossini left Rome for Milan, to fulfil a new commission from the Teatro alla Scala, where his most recent opera for Milan, *Il Turco in Italia*, had been so ungraciously received in 1814. The libretto he was given upon his arrival was *La Gazza ladra* (The Thieving Magpie), with which a Milanese poet and philologist, Giovanni Gherardini, had won a competition. Based on a recent French play, *La pie voleuse* by T. Badouin d'Aubigny and Louis-Charles Caigniez, which had been a success in Paris in 1815, Gherardini's libretto pleased Rossini who wrote to his mother that he thought it 'bellissimo'.

Its action is set in a village ('un grosso villagio', the libretto insists) not far from Paris. Ninetta, a servant-girl engaged to Giannetto, the son of the wealthy farmer in whose household she is employed, is accused of stealing silverware from her employer. When the obnoxious Mayor, whose amorous advances Ninetta has repulsed, insists that she be brought to trial, she is found guilty and condemned to death. It is only as Ninetta is being led to execution that the real thief is discovered to be a magpie.

At its Milan première on 31 May 1817, *La Gazza ladra* was an unqualified success. Within months it was produced in Munich, and in addition to being staged in several Italian cities it was soon making its way across Europe, from Amsterdam to St Petersburg. Its first London performance was at Her Majesty's Theatre in 1821, in Italian. With Rossini's music adapted by Sir Henry Bishop it reached Covent Garden in 1830 in English, as *Ninetta, or The Maid of Palaiseau*. The first American performances of the opera, in Philadelphia (1827) and New York (1830), were sung in French. There were well received English-language productions by English National Opera in London in 1978 and by Opera North in Leeds and elsewhere in 1992.

The work belongs to the genre of *opera semiseria*, containing potentially tragic as well as comic elements, but ending happily. (*La Cenerentola* could be said to fit, less decisively, into the same category.) Though *La Gazza ladra* is an inordinately lengthy opera, in two acts of about one-and-three-quarter hours each, it seems shorter in performance, for Rossini's score, comparatively free of the vocal pyrotechnics which can sometimes tend to overshadow the dramatic content of his operas, displays an agreeable simplicity and directness. The composer has responded imaginatively to the odd but affecting plot, based by the French playwrights upon an actual case in which a French peasant girl's innocence and a magpie's guilt were established only after the girl had been executed.

Once it has gained attention with its opening drumrolls, Rossini's overture (which has long been a favourite concert item) reveals itself to be a graceful piece culminating in the by now expected *crescendo*. Ninetta's opening cavatina, 'Di piacer mi balza il cor', with its artless cabaletta, 'Tutto sorridere', in which she looks forward to being reunited with her father (a deserter from the army) immediately establishes her attractively innocent personality. Her tenor suitor, Giannetto, introduces himself in an attractive aria, 'Vieni fra queste braccia', with an impressively decorated cabaletta, and Ninetta's duet with her father, Fernando, almost anticipates some of Verdi's great father–daughter duets in its tenderness.

The Mayor's opening cavatina, 'Il mio piano è preparato', would appear to establish him as a conventional comic character, but his darker side soon emerges. The scene in which Ninetta deceives him by changing the description of the deserter in the letter which she is reading aloud puts one in mind of a similar situation in *Boris Godunov* (both Pushkin's play and Mussorgsky's opera: Pushkin is known to have seen *La Gazza ladra* in the 1820s). The trio ('O nume benefico') for Ninetta, her father and the Mayor, is taut and dramatically compelling, and the finale, with its affecting cry of despair from Giannetto ('Ninetta! Ninetta! Tu dunque sei rea?') when the evidence persuades him to believe her guilty, makes an exciting and cliffhanging conclusion to Act I.

Act II opens with a too lengthy passage of recitative before Ninetta and Giannetto are allowed a two-part duet, and the Mayor an aria, 'Si per voi, pupille amate', in whose brilliant cabaletta ('Udrai la sentenza') he is joined by a chorus of villagers while the orchestra contributes the *crescendo* from the overture. Though often omitted from performances of what is, admittedly, an opera which could be shortened with impunity, Fernando's 'Accusata di furto' is a fascinating aria shaped by dramatic rather than by musical considerations. Almost invariably at his best when writing duets for soprano and contralto, Rossini provides an exquisite *andantino* for Ninetta and Pippo in 'E ben, per mia memoria', which makes use of music already heard in the overture.

A powerful and affecting chorus, 'Tremate, o popoli', opens the trial scene, but the ensemble which ensues after the judge has pronounced sentence of death upon Ninetta is disappointingly conventional, and Giannetto's protestations of his beloved's innocence are delivered in inappropriate roulades of *fioriture*. The scene recovers, however, after the intervention of Ninetta's father, culminating in a highly dramatic ensemble. The final scene in the village square is splendidly written throughout. Even Lucia's dramatically expendable aria, 'A questo seno', which holds up the action at the beginning of the scene, is gently affecting until its stretta in which words and music are clearly at loggerheads. From the sombre funeral march which frames Ninetta's moving prayer, 'Deh, tu reggi', as she is being led to execution, to the joyous end of the opera after the real culprit has been discovered, Rossini's choral and orchestral writing is deeply impressive. Though *La Gazza ladra* may never become as popular as its overture, it is an ambitious work which certainly deserves to retain a place in the operatic repertoire.

Armida

opera seria in three acts

Principal characters:

Armida   (soprano)
Rinaldo   (tenor)
Carlo   (tenor)
Goffredo   (tenor)
Eustazio   (tenor)
Gernando   (tenor)
Ubaldo   (tenor)
Idraote   (bass)
Astarotte   (bass)

LIBRETTO by Giovanni Federico Schmidt

TIME: The period of the Crusades
PLACE: The country near Jerusalem

FIRST PERFORMED at the Teatro San Carlo, Naples, 11 November 1817, with Isabella Colbran (Armida); Andrea Nozzari (Rinaldo); Giuseppe Ciccimarra (Goffredo); Michele Benedetti (Idraote); Claudio Bonoldi (Gernando and Ubaldo)

Within a few weeks of the première of *La Gazza ladra* at La Scala, Rossini was back in Naples where, at the beginning of August, he began work on his next opera for the rebuilt Teatro San Carlo. This was *Armida*, whose libretto by Giovanni Schmidt (the librettist of *Elisabetta, regina d'Inghilterra* in 1815) is derived from the famous verse epic about the First Crusade, *Gerusalemme liberata*, by the sixteenth-century Italian poet, Torquato Tasso.

Tasso's *Gerusalemme liberata* had already frequently been plundered by opera composers and librettists, and the tale of the pagan enchantress Armida and the Christian knight Rinaldo had been told in at least a dozen operas before Rossini made use of the subject. The earliest, Benedetto Ferrari's *Armida*, staged in Venice in 1639 (now lost), was followed by Lully's *Armide* (Paris, 1686), Handel's *Rinaldo* (London, 1711), Salieri's *Armida* (Vienna, 1771), Gluck's *Armide* (Paris, 1777), Haydn's *Armida* (Eszterháza, 1784) as well as operas by minor composers such as Pallavicino, Jommelli, Sacchini, Naumann and Mysliveček. (The most recent *Armida* is Dvořák's, first performed in Prague in 1904.)

At its première on 11 November 1817, although Rossini's *Armida* was lavishly staged, displaying (according to the composer's biographer, Radiciotti) 'Armida's palace and enchanted garden, appearances and disappearances of demons, furies, spectres, chariots pulled by dragons, dances of nymphs and cherubs, characters swept up into the sky and descending from artificial clouds', it was only moderately well received, the general critical opinion being that it was 'too German' which may have been a way of recognising an increasing romanticism in Rossini's music.

Armida became fairly popular for a time outside Italy in a German version first performed in Vienna in 1821; but after 1838, when it was produced in Budapest in Hungarian, the opera disappeared from the repertoire until it was revived at the 1952 Maggio Musicale in Florence, with Maria Callas in the title-role. Subsequent productions in Venice (1970), Bregenz (1973, both with Cristina Deutekom), and Aix-en-Provence (1988, with June Anderson) have led to the reappraisal of a work which writers on Rossini formerly tended to reject out of hand. *Armida* has yet to be staged in Great Britain. The first performance in the United States was given in Tulsa on 29 February 1992 (in a co-production by Tulsa Opera and Minnesota Opera).

Plot, in *Armida*, is subservient to situation. Francis Toye described the opera as one long love scene whose sole merit lay in the fact that it inspired Rossini to write three splendid love duets, containing 'some of the most voluptuous music he ever composed'. (The more than usually passionate nature of the love duets may have some connection with the fact that Isabella Colbran, for whom Rossini wrote the role of Armida, was shortly to become his wife.) What plot there is concerns itself with the enslavement of the Crusader, Rinaldo, by the enchantress Armida who, in turn, falls in love with him. When Rinaldo is rescued by his fellow-Crusaders, the distraught Armida calls on demons to destroy her palace, while she ascends to higher realms in a chariot drawn by dragons.

Though Rossini, who had even contrived to have the magic element removed from *Cinderella*, is known to have disliked opera plots which involved supernatural elements, he seems to have accepted *Armida* without quibbling, and to have composed the opera with his usual celerity. It is indeed, as Toye observed, virtually a love duet in three acts with interruptions, its other unusual feature being that there is only one female role, that of Armida, and six roles (three of them major ones) for tenors. These four principal roles are, even for Rossini, unusually demanding in the range and agility they require of their performers. Rossini's vocal writing can hardly be described, therefore, as 'too German', though a certain Viennese influence can perhaps be detected in the richness of the opera's instrumentation.

The overture to *Armida*, more attuned to the atmosphere of the opera which follows than is sometimes the case with Rossini, is, for most of its length, a stately *maestoso* march which alternates with a lively *vivace*. After the opening chorus of Paladins, Goffredo's heroic cavatina ('Ah, no, sia questo di tregua il giorno') and cabaletta establish the Crusaders' mood of heroic fervour, into which Armida is soon to intrude so spectacularly, but not before Eustazio has made his entrance to the accompaniment of a jaunty figure in the orchestra which was to reappear in *Mosè in Egitto* four months later.

Making her first appearance in a scene of accompanied recitative, Armida soon launches the great dramatic quartet, 'Sventurata! or che mi resta?', with a vocal line of threatening bravura. The central *andante* of the quartet is built around a phrase which, perhaps unconsciously, plagiarises the opening bars of the popular eighteenth-century canzonetta, 'Caro mio ben', which is usually attributed to Giuseppe Giordani (1753–1798). Gernando's aria, 'Non soffrirò l'offesa', follows, notable more for its fearsome coloratura than for any musical individuality. Beginning and ending in fiercely decorative vocal ardour, with a central lyrical section of sensuous beauty, the first of the Armida–Rinaldo love duets, 'Amor, possente nome', extends its influence into the elaborate Act I finale whose stretta exhibits the kind of raw energy more usually associated with the young Verdi of more than twenty years later. It was of 'Amor, possente nome' that Stendhal wrote, 'Rossini has given us a hundred different portraits of the joys of love, and one at least (the duet from *Armida*) which resembles nothing that was even dreamed of before'.

Rossini's writing for chorus and orchestra (with an unusually preponderant brass section) at the beginning of Act II anticipates the romantic supernatural world of the Wolf's Glen scene in Weber's *Der Freischütz*; but after the demons have had their say in their two choruses separated by Astarotte's recitative, a more tender mood returns in the love duet, 'Dove son io?', a solo cello introducing and accompanying the voices of Rinaldo and Armida. Delightful ballet music accompanies the entertainment conjured up by Armida, the only ballet to be found in any of Rossini's Italian operas, and the enchantress displays her pyrotechnical vocal prowess in the aria, 'D'amore al dolce impero'.

Act III opens with a duet, 'Come l'aurette placide', for two tenors, the knights Ubaldo and Carlo, the pastoral innocence of its *andante grazioso* soon giving way to a frightened *allegro* as the knights become aware of the atmosphere surrounding them. A rather charming chorus of spectres ('Qui tutto è calma') is followed by the last and least impressive of the Armida–Rinaldo duets, 'Soavi catene', an *andante grazioso* in which the two voices are joined by a solo violin. An exciting C major trio, 'In quale aspetto imbelle', follows for three tenors, Rinaldo and the two knights, Ubaldo and Carlo, who have come to rescue him. Rinaldo especially is called upon to perform prodigious feats of virtuosity which severely test the singer's vocal flexibility and range. Rossini's score brings them to a unison conclusion on the C above middle C, but it would be a faint-hearted threesome who did not elect instead to end an octave higher. The imaginatively scored finale finds room for another great outburst of passion and fury from Armida in 'Se al mio crudel tormento', whose central *andante* briefly recalls the ecstasy of her love for Rinaldo before she is carried aloft by her demons in a final *allegro* flourish.

Adelaide di Borgogna

dramma in two acts

Principal characters:

Ottone, Emperor of Germany	(contralto)
Adelaide, widow of Lotario	(soprano)
Adalberto	(tenor)
Berengario, father of Adalberto	(bass)

Eurice, wife of Berengario   (soprano)
Iroldo, Governor of Canosso   (tenor)
Ernesto, an officer of Ottone   (tenor)

LIBRETTO by Giovanni Federico Schmidt

TIME: The tenth century
PLACE: Italy

FIRST PERFORMED at the Teatro Argentina, Rome, 27 December
1817, with Elisabetta Manfredini-Guarmani (Adelaide);
Elisabetta Pinotti (Ottone); Anna Maria Muratori (Eurice); Luisa
Bottesi (Iroldo); Savino Monelli (Adalberto); Antonio Ambrosi
(Berengario); Giovanni Puglieschi (Ernesto)

Even for Rossini, the quickness with which his next opera reached
the stage was exceptional. Shortly after *Armida*'s première on 11
November 1817, the twenty-five-year-old composer travelled from
Naples to Rome where, on 27 December, *Adelaide di Borgogna*, which
he may well have composed in less than three weeks, was produced
at the Teatro Argentina. It was not much liked: Prince Chigi-
Albani, a member of the first-night audience, noted in his diary that
'everything turned out rather badly', and within two or three weeks
the opera was withdrawn. Described by Stendhal in one word –
'failure' – and later denounced by its composer's twentieth-century
biographer Radiciotti as 'the worst of Rossini's serious operas',
Adelaide di Borgogna seems, after a few performances in other Italian
towns, not to have been heard again until 1979 when a concert
performance at the Queen Elizabeth Hall, London, revealed it to be,
though clearly no masterpiece, a not unenjoyable *opera seria*. It was
subsequently staged, for the first time in more than a hundred and
fifty years, in Italy at the 1984 Valle d'Itria Festival.

Giovanni Schmidt's libretto, set in tenth-century Italy, tells the
story of Adelaide, whose husband, Lotario, King of Italy, has been
murdered by Berengario. Adelaide can be restored to the throne
only if she agrees to marry Adalberto, Berengario's son. However,
the German Emperor, Ottone, comes to her aid, and eventually all
ends well with the defeat of Berengario, and Ottone and Adelaide in
love and triumphant.

Rossini appears not to have lavished a great deal of care and
attention upon *Adelaide di Borgogna*. Its overture is that of the 1810 *La*

Cambiale di matrimonio with its orchestration only slightly altered, and the composition of more than one number was left to Michele Carafa, a Neapolitan nobleman and minor composer. Rossini's choral writing, however, is impressive, especially in the opening chorus, 'Misera patria oppressa' and the triumphal 'Serti intrecciar le vergini' in Act II. A duet for Adelaide (soprano) and Ottone (whose role is written for a female contralto *en travesti*), 'Mi dai corona e vita', is attractive, as is a more dramatic duet, 'Della tua patria ai voti', for Adelaide and the tenor Adalberto. Act II is livelier than Act I, with a splendid quartet, 'Oh Ciel, che vedo' and an exciting final rondo, replete with coloratura, allotted not to the eponymous Adelaide but to the victorious Ottone.

Mosè in Egitto
(Moses in Egypt)

azione tragico-sacra in three acts

Principal characters:

Mosè (Moses), leader of the Israelites	(bass)
Aronne (Aaron), his brother	(tenor)
Faraone (the Pharaoh), King of Egypt	(baritone)
Osiride, the Pharaoh's son	(tenor)
Mambre, an Egyptian officer	(tenor)
Elcia, a Jewish maiden	(soprano)
Amenosi, Elcia's confidante	(mezzo-soprano)
Amaltea, the Pharaoh's wife	(soprano)

LIBRETTO by Andrea Leone Tottola

TIME: Around 1230 B.C.
PLACE: Egypt

FIRST PERFORMED at the Teatro San Carlo, Naples, 5 March 1818, with Isabella Colbran (Elcia); Friderike Funk (Amaltea); Maria Manzi (Amenosi); Michele Benedetti (Mosè); Andrea Nozzari (Osiride); Giuseppe Ciccimarra (Aronne); Raniero Remorini (Faraone); Gaetano Chizzola (Mambre)

Back in Naples after the failure in Rome of *Adelaide di Borgogna*, Rossini turned his attention to the next opera he was to write for the Teatro San Carlo. As it was to be performed during Lent when secular subjects were not allowed on the stage, the opera had to have a sacred theme. Andrea Leone Tottola, a local librettist who had revised Palomba's libretto for Rossini's *La Gazzetta* in 1816, and who would provide libretti for four future operas by Rossini, was commissioned by the San Carlo Theatre to prepare an *azione-sacra* or oratorio. He took as his subject the Old Testament story from the Book of Exodus of the enslavement of the Jews in Egypt, and their eventual deliverance when 'Moses stretched out his hand over the sea; and the Lord caused the sea to go back by a strong east wind all that night, and made the sea dry land, and the waters were divided'. (Exodus 14.21)

In order to provide a leading role for Isabella Colbran, Tottola introduced a love interest. The Pharaoh's reluctance to respond to the plea of Moses, 'Let my people go', insufficiently motivated in the Bible, is now explained. Tottola's libretto, which is in fact based on a play, *L'Osiride*, by Padre Francesco Ringhieri, first staged in Padua in 1760, describes how the Pharaoh, impressed by the plagues visited upon Egypt by the God of the Jews, intends to set Moses and his people free, but is dissuaded by his son Osiride, who is in love with Elcia, a Jewish girl (who, in the later French version of the opera, becomes specifically the niece of Moses). Only after Osiride is killed by a stroke of lightning are the Israelites able to leave Egypt. Pursued by the Pharaoh and his forces who swear revenge for the death of Osiride, the Israelites reach the Red Sea which, when touched by the rod of Moses, parts to let them across and then closes over the pursuing Egyptians.

Though he was, as usual, working against time, Rossini called on Michele Carafa to provide only one aria (Pharaoh's 'A rispettarmi') and kept his self-borrowings to a minimum. At its première on 5 March 1818, *Mosè in Egitto* was an immediate success, even though, according to Stendhal who was present, the parting of the Red Sea failed to achieve its desired effect:

> The stage technician of the San Carlo, desperately intent upon finding a solution to an insoluble problem, had finished up by producing a real masterpiece of absurdity. Seen from the pit, the 'sea' rose up into the air some five or six feet above its retaining 'shores'; whereas the occupants of the boxes, who were favoured with a bird's-eye view of the 'raging

billows', also had a bird's-eye view of the little rascals whose job it was to 'divide the waters' at the sound of Moses' voice! ... The scene was greeted with a gale of laughter, and the general merriment was so frank and so open that no one really had the heart to turn surly and whistle.

Mosè in Egitto soon began to go the rounds of other cities in Italy and abroad. Biblical subjects not being allowed on the stage in England, the opera was first heard in London in concert form, as an oratorio, at Covent Garden on 30 January 1822. Later in the same year it was staged at the King's Theatre, but with a changed, secular plot and a new title, *Pietro l'Eremita* (Peter the Hermit). The first New York staging of *Mosè in Egitto* was on 2 March 1835, but it had been preceded by a concert performance at the Masonic Hall on 22 December 1832.

The choral prayer led by Moses, 'Dal tuo stellato soglio', which became the most popular number in the opera, was not heard at the first performances in 1818, but was composed by Rossini for a revival of *Mosè in Egitto* at the Teatro San Carlo in March of the following year.

A French version of the opera, *Moïse et Pharaon*, was produced by Rossini for the Paris Opéra where it was staged in 1827. This was subsequently translated back into Italian for performance in Italy where it became known as *Il Mosè nuovo*, and it is not always clear whether later nineteenth-century stagings were of the original Italian opera, the later French version, or a conflation of the two. In one version or another, Rossini's *Moses* never entirely disappeared from the repertoire, and has enjoyed a number of productions in recent years. The version performed nowadays is almost invariably the 1827 Paris revision, *Moïse et Pharaon* (though this is sometimes sung in Calisto Bassi's Italian translation under the misleading title of *Mosè in Egitto*). A discussion of the 1827 French opera will be found on pp 125–127. What follows here refers to *Mosè in Egitto*, the 1818 Italian opera as revised for its performances in 1819.

There is no overture. C major chords grasp the audience's attention, and the curtain rises on the terrified Egyptians whose land has been plunged into total darkness. Their opening chorus is a gravely beautiful *andante maestoso* with solo contributions from the Pharaoh, his wife Amaltea and their son Osiride. This is followed by accompanied recitative – there is no *recitativo secco* in the opera – leading to Moses' dramatic invocation, 'Eterno! immenso! incomprensibil Dio!', with the orchestra's wind instruments emphasising its solemnity and, after Moses has turned the darkness to light, a great choral cry of wonder. The F major *andante* quintet, 'Celeste man placata', begun by Moses, is one of Rossini's finest and most affecting ensembles with some glorious writing for the horn, and its *vivace* stretta is fiercely energetic. A graceful, touching yet quite lively duet of farewell ('Ah! se puoi così lasciarmi') for Osiride and Elcia precedes the Pharaoh's florid two-part aria, 'Cade dal ciglio il velo' (added by Rossini four years after the première), and the large-scale Act I finale which, in a moment of repose, incorporates a charming duet for Elcia and her confidante, Amenosi.

In Act II the Osiride–Faraone duet, 'Parlar, spiegar non posso', is one of Rossini's attractive, all-purpose numbers, its vocal line bearing little relation to the sense of the words, and its principal theme deriving from part of a duet in the previous year's *La Gazza ladra*. Amaltea's aria, 'La pace mia smarrita', sounds agreeable but inappropriate, which is hardly surprising since its music was first heard six years earlier in *Ciro in Babilonia*. The highlights of the act are the duet, 'Quale assalto, qual cimento!', for the lovers Elcia and Osiride, and the quartet which ensues with the arrival of Amaltea and Aronne ('Mi manca la voce'). Mosè contributes a belligerent aria, 'Tu di ceppi m'aggravi la mano' (composed for Rossini by another hand, time being pressing), and the Egyptians a chorus ('Se a mitigar tue cure') which contrives to sound both militant and jolly, and which had already been heard less than three months earlier in Rome in *Adelaide di Borgogna*. The finale of the act takes the form of a tender aria ('Porgi la destra amata'), followed by a superb, grief-ridden cabaletta ('Tormenti, affani e smanie') when the Pharaoh's son Osiride is struck by lightning and falls lifeless to the ground.

Act III contains little more than the great choral prayer, 'Dal tuo stellato soglio', launched by Moses, with stanzas contributed also by Aronne and Elcia. Its simple melody, with harp and wind accompaniment, is one of Rossini's most memorable. As the Egyptians are engulfed by the Red Sea whose waves had parted only to allow access to the fleeing Hebrews, the orchestra alone brings Rossini's fascinating and often very beautiful opera to a triumphant conclusion.

5

From *Adina* to *La Donna del lago*

Adina

farsa in one act

Principal characters:

Adina, a young slave and intended bride of the Caliph	(soprano)
Selimo, a young childhood friend of Adina, and her fiancé	(tenor)
Alì, keeper of the Caliph's harem	(tenor)
Mustafà, servant of Selimo and harem gardener	(bass)
Caliph of Baghdad	(bass)

LIBRETTO by Gherardo Bevilacqua-Aldobrandini

TIME: The remote past
PLACE: Baghdad

FIRST PERFORMED at the Teatro Sao Carlos, Lisbon, 22 June 1826 (together with Act II of *Semiramide* and a short ballet), with Luigia Valesi (Adina); Luigi Ravaglia (Selimo); Gaspare Martinelli (Alì); Filippo Spada (Mustafà); Giovanni Orazio Cartagenova (Caliph)

Three months after the première of *Mosè in Egitto* in Naples, a new opera house in Pesaro was opened in June with a revival, supervised by Rossini, of *La Gazza ladra*. Later in the year, in Bologna where he was visiting his parents, the composer dashed off a one-act comedy,

Adina, at the behest of the son of the Lisbon prefect of police, who may or may not have been acting on behalf of the Teatro Sao Carlos in Lisbon. For some unknown reason *Adina* was not staged until eight years later, when it was performed at the Teatro Sao Carlos on 22 June 1826, together with Act II of Rossini's *Semiramide* (first seen in Venice in 1823) and a ballet. Apparently *Adina* was given only one performance, which its composer did not travel to Portugal to attend, after which it was not staged again until 1963 in Siena. Its first and, so far, only British production was at the Holywell Music Room on 27 June 1968 as part of the Oxford Festival. It has yet to be performed in the United States. In 1992, to celebrate the two hundredth anniversary of the birth of Rossini, it was performed in Rome.

The libretto of *Adina* or *Il Califfo di Bagdad* (The Caliph of Baghdad), written for Rossini by his Bolognese friend the Marchese Gherardo Bevilacqua-Aldobrandini, was based on Felice Romani's libretto for a now forgotten composer, Francesco Basili, whose opera, *Il Califfo e la schiava*, had been produced at La Scala, Milan, in 1819. It may also derive, in part, from Andrea Leone Tottola's version (written for Manuel Garcia's *Il Califfo di Bagdad*) of Claude Godard d'Aucour de Saint-Just's libretto for Boieldieu's *Le Calife de Bagdad* (1800).

Notwithstanding so complex a provenance, the plot of *Adina* is little more than a variant of that of Gluck's *La rencontre imprévue*, Mozart's *Die Entführung aus dem Serail*, and several other operas. Accompanied by his servant Mustafà, Selimo arrives in Baghdad in search of his lost love, Adina, who is about to be married to the Caliph. Selimo's attempt to rescue Adina from the Caliph's harem is unsuccessful, and the lovers are sentenced to death. Fortunately the Caliph discovers, from a medallion worn by Adina, that she is his daughter by a former love. Father and daughter are reunited, and father agrees to daughter's marriage to the man she really loves.

In his *Rossini*, Francis Toye wrote that the composer had gone to Bologna in the summer of 1818 to see his parents 'and incidentally to write an entirely worthless comic opera for Lisbon called *Adina*, which was only performed once, and should, apparently, neither have been written nor performed at all'. Toye had, of course, never seen the opera, and he cannot have bothered to look at a score, for *Adina* is by no means worthless. It is admittedly a slight piece with a mediocre libretto, but its score reveals that Rossini had lost none of his flair for *opera buffa*.

There is no overture, the tight-fisted or at least immensely practical composer having refused to provide one since it had not been specified in the contract. There is also, as in *Armida*, only one female voice, that of the eponymous heroine, even the chorus consisting entirely of male slaves and gardeners. The general mood of the work is one of tenderness rather than comic boisterousness. Adina's cavatina, 'Fragolette fortunate', has a wistful charm, and her duet with the Caliph, 'Se non m'odi, o mio tesoro', is a delicate expression of affection between the young woman and the man who is her captor, who wants to be her husband, and who will turn out to be her father! The Caliph's *allegro* aria, 'D'intorno al seraglio', has an especially attractive *larghetto* middle section. Selimo's tender 'Giusto cielo' with its cor anglais obbligato is a piece borrowed from *Sigismondo*, and a graceful *sotto voce* chorus, 'Apri i begli occhi al dì', is almost Mozartian in feeling and shapeliness of phrase. 'Nel lasciarti, o caro albergo', which begins as a cavatina for Adina, and then continues as a duet with Selim before developing into a quartet, is reminiscent of the Rossini of *Il Barbiere di Siviglia*, and not only in its engaging *crescendo*. Only the 'aria di sorbetto' for Ali, the keeper of the harem, is dull, and it was probably not by Rossini.

Ricciardo e Zoraide

opera seria in two acts

Principal characters:

Zoraide, Asian princess	(soprano)
Zomira, Agorante's Queen	(mezzo-soprano)
Fatima	(mezzo-soprano)
Elmira	(mezzo-soprano)
Ricciardo, a Christian knight	(tenor)
Agorante, King of Nubia	(tenor)
Ircano, father of Zoraide	(bass)
Ernesto, Christian Ambassador	(tenor)

LIBRETTO by Francesco Berio di Salsa

TIME: The mythical past

PLACE: Asia

FIRST PERFORMED at the Teatro San Carlo, Naples, 3 December 1818, with Isabella Colbran (Zoraide); Rosmunda Pisaroni (Zomira); Maria Manzi (Fatima); Raffaela De Bernardis (Elmira); Giovanni David (Ricciardo); Andrea Nozzari (Agorante); Michele Benedetti (Ircano); Giuseppe Ciccimarra (Ernesto)

After *Mosè in Egitto*, Rossini's next opera for the Teatro San Carlo later in the same year was *Ricciardo e Zoraide*, an *opera seria* whose libretto by the Marchese Berio di Salsa was based on an early eighteenth-century drama, *Ricciardetto* by Niccolò Forteguerri. The successful première of *Ricciardo e Zoraide* took place on 3 December 1818, postponed from the previous week because the prima donna, Isabella Colbran, had injured herself in a fall. In the following year it was not only revived in Naples but also produced, in German translation, in Vienna. Within the next few years it was seen in Lisbon, Madrid, Munich, Paris and several other cities. Its first London performance was at the King's Theatre on 5 June 1823. However, after a production at La Scala in 1846, *Ricciardo e Zoraide* disappeared until it was revived at the Pesaro Festival in 1990. It has not yet been staged in America.

The opera is set in Dongola, ancient capital of Nubia, on the upper Nile. Ricciardo is a Christian knight in love with Zoraide, an Asian princess also loved by Agorante, King of Nubia, who has captured her father, Ircano, an Arab chieftain with designs on the Nubian throne. An absurd and complicated plot also involves Zomira, the most favoured of Agorante's wives, who is responsible for the capture of Zoraide and Ricciardo, who has attempted to rescue Zoraide from Agorante's harem. The opera ends with Christian knights defeating the Arabs, and Ricciardo magnanimously sparing Agorante's life.

The overture is unusual in that, following an introductory *largo* section of no more than eleven bars, the curtain rises and an on-stage band is introduced in a march. After an *andante* section, the march is repeated, and then the chorus joins in. In an uneven score the most effective numbers are, as the French composer Ferdinand Hérold confided to his diary after hearing the opera in Florence in 1821, 'three enchanting duets, a delightful quartet and tuneful and energetic choruses'. The Act II duet for Zoraide and Ricciardo is indeed quite powerful, and there is also a splendid trio in Act III for Agorante, Zomira and Zoraide. But the most impressive and original number in the score is the three-movement quartet, 'Contro cento, e cento prodi', although there are fleeting but disconcerting reminiscences in its opening section of the Almaviva–Figaro duet, 'All' idea di quel metallo', from *Il Barbiere di Siviglia*.

Though it contains some delightful music, *Ricciardo e Zoraide* does not really succeed in rising above the mediocrity of its libretto. It is unlikely to enter the operatic repertoire.

Ermione

azione tragica in two acts

Principal characters:

Ermione (Hermione)	(soprano)
Andromaca (Andromache)	(mezzo-soprano)
Cleone	(soprano)
Cefisa (Cephissa)	(mezzo-soprano)
Pirro (Pyrrhus)	(tenor)
Oreste (Orestes)	(tenor)
Fenicio (Phoenix)	(bass)
Pilade (Pylades)	(tenor)
Attalo	(tenor)

LIBRETTO by Andrea Leone Tottola

TIME: Around 430 B.C.
PLACE: Epirus, Greece

FIRST PERFORMED at the Teatro San Carlo, Naples, 27 March 1819, with Isabella Colbran (Ermione); Rosmunda Pisaroni (Andromaca); Maria Manzi (Cleone); De Bernardis *minore* (Cefisa); Andrea Nozzari (Pirro); Giovanni David (Oreste); Michele Benedetti (Fenicio); Giuseppe Ciccimarra (Pilade); Gaetano Chizzola (Attalo)

A mere three months after the première of *Ricciardo e Zoraide*, Rossini's next opera was ready for the San Carlo. This was *Ermione*, its libretto an adaptation by Andrea Leone Tottola of Racine's great tragedy, *Andromaque*. Unlike *Ricciardo e Zoraide*, *Ermione* was received with indifference by the Neapolitans at its première on 27 March 1819 at the Teatro San Carlo with Isabella Colbran in the title-role, and it was neither revived in Naples nor performed again anywhere until 1977 when a concert performance was given in Siena, followed in 1986 by another concert performance in Padua. On 22 August 1987 the opera was staged at the Rossini Festival in Pesaro. *Ermione* had to wait until 1988 to achieve its second performance at the Teatro San Carlo, and it was also produced in Madrid in that year. In all three stage productions of 1987–1988, the role of Ermione was sung by Montserrat Caballé. A production at the Teatro dell' Opera in Rome in 1991 was enthusiastically received, as was *Ermione*'s first London performance, given in concert form at the Queen Elizabeth Hall on 10 April 1992, conducted by Mark Elder. The opera was first heard in the United States, also in concert performance, at the War Memorial Opera House, San Francisco, on 26 June 1992. The American stage première followed on 11 September in Omaha, in a production by Jonathan Miller.

Andromache, the wife of Hector, appears in Homer's *Iliad* and Euripides' *The Trojan Women*, and is the heroine of Euripides' *Andromache*. Racine's *Andromaque* (1667), though based on the Greek legend, differs from it in several details. His play is set in Epirus after the fall of Troy and the death of Hector. Andromache (Andromaca) is loved by her captor Pyrrhus (Pirro), whom she hates. Pyrrhus threatens to deliver her son Astyanax to the Greeks if she will not yield to him. Andromache agrees to marry Pyrrhus, but secretly intends to kill herself after the wedding. Orestes (Oreste) arrives to demand that Astyanax be handed over to the Greeks, and Hermione (Ermione), the rejected lover of Pyrrhus, persuades Orestes to murder Pyrrhus. After the murder, she reviles Orestes and kills herself on the funeral pyre of Pyrrhus. Tottola's libretto follows Racine reasonably closely, except that his Ermione does not kill herself, but merely falls in a swoon. (Death and swooning are not always clearly differentiated in Italian *opera seria*.)

One can only assume that the Neapolitan audience of 1819 must have found itself puzzled by *Ermione*, for it is one of the most original in structure of Rossini's serious operas and a work of great power and intensity, quite undeserving of its neglect. Its originality is proclaimed from the very beginning, for the overture to *Ermione* is not one of those interchangeable, all-purpose Rossini overtures. Its mood is that of the work to follow, and none other, and it incorporates the cries of an off-stage chorus lamenting the fall of Troy in motifs which will occur again after the rise of the curtain in the opening chorus, 'Troja! qual fosti un dì'.

Andromaca's *andantino* cavatina, 'Mia delizia! un solo istante', is Rossini in his most melting vein; the *allegro* duet, 'Non proseguir', for Ermione and Pirro is dramatically arresting; and the scene of Oreste's arrival ('Reggia abborrita') with his confidant, Pilade, is unusual in that Oreste's cavatina, 'Che sorda al mesto pianto', virtually turns into a duet with Pilade, though of course it is Oreste who has the spectacular high notes both in the *andante* and in the *allegro* concluding section. Pirro's three-part aria, 'Balena in man del figlio', threads its way through the utterance of the chorus and the other characters, and from the beginning of the Ermione–Oreste duet, 'Amarti?', to the end of the first act whose finale is dominated by Ermione, the drama proceeds inexorably, with Rossini's writing for the voices at its most expressive, and nowhere a hint of vocal gymnastics for their own sake. The *andante* ensemble, 'Sperar poss'io?', and its *marziale* conclusion are positively Verdian in their dramatic pulse and energy.

Act II, which begins with a superb duet, 'Ombra del caro sposo', for Andromaca and Pirro, is dominated by Ermione's *gran scena*, 'Dì che vedesti piangere', an aria in several parts in which she encompasses a wide range of conflicting emotions. Split into separate sections by recitatives and a funeral march, this huge aria is an encapsulation of the entire drama. After a brief duet, 'A così triste immagine', for Fenicio and Pilade, Ermione launches the powerful finale.

This is the opera of which the usually sensible Stendhal wrote: 'Rossini has attempted to imitate the style of Gluck, and the characters are, to all intents and purposes, given nothing to portray except bad temper.' However, Rossini was not imitating Gluck; he was simply continuing to develop his own style. *Ermione* may share with Gluck a certain gravity and elevation of manner, but it is a thoroughly Rossinian *opera seria* which deserves to be more widely known. Writing in 1934, Francis Toye dismissed *Ermione* out of hand ('a bungled version of Racine's *Andromaque*'), but the leading Rossini scholar of today, Philip Gossett, considers it 'one of the finest works in the history of nineteenth-century Italian opera'.

Eduardo e Cristina

dramma in two acts

Principal characters:

Cristina	(soprano)
Eduardo	(mezzo-soprano)
Carlo, King of Sweden	(tenor)
Giacomo, Prince of Scotland	(bass)
Atlei	(tenor)

LIBRETTO by Giovanni Federico Schmidt, revised by Andrea Leone Tottola and Gherardo Bevilacqua-Aldobrandini

TIME: The distant past
PLACE: Sweden

FIRST PERFORMED at the Teatro San Benedetto, Venice, 24 April 1819, with Rosa Morandi (Cristina); Carolina Cortesi (Eduardo); Eliodoro Bianchi (Carlo); Luciano Bianchi (Giacomo); Vincenzo Fracalini (Atlei)

Less than a month separates the first (and only) performance of *Ermione* in Naples, and the première of Rossini's next opera, *Eduardo e Cristina*, in Venice, so it is hardly surprising that nineteen of the new opera's twenty-six musical numbers were taken from existing works by Rossini: nine from *Adelaide di Borgogna*, three from *Ricciardo e Zoraide*, and seven from the recent *Ermione*. The libretto by Giovanni Federico Schmidt, written for the opera *Edoardo e Cristina* by Stefano Pavesi (which was performed in Naples in 1810), was revised for Rossini by Tottola and Bevilacqua-Aldobrandini to fit the pieces from earlier operas which the composer intended to use again. Rossini supplied cembalo-accompanied recitative and seven new numbers, as well as an overture cobbled together from parts of the overtures to *Ricciardo e Zoraide* and *Ermione*, but this pastiche whose subject is the secret marriage of a Swedish soldier can hardly be regarded as an original Rossini opera.

Ironically, in view of the failure four weeks earlier of *Ermione*, the cynically concocted *Eduardo e Cristina* was a huge success, the Venetian *Gazzetta* reporting 'a triumph like no other in the history of our musical stage'. The audience at the première encored almost all the numbers, and called Rossini out on to the stage many times throughout the evening. Byron, who was in Venice at the time, wrote to John Hobhouse: 'There has been a splendid opera lately at the San Benedetto, by Rossini, who came in person to play the harpsichord. The people followed him about, cut off his hair "for memory"; he was shouted, and sonnetted, and feasted, and immortalised much more than either of the Emperors.'

Twenty-five performances of *Eduardo e Cristina* were given during the season, and the following year it was staged in Venice again, this time at the more prestigious Teatro La Fenice. There were several productions in other Italian cities and abroad, though few, if any, after 1840. The opera reached New York on 25 November 1834, but has not yet been performed in Great Britain.

La Donna del lago
(The Lady of the Lake)

melodramma in two acts

Principal characters:

Elena	(soprano)
Albina, her confidante	(mezzo-soprano)
Malcolm Graeme	(mezzo-soprano)
Giacomo (James V), King of Scotland	(tenor)
Douglas d'Angus, Elena's father	(bass)
Serano, Douglas's retainer	(tenor)
Rodrigo di Dhu	(tenor)

LIBRETTO by Andrea Leone Tottola

TIME: The sixteenth century
PLACE: Scotland

FIRST PERFORMED at the Teatro San Carlo, Naples, 24 September 1819, with Isabella Colbran (Elena); Rosmunda

Pisaroni (Malcolm); Maria Manzi (Albina); Giovanni David (Giacomo); Andrea Nozzari (Rodrigo di Dhu); Michele Benedetti (Douglas d'Angus); Gaetano Chizzola (Serano)

From Venice, after the hugely successful première of *Eduardo e Cristina*, Rossini travelled via Pesaro to Naples where he was to compose his next opera for the Teatro San Carlo. This was *La Donna del lago*, its libretto by his usual San Carlo librettist, Andrea Leone Tottola, based on Sir Walter Scott's long narrative poem, *The Lady of the Lake*. Nothing by Scott had at this time been published in Italian: it was the French translation of the poem which aroused Rossini's interest and led to his composing the earliest of the many operas to be inspired by the romantic poems and novels of the Scottish author, the most famous of which is Donizetti's *Lucia di Lammermoor* of 1835. (By 1840 there were at least twenty-five Italian operas based on Scott, as well as operas by German, French and English composers such as Flotow, Marschner, Nicolai, Auber, Adam and Bishop.)

Rossini had arrived back in Naples at the beginning of June. By early September he had completed *La Donna del lago*, and the opera was performed at the San Carlo on 24 September 1819 before a largely indifferent audience who, according to the *Giornale*, were roused to enthusiasm only by the final rondo sung by their favourite prima donna, Isabella Colbran. The audience at the second performance seemed to enjoy the opera more, and from then on it became increasingly popular, in Naples and elsewhere. It remained in the San Carlo's repertoire for the next twelve years, was staged in many other Italian towns, and went the European rounds with productions in Dresden, Munich, Lisbon, Vienna, Malta, Budapest, Barcelona, St Petersburg, Paris, Graz and Amsterdam, all within five years of its Naples première.

La Donna del lago was produced at Her Majesty's Theatre, London, on 18 February 1823 in Italian, and at the Theatre Royal, Drury Lane, on 4 January 1827 in English. Its first New York production, on 25 August 1829, was in French, and its second, on 16 December 1833, in Italian. After 1860, the opera disappeared from view until it was revived in Florence in 1958. Since then it has begun to creep back into the repertoire. The first modern English staging was a modest affair at the 1969 Camden Festival with the young Kiri Te Kanawa as Elena, while its first modern American staging was that of Houston Grand Opera in 1981 with Frederica von Stade as

Elena and Marilyn Horne as Malcolm. In 1985, with the same singers, the Houston production was seen in London at the Royal Opera House, Covent Garden. In 1992, Rossini's bi-centennial year, *La Donna del lago* was staged at La Scala, Milan, conducted by Riccardo Muti.

The limp verses of Tottola's cliché-ridden libretto necessarily compressed and simplified Scott's poem which, set in sixteenth-century Scotland, tells the story of Ellen Douglas who lives with her father near Loch Katrine, and of the varied fortunes of her suitors in troubled times of border warfare. One of Ellen's suitors is the disguised Scottish King, James V, but she finally chooses the bold young Highlander, Malcolm Graeme. In the opera, Giacomo (King James) loses his way during a hunt and, calling himself Uberto, seeks shelter in the house of his enemy, Douglas, whose daughter Elena is being forced to marry the rebel chief Rodrigo. When Rodrigo is killed in the uprising, Elena secures an audience with the King, who she is surprised to find is none other than Uberto, who had declared his love for her. She successfully pleads with him both for the life of her father and for permission to marry the man she really loves, Malcolm Graeme.

There is no overture; presumably, this time, not because the contract did not specify one, but because Rossini wanted instead to conjure up the atmosphere of the Scottish Highlands in sixteen bars of orchestral introduction before taking the curtain up on a picturesque scene of mountain and valley with Loch Katrine in the foreground, and a chorus of shepherds and shepherdesses singing a light-hearted chorus, 'Del dì la messaggiera', echoed by the voices of hunters in the distance. Elena appears in a boat on the lake, no doubt giving a headache to scenic designers and stage management, but singing a charming *andantino* aubade, 'O, mattutini albori!' The distant horns of the hunters bring her beloved Malcolm to mind. However, as she nears the shore, it is not Malcolm who emerges from the woods, but a stranger, Uberto, seeking direction. Their duet, 'Scendi nel piccol legno', a gentle *andantino moderato*, borrows the graceful melody of Elena's earlier song. The horns are heard again, heralding a vigorous chorus of Uberto's hunting colleagues in search of him.

The melody of Elena's song is heard again as the scene changes to her cottage, where the action is advanced in expressive recitative. The female chorus of Elena's friends and companions is given music of lightness and charm with a delightful *tremolo* string accompaniment and a Scottish snap in the crispness of its rhythms. Malcolm makes his first appearance with a Bellini-like solo scene of recitative, *andantino* cavatina ('Elena! o tu, che chiamo!') and florid *allegro* cabaletta ('O quante lacrime'). Although it was in decline, the practice of writing male roles for female contraltos or mezzo-sopranos was to persist for some years, but one cannot help feeling that Rossini has placed the youthful Malcolm (one of three admirers of Elena, the other two of whom are tenors) at something of a disadvantage by requiring him to be portrayed by a woman. A note in the French libretto suggests that the role can be sung by a baritone if a suitable contralto is not available.

Douglas's vigorous cavatina, 'Taci, lo voglio, e basti!', is effective enough in context, and the *andantino* duet ('Vivere io non potrò') in which Elena and Malcolm plight their troth is typical of the engaging tunefulness which pervades Rossini's romantic score. Preceded by a splendid chorus of his clansmen, the warrior Rodrigo introduces himself in an extremely florid aria, 'Eccomi a voi, miei prodi', with a tender *andantino* section in which his thoughts turn to Elena, and an exciting *allegro* conclusion. The highly dramatic Act I finale contains the Chorus of Bards, accompanied by harp, violas and pizzicato cellos, which was to become a favourite with Italian patriots during the following half-century as their peninsula struggled towards unity and independence.

Act II is considered by some writers on Rossini to be less satisfactory than Act I, and has even been described as little more than a concert in costume. All that this means, however, is that, structurally, it is less adventurous than Act I. Musically, Rossini's inspiration remains at a high level. Uberto's *andante* cavatina, 'O fiamma soave', is a winning combination of flowing lyricism and agile coloratura, and even more impressive is his *allegro* duet with Elena, 'Alla ragion, deh rieda', whose cabaletta becomes a trio with the arrival of Rodrigo, the two tenors vying excitingly with each other in high-lying vocal agility, and Uberto's top D presumably winning the day. The subsequent trio in which Rodrigo and Uberto prepare to fight a duel is augmented by the sudden emergence of Rodrigo's clansmen from their hiding-place.

Malcolm's majestic aria 'Ah! si pera', attractive in itself, is dramatically redundant, though its cabaletta, 'Fata crudele, e rio!', when he learns of the defeat of his fellow rebels, makes an exciting end to the opera's penultimate scene. The melody of Elena's 'O mattutini albori' returns in the King's sad off-stage song at the beginning of the last scene, and the opera ends conventionally with Elena's rondo ('Tanti affetti') and cabaletta ('Fra il padre, e fra l'amante'). It is all rather like the finale of *La Cenerentola*, which is perhaps not how a tale of rivalry among fierce Highland warriors ought to end, but it makes a highly agreeable conclusion to what is, after all, a generously tuneful, delicately orchestrated opera of innocent romantic charm.

The Italian poet Leopardi, who saw *La Donna del lago* at the Teatro Argentina in Rome four years after its Naples première, wrote: 'It is stupendous music and would move me to tears if the gift of tears had not been removed from me.' It is certainly music to soothe the savage breast, an opera which respects and preserves the spirit of Sir Walter Scott's poem despite being saddled with a libretto which is virtually a travesty of that spirit. *La Donna del lago* conjures up the atmosphere of the Scottish Highlands, anticipating *Guillaume Tell* in which Rossini was to do much the same for the not dissimilar Swiss Alpine landscape.

6

From *Bianca e Falliero* to *Semiramide*

Bianca e Falliero

melodramma in two acts

Principal characters:

Bianca, daughter of Contareno	(soprano)
Falliero, a Venetian general	(mezzo-soprano)
Contareno, a senator	(tenor)
Capellio, a senator	(bass)
Friuli, Doge of Venice	(bass)
Costanza, Bianca's nurse	(soprano)

LIBRETTO by Felice Romani

TIME: The seventeenth century
PLACE: Venice

FIRST PERFORMED at the Teatro alla Scala, Milan, 26 December
1819, with Violante Camporesi (Bianca); Carolina Bassi
(Falliero); Adelaide Chinzani (Costanza); Claudio Bonoldi
(Contareno); Alessandro De Angeli (Friuli); Giuseppe Fioravanti
(Capellio)

After the first performances of *La Donna del lago*, Rossini took
another of his frequent leaves of absence from Naples, to travel to
Milan where he had accepted a commission to write an opera to
open the carnival season at La Scala on 26 December. He was in
Milan by the beginning of November, where he met Stendhal and

Meyerbeer and conferred with Felice Romani who, only three years the composer's senior, was already establishing a fine reputation as a librettist. Romani handed Rossini a libretto which he had based on a 1798 French play, *Blanche et Montcassin* by Antoine-Vincent Arnault. This became the opera, *Bianca e Falliero*, which, though received indifferently by the first-night audience, was successful enough to be performed thirty-nine times during the season in Milan, after which it was staged elsewhere in Italy as well as in Lisbon (1824), Vienna (1825) where Rossini's operas were especially popular, and Barcelona (1830). After 1846 when it was staged in Cagliari, Sardinia, *Bianca e Falliero* disappeared until its revival in 1986 at the Rossini Festival in Pesaro, with Katia Ricciarelli as Bianca, Marilyn Horne as Falliero and Chris Merritt as Contareno. On 7 December 1987 it reached the United States in a production by Greater Miami Opera at the Dade County Auditorium in Miami. It has yet to be staged in Great Britain.

Set in seventeenth-century Venice, the plot concerns a nobleman, Contareno, who for reasons of political advantage intends to marry his daughter, Bianca, to Capellio, a senator. Bianca, however, is in love with Falliero, a Venetian general. Falliero is unjustly accused of treason and sentenced to death, but is saved (in the opera, though not in Arnault's play) by the intervention of Bianca with the help of Capellio.

It may not represent its composer at his highest level of invention, but *Bianca e Falliero* is an opera certainly worth occasional revival, for it contains some highly attractive music. Rossini's habit of self-borrowing is kept fairly well under control, though the overture, once past its opening *allegro vivace*, is patched together from an *andante* already heard in *Ricciardo e Zoraide* and *Eduardo e Cristina*, a tune from Act I of *La Donna del lago*, and a crescendo from the overture to *Eduardo e Cristina*. After the opening chorus, Contareno and Capellio are introduced in a mellifluous duet. Rossini assigned the role of Bianca's father, Contareno, a highly unsympathetic character, to the leading tenor, and perversely made Bianca's lover, the heroic Falliero, a *travesti* role for a female singer.

Falliero's recitative, aria ('Se per l'Adria il ferro io strinsi') and fearsome cabaletta ('Il ciel custode') in Act I offer splendid opportunities to the singer to display her coloratura agility, but Bianca's aria, 'Della rosa il bel vermiglio', lacks individuality, and its cabaletta, 'Oh! serto beato', is somewhat plodding. Contareno's sequence of recitative, aria and cabaletta is more interesting, with a real fury exploding in the cabaletta ('Il piacer di mia ventura'). The finale, which builds up inexorably through duet, trio and quartet to an energetic ensemble, redeems a first act which is baldly conventional in form as well as musically uneven.

It is in Act II that *Bianca e Falliero* shows itself most worthy of revival, for the act contains a graceful duet for the lovers ('Va crudel, vedrai l'effetto'), a highly dramatic scene for father and daughter in which Contareno uses his high notes to splendidly threatening effect, and a fine extended scena, aria ('Alma, ben mio, si pura') and cabaletta ('Ma più che onore e vita') for Falliero. Most impressive of all is the quartet, 'Cielo, il mio labbro ispira', which remained popular long after the rest of the opera had been forgotten, and of which a rival composer, Pacini, declared that it alone was worth the entire score of his own new opera that same season at La Scala. Typically, Stendhal wrote that 'this quartet (and, in particular, the clarinet part in the accompaniment) must rank among the noblest conceptions with which any maestro in the world has ever been inspired'.

Bianca e Falliero ends conventionally with a joyous aria ('Teco io resto') and cabaletta ('Oh padre! oh Eroe benefico') for Bianca, in which the finale of *La Donna del lago*, Elena's 'Tanti affetti', finds itself recycled.

Maometto II

dramma in two acts

Principal characters:

Anna Erisso	(soprano)
Calbo, Venetian warrior	(mezzo-soprano)
Paolo Erisso, Anna's father, Venetian Governor	(tenor)
Maometto II	(bass)
Condulmiero, Venetian warrior	(tenor)
Selimo	(tenor)

LIBRETTO by Cesare della Valle

TIME: 1470

PLACE: Negroponte, in the Aegean

FIRST PERFORMED at the Teatro San Carlo, Naples, 3 December 1820, with Isabella Colbran (Anna Erisso); Adelaide Comelli (Calbo); Andrea Nozzari (Paolo Erisso); Filippo Galli (Maometto II); Giuseppe Ciccimarra (Condulmiero); Gaetano Chizzola (Selimo)

Rossini's hectic pace of composition now began to show signs of slowing down. Almost a full year separates the premières of *Bianca e Falliero* on 26 December 1819 and his next opera, *Maometto II*, on 3 December 1820. Although *Matilde di Shabran* was then to follow within weeks, Rossini was subsequently to compose no more than one opera each year until his premature retirement from operatic composition with *Guillaume Tell* in 1829.

Bianca e Falliero was the thirtieth opera of its twenty-eight-year-old composer who, five weeks after its première, found himself supervising the rehearsals at the Teatro San Carlo of an opera composed not by himself but by his older contemporary, Gasparo Spontini (1774–1851). This was *Fernando Cortez*, a revised version of an opera which had already been performed in Paris. The Italian première of *Fernando Cortez* on 4 February 1820 was received with indifference by the Neapolitans, after which Rossini turned to the composition of a Mass, the *Messa di Gloria*, which was performed in March in a Naples church. In April the father of Isabella Colbran, the prima donna of Rossini's Neapolitan operas, died. The composer, who was almost certainly Isabella's lover by this time, and who was to marry her two years later, commissioned a sculptor to provide a monument for her father's tomb.

It was not until May that Rossini began work on his next opera for Naples, a *dramma* or *opera seria* entitled *Maometto II*, its libretto by Cesare della Valle, Duke of Ventignano, based on the librettist's own verse drama, *Anna Erizo*, which in turn had been derived, in part, from Voltaire's *Mahomet, ou Le Fanatisme* of 1742. (Cesare della Valle was reputed to possess the *mal occhio* or evil eye, and it is said that the superstitious Rossini composed most of the opera with the index and little fingers of his left hand extended to form the sign of the devil's horns, a gesture which is still in use in Italy today as protection against the *mal occhio*.)

Composition of *Maometto II* was interrupted by the political events of the year in Naples. In July a group of disaffected army officers and priests led an uprising against King Ferdinand I, threatening revolution if the King did not proclaim a constitution. Ferdinand gave in to their demands, but within weeks Austria had threatened to intervene, by October two British frigates had arrived in the Bay of Naples, and in November the Austrian Emperor, the King of Prussia and the Tsar of Russia summoned King Ferdinand to a conference in Laibach (now Ljubljana). Greeted by crowds of cheering citizens, the Austrian army entered Naples in March of the following year, and Ferdinand's absolute rule was restored.

Theatrical activity in Naples had been seriously disrupted by this period of civic disorder, during which Rossini apparently served for a short time in the *guarda nazionale*, probably in some musical capacity. But he continued to work on *Maometto II*. Filippo Galli, the bass who was to create the title-role, wrote to a colleague on 28 November 1820, 'I can tell you that, from what I have heard of it up to now, it seems to be a masterpiece, but that [Rossini] still has not completed it.'

Whether or not Rossini had completed his opera by 28 November, it was given its première five days later, on 3 December 1820. *Maometto II* was not much liked by the Neapolitans, but was well received when Rossini revised it for performance in Venice at the Teatro La Fenice in December 1822. The opera was produced in Vienna in 1823 and managed to achieve fifteen performances in Milan in 1824. In October 1826 it was staged in Lisbon, while at the same time Rossini was busy, in Paris, adapting a large part of its score to a new French libretto. It was in its French version that the opera, now called *Le Siège de Corinthe*, achieved a great success (see pp 122–125). The Italian *Maometto II* of 1820 and 1822 seems not to have performed again until its revival in 1985 at the Rossini Festival in Pesaro. Its American première was at the San Francisco Opera House on 19 September 1988, but it has yet to be staged in Great Britain.

The fictional plot of *Maometto II* is set against the background of an historical event, the war between the Venetians and the Turks which culminated in a Turkish victory at Negroponte in 1470. The Venetian Governor of Negroponte (now the modern Euboea, largest of the Greek islands in the Aegean), Paolo Erisso, intends his daughter, Anna, to marry Calbo, a Venetian soldier. Anna, however, is in love with a man whom she had met in Corinth, who told

her his name was Uberto. Erisso is able to convince Anna that the
real Uberto, a valiant soldier, was in Venice at the time. When
Erisso and Calbo are taken prisoner by the army of Mohammed the
Conqueror (Maometto II), Anna pleads for the lives of her father
and Calbo, who she pretends is her brother, and is horrified to
discover that Mohammed is none other than her beloved Uberto.
Mohammed offers to make her his queen, but she rejects him,
marries Calbo, and, after the decisive battle, stabs herself at
Mohammed's feet.

It is not easy now to understand why Rossini's Neapolitan
audience should have acclaimed one opera while rejecting another,
for it is not simply a question of a composer being slightly ahead of
his audience's taste. The Neapolitans appear not to have been at all
consistent in their preference, either for the comic Rossini as
opposed to the serious, or for the conventional as distinct from the
innovative. It may well be that their response to each new work was
dictated largely by the standard of the actual performance they were
witnessing. Though Naples was indifferent to *Maometto II*, it is one of
the most immediately attractive of Rossini's serious operas, its
orchestration rich and varied, its structure sound and imposing, and
its dramatic impact striking. (*Le Siège de Corinthe* is even better.)

There is no overture, merely a short, brass-dominated orchestral
introduction preceding the grave opening chorus of Venetian
warriors. The ensuing scene introduces Erisso, Calbo and their
colleague Condulmiero, whose ferocious utterance arouses the
fighting spirit of the warriors. Anna is introduced in a sad, graceful
cavatina, 'Ah! che invan su questo ciglio', but the central number of
Act I is the extended ensemble which Rossini labelled *terzettone* or
'huge trio', a trio for Anna, her father and Calbo (one of Rossini's
contralto heroes *en travesti*) which survives the noise of distant battle,
a change of scene, and the intrusion of a female chorus supporting
Anna in prayer. Indeed, this *terzettone* never actually comes to a
formal end, but eventually merges into a somewhat comical, indeed
operetta-like chorus of Moslem soldiers.

Maometto's cavatina, 'Sorgete: e in sì bel giorno', though somewhat florid, retains a certain dignity, but its cabaletta's flamboyant
air of self-glorification takes the singer into such a whirl of
coloratura that he is in danger of sounding more like a high-spirited
reveller than a leader whose troops have just acclaimed him
conqueror of the world. In the Act I finale, powerful accompanied

recitative leads to a lilting trio ('Giusto Ciel, che strazio è questo!') and a ferocious ensemble which, if it were set to other words, could easily be described as joyous.

Amiability, high spirits and a gentle nostalgia – that 'candeur virginale' which so impressed Stendhal – are the qualities nearest to the surface of Rossini's personality, and he tended to alternate them on appropriate and inappropriate occasions alike. However, whether the chorus of Moslem maidens attending Anna at the beginning of Act II is dramatically apt seems hardly to matter when the *vivace* chorus itself ('È follia sul fior degli anni') is so joyous, and its orchestration so light and airy. The duet between Anna and Maometto ('Anna, tu piangi?') is equally impressive, particularly Anna's serene *larghetto*, 'Lieta innocente un giorno'; and Maometto's aria, 'All' invito generoso', its gesture towards a cabaletta truncated by the chorus of impatient Moslem soldiers, is both mellifluous and formally interesting. Calbo's aria, 'Non temer', with its extremely florid cabaletta ('E d'un trono alla speranza'), is equally attractive though less original.

After an affecting trio ('In questi estremi istanti') for Anna, Calbo and Erisso, Anna's solo scene with an off-stage chorus of Venetian women praying for victory leads to the opera's dramatically confused but musically exciting finale. This takes the form of an extended aria for Anna, its final section ('Madre, a te') not the usual lively cabaletta, whether of grief, rage or joy, but a devout prayer to the soul of her dead mother. The end of the opera then comes swiftly with a brief exchange between Anna and her captor-lover, Maometto, followed by Anna's suicide and the horrified reaction of Maometto, his Moslem followers and the Venetian women.

Matilde di Shabran

melodramma giocoso in two acts

Principal characters:
Matilde   (soprano)
Edoardo   (mezzo-soprano)
Corradino (tenor)
Aliprando (bass)

Isidoro   (bass)
Ginardo   (bass)
Egoldo   (tenor)
Rodrigo   (tenor)
Raimondo (bass)

LIBRETTO by Jacopo Ferretti

TIME: The middle ages
PLACE: Spain

FIRST PERFORMED at the Teatro Apollo, Rome, 24 February 1821, with Caterina Lipparini (Matilde); Annetta Parlamagni (Edoardo); Giuseppe Fusconi (Corradino); Giuseppe Fioravanti (Aliprando); Antonio Parlamagni (Isidoro); Antonio Ambrosi (Ginardo); Carlo Moncada (Raimondo); Gaetano Rambaldi (Egoldo and Rodrigo)

A week or two after the première of *Maometto II*, Rossini left Naples for Rome where he had agreed to provide a new opera for the Teatro Apollo's carnival season. He had already composed the first act of an opera based on a French play, *Mathilde de Morwel*, but had become increasingly dissatisfied both with the quality of the libretto and the slowness with which it was being delivered to him piecemeal. In Rome, therefore, he approached Jacopo Ferretti (the librettist of his *Cenerentola*), who, it transpired, had been working in his spare time on adapting the libretto which François Benoit Hoffmann had derived from Voltaire for the opera, *Euphrosine et Coradin* by Méhul, first performed in Paris in 1790.

Since Rossini's new opera had already been announced as *Matilde*, Ferretti changed the names of the characters in *Euphrosine et Coradin*, which he retitled *Matilde Shabran* before offering his libretto to Rossini. (Soon after its initial Rome performances, the opera began to be known as *Matilde di Shabran*.) Working against time as usual, Rossini enlisted the aid not only of one or two of his earlier operas but also of another composer, Giovanni Pacini, whose first opera had been staged in Vienna in 1813 and who was in Rome following the successful première at the Teatro Valle of his latest opera, *La Gioventù di Enrico V*, its libretto (also by Ferretti) derived from Shakespeare's *Henry V*. Rossini prevailed upon Pacini to compose three of the numbers for *Matilde di Shabran*.

The conductor of the Teatro Apollo having died of apoplexy during rehearsals, the première of Rossini's new opera was conducted by the famous violinist, Niccolò Paganini. It was an unusually lively occasion, with not only a mixed reception for the opera in the auditorium but also a street brawl after the performance between Rossini's admirers and his detractors.

After the première, displeased at the reception accorded to the opera and also at discovering that the work was not all new and not all by Rossini, the impresario of the Teatro Apollo refused to pay the composer the fee that had been agreed. Rossini immediately removed his score and orchestral parts from the theatre, and wrote a letter of complaint to the Governor of Rome. This action seems to have resulted in his fee being paid: *Matilde (di) Shabran* certainly continued to be performed in repertory at the Teatro Apollo until the end of the season. Later in the year it was performed in Naples, and thereafter went the rounds of other Italian cities. It was also widely performed throughout Europe and in the New World, reaching London on 3 July 1823 (at Her Majesty's Theatre) and New York on 10 February 1834. After 1892 in Florence, *Matilde di Shabran* appears not to have been revived anywhere until 1974 when it was staged in Genoa.

The plot of the opera is a senseless and complicated affair involving Corradino, his young prisoner Edoardo (son of his enemy, Raimondo), and Corradino's ward, Matilde, who falls in love with Edoardo. Some of the numbers, however, are more enjoyable than the work's disappearance from the repertory for nearly a century would seem to suggest. For the overture, Rossini used the piece he had put together the previous year for *Eduardo e Cristina*, and in the opera he also recycled a chorus and part of a duet from his *Ricciardo e Zoraide* of two years earlier.

An opening *allegretto* chorus, 'Zitti nessun qui v'e', gives way to Ginardo's lively narrative describing Corradino's ferocious character. The itinerant poet, Isidoro, is given an aria, 'Intanto Erminia', whose tedious opening *allegro moderato* gives way to a *vivace* which is a poor imitation of Figaro's 'Largo al factotum'. An extended quartet, 'Alma rea', for tenor (Corradino) and three basses, is one of the liveliest numbers of the entire score with its highly decorated tenor part, but Edoardo's mezzo-soprano aria, 'Piange il mio ciglio' is disappointing, and the soprano–bass duet, 'Di capricci di smorfiette', for Matilde and Aliprando is only intermittently engaging until its spirited *allegro* concluding section, 'Ah, di veder già parmi'. The most successful (though rather too lengthy) number in the first act is a bustling *allegro maestoso* quintet, 'Questa è la Dea', especially its lilting central *andante*, 'Dallo stupore oppresso', launched by the tenor, Corradino. The finale to the act, 'Ah, capisco', begun by Matilde, is not one of Rossini's most sparkling, except for its hectic love duet for Corradino and Matilde, cut short by a march (borrowed from *La Donna del lago*) which heralds the arrival of Corradino's father. The final *allegro* ensemble, however, is typically Rossinian and quite exhilarating.

Act II is no less uneven. Raimondo's aria, 'Ah, perchè, perchè la morte', reveals a certain dignity, as does the trio, 'Deh, serena il mesto ciglio', but individuality is lacking. The act continues with an impressive *maestoso* sextet ('E palese il tradimento') in which Corradino has several opportunities to display his high C. After the sextet's hectic *vivace* conclusion, a fine *andante–allegro* duet ('No, Matilde non morrai') ensues for the soprano and mezzo-soprano characters of Matilde and Edoardo. Writing for two female voices in duet seemed to inspire Rossini as it would Bellini and, in the following century, Richard Strauss. Corradino's *andante* cavatina, 'T'arrendi al mesto pianto', borrowed from *Ricciardo e Zoraide*, has an effective though all too brief cabaletta, and Matilda's aria 'Ami alfin' brings the opera to a rousing conclusion. 'Execrable libretto, but pretty music – such was the general verdict', according to Stendhal.

Zelmira

dramma in two acts

Principal characters:

Zelmira	(soprano)
Emma	(contralto)
Ilo	(tenor)
Antenore	(tenor)
Polidoro	(bass)
Leucippo	(bass)
Eacide	(tenor)
Gran Sacerdote	(bass)

LIBRETTO by Andrea Leone Tottola

TIME: The remote past
PLACE: The island of Lesbos

FIRST PERFORMED at the Teatro San Carlo, Naples, 16 February 1822, with Isabella Colbran (Zelmira); Anna Maria Cecconi (Emma); Antonio Ambrosi (Polidoro); Giovanni David (Ilo); Andrea Nozzari (Antenore); Michele Benedetti (Leucippo); Gaetano Chizzola (Eacide); Massimo Orlandini (Gran Sacerdote)

On his return to Naples after the Rome première of *Matilde di Shabran*, Rossini found that the impresario Barbaja had arranged for his Naples company to appear in Vienna. The new opera they would perform there was to be Rossini's *Zelmira*, which would first, however, be performed in Naples. *Zelmira*, its libretto by Tottola drawn from a 1762 French tragedy, *Zelmire*, by Dormont de Belloy (the pseudonym of Pierre-Laurent Buyrette), was warmly received at its Naples première on 16 February 1822. Three weeks later, the day after its final performance of the season and one week after his thirtieth birthday, Rosini and the opera's prima donna Isabella Colbran set out for Vienna with three other members of the cast, stopping at Castenaso near Bologna, where Isabella Colbran had a villa. There, she and Rossini were married.

Already Vienna's favourite opera composer, Rossini found himself being fêted when he and Colbran arrived in the Austrian capital at the end of March. From April to July the Kärntnertor Theater mounted a Rossini festival, beginning on 13 April with the new *Zelmira* which the Viennese audience received with great enthusiasm. During the year, *Zelmira* was performed in several Italian cities, and the following year in Lisbon. Its first London performance was given at the King's Theatre on 24 January 1824, conducted by Rossini, with Isabella Colbran in the title-role. In the same year it was also staged in Barcelona, Dresden and Prague. Its only performance in the United States appears to have been in New Orleans around 1835. *Zelmira* returned to Naples and the Teatro San Carlo in 1965 with Virginia Zeani in the title-role, but to no great acclaim. A concert performance in Venice at the Teatro La Fenice in 1988 conducted by Claudio Scimone was much more successful, as was a production at the Rome Opera in 1989.

Dormont de Belloy's tragedy is a tedious and dully written piece, and Tottola's mindless libretto is no improvement upon it. Set on the island of Lesbos, it tells an absurd and complicated tale involving old King Polidoro, whose daughter Zelmira has hidden him among the tombs in order to save him from being murdered by the usurper, Azor, who is killed by Antenore, pretender to the throne of Mytilene. (All of this occurs before the opera begins.) Zelmira's husband, Ilo, a Trojan prince, almost loses his life as well, and his would-be assassins persuade him that it was his wife who had been about to kill him. Zelmira is led off to prison, but in due course all ends happily, with Polidoro, who had been presumed dead, returned to the throne, and Zelmira reunited with her husband.

It can hardly be claimed that *Zelmira* is one of Rossini's greatest operas (though Claudio Scimone, who conducted it in Venice in 1988, has referred to it as 'the happiest and most harmonious of Rossini's works'). Nevertheless, in performance it is more than capable of rising above the absurdity of its dramatic action through the vigour and skill of its score. There is no overture, merely a few bars of dramatic orchestral comment before the curtain rises on a chorus of warriors who have just discovered that their leader has been killed. Throughout the opera, the particular care taken with the orchestration makes it clear that Rossini was writing with Vienna in mind. Stendhal compared *Zelmira* with Mozart's *La Clemenza di Tito*, adding the perceptive comment that 'while Mozart would probably, had he lived, have grown completely Italian, Rossini may well, by the end of his career, have become more German than Beethoven himself!'

Antenore's aria, 'Che vidi amici!', is difficult to bring off in performance, the transparent candour of Rossini's melody being at variance with the real feelings of Antenore who is merely feigning distress, but the fierce cabaletta, 'Sorte! Secondami!', in which he expresses his ambition to seize the throne, is vocally irresistible. Polidoro's cavatina, 'Ah! già trascorso il dì', is impressive in its solemnity, and the orchestrally accompanied recitative throughout both acts gives the opera a stature which makes Stendhal's reference to *La Clemenza di Tito* understandable. The Act I trio for Polidoro, Zelmira and Emma could almost be by the Weber of *Der Freischütz*, but Ilo's aria ('Terra amica') and cabaletta ('Cara! deh attendimi'), which so exhilaratingly display the tenor's virtuoso range and agility, could only be by Rossini.

In the duet for Ilo and Zelmira, 'A che quei tronchi accenti?',
Rossini writes both for the voices and for the orchestra with an
originality and a concern for the dramatic situation which he used
not always to display, the anxiety of husband and wife vividly
conveyed in their nervous coloratura. Antenore's aria, 'Mentre qual
fiera ingorda', is more conventional but no less fierce in its
vertiginous vocal demands, especially in its cabaletta, 'Ah! dopo
tanti palpiti', while by contrast the delicate F minor duet, 'Perchè mi
guardi', for Zelmira and Emma, accompanied only by harp and cor
anglais, offers an oasis of tenderness in the middle of the surrounding fury. The Act I finale is much more impressive musically than
dramatically, Leucippo's attempted murder of Ilo and his subsequent placing of the blame successfully upon Zelmira being almost
impossible to take seriously. However the quintet, 'La sorpresa, lo
stupore', and the final ensemble are effective.

Emma's aria and cabaletta, which Rossini added to the score for
Fanny Eckerlin, the Emma of the Vienna performances, are
musically dull and dramatically redundant, but the rest of Act II is
first-rate. The scene in which Ilo encounters Polidoro, whom he had
thought killed by Zelmira, is the finest in the opera, the outburst of
joy by the two men ('In estasi di gioia') quite irresistibly exciting.
The quintet, 'Ne' lacci miei cadesti', is lively and affecting by turns,
but the finale of the opera, consisting of an aria ('Stelle! e fia ver?')
and cabaletta ('Deh, circondatemi') for Zelmira, is not one of
Rossini's more striking solo rondo finales.

Semiramide

melodramma tragico in two acts

Principal characters:

Semiramide   (soprano)
Arsace   (contralto)
Idreno   (tenor)
Azema   (soprano)
Assur   (bass)
Oroe   (bass)

LIBRETTO by Gaetano Rossi

TIME: Antiquity
PLACE: Babylon

FIRST PERFORMED at the Teatro La Fenice, Venice, 3 February
1823, with Isabella Colbran (Semiramide); Rosa Mariani
(Arsace); Matilde Spagna (Azema); John Sinclair (Idreno);
Filippo Galli (Assur); Luciano Mariani (Oroe)

One of Rossini's first actions on his arrival in Vienna towards the
end of March 1822 was to write to the impresario Giovanni Battista
Benelli in London. 'I do not want to return to Naples after Vienna,'
he informed Benelli, 'nor do I want my wife to return there.' If
Benelli had not yet engaged his leading soprano for the following
year, Rossini would be willing to come to London with Isabella,
compose a new opera, and stage some of his others.

In Vienna, Rossini attended a performance of Weber's *Der
Freischütz* conducted by the composer and, once the successful
launching of the Viennese Rossini festival with *Zelmira* was past,
paid a visit to Beethoven in the company of Giuseppe Carpani, the
Austrian Court Poet. Describing the occasion to Wagner nearly
forty years later, Rossini recalled that he and Carpani

> went up the stairs leading to the poor lodgings in which the great man
> lived. I had some difficulty in containing my emotion. When the door
> was opened, I found myself in a kind of hovel, so dirty as to testify to
> frightening disorder. ... When we first entered, he paid no attention to
> us, but for some moments remained bent over a piece of printed music
> which he was correcting. Then, raising his head, he said to me brusquely
> in quite comprehensible Italian, 'Ah, Rossini, you are the composer of *Il
> Barbiere di Siviglia*? I congratulate you, it is an excellent comic opera. I
> read it with pleasure, and it delights me. It will be performed as long as
> Italian opera exists. Never try to do anything other than *opera buffa*.'

When Carpani attempted to mention Rossini's serious operas,
Beethoven spoke dismissively of them. Italians lacked the musical
knowledge to deal with real drama, 'and how could they acquire it in
Italy?' Rossini felt secure enough not to resent Beethoven's attitude.
Indeed, while he was in Vienna he considered attempting to raise
funds by subscription for Beethoven who, about to begin work on his
Ninth Symphony, was in ill health and harassed by creditors. But
there was little support from the Viennese for Rossini's suggestion.

The Rossini operas staged in Vienna between April and July were *Cenerentola*, *Matilde di Shabran*, *Elisabetta, regina d'Inghilterra*, *La Gazza ladra* and a one-act version, arranged by the composer, of *Ricciardo e Zoraide*, after the performance of which a vast crowd gathered outside the house in which the Rossinis and their colleagues were having supper. The crowd was rewarded with an impromptu concert of Rossini arias, but it was two o'clock in the morning before they could be persuaded – by the police – to disperse. Vienna was well and truly in the grip of Rossini fever: it is small wonder that Beethoven was envious.

Rossini and Isabella Colbran left Vienna at the end of July. Later in the year, the composer was invited by Prince Metternich, the Austrian Chancellor, to participate in an international congress in Verona. Rossini, Metternich told the composer, was the God of harmony, and harmony would be needed very badly at the congress. During his several weeks' stay in Verona, Rossini attended parties given by Metternich, and was presented to the Austrian Emperor Francis I, Tsar Alexander I, and the Duke of Wellington. For performance during the period of the congress, he composed five cantatas. By the middle of December, Rossini and Colbran had left Verona for Venice where Rossini had agreed, for the then unprecedented sum of 5000 francs, to compose an opera for the Teatro La Fenice. First, however, he staged at the Fenice, on 26 December, a slightly revised version of *Maometto II* which was not well received, most probably because Isabella Colbran was in poor vocal health and sang badly.

The new opera was *Semiramide*, its libretto by Gaetano Rossi based on Voltaire's 1748 tragedy, *Sémiramis*, about the legendary Assyrian Queen who married King Ninus, and after his death built Babylon and other great cities. In Rossini's opera, Semiramide, Queen of Babylon, and her lover, Assur, murder the King, but Semiramide then falls in love with Arsace, the young Commander of the Assyrian army, whom she plans to marry. Before the ceremony can take place, Arsace is revealed to be her son. Defending himself against an attack by Assur, Arsace accidentally kills Semiramide. He is proclaimed King and hailed as the avenger of his father's murder.

At its première on 3 February 1823, *Semiramide*, which Rossini claimed he had composed in thirty-three days, was favourably received. It was performed twenty-eight times until the end of the season, and was immediately taken up by other opera houses in Italy and abroad. Rossini was now beyond doubt the most successful composer of his day, his operas staged throughout Europe, as well as in the Americas. Stendhal, writing in the year of *Semiramide*'s première, said of its composer, 'The glory of this man is only limited by the limits of civilisation itself; and he is not yet thirty-two.'

London first saw *Semiramide* at His Majesty's Theatre in the Haymarket on 15 July 1824. The opera did not reach New York until 3 January 1845, although parts of it had been performed there in 1835. The first complete performance in the United States was at the St Charles Theatre, New Orleans, on 1 May 1837.

Semiramide remained popular until the end of the century, after which it was neglected until revived in Rostock (in German translation) in 1932 and at the Florence Maggio Musicale in 1940. A much acclaimed production at La Scala, Milan, in 1962 with Joan Sutherland in the title-role and Giulietta Simionato as Arsace gave *Semiramide* a new lease of life and led to productions in many leading opera houses throughout Europe, the Americas and Australia. The dismissive comment still to be found in Kobbé's *Complete Opera Book* – '*Semiramide* seems to have had its day' – would appear to be overdue for revision. Though it is an uneven work *Semiramide* can still hold the stage, given intelligent production and singers capable of rising to its vocal demands. It was performed at the Rossini Festival in Pesaro in 1992.

The overture, constructed on themes from the opera itself, is an imposing piece which has become popular as a concert item. The opening scene, once past Oroe's dull recitative, is enlivened by a perhaps inappropriately jaunty chorus in praise of Baal, but the ensuing trio ('Là dal Gange') is undistinguished. After another somewhat eccentric chorus, Semiramide makes her first appearance in the quartet, 'Di tanti regi e popoli', during which the dramatic action finally gets under way with a blinding flash extinguishing the sacred flame on the altar, sending Semiramide into a flurry of agitated coloratura.

Arsace's *andantino* aria, 'Ah! quel giorno', is preceded by an impressive orchestral introduction and dramatic recitative in which the young warrior ponders upon why he has been summoned back to Babylon. The aria, despite its joyous cabaletta, makes less of an effect than Arsace's ensuing duet ('Bella imago') with Assur. Semiramide's brilliant cavatina, 'Bel raggio lusinghier', is justly famous, but no less dazzling is the concluding section of her beautiful *andantino* duet with Arsace, 'Serbami ognor', which incorporates between its verses a *crescendo* from the overture. In the magnificent Act I finale, her court swears loyalty to Semiramide to the tune of the overture's *andantino*; an ensemble led by the Queen ('Qual mesto gemito'), its solemn *ostinato* an anticipation of the 'Miserere' in Verdi's *Il Trovatore*, is interrupted by the ghost of Ninus which makes its displeasure known in utterances not unworthy of the Commendatore in *Don Giovanni*; and Rossini's famous *crescendo* brings the final *vivace* ensemble to a hugely exciting conclusion.

There is an adumbration of Verdi again – *Macbeth* this time – in 'Se la vita ancor t'è cara', the *allegro* duet for the guilty couple, Semiramide and Assur, which begins Act II. The mood of Arsace's *andante* aria, 'In sì barbara sciagura', ranges widely from despair to heroic determination, and his *allegro agitato* duet ('Ebben, a te') with Semiramide when she discovers that her love for him is incestuous reveals Rossini at his most powerful, in its balance of musical and dramatic requirements. 'La speranza più soave', the *andantino* tenor aria in which Idreno presses his suit upon the Princess Azema, is a nondescript piece and peripheral to the action, as indeed is the character of Idreno.

In the opera's dramatic penultimate scene, Assur, lurking near the tomb of Ninus intent on killing Arsace, is beset by fearsome visions. Again one is reminded of Verdi's *Macbeth*. Semiramide's prayer, 'Al mio pregar t'arrendi', is affecting, and the dénouement arrives in a trio, 'L'usato ardir', with the protagonists circling around one another in the dark. The final chorus is both perfunctory and inappropriately cheerful. It is due to its masterly ensembles and the duets for Semiramide and Arsace that *Semiramide* continues to be enjoyed by modern audiences.

7

From *Il Viaggio a Reims* to *Guillaume Tell*

Il Viaggio a Reims
(The Journey to Rheims)

dramma giocoso in one act

Principal characters:

Corinna	(soprano)
La Contessa di Folleville	(soprano)
Madama Cortese	(soprano)
La Marchesa Melibea	(contralto)
Il Cavalier Belfiore	(tenor)
Il Conte di Libenskof	(tenor)
Lord Sidney	(bass)
Don Profondo	(bass)
Il Barone di Trombonok	(bass)
Don Alvaro	(bass)

LIBRETTO by Luigi Balocchi

TIME: 1825
PLACE: An inn in Plombières, France

FIRST PERFORMED at the Théâtre-Italien, Paris, 19 June 1825, with Giuditta Pasta (Corinna); Laure Cinti-Damoreau (La Contessa di Folleville); Ester Mombelli (Madama Cortese); Adelaide Schiassetti (La Marchesa Melibea); Domenico Donzelli (Il Cavalier Belfiore); Marco Bordogni (Il Conte di Libenskof);

Carlo Zucchelli (Lord Sidney); Felice Pellegrini (Don Profondo);
Francesco Graziani (Il Barone di Trombonok); Nicholas-Prosper
Levasseur (Don Alvaro)

After the première of *Semiramide* the Rossinis left Venice in March
1823, spent the summer in Bologna and Castenaso, and in
November made their way to London via Paris where they stayed
for a month as guests of the Genoese writer, Nicola Bagioli, a month
during which the Parisians proved that they were no more immune
to 'Rossini fever' than the Viennese. A rough channel crossing to
England in December reduced Rossini to a state of nervous collapse,
and it was not until two weeks after he and Isabella had settled into
their London apartment at 90 Regent Street that the composer felt
well enough to accept King George IV's invitation to Brighton,
where the King was in residence at the Pavilion. Here Rossini
delighted the entire court with his performance of Figaro's 'Largo al
factotum', followed by Desdemona's Willow Song from *Otello* which
he sang in falsetto. This caused the *Quarterly Musical Magazine* later
to express its outrage that he should have imitated those 'eunuchs
who have been banished from the stage for many years because they
offended against the modesty and humanity of the English'. However, George IV appears not to have been shocked, and on a later
occasion he actually raised his uningratiating bass voice in duet with
Rossini. When the King apologised for singing a few wrong notes,
Rossini replied, 'Sire, you have every right to do as it pleases you. I
will follow you to the grave.'

London, too, succumbed to Rossini mania, and with much of his
time spent at fashionable parties, where he charged fifty pounds an
appearance, the composer failed to complete *Ugo, Re d'Italia*, the
opera he had been contracted to write for performance in London.
How much of the opera was actually composed is not known, for
when Rossini left England after seven months he left as much of the
score as he had written with the London impresario's bankers. *Ugo,
Re d'Italia* now seems to be irretrievably lost.

Though he left an incomplete opera behind, Rossini took with
him several thousand pounds which he had earned in London from
his social appearances and from accompanying singers in performances of his music. It is hardly surprising that he often expressed a
deep love of London. 'During my stay in England,' he said later, 'I
received attentions which it would be difficult to parallel elsewhere.'

Nevertheless, when he left London in August 1824 for Paris, Rossini was welcomed by the Parisians with open arms as one of the most celebrated of living composers, and given the general management of the Théâtre-Italien, the Paris theatre in which Italian operas were performed in their original language.

It was, of course, hoped and expected that Rossini would immediately begin to compose new operas for performance in Paris, but this was not to be. The composer mounted productions of such existing operas of his as *Cenerentola*, *La Donna del lago* and *Otello*, as well as works by other composers, but it was not until the following year that he wrote his first and only opera for the Théâtre-Italien. This was *Il Viaggio a Reims*, an occasional piece produced to celebrate the coronation of Charles X in Rheims Cathedral in June 1825. The première of the opera took place on 19 June, two weeks after the coronation, and was hugely successful. That some writers on Rossini have described it as a failure can only be due to their having taken at face value the entry in Loewenberg's *Annals of Opera*, which records tersely: 'Complete failure, three nights only.' But it was Rossini who withdrew the piece after three sold-out and enthusiastically received performances, almost certainly because he considered it purely a *pièce d'occasion*, and already had plans for the recycling of much of its score.

Rossini was, in fact, prevailed upon to allow a fourth performance of the opera some months later, as a benefit for the victims of a fire in the small French town of Salins-les-Bains. Three years later, in 1828, he was to re-use five of *Il Viaggio a Reims*'s nine numbers in *Le Comte Ory*, but an unauthorised adaptation of the original *Viaggio* was performed at the Théâtre-Italien in the middle of the 1848 Revolution, as *Andremo a Parigi?*, with the characters *en route* not to a coronation but to the Parisian barricades. The opera was also staged in Vienna in 1854 as *Il Viaggio a Vienna*, to celebrate the wedding of the Emperor Franz Josef and Elisabeth of Bavaria.

After this, *Il Viaggio* was not heard again until 1984 when, some of the individual parts having been found in the library of the Paris Conservatoire, Rossini's autograph manuscript of the numbers that were not used again in *Le Comte Ory* having come to light in a basement storeroom of the Santa Cecilia Library in Rome, and the 1854 Viennese copy of the score having been unearthed in the Austrian National Library, the American Rossini scholar Philip Gossett was able to reconstruct virtually the complete work, which was staged at the Pesaro Rossini Festival in 1984. Since then *Il Viaggio a Reims* has been performed at La Scala, Milan, in 1985, and given its American première by the Opera Theater of St Louis, Missouri, in 1986, in an English translation which was used again for the opera's British première in a student production by the Guildhall School of Music, London, in 1987. A missing chorus was finally unearthed in time for the first professional staging of *Il Viaggio a Reims* in Great Britain, which took place at the Royal Opera House, Covent Garden, on 4 July 1992.

Though the libretto of *Il Viaggio a Reims ossia l'Albergo del giglio d'oro* (The Journey to Rheims or The Golden Lily Inn) describes itself as a *dramma giocoso*, Rossini's manuscript score defines the work as a *cantata scenica* (cantata for the stage). From Madame de Staël's novel, *Corinne, ou l'Italie* (1807), on which it is supposed to be based, Luigi Balocchi's libretto has borrowed a character, Corinna, and some caricatures of various national types. In the novel Oswald Nevil, an English nobleman recuperating in Rome, meets Corinne, a famous poetess who, though half-English, prefers to live in Italy. They fall in love, but Corinne refuses to leave the delights of Italy for the restrictive English life she once knew. Oswald returns to England and later marries Lucile, the English half-sister of Corinne who, upon learning of the marriage, dies of grief.

Rossini's opera is about a group of travellers from various countries, one of whom happens to be Corinna, a famous Roman improvising poetess or *improvvisatrice*. All of them intend to leave the spa hotel in Plombières where they have been taking the cure, in order to attend the coronation of Charles X in Rheims Cathedral. The opera concerns itself with their attempts to depart. At the same time, it contrives to present an affectionate satire on the kind of romantic novel in which Madame de Staël specialised, to offer ten leading roles for brilliant singers, and, in its final scene, to pay tribute to the new King, Charles X. Some of the most famous opera singers of the time participated in the 1825 royal première, among them Giuditta Pasta, Ester Mombelli, Domenico Donzelli, Felice Pellegrini and Nicholas-Prosper Levasseur.

According to a report in the *Journal des Débats*, at its première the opera was performed without an overture. However, among the musical manuscripts left by Rossini to the Liceo in Pesaro is one (not in the composer's hand) which bears the superscription, '*Gran Sinfonia scritta per l'Opera Reale nel Melodramma Un Voyage à Reims*'

(Grand symphony [i.e. overture] written for the royal opera in the melodrama, A Journey to Rheims).

The performance of the opera at its première is said to have lasted three hours. This would make *Il Viaggio* one of the longest of one-act operas, along with Wagner's *Das Rheingold* and the original version of *Der fliegende Holländer*. The score as published by the Fondazione Rossini in Pesaro in 1983 (still without overture) takes approximately two and a quarter hours to perform.

After a brief orchestral introduction anticipating the bustle of the Golden Lily Inn, the curtain rises on a spacious reception room in the hotel where Maddalena, the housekeeper, is busily exhorting her somewhat insolent staff of maids and waiters to work a little harder. She is followed by the spa's doctor, Don Prudenzio, who is concerned to inspect the menu being offered for the day, and by Madama Cortese, the Tyrolean owner of the hotel who, after a graceful aria ('Di vaghi raggi adorno') in which she wishes that she could accompany her guests to the coronation, explains to the staff in a lively cabaletta (replete with *crescendo* when they respond enthusiastically) that they must be ready to talk with each guest about his or her special interest: with the Cavalier Belfiore about beautiful women, with the Marchesa Melibea about fantastic ideas, with the German visitor about musical counterpoint, and so on.

The first of the guests to appear is a Parisian lady of fashion, the Contessa di Folleville, whose elegantly grief-stricken aria, 'Partir, oh ciel! desio', is occasioned by the loss of her luggage in an accident *en route* to the spa. Rossini gently pokes fun both at the excesses of the romantic movement and at his own brand of languid melancholy. To the amusement of the onlookers, when her maid arrives with a beautiful hat salvaged from the wreck the Contessa cheers up sufficiently to launch into a joyous cabaletta whose grandeur is delightfully disproportionate to the situation occasioning it.

Several other characters now begin to appear: the German Baron von Trombonok (Barone di Trombonok) who seems to have been elected treasurer of the group of travellers; Don Profondo who has returned from visiting a nearby site of antiquity; Don Alvaro, a Spanish admiral, escorting the Marchesa Melibea, the Polish widow of an Italian general; and the Conte di Libenskof, a Russian general and Alvaro's jealous rival for the affections of Melibea. By the time Madama Cortese has reappeared to explain that their departure will have to be delayed as the courier has not returned with the horses, the Spaniard and the Russian are preparing to fight a duel over Melibea. All express their feelings in a spacious sextet ('Sì, di matti una gran rabbia'), begun *allegro giusto* by Trombonok, with a beautiful central *andante* ('Non pavento alcun periglio') which is followed not, as one might expect, by a concluding *allegro* but by the off-stage voice of the poetess, Corinna, improvising to harp accompaniment a wistful ode to the dawning of a golden age of brotherly love ('Arpa gentil'), its main theme derived from a tune Rossini had used in *Armida*. Corinna's sentiments are echoed by the on-stage characters, at first piously and then, in a brilliant stretta, enthusiastically, all thoughts of duels and jealousy dispelled. This appealing sextet is one of Rossini's finest ensembles. As other commentators have noted, it sounds like a fully-fledged Act I finale, and indeed it is possible to stage *Il Viaggio* in three comparatively short acts, ending Act I with the sextet.

In a florid aria ('Invan strappar dal core') and cabaletta with a virtuoso flute obbligato, the English nobleman Lord Sidney sings of his hopeless passion for Corinna. The Cavalier Belfiore, also in love with Corinna, plucks up the courage to discuss the matter with her personally in a charming duet ('Nel suo divin sembiante') in which, however, she indignantly rejects him. Don Profondo's strophic patter aria, 'Medaglie incomparabili', listing the various travellers' effects, bursts into melodic bloom only in its final section. (Rossini was to adapt it to a different situation in *Le Comte Ory*.)

When the courier finally arrives, it is to announce, to the consternation of the assembled travellers, that there are no horses available for the coaches which were to take them to Rheims. There follows the opera's most delightful number, the superb *Gran pezzo concertato a quattordici voci* (Grand Ensemble for fourteen voices), 'Ah! A tal colpo inaspettato', in which the ten principal characters plus Delia (a young Greek orphan travelling with Corinna), Don Prudenzio (the spa's doctor), Modestina (the Contessa di Folleville's chambermaid) and Zefirino (the courier) all take part. In the course of the ensemble Madama Cortese receives a letter from her husband informing her that, immediately after the coronation, King Charles X will return to Paris where magnificent festivities are being planned. The travellers decide that, as they cannot get to Rheims, they will take part instead in the celebrations in Paris, proceeding there the very next day by the public stagecoach. The Contessa di Folleville, whose home is in Paris, offers them accommodation.

With the money they have saved by not proceeding to Rheims, the company decides to give a banquet that evening at the inn, to which they will invite the villagers. This *Gran pezzo concertato* makes an exhilarating conclusion to Act II if the opera is being staged in three acts.

After the duet, 'D'alma celeste, oh Dio!', in which the lovers' quarrel between the Marchesa Melibea and the Conte di Libenskof is mellifluously resolved, the opera's final scene takes place in the brightly illuminated garden of the inn where a table has been laid for the banquet. Entertainment is provided by a company of itinerant musicians and dancers who have serendipitously arrived – a chorus, at this point, remained lost until shortly before the opera's 1992 production in London – after which Baron von Trombonok proposes a round of toasts to the royal family and to a harmonious future for Europe, contributed to by each of the travellers in the style of his or her country.

Trombonok begins, to the tune of Haydn's 'Gott erhalte Franz den Kaiser', and is followed by the Marchesa Melibea with a Polonaise, the Conte di Libenskof with an ebullient Russian tune, and Don Alvaro with a Spanish song, to each of which the assembled company adds a refrain. Lord Sidney, claiming to know only one song, offers his highly decorated version of 'God Save the King'. His attempt at a cadenza is cut short by Trombonok, after which the French couple, the Cavalier Belfiore and the Contessa di Folleville, combine in a French song. Madama Cortese and Don Profondo follow with a Swiss Tyrolienne complete with somewhat tentative yodelling effects. Invited to improvise, Corinna allows the other guests to choose a subject. From a number of suggestions – some considerably more arcane than others – including Joan of Arc, the Battle of Tolbiac, Clovis, Hugh Capet and 'Las tres estirpes reales de Francia', the one chosen is, fortunately, Charles X, King of France. After Corinna's graceful aria in praise of Charles ('All' ombra amena del Giglio d'Or'), portraits of the French royal family are produced and everyone joins in a final chorus in praise of France.

A Parisian critic, writing after the première, praised the *Gran pezzo concertato*, but concluded that 'the rest is noise, *crescendos*, and the other culminating forms that now are used and abused to satiety'. *Au contraire*, Rossini's final Italian opera (and his first opera to be composed for Paris) is an enchanting oddity.

Le Siège de Corinthe
(The Siege of Corinth)

tragédie lyrique in three acts

Principal characters:

Pamyre	(soprano)
Néocles	(tenor)
Mahomet II	(bass)
Cléomène	(tenor)
Hiéros	(bass)
Omar	(bass)
Ismène	(mezzo-soprano)
Adraste	(tenor)

LIBRETTO by Luigi Balocchi and Alexandre Soumet

TIME: 1459
PLACE: Corinth

FIRST PERFORMED at the Paris Opéra, 9 October 1826, with
Laure Cinti-Damoreau (Pamyre); Adolphe Nourrit (Néocles);
Henri Étienne-Dérivis (Mahomet II); Louis Nourrit (Cléomène);
Alex Prévost (Hiéros); Ferdinand Prévost (Omar); Mlle Frémont
(Ismène); M. Bonel (Adraste)

Rossini took his duties as Director of the Théâtre-Italien seriously,
devoting to them time and energy which would otherwise have been
used for composition. It was more than a year after the performances of *Il Viaggio a Reims* that his next opera, and his first to be
composed to a French text, was heard in Paris, and even then it was
not a completely new work, but *Le Siège de Corinthe*, a revision of his
Maometto II of six years earlier. Its production at the Paris Opéra on
9 October 1826 was preceded in September by another opera with
music by Rossini, staged at the Théâtre de l'Odéon. This was
Ivanhoé, based on the novel by Sir Walter Scott, a pastiche put
together by Antonio Pacini, using numbers from six Rossini operas:
Tancredi, *Cenerentola*, *La Gazza ladra*, *Mosè*, *Zelmira* and *Semiramide*.
(Antonio Pacini [1778–1866] is not to be confused with Giovanni
Pacini [1796–1867], a successful and prolific imitator of Rossini,

who also composed an *Ivanhoe* which was produced at the Teatro La Fenice, Venice, in 1832.)

The new or, at any rate, authentic Rossini opera, *Le Siège de Corinthe*, utilised the plot of *Maometto II* but moved the action back a decade or so to Corinth, besieged by Mohammed's forces in 1459. In doing this, it cleverly took advantage of French pro-Greek and anti-Turkish sentiment at a time when the cause of Greek independence was very much in the air, the fighting between Greece and Turkey was at its height, and the Turks' siege of Missolonghi (where Byron had died in 1824) was in all the newspapers. (On 3 April 1826 Rossini conducted a charity concert in Paris on behalf of Greek patriots.) Luigi Balocchi (the Italian librettist at the Théâtre-Italien who had written *Il Viaggio a Reims*) and Alexandre Soumet (the author of a play, *Norma*, which would later be turned into an opera by Bellini) recast Cesare della Valle's two-act *Maometto II* libretto in three acts, turning it into a salute to Greece, and Rossini extensively revised his earlier score, writing new music and giving the ensembles a more important role. He also turned the contralto role of Calbo, Anna's suitor, into the tenor role of Néocles, Pamyre's suitor, characters *en travesti* being less acceptable to Parisian audiences than to Italians. However, although detail is changed, the basic plot remains the same. It is now Pamyre, daughter of the Governor of Corinth, not Anna, daughter of the Governor of Negroponte, who is in love with a man who turns out to have been Mahomet II using a false name. Like Anna, Pamyre kills herself rather than live as the consort of the tyrant who has conquered her country.

Le Siège de Corinthe was received at its première with immense enthusiasm. 'Nothing was lacking from the composer's triumph,' wrote the critic of *La Quotidienne*, 'for not only was every number greeted with a triple salvo of applause, but also after the performance the entire audience wanted to enjoy Rossini's presence. For almost half an hour the maestro was called persistently on to the stage.' The opera reached its hundredth performance in 1839, and remained in the repertoire of the Paris Opéra until 1844. In an Italian translation by Calisto Bassi it was staged in Barcelona in 1827 as *L'Assedio di Corinto*, in which form it reached Italy the following year with productions in Parma, Venice, Naples and, in a different translation, Genoa. The opera became popular throughout Europe until towards the end of the century, when it disappeared until its revival in Florence in 1949, with Renata Tebaldi as Pamira

(Pamyre). It was in Italian, too, that it was first heard in London, at Her Majesty's Theatre, on 5 June 1834, and in New York, at the Italian Opera House, on 6 February 1835. An unsatisfactory conflation of *Maometto II* and *L'Assedio di Corinto*, described by one of its two editors, the conductor Thomas Schippers, as 'eighty per cent Naples, twenty per cent Paris', was first staged at La Scala, Milan, in 1969 as *L'Assedio di Corinto* with Beverly Sills as Pamira and Marilyn Horne as a *travesti* Neocle. *Le Siège de Corinthe* was not heard in French in Italy until 1992 when it was staged in Genoa. In the same year, a concert performance in French was given at the Queen Elizabeth Hall, London.

Unlike *Maometto II*, *Le Siège de Corinthe* has an overture. It incorporates part of the opening *allegro vivace* of the overture to *Bianca e Falliero*, and also quotes from Rossini's *Messa di Gloria*, composed and performed in Naples in 1820. Unusually for a composer who rarely resorted to plagiarism, the forceful overture's slow march is taken from Giovanni Simone Mayr's *Atalia*, an opera which Rossini had conducted in Naples in 1822. (But apparently Mayr had lifted the tune from Benedetto Marcello's 'Estro poetico-armonico'.)

Although very few pieces in *Le Siège de Corinthe* are entirely new, every number in the score was revised to a greater or lesser extent, and the expressive recitatives were freshly composed. The solemn hymn, 'Divin prophète', in Act II is one of the most effective of the huge choruses, and the new Act II finale with its tuneful and eloquent trio for Mahomet, Pamyre and Néocles demonstrates that Rossini was able to write as fluently and confidently to a French text as to an Italian one. In Act II the blessing of the Greek banners ('Quel nuage sanglant') is positively Verdian in its vigorous incitement to national fervour, and the opera's finale depicting the sacking of Corinth, which makes use of parts of the *Maometto II* finale, is both powerful and original, the orchestra pushing the action furiously to its conclusion.

Francis Toye wrote that, with this work, Grand Opera had been born. Perhaps the essentially French *grand opéra* was not really to come to birth until three years later with *Guillaume Tell*, but *Le Siège de Corinthe* is certainly a significant step towards the emergence of the genre, and it is to be preferred to its earlier Italian version, *Maometto II*, not only for the strength of its choruses and the comparative tautness of its dramatic structure but also for the greater psychological depth and credibility of its characters.

Moïse et Pharaon (Moses and Pharaoh)	*Mosè*
grand opéra in four acts	(Italian translation by Calisto Bassi)

Principal characters:

Moïse, leader of the Israelites	(bass)	Mosè
Eliézer, his brother	(tenor)	Elisero
Pharaon, King of Egypt	(bass)	Faraone
Aménophis, his son	(tenor)	Amenofi
Orphide, an Egyptian officer	(tenor)	Aufide
Osiride, priest of Isis	(bass)	Osiride
Marie, sister of Moses	(mezzo-soprano)	Maria
Anaï, her daughter	(soprano)	Anaide
Sinaïde, the Pharaoh's wife	(soprano)	Sinaide

LIBRETTO by Luigi Balocchi and Victor-Joseph-Etienne de Jouy, based on Andrea Leone Tottola's libretto of *Mosè in Egitto*.

TIME: Around 1230 B.C.
PLACE: Egypt

FIRST PERFORMED at the Paris Opéra, 26 March 1827, with Nicholas-Prosper Levasseur (Moïse); Alexis Dupont (Eliézer); Henri-Bernard Dabadie (Pharaon); Adolphe Nourrit (Aménophis); Ferdinand Prévost (Orphide); M. Bonel (Osiride); Mlle Mori (Marie); Laure Cinti-Damoreau (Anaï); Louise-Zulme Dabadie (Sinaïde)
Italian translation first staged in Perugia, 4 February 1829

Less than six months after the première of *Le Siège de Corinthe*, the second of Rossini's French revisions of earlier Italian works was staged at the Opéra. This was *Moïse et Pharaon*. Luigi Balocchi and Victor-Joseph-Etienne de Jouy were responsible for putting together a French text, based on Tottola's libretto for the Italian

Mosè in Egitto of 1818, and Rossini provided much new music as well as adapting parts of his earlier score. The success of *Moïse* was immediate and even greater than that of *Le Siège de Corinthe*, and the opera soon began to be staged abroad. Italy first heard *Moïse* in a concert performance given in Rome some months after the opera's Paris première, but the first Italian stage production was in Perugia, on 4 February 1829 (as *Mosè e Faraone*). An opera staged in London at Covent Garden in 1833 under the title of *The Israelites in Egypt, or The Passage of the Red Sea* was, in fact, a conflation by one Michael Rophino Lacy of Rossini's opera with Handel's oratorio, *Israel in Egypt*! (Lacy, an Irish musician, had been responsible in 1829 for another spurious Rossini opera at Covent Garden: *The Maid of Judah*, adapted from Scott's *Ivanhoe*, and consisting for the most part of music from *Semiramide*.) The authentic *Moïse* arrived at Covent Garden in Italian on 20 April 1850, entitled *Zora* (to conceal its biblical origins from the puritanical English), and reached New York, still in Italian, in 1860 (the original Italian *Mosè in Egitto* having been heard there in 1835). Modern performances are almost invariably of the Paris version, though usually in its Italian translation.

In *Moïse*, several of the characters have undergone changes of name, among them Moses' brother who is no longer Aronne (Aaron) but Eliézer or, in the Italian translation, Elisero. The opera is now in four acts, of which the first is, in theory, new, although it incorporates much already existing music. Dramatically, nothing is added. This new first act serves merely to give an earlier instance of the Pharaoh's reluctance to let the Jews depart and of Jehovah's virtuosity in dispensing plagues. An orchestral prelude whose opening *andante* gives way to a jaunty *allegro* leads into a tuneful chorus of Jews and Midianites who pray for deliverance from their Egyptian masters, and are then addressed by their leader, Moses. This lively beginning to the opera draws on material from *Armida* and *Bianca e Falliero*, but the following scene, chorus and solemn quartet, 'Dieu de la paix' ('Dio! possente in pace e in guerra'), as Moses presents the tablets of the law to his people, is new. It is followed by recitative and an ardent duet for the lovers Anaï (Anaide) and Aménophis (Amenofi), formerly known as Elcia and Osiride, taken from *Mosè in Egitto*'s Act I ('Ah! se puoi così lasciarmi'). Apart from slight changes of text, the remainder of the act follows Act I of the earlier version. The *andante* duet for Anaï and

Marie is Rossini at his most delicate, and the dramatic Act I finale, in which Moses causes a tempest to devastate the land of Egypt, is cleverly built up by the repetition of short solo phrases until the concluding stretta which involves the entire ensemble.

Act II begins (as does Act I of *Mosè in Egitto*) with three reiterated C major chords, and follows the earlier version in its first two numbers, a solemn *andante maestoso* ensemble of frightened Egyptians and the gravely beautiful *andante* quintet which ensues after the arrival of Moses (whose prayer to the 'Eterno! immenso! incomprensibil Dio!' now becomes 'Arbitre suprême du ciel et de la terre'). However, after the quintet's jubilant *vivace* stretta launched by Sinaïde, the duet, 'Parlar, spiegar non posso', for the Pharaoh and Aménophis (formerly Osiride) from Act II of *Mosè* is slotted in. The Act II finale of *Moïse* is that of the earlier version's Act II, omitting the death of the Pharaoh's son, who in *Moïse* stays alive until the final catastrophe for the Egyptians in the Red Sea. Elcia's *adagio* aria, 'Porgi la destra amata', is now equipped with a new text ('Ah! d'une tendre mère'), and given to the Pharaoh's wife, Sinaïde.

In Act III, after an introductory march and chorus, the obligatory ballet music for the Paris audience is, of course, new to the opera, though it is based on the music Rossini had provided for the ballet in *Armida*. The great ensemble, 'Mi manca la voce', when at a gesture from Moses the sacrificial fire of the Egyptian altar is extinguished, retains its central place in the finale of the act which culminates in a conventional but vigorous ensemble.

Act IV opens by finding a place, albeit an inappropriate one, for the attractive love duet for Anaï and Aménophis, 'Quale assalto! qual cimento!' from Act II of *Mosè*, and follows it with a completely new two-part *allegro* aria for Anaï (formerly Elcia) and ensemble, the powerful 'Quelle horrible destinée' ('Qual orribile sciagura' in the Italian version). The great prayer begun by Moses, 'Des cieux où tu résides' ('Dal tuo stellato soglio'), is still there, with its simple emotional appeal almost the equal of that more famous chorus of captive Jews in Verdi's *Nabucco* fifteen years later; but, as the Egyptians sink beneath the waves of the Red Sea to the accompaniment of a slow and compassionate melody, *Moïse* ends *sotto voce* instead of with the emphatic orchestral stretta which had brought *Mosè in Egitto* to its triumphant conclusion.

Le Comte Ory
(Count Ory)

opéra comique in two acts

Principal characters:

La Comtesse Adèle	(soprano)
Isolier, page to Le Comte Ory	(mezzo-soprano)
Ragonde, companion to La Comtesse Adèle	(contralto)
Le Comte Ory	(tenor)
Le Gouverneur, tutor to Le Comte Ory	(bass)
Raimbaud, friend of Le Comte Ory	(baritone)

LIBRETTO by Eugène Scribe and Charles-Gaspard Delestre-Poirson

TIME: The Crusades
PLACE: Touraine

FIRST PERFORMED at the Paris Opéra, 20 August 1828, with Laure Cinti-Damoreau (La Comtesse Adèle); Constance Jawureck (Isolier); Mlle Mori (Ragonde); Adolphe Nourrit (Le Comte Ory); Henri-Bernard Dabadie (Raimbaud); Nicholas-Prosper Levasseur (Le Gouverneur)

During the rehearsals of *Moïse et Pharaon*, Rossini had received news that his mother, in Bologna, was seriously ill. She died on 20 February 1827 at the age of fifty-five, and the composer persuaded his father to come to live with him in Paris. Rossini had already agreed to write *Guillaume Tell*, his first (and, as it happened, his last) completely new opera for Paris, but before doing so he turned his hand to a lighter work, *Le Comte Ory*, making use of several numbers from his occasional piece of 1825, *Il Viaggio a Reims*, but composing new music as well.

The libretto of *Le Comte Ory* had begun life as a one-act comedy written in 1817 by Eugène Scribe and Charles-Gaspard Delestre-Poirson, based on a Crusaders' ballad from Picardy, collected by Antoine de la Place in 1785, about Count Ory and his followers who disguise themselves as a group of nuns in order to gain entry to the Castle of Formoutiers so that Ory can attempt to win the affections of the Countess while her brother is absent at a Crusade. For Rossini, Scribe added a prefatory act which is little more than a variation on the same plot.

Le Comte Ory was a huge success at its première at the Paris Opéra in August 1828, and played to delighted audiences throughout the season, remaining in the repertoire of the Opéra for many years. Rossini sold the score to the French publisher Troupenas for the then immense sum of 16,000 francs. The opera reached London, at His Majesty's Theatre in the Haymarket, in an Italian translation, on 28 February 1829. Its first performance in New York (in French) was on 22 August 1831, and it was heard in London in French at the St James's Theatre on 20 June 1849. There have been several productions since its revival at the 1952 Maggio Musicale in Florence in Italian as *Il Conte Ory*, and at the Edinburgh Festival in its original French by Glyndebourne Festival Opera in 1954.

The plot of the opera is simple. When her brother leaves to go on one of the Crusades, the Countess Adèle retreats with her ladies-in-waiting to the family castle. The licentious Count Ory attempts to gain entrance to the castle by disguising himself, first as a hermit and then, when this fails, as the Mother Superior of a group of nuns, who are really his own men in disguise. Ory's plans are thwarted by his young page, Isolier, who is in love with the Countess, and also by the return of the Crusaders at a crucial moment.

After a brief orchestral introduction, the opening number, 'Jouvencelles, venez vite', in which Ory's companion Raimbaud summons the sceptical peasants to the hermit's presence, makes use of the music of *Il Viaggio*'s opening number, in which the manager of a hotel exhorted her staff to work harder. After Ory, as the hermit, has delivered his graceful C major cavatina, 'Que les destins prospères', the crowd gathers around excitedly to consult him. The rather florid F major *andantino* aria ('Veiller sans cesse') sung by Ory's tutor is new, as is Isolier's delightful duet with the disguised Count Ory ('Une dame de haut parage'). Adèle's elaborate aria, 'En proie à la tristesse', prefaced by an orchestral introduction lifted from *Bianca e Falliero*, is the Contessa di Folleville's aria, 'Partir, o ciel! desio', from *Il Viaggio a Reims* with some changes in orchestration, its music this time asked to express real feeling instead of parody. This is virtually the only instance in *Le Comte Ory* of that virtuoso writing for the voice which Rossini's earlier soprano heroines were generally expected to master. The finale to Act I ('Ciel! ô terreur, ô peine extrême') is the

Gran pezzo concertato from *Il Viaggio*, the fourteen solo voices of its former manifestation now reduced to seven soloists plus chorus, but the charm of its unaccompanied opening section and the comic verve of its spirited *allegro* conclusion left intact.

Two of the numbers in Act II are taken over from *Il Viaggio*. The A major duet, 'Ah, quel respect, madame', for Ory (in his guise as Mother Superior) and Adèle is *Il Viaggio*'s 'Nel suo divin sembiante' in which Corinna rejected the advances of the Cavalier Belfiore; and Raimbaud's patter song, 'Dans ce lieu solitaire', when he describes his raid upon the castle's wine cellar, is Don Profondo's 'Medaglie incomparabili'. Act II's new music is delightful, from the gentle quartet of nuns begging the 'noble châtelaine' of the castle for refuge from the wicked Count Ory, to the ebullient drinking chorus ('Buvons!') of all the nuns once they are inside the castle, their carousing alternating with the pseudo-devout unaccompanied prayer of the quartet whenever they realise they are being over-heard.

The highlight of the score is an exquisite trio, 'A la faveur de cette nuit', in which Ory finds himself soliciting his page, Isolier, by mistake. The situation recalls Act IV of *Le Nozze di Figaro*, and indeed the music is positively Mozartian in its delicacy and wit. Berlioz, hearing *Le Comte Ory* at a revival in 1839, wrote favourably of it in the *Journal des débats*, declaring the trio to be the composer's masterpiece. As occasionally happens with Rossini, the finale of the opera is rushed and perfunctory, in this instance more so than usual. Nevertheless, *Le Comte Ory* is one of its composer's finest comic operas, not in the ebullient manner of *Il Barbiere di Sivilgia* and the other Italian comedies, but in a style which might be said to have initiated the genre of French operetta. This is an opera which looks back to Mozart and forward to Offenbach. As Berlioz concluded, it consists of 'a collection of diverse beauties which, if divided up ingeniously, would suffice to make the fortune of not one, but two or three operas'.

Guillaume Tell
(William Tell)

opéra in four acts

Principal characters:

Mathilde, Princess of the House of Habsburg	(soprano)
Jemmy, son of Guillaume Tell	(soprano)
Hedwige, Tell's wife	(soprano)
Guillaume Tell	(baritone)
Arnold Melcthal	(tenor)
Gessler, Governor of the cantons of Schwyz and Uri	(bass)
Walter Furst	(bass)

LIBRETTO by Victor-Joseph Étienne de Jouy, Hippolyte-Louis-Florent Bis and Armand Marrast

TIME: The thirteenth century
PLACE: Switzerland

FIRST PERFORMED at the Paris Opéra, 3 August 1829, with Laure Cinti-Damoreau (Mathilde); Louise-Zulme Dabadie (Jemmy); Mlle Mori (Hedwige); Henri-Bernard Dabadie (Guillaume Tell); Adolphe Nourrit (Arnold); Ferdinand Prévost (Gessler); Nicholas-Prosper Levasseur (Walter Furst)

In September 1823, several months before the composer's period of residence in Paris had begun, Stendhal wrote in the Preface to his *Life of Rossini*: 'Napoleon is dead; but a new conqueror has already shown himself to the world; and from Moscow to Naples, from London to Vienna, from Paris to Calcutta, his name is constantly on every tongue.' Now, five years later, after the appearance of his Paris operas, *Il Viaggio a Reims*, *Le Siège de Corinthe*, *Moïse et Pharaon* and *Le Comte Ory*, Rossini's fame was greater than ever, and his new French *grand opéra* was being eagerly awaited.

The opera was *Guillaume Tell*, its libretto drawn from Schiller's *Wilhelm Tell*, the German poet's last completed play which was staged at Weimar in 1804. The writing of the libretto was entrusted to Victor-Joseph Étienne de Jouy, but his unwieldy version had to be edited and partly rewritten by Hippolyte-Louis-Florent Bis, and

further changes to one scene required by Rossini were made by
Armand Marrast. The scope of Schiller's drama about William Tell,
the thirteenth-century Swiss patriot (who, like Robin Hood, may or
may not have existed), is lessened in its transposition to the operatic
stage, though Rossini's opera is itself immensely long and, for its
subject, curiously leisurely in pace. A fictional plot concerning the
love of Arnold, a Swiss follower of William Tell, for the Austrian
Princess Mathilde is fitted into a representation of the uprising of
the Swiss against their Austrian overlords. The famous incident in
which Tell is forced to shoot an apple from the head of his son is
included.

At its première on 3 August 1829 the opera was politely rather
than enthusiastically received, though critical opinion was
extremely favourable. Soon after the first performance, cuts began
to be made in order to reduce the score to a manageable length.
Some years later, when Duponchel, the director of the Paris Opéra,
mentioned to Rossini that the second act of *Guillaume Tell* was to be
performed, the composer exclaimed in mock astonishment, 'What,
the whole of it?'

There were difficulties, too, with the tenor role of Arnold whose
fearsome tessitura has taken its toll of many singers over the years.
The creator of the role, Adolphe Nourrit, found it very difficult to
sing, and his successor, Gilbert-Louis Duprez, the first to sing
Arnold's top Cs from the chest instead of with supported falsetto,
had his C unkindly likened by Rossini to 'the squawk of a capon
having its throat cut'. When the Irish tenor John O'Sullivan sang
Arnold at the Paris Opéra in 1929, his admirer James Joyce, the
novelist, commented, 'I have been through the score of *Guillaume
Tell*, and I discover that Sullivan sings 456 Gs, 93 A flats, 54 B flats,
15 Bs, 19 Cs and 2 C sharps. Nobody else can do it.' Pavarotti
refused to make his debut at La Scala as Arnold, claiming that the
role would have ruined his voice, and in recent years only Nicolai
Gedda, on record and at the Florence Maggio Musicale of 1972
when the opera was performed in its entirety, has been able to
encompass all of Arnold's notes mellifluously.

Because of its overtly political subject, *Guillaume Tell* had to be
performed in some countries under different titles and with many
changes to its libretto. In Riga it was given as *Karl der Kühne* up to the
end of the nineteenth century. St Petersburg and Warsaw heard the
opera as *Carlo il Temerario*, in Milan it was *Guglielmo Vallace* and in

Rome *Rodolfo di Sterlinga*. It was first seen in London at the Theatre Royal, Drury Lane, on 1 May 1830, as *Hofer, or The Tell of the Tyrol*, adapted by the librettist James Robinson Planché, with its music arranged by Sir Henry Bishop. In 1838 it was performed again at Drury Lane, in a new English version by Alfred Bunn, but still in Bishop's arrangement. At Her Majesty's Theatre in 1839 it was staged in Italian, the original French version of the opera finally reaching England at Covent Garden on 6 June 1845. New York first heard the opera on 19 September 1831 in English, and subsequently in 1845 in French, in 1855 in Italian, and in 1866 in German.

The famous overture, which must surely be in the repertoire of every orchestra – and brass band – in the world, is a magnificent piece in four distinct sections. Its opening passage for five cellos conjures up an atmosphere of blissful contentment or, as Berlioz described it, 'the calm of profound solitude, the solemn silence of nature, when the elements and the human passions are at rest.' The second section, a spirited *allegro*, is one of Rossini's finest depictions of a storm, and the third, an *andante*, introduces on cor anglais and flute the *ranz des vaches* or Swiss pastoral melody which will recur later in the opera. A trumpet fanfare introduces the final hectic and archetypal Rossinian galop.

A pastoral atmosphere permeates the music of Act I, set on the outskirts of a Swiss mountain village. The opening chorus is charming, and the young fisherman's song accompanied by two harps epitomises the sense of leisurely content soon to be shattered by passion and patriotism. The duet for Tell and Arnold ('Où vas-tu?') is really an aria and cabaletta for the tenor who carries the principal melody, with the baritone, Tell, rather dully inserting his comments. The impassioned tune (rising, the second time, to the tenor's high C) with which Arnold apostrophises the absent Mathilde can be most exciting in performance. The peasant festivities are encompassed in happy choruses, music to accompanying dances (a delightful *pas de six*), and an archery contest. The finale to the act shows Rossini at his most vigorous.

Act II, which takes place on the heights above Lake Lucerne, is generally regarded as being the opera's musical and dramatic peak. Donizetti remarked that the acts preceding and following it might be by Rossini, but that Act II was by God. Rossini's interest in the psychology of his characters seems to have been awakened in this act, with Mathilde's beautifully expressive recitative and elegantly melancholy aria, 'Sombre forêt', her C major duet with Arnold ('Oui, vous l'arrachez à mon âme'), and the superb trio ('Quand l'Helvétie est un champ de suppices') when, in an ensemble with the melodic pulse and the dramatic energy of Verdi, Arnold learns of his father's death at the hands of the Austrians. The hunting chorus and its juxtaposition with a calm evening song heard in the distance make an effective beginning to the act, and the finale in which the men of the three cantons assemble and are inspired by Tell to rise against their oppressors is magnificent in its power and originality. Act II concludes not with a conventional *allegro* stretta but with a drum-roll to greet the dawn, a threefold cry of 'Aux armes' and sixteen bars of violent orchestral coda.

In the often omitted scene at the beginning of Act III in which Mathilde and Arnold part, Mathilde's aria and cabaletta are fascinating, vocal virtuosity (largely absent from Mathilde's music) being confined to the aria, 'Pour notre amour plus d'espérance', while its cabaletta ('Sur la rive étrangère') is unadorned and sweetly plaintive in tone. The remainder of Act III takes place in the main square in Altdorf. This is the scene in which Tell is made to shoot an apple from his son Jemmy's head. ('The Englishman', wrote Francis Toye, 'finds it not so much difficult as impossible to take the familiar episode of the apple seriously as the climax of a drama; the more so when he discovers that William Tell has christened his son Jemmy, repeatedly addressing him by this depressing name at the most poignant moment in the opera!') Rossini takes his time over this scene, with marches, choruses and dances, including a Tyrolean dance accompanied only by the voices of the chorus. But when it eventually arrives introduced by a solo cello, Tell's 'Sois immobile', addressed to his son, is not only extremely moving in its simplicity and sincerity but also impressive in the way in which its free and declamatory vocal line is dictated by, and thus perfectly suited to, the rhythm of the words. Many years later Rossini was to tell Wagner, 'The sentiment that moved me most during my life was the love I had for my mother and my father, and which they repaid at usurious rates. It was there, I think, that I found the note that I needed for the scene of the apple.'

One of the finest numbers in the score is to be found at the beginning of Act IV. This is Arnold's lyrical aria ('Asile héréditaire') with fierce cabaletta ('Amis, amis, secondez ma vengeance'), extremely taxing for the tenor but exhilarating for the audience. The final scene brings a delicately scored trio, 'Je rends à votre amour', for Mathilde, Jemmy and Hedwige (his mother), and a great choral prayer ('Toi, qui du faible es l'espérance') launched by Hedwige, which leads into the storm and the hectic and not very convincing dénouement in which Tell's arrow despatches Gessler thereby apparently bringing instant freedom to the whole of Switzerland. Harps and horns herald a symbolic new dawn, the *ranz des vaches* is heard, and a mood of hushed radiance descends upon all as they praise the beauty of nature and salute their new-found liberty. Confident C major chords in the orchestra bring the curtain down on what was to prove Rossini's final opera.

An uncut performance of *Guillaume Tell* would take about four hours without intermissions, so it is not surprising that cuts are frequently made. The opera works best, however, when it is staged complete, and allowed to present itself in its own somewhat leisurely style. Is Act II really so superior to the other three acts? One would not want to be without Arnold's music in Acts I and IV or Tell's address to his son in Act III. Verdi, who admired the work, nevertheless felt that it had about it 'this fatal atmosphere of the [Paris] Opéra' and that at times 'you feel there's too much here, not enough there, and that it doesn't move with the honesty and security of *Il Barbiere*'. This is self-evidently true, but *Guillaume Tell* is nevertheless an opera one can grow to love.

Rossini had for some time been thinking about retiring from his profession of opera composer. After *Guillaume Tell* he did consider other operatic projects, but before long it became clear, not only to the composer himself but also to his colleagues in the musical world, that he had written his last opera. Aged only thirty-seven at the time of the première of *Guillaume Tell*, Rossini lived on until his seventy-seventh year, composing some of his finest music in the *Stabat Mater* (1832) and the *Petite Messe Solennelle* (1864) as well as a great many delightful miniatures in the intervening years, thirteen volumes of which were collected under the title, chosen by the composer himself, of *Péchés de vieillesse* (Sins of Old Age).

II

Gaetano Donizetti

1797–1848

8

From *Il Pigmalione* to *Il Fortunato inganno*

Il Pigmalione

scena lirica in one act

Principal characters:
Pigmalione   (tenor)
Galatea   (soprano)

LIBRETTO adapted from Antonio Simone Sografi's libretto for *Pimmalione* by Giambattista Cimadoro (Venice, 1790), itself based on Jean-Jacques Rousseau's *Pygmalion* (1770)

TIME: The classical past
PLACE: Cyprus

FIRST PERFORMED at the Teatro Donizetti, Bergamo, 13 October 1960, with Orianna Santunione (Galatea); Doro Antonioli (Pigmalione)

Gaetano Donizetti was born in the provincial north Italian town of Bergamo on 29 November 1797, the son of a tradesman who became porter to the civic Monte di Pietà or pawnshop when Gaetano was eleven years old. There were six children, two of whom, Gaetano and his elder brother Giuseppe, were to take up musical careers. (Giuseppe became a bandsman in Napoleon's army, and ended his days in Constantinople as Chief of Music to the Ottoman Armies, with the title of Donizetti Pasha.) It seems most likely that the family had moved to Bergamo from elsewhere in Lombardy some time during the eighteenth century.

When the young Gaetano showed that he had some talent for music, his father allowed him to study at the local Musical Institute in Bergamo. Here he was especially fortunate to have as his first teacher a distinguished composer, Johann Simon Mayr. Mayr, a Bavarian, was professor of composition at the Institute, and had composed a number of highly successful Italian operas, among them *Saffo* (1794), *Ginevra di Scozia* (1801) and *Alonso e Cora* (1803). The young Donizetti came under Mayr's influence, and was to admit his debt to the older composer for the rest of his life. He was soon sufficiently advanced in his studies to be sent on to the Liceo Filarmonico in Bologna, to work under another famous teacher, Stanislao Mattei, who had also taught the young Rossini. By the time he was twenty, Donizetti was back in Bergamo, uncertain how next to proceed. His father strongly urged him to take up an academic career but, unwilling to do so, he began instead to compose music for a number of local music societies. Several string quartets, as well as choral and instrumental pieces, were written at this time.

It was not as the result of a commission but while he was still a student in Bologna that Donizetti wrote his first opera, shortly before his nineteenth birthday. This was a one-act comedy, *Il Pigmalione*, whose autograph score bears a note in the composer's hand to the effect that it was begun on 15 September 1816 and finished on 1 October 'at almost two in the morning'. It is not known who adapted the libretto which derives from Antonio Simone Sografi's libretto for a *Pimmalione* by the Venetian composer Cimadoro, performed in Venice in 1790, which in turn derives from Rousseau and, ultimately, from Book X of Ovid's *Metamorphoses*.

Il Pigmalione seems not to have been performed in Donizetti's lifetime. It had to wait until 13 October 1960 for its première, when it was staged in Bergamo at the theatre named after the composer. The only productions subsequently have been in Barga in 1977 and at the Buxton Festival in 1987. (Cimadoro's one-act *Pimmalione*, by contrast, was hugely successful throughout Europe during its composer's lifetime and after. Giovanni Battista Cimadoro, who was born in Venice in 1761, eventually settled in England where he abbreviated his name to Cimmador. He died in Bath in 1805. His

Pimmalione was revived by the Warsaw Chamber Opera at the Valle d'Itria Festival in 1978.)

Pygmalion was the sculptor and King of Cyprus in Greek legend who, though he hated women, fell in love with his own statue of Aphrodite. When he prayed to Venus, the goddess brought the statue to life as Galatea who happily reciprocated Pygmalion's love. The story is first told in Ovid's *Metamorphoses*. Donizetti's version, lasting less than thirty minutes, is virtually a solo piece for the tenor, Pygmalion, with a short orchestral introduction followed by accompanied recitative alternating with quite pleasant but un-memorable arias, the first of which, 'Voi che intorno', is the most attractive. Galatea joins Pygmalion only in the final recitative and disappointingly stately, somewhat nondescript duet. *Il Pigmalione* makes a not very lively start to Donizetti's *oeuvre*.

At some time during his student days, Donizetti had composed a duet from Metastasio's *Olimpiade*, a libretto first set by Caldara in 1733, and subsequently by Vivaldi, Pergolesi, Hasse, Cimarosa and several other composers. But after his next student attempt to write an opera, *L'Ira d'Achille* (The Anger of Achilles), of which he composed one act and part of a second before abandoning it, Donizetti never again made use of a subject from mythology.

Enrico di Borgogna

opera semiseria in two acts

Principal characters:

Enrico   (mezzo-soprano)
Elisa   (soprano)
Geltrude   (mezzo-soprano)
Pietro   (tenor)
Guido   (bass)
Gilberto   (bass)
Brunone   (baritone)

LIBRETTO by Bartolomeo Merelli

TIME: The middle ages
PLACE: Burgundy

FIRST PERFORMED at the Teatro San Luca, Venice, 14 November 1818, with Fanny Eckerlin (Enrico); Adelaide Catalani (Elisa); Adelaide Cassago (Geltrude); Giuseppe Fosconi (Pietro); Giuseppe Spech (Guido); Andrea Verni (Gilberto); Giuseppe Fioravanti (Brunone)

After composing *Il Pigmalione*, the student Donizetti worked on two other operas, both of which he left incomplete. One, *L'Ira d'Achille*, has already been mentioned. Of the other, *L'Olimpiade*, he appears to have composed only one duet. His first commission came in the spring of 1818 from an impresario, Paolo Zancla, who engaged the young composer to write a two-act opera for performance in the autumn at the Teatro San Luca in Venice. The librettist, Bartolomeo Merelli (who, many years later when he was in charge of La Scala, Milan, was to commission from Verdi his first opera), derived his subject from a play by the German dramatist, August von Kotzebue, *Der Graf von Burgund*, which had been performed in Vienna in 1795.

The plot of the opera, *Enrico di Borgogna*, involves the exiled Enrico, son of the murdered Count, in preventing Guido, the son of his father's murderer, from succeeding to the title and marrying Elisa whom Enrico loves. At the first performance on 14 November 1818 (two weeks before its composer's twenty-first birthday), the prima donna, Adelaide Catalani, who was appearing on the operatic stage for the first time, fainted from stage fright at the end of Act I, which necessitated the omission of some of her music in Act II and her replacement in the finale by another singer. The critic of the *Nuovo osservatore veneziano* mentioned that several pieces were applauded, among them the overture, a trio and a *buffo* aria in Act I, and a duet in Act II, and thought that 'there would have been more applause were it not for the unexpected indisposition of Adelaide Catalani'. The review continued: 'If it is possible now to judge tranquilly after such disagreeable circumstances the merit of the music, one cannot but recognise a regular handling and expressive quality in his style. For these, the public wanted to salute Signor Donizetti on stage at the end of the opera.'

Enrico di Borgogna, which has not been staged since its initial performances in Venice in 1818, contains much agreeable and dramatically expressive music. Enrico's entrance aria ('Care aurette') and cabaletta would not seem out of place in any mature

Donizetti opera, and in fact the cabaletta was to appear again twelve years later, greatly transformed, as Anna's 'Al dolce guidami' in *Anna Bolena*. The influence of Rossini can be discerned in the florid writing of Enrico's rondo, 'Mentre mi brilli intorno', but the individual voice of Donizetti makes itself heard in the vigorous ensembles.

Il Falegname di Livonia
(The Livonian Carpenter)

opera buffa in two acts

Principal characters:

Carlo   (tenor)
Annetta   (soprano)
Madama Fritz   (mezzo-soprano)
Firman   (baritone)
Pietro   (bass)
Caterina   (soprano)
Ser Cuccupis   (bass)

LIBRETTO by Gherardo Bevilacqua-Aldobrandini

TIME: The late-seventeenth century
PLACE: The Baltic State of Livonia

FIRST PERFORMED at the Teatro San Samuele, Venice, 26 December 1819, with Giovanni Battista Verger (Carlo); Angela Bertozzi (Annetta); Caterina Amati (Madama Fritz); Giuseppe Guglielmini (Firman); Vincenzo Botticelli (Pietro); Adelaide Raffi (Caterina); Luigi Martinelli (Ser Cuccupis)

A month after the première of *Enrico di Borgogna*, the Teatro San Luca staged another piece by Donizetti. This was a one-act farce, *Una follia*, which shared a double-bill on 17 December 1818 with a revival of Rossini's *L'Inganno felice* of 1812. *Una follia* (whose librettist, Bartolomeo Merelli, in a pamphlet more than fifty years later referred to it under a different title, *Il Ritratto parlante*) was not performed again, and its score has not been found. In 1819, for a student performance in Bologna, Donizetti contributed at least two numbers, an *Introduzione* and an aria with chorus, to a pasticcio, *I Piccioli virtuosi ambulanti,* assembled by his old teacher, Mayr. Later in the same year, for the Teatro San Samuele in Venice Donizetti composed *Il Falegname di Livonia, ossia Pietro il grande, Tsar delle Russie* (The Livonian Carpenter, or Peter the Great, Tsar of the Russias). Its libretto by the Marchese Gherardo Bevilacqua-Aldobrandini was based on the comedy *Le Menuisier de Livonie* by Alexander Duval (first performed in Paris in 1805), but also drew upon Felice Romani's libretto for Giovanni Pacini's opera of the same title which had been staged in Milan earlier in 1819. There are at least seventeen other operas about Peter the Great, including another by Donizetti, *Il Borgomastro di Saardam* (see pp 169–171).

Although *Il Falegname di Livonia* was only moderately well received at its première, it was the earliest of Donizetti's operas to achieve more than one production. In 1823 it opened the carnival season in Bologna, and within the following six years it was staged in Verona, Padua, Spoleto and again in Venice (at a different theatre, the San Benedetto). It has not been performed since 1829.

The opera's plot concerns Carlo, a young carpenter in the Baltic state of Livonia, who is eventually discovered to be the missing nephew of the Tsarina, in search of whom a disguised Tsar and Tsarina have come to Livonia. There are still traces of Rossini in Donizetti's vocal writing, especially for Pietro. The most effective numbers in the score are the Act I finale and a sextet, 'Ah qual colpo', which occurs in Act II when Annetta, whom Carlo wishes to marry, is revealed to be the daughter of the Tsar's enemy, Mazeppa.

Le Nozze in villa
(The Wedding in the Villa)

opera buffa in two acts

Principal characters:
Sabina   (mezzo-soprano)
Claudio   (tenor)
Trifoglio   (bass)

LIBRETTO by Bartolomeo Merelli

TIME: The eighteenth century

PLACE: A small town in Germany

FIRST PERFORMED at the Teatro Vecchio, Mantua, during the carnival season of 1820–1821, with Fanny Eckerlin (Sabina)

A failure at its première, *Le Nozze in villa* was subsequently performed in Genoa in the spring of 1822 as *I Provinciali, ossia Le Nozze in villa*, after which it disappeared. No further performances have been traced, nor has Donizetti's autograph score been found, but there is an incomplete copy – a quintet from Act II is missing – in the library of the Paris Conservatoire. The opera's librettist, Bartolomeo Merelli, wrote in his *Cenni biografici* that 'in spite of many successful numbers it could not maintain itself, on account of the caprices and ill will of several of the singers, especially the prima donna'. His libretto, based on the play *Die Deutschen Kleinstädter* by August von Kotzebue, which was staged in Vienna in 1802, describes the attempts of two suitors to win the hand in marriage of Sabina. One of them, the village schoolteacher Trifoglio, withdraws when he discovers that her dowry is inadequate, leaving the way clear for the wealthy Claudio whom Sabina prefers, and who is happy to accept her without a dowry.

Zoraida di Granata

opera seria in two acts

Principal characters:

Zoraida   (soprano)
Abenamet   (contralto)
Ines   (mezzo-soprano)
Almuzir   (tenor)
Ali Zegri   (bass)
Almanzor   (bass)

LIBRETTO by Bartolomeo Merelli

TIME: 1480
PLACE: Spain

FIRST PERFORMED at the Teatro Argentina, Rome, 28 January

1822, with Ester Mombelli (Zoraida); Mazzanti (Abenamet); Gaetana Corini (Ines); Domenico Donzelli (Almuzir); Alberto Torri (Ali Zegri); Gaetano Rambaldi (Almanzor)

It was with *Zoraida di Granata*, commissioned by the Teatro Argentina in Rome, and produced there in 1822, that the young Donizetti made his decisive breakthrough into the career of a full-time professional composer of operas. *Zoraida* was acclaimed with great enthusiasm in Rome, and after the third performance Donizetti and his tenor, Domenico Donzelli, left the theatre in a carriage to the accompaniment of a loud military band along a route illuminated with torches in the composer's honour. The weekly *Notizie del giorno* wrote:

> A new and very happy hope is rising for the Italian musical theatre. The young Maestro Gaetano Donizetti, a pupil of the most famous professors of music, has launched himself strongly in his truly serious opera, *Zoraida di Granata*. Unanimous, sincere, universal was the applause he justly collected from the capacity audience, which decreed a triumph for his work. Every piece was received with particular pleasure.

While Donizetti was composing *Zoraida*, the tenor Americo Sbigoli who had been cast in the important role of Abenamet burst a blood vessel in his throat during a performance of Pacini's *Cesare in Egitto*, and died within a few days. As there was no suitable tenor available to replace him, Donizetti rewrote the role of Abenamet at short notice for a contralto named Mazzanti, a change which necessitated the omission of three numbers. Nevertheless the opera succeeded, its audiences appreciating Donizetti's melodic gift and his skill in handling the concerted numbers. The composer himself wrote to his teacher, Mayr, 'I limit myself to saying that the outcome has been extremely happy.'

When *Zoraida di Granata* was revived in Rome two years later, on 7 January 1824, its libretto had been extensively revised by Jacopo Ferretti, to whom Donizetti's teacher, Mayr, had given the composer a letter of introduction. Merelli's libretto had been based on Luigi Romanelli's for the opera *Abenamet e Zoraide* by Giuseppe Nicolini (Milan, 1804), which in turn derived from the play, *Gonzalve de Cordove* by Jean-Pierre-Claris de Florian, produced in Paris in 1793. Despite the success of Donizetti's *Zoraida di Granata* in Rome, at least on its first appearance in 1822, the opera seems to have been revived only once, in Lisbon in the winter of 1825.

The opera is set in Spain in 1480. Almuzir, who has murdered the King of Granada and usurped his throne, wishes to marry Zoraida, the late King's daughter, and threatens to kill her beloved Abenamet if she refuses him. Zoraida agrees to marry Almuzir, survives an accusation of infidelity by Abenamet and a sentence of death imposed by Almuzir, and is finally, and improbably, allowed by the usurper to marry Abenamet. A duet, 'Là nel tempio', was the most vigorously applauded piece at the 1824 Rome revival, though Zoraida's gently plaintive aria, 'Rose, che un dì spiegaste', in Act II was also liked.

La Zingara
(The Gypsy Maiden)

opera seria in two acts

Principal characters:

Ines	(soprano)
Argilla	(mezzo-soprano)
Don Sebastiano	(baritone)
Don Ranuccio	(baritone)
Pappacione	(bass)
Ferrando	(tenor)
Duca di Alziras	(tenor)

LIBRETTO by Andrea Leone Tottola

TIME: The middle ages
PLACE: Spain

FIRST PERFORMED at the Teatro Nuovo, Naples, 12 May 1822, with Monticelli (Ines); Giacinta Canonici (Argilla); Giuseppe Fioravanti (Don Sebastiano); Carlo Moncada (Don Ranuccio); Carlo Casaccia (Pappacione); Marco Venier (Ferrando); Alessandro Busti (Duca di Alziras)

In March 1822, Donizetti entered into an agreement with the impresario of the Teatro Nuovo, Naples, to provide an opera to be staged in May. This was *La Zingara*, its libretto by the Neapolitan

poet Andrea Leone Tottola who had written the libretti of four
Rossini operas, the most recent of which, *Zelmira*, had been given its
première in Naples at the Teatro San Carlo some weeks previously.
Donizetti set to work, as he put it, '*precipitevolissimevolmente*, in order
to facilitate the staging', and *La Zingara* was performed on 12 May at
the Teatro Nuovo whose audience greeted it with wild enthusiasm.
'The audience was certainly not miserly with its compliments,'
Donizetti wrote to a friend in Rome, modestly attributing most of his
success to the excellence of the singers and to Tottola's libretto. The
critic of the *Giornale del Regno delle Due Sicilie* wrote next morning that
'this new work by our young composer was crowned with a success
that sustains the reputation he acquired in the first test of his music
in Rome'.

La Zingara was popular enough be given twenty-eight consecutive
performances at the Teatro Nuovo and then to stay in the repertoire
for the rest of the year. The young Bellini, who attended some of the
later performances, was especially impressed by a septet in the
penultimate scene. Introduced to Donizetti by another composer,
Carlo Conti, Bellini told a friend that, in addition to his great talent,
Donizetti possessed a handsome, noble physiognomy which
inspired respect.

Tottola's libretto for *La Zingara* was based on the play, *La petite
bohémienne* by Louis-Charles Caigniez, which had been produced in
Paris in 1816 and was itself, according to its title-page, 'imitated
from Kotzebue'. The opera tells the story of the gypsy Argilla who
brings the lovers Ferrando and Ines together, foils the villainous
Ranuccio's plot to assassinate the Duke of Alziras, and secures the
freedom of Don Sebastiano who had been imprisoned by Ranuccio.
Eventually, Argilla is discovered to be the long-lost daughter of Don
Sebastiano.

The musical numbers, separated not by recitative but by dialogue, include in Act I a lively entrance aria for Argilla, and in Act
II the aforementioned septet, an adumbration of the celebrated
sextet in *Lucia di Lammermoor*, still thirteen years away in the future.

La Lettera anonima
(The Anonymous Letter)

farsa in one act

Principal characters:

Rosina   (soprano)
Melita   (mezzo-soprano)
Lauretta   (soprano)
Contessa   (soprano)
Filinto   (tenor)
Don Macario   (bass)

LIBRETTO by Giulio Genoino

TIME: The seventeenth century
PLACE: France

FIRST PERFORMED at the Teatro del Fondo, Naples, 29 June 1822, with Flora Fabbri (Contessa Rosina); Teresa Cecconi (Melita); Raffaela de Bernardis (Lauretta); Giovanni Battista Rubini (Filinto); De Franchi (Don Macario)

This one-act farce was produced at the Teatro del Fondo in Naples a mere six weeks after *La Zingara* had been staged at the Teatro Nuovo. Though, according to its composer, it was 'half ruined by a novice singer' (Teresa Cecconi), it was well received, and was given twenty performances during the season before lapsing into obscurity. The libretto by Giulio Genoino, a former monk, is based on a farce by Genoino himself, which in turn derives from Corneille's *Mélite, ou Les fausses lettres*, a play staged in Paris in 1630.

Genoino's libretto is a trivial affair about an anonymous letter read by the wrong person and misinterpreted, but Donizetti's music, consisting of a prelude and ten numbers, is rather engaging. The quartet ('Stelle che intesi') was praised by the critic of the *Giornale del Regno delle Due Sicilie* for having made fresh again 'the old-time procedure of our so-called concerted pieces, avoiding those cabalettas and that symmetrical repetition of motifs which obliges all the performers to repeat the same musical phrases no matter what very different emotions may agitate them'. It is interesting to note that, as early in his career as this, Donizetti's prime concern was with opera as drama, and that to achieve his theatrical effects he was willing to break a few musical rules. The score of *La Lettera anonima* is hardly memorable; but, in addition to the quartet, the *allegro* prelude and the introductory ensemble are lively, and the duet, 'Questo giorno', for Rosina and Filinto is pleasantly eccentric, keeping both tenor and soprano well in the middle of their range. The trio, 'Signor il Ciel vi dia fortuna e sanità', is dull, but the solo ('Maître de danse par excellence') which follows it (apparently a last-minute addition to the score as it is numbered 3 bis) is an amusing interpolation for the *buffo* bass Calvarola who made a cameo appearance as Flagiolet, a French dancing-master. The rest of the score, especially an attractive duet for Rosina and Melita, is agreeable enough in context.

Chiara e Serafina

opera semiseria in two acts

Principal characters:

Chiara   (soprano)
Serafina   (soprano)
Don Ramiro   (tenor)
Don Fernando   (bass)
Don Alvaro   (bass)
Picaro   (baritone)

LIBRETTO by Felice Romani

TIME: The seventeenth century
PLACE: Spain

FIRST PERFORMED at La Scala, Milan, 26 October 1822, with Isabella Fabbrica (Chiara); Rosa Morandi (Serafina); Savino Monelli (Don Ramiro); Carlo Poggioli (Don Fernando); Carlo Pizzochero (Don Alvaro); Antonio Tamburini (Picaro)

Shortly after the production of *La Lettera anonima* in Naples, Donizetti was commissioned by the leading Italian theatre, La

Scala, Milan, to compose an opera in collaboration with Felice Romani, the foremost Italian librettist of the day. Romani agreed to deliver his libretto to Donizetti within seven weeks, but lived up to his reputation of failing to meet his deadlines. Three weeks before the date of the première, he had produced only the first act. Donizetti was forced to compose the opera, *Chiara e Serafina, o I Pirati* (Chiara and Serafina, or The Pirates), in less than two weeks; after a further two weeks in rehearsal, it reached the stage, only to be greeted with a distinct lack of enthusiasm. The critic of the *Gazzetta di Milano* wrote that 'with faces of bronze the audience watched the final curtain descend'. Twelve performances were given at La Scala between 26 October and 26 November, after which *Chiara e Serafina* disappeared from the repertoire. There seem to have been no subsequent performances anywhere.

Since it was conceived and written in such haste, it is hardly surprising that *Chiara e Serafina* was not a success. Donizetti had anticipated this. In a letter to his old teacher, Mayr, ten days before the première, he had written: 'I suggest that you bring a Requiem to the performance, for I shall be slaughtered, and thus the funeral rites can be taken care of.' The progress of a major treason trial in Milan at the time, and a consequent reluctance on the part of the Milanese to go to the theatres, which were under police surveillance, no doubt contributed to the failure of Donizetti's first opera for La Scala. It was to be almost ten years before that theatre invited him to compose another.

Romani's libretto, based on the melodrama *La Cisterne* by René-Charles-Guilbert de Pixérécourt which was staged in Paris in 1809, describes how Don Alvaro, captured by Algerian pirates with his daughter Chiara, returns to Spain just in time to save his other daughter Serafina from the machinations of his enemy Don Fernando who has designs upon Serafina's wealth. The hastily composed score is hardly one of Donizetti's most exciting: its most attractive number is Chiara's aria ('Queste romite sponde') with cabaletta.

Alfredo il Grande
(Alfred the Great)

opera seria in two acts

Principal characters:
Amalia   (soprano)
Alfredo   (tenor)
Edoardo   (bass)
Atkins   (bass)
Guglielmo   (tenor)

LIBRETTO by Andrea Leone Tottola

TIME: The ninth century
PLACE: Athelney, Somerset

FIRST PERFORMED at the Teatro San Carlo, Naples, 2 July 1823, with Elisabetta Ferron (Amalia); Andrea Nozzari (Alfredo); Giovanni Botticelli (Edoardo); Michele Benedetti (Atkins); Antonio Orlandini (Guglielmo)

At the beginning of April 1823, five months after the unsuccessful première of *Chiara e Serafina*, Donizetti told the Roman librettist Jacopo Ferretti that he was at work on 'the one-act opera of Schmidt' and then 'Tottola's *Alfredo il Grande*'. The 'one-act opera', with a libretto by Giovanni Federico Schmidt, was, in fact, not an opera but *Aristea*, an *azione pastorale* or pastoral cantata, and its composer correctly described it as such to another correspondent. *Aristea* was performed at the Teatro San Carlo, Naples, on the King's name-day, 30 May. By then Donizetti was already at work on *Alfredo il Grande*, the first of his forays into English history, promised to the San Carlo. At its première in Naples on 2 July 1823, with an English soprano, Elisabetta Ferron, as Alfred's Queen, *Alfredo il Grande* failed to please. It is still awaiting its second performance, any-where.

Andrea Leone Tottola's libretto may have been based on one which Bartolomeo Merelli had provided five years earlier for an opera with the same title by Donizetti's teacher, Johann Simon Mayr. Set in Athelney, Somerset, the hiding-place of Alfred the

Great (*c*.849–*c*.900), it describes the search of Alfred's Queen Ealswith (for Italian operatic purposes understandably renamed Amalia) for her husband. She and Edoardo, a general, are followed by a Danish general with the distinctly un-Danish name of Atkins. There is a battle at which Alfred and his army defeat the Danes, but Atkins captures the Queen and holds her as hostage. In due course the English army arrives, the Queen is set free, and Alfredo is hailed as the saviour of his country.

Donizetti's highly Rossini-influenced score contains some jaunty marches and much florid vocal writing for Alfredo, Amalia, and virtually everyone else. *Alfredo il Grande* might provide a certain amount of innocent merriment if it were to be staged today, but there are worthier candidates for revival among Donizetti's forgotten operas.

Il Fortunato inganno
(The Happy Deception)

opera buffa in two acts

Principal characters:

Aurelia	(soprano)
Eugenia	(soprano)
Lattanzio Latrughelli	(bass)
Franceschetti, a colonel	(baritone)
Edoardo, a lieutenant	(tenor)

LIBRETTO by Andrea Leone Tottola

TIME: The early-nineteenth century
PLACE: A town in Italy

FIRST PERFORMED at the Teatro Nuovo, Naples, 3 September 1823, with Teresa Melas (Aurelia); D'Auria (Eugenia); Carlo Casaccia (Lattanzio Latrughelli); Giuseppe Fioravanti (Colonnello Franceschetti); Marco Venier (Edoardo)

In the spring of 1823, while he was at work on *Alfredo il Grande* for one Neapolitan theatre, the San Carlo, Donizetti had already promised another, the Teatro Nuovo (where his serious opera *La Zingara* had been successfully staged the previous year), that he would provide a new comic opera for the autumn. This was *Il Fortunato inganno*, and again the librettist was that busy Neapolitan hack, Andrea Leone Tottola. Donizetti composed the opera during the summer, and it was given its première on 3 September 1823. Unfortunately it failed to please, and was withdrawn after three performances, never to be seen again.

The opera's musical numbers are separated by dialogue in Tottola's story of a troupe of opera singers, one of whom, Eugenia, is in love with Edoardo, a young lieutenant. The 'happy deception' of the title is practised by Aurelia, the troupe's leading soprano and Eugenia's aunt, upon Edoardo's uncle, a colonel with a prejudice against theatre people. Eventually, the colonel gives his consent to the wedding of the young couple. Donizetti's score contains a good deal of amiable satire on the operatic conventions of the time and on the foibles of singers.

Perhaps some enterprising music festival should mount a few performances of *Il Fortunato inganno* which, shorn of large stretches of Tottola's copious dialogue, might prove more enjoyable than some of the other unfamiliar eighteenth- and early nineteenth-century operas which have been subjected to attempts at resuscitation.

9

From *L'Ajo nell'imbarazzo* to *Il Giovedì grasso*

L'Ajo nell'imbarazzo
(The Tutor Embarrassed)

opera buffa in two acts

Principal characters:

Gilda	(soprano)
Leonarda	(mezzo-soprano)
Enrico	(tenor)
Don Giulio	(baritone)
Don Gregorio	(bass)
Pipetto	(tenor)

LIBRETTO by Jacopo Ferretti

TIME: The early-nineteenth century
PLACE: An Italian city

FIRST PERFORMED at the Teatro Valle, Rome, 4 February 1824, with Ester Mombelli (Gilda); Agnese Loyselet (Leonarda); Savino Monelli (Enrico); Antonio Tamburini (Don Giulio); Carlo Casaccia (Don Gregorio); Giovanni Puglieschi (Pipetto)

After the disappointing première of *Il Fortunato inganno*, Donizetti left for Rome, where his commitments included presenting a revised version of *Zoraida di Granata* at the Teatro Argentina, the theatre of its 1822 première, and composing a new opera, *L'Ajo nell'imbarazzo*, which was greeted with wild enthusiasm at its première at the Teatro Valle on 4 February 1824. It is with this opera, which a newspaper next morning described as having 'spontaneity, fecundity, clarity, and originality of ideas', that Donizetti had his first really lasting success.

L'Ajo nell'imbarazzo was performed frequently at the Teatro Valle throughout the season, was staged in a number of other Italian towns, and became the earliest of Donizetti's operas to make its way abroad, with productions in Vienna, Dresden, Barcelona and Rio de Janeiro over the next few years. Before its Naples production in 1826 Donizetti revised the work, and it was under the title of *Don Gregorio* that it was staged in Naples and in several other cities. Donizetti made more changes for its first performance at La Scala, Milan, also in 1826. As late as 1845, he was still considering further changes to the work, but by then was too ill to complete the task.

It was as *Don Gregorio* that the opera was given its London première at Her Majesty's Theatre, on 28 July 1846. After a Venice revival in 1879, it seems to have disappeared from view until it turned up again in Italy in the twentieth century, at first in a trunctated version in the thirties, and then in a new edition by Adolfo Camozzo, also somewhat abbreviated, at the Teatro Donizetti in Bergamo in 1959. However, it was a production at the Wexford Festival in 1973 which gave *L'Ajo nell'imbarazzo* a new lease of life, since when it has been successfully staged in Berne (1975), Vienna (1981), Turin (1984) and Batignano (1990).

Ferretti had based his libretto on a comedy of the same title by Giovanni Giraud, which had been performed at the Teatro Valle in 1807, had since been used as the basis of four operas by Guarnaccia, Pilotti (who had been Donizetti's counterpoint teacher at Bologna), Celli and Mosca, and was to be used again, in 1825, by Nicelli. The plot concerns the misogynistic Don Giulio who has engaged a tutor, Don Gregorio, to educate his two sons, Enrico and Pipetto, so strictly that they will know nothing of life's diversions, and of women in particular, before reaching the age of forty. However, the system has failed. Enrico, the elder son already in his twenties, has married a charming neighbour, Gilda, and has fathered a son, while Pipetto, his young brother, has been making advances to his father's senile housekeeper, Leonarda. Learning of Enrico's marriage, the tutor, Don Gregorio, attempts to help him and Gilda, but when Gilda is discovered in the tutor's room, she is assumed by Don Giulio to be his mistress. Eventually the truth is revealed, Don Giulio is persuaded to accept the situation, and Gilda suggests that a trip around the world will cure young Pipetto of his infatuation with the unsuitable Leonarda.

It may well have been Ferretti's libretto, certainly a distinct improvement upon those of Tottola, which was to a large extent responsible for the huge success of *L'Ajo nell'imbarazzo* in Rome and elsewhere. Donizetti's score is engaging, but not one of his most individual. The eloquent melodic vein of *Don Pasquale* and *L'Elisir d'amore* has yet to be achieved, and much of the action is advanced in concerted numbers which rely on the traditional *buffo* formulas of the time. A trio ('Come, come! Un Bernardino') for Gregorio, Enrico and Gilda in Act I is delightful, as is the gentle duet ('Sempre fidele a te') for Gilda and Enrico in Act II. The middle section ('A chi de' figli') of Don Giulio's aria makes him seem a more sympathetic character than he appears to be for the rest of the work, and Gilda's aria ('Figlia son d'un colonnello') is quite lively. Gilda's rondo finale ('Quel tuo sorriso') is disappointingly bland, though presumably the composer thought otherwise, for he used it again some years later in *I Pazzi per progetto*.

Given a reasonably good performance, *L'Ajo nell'imbarazzo* is an opera which falls easily on the ear though it is unlikely to remain in the memory.

Emilia di Liverpool

opera semiseria in two acts

Principal characters:

Emilia	(soprano)
Candida	(soprano)
Federico	(tenor)
Claudio	(bass)
Don Romualdo	(bass)

LIBRETTO revised by Giuseppe Checcherini, derived from the play, *Emilia di Laverpaut* by Stefano Scatizzi, which in turn was based on *Emilia* by August von Kotzebue.

TIME: The past
PLACE: A village near Liverpool

FIRST PERFORMED 28 July 1824 at the Teatro Nuovo, Naples,
with Teresa Melas (Emilia); Francesca Checcherini (Candida);
Domenico Zilioli (Federico); Giuseppe Fioravanti (Claudio);
Carlo Casaccia (Don Romualdo)

Shortly after returning to Naples after the Rome success of *L'Ajo
nell'imbarazzo*, Donizetti was asked by the Teatro Nuovo to compose
a new opera and to revise *L'Ajo nell'imbarazzo* to suit the Nuovo and
its audience. The new opera, *Emilia di Liverpool*, was a failure at its
première in July 1824, and disappeared from the repertoire after
eight performances. Four years later, Donizetti revised *Emilia*,
removing eight numbers and adding four new ones, while Giuseppe
Checcherini (whose wife Francesca had sung in the 1824 première)
modified the anonymous libretto, renaming some of the characters.
Now retitled *L'Eremitaggio di Liwerpool* (The Hermitage of Liverpool), the opera was presented again at the Teatro Nuovo on 8
March 1828, but was no more successful than it had been in 1824,
receiving this time only six performances. The first version was
revived at the Teatro Nuovo in 1838 for three performances, and
again in 1871, but appears not to have been staged anywhere other
than Naples until 12 June 1957 when, as part of the festivities for
the 750th anniversary of the granting of a charter to the city of
Liverpool, a concert performance of the 1828 revision was given in
Liverpool, conducted by Fritz Spiegl, with Doreen Murray as
Emilia and the plot narrated satirically by Bernard Miles. Later in
the year, an abridged version was broadcast by the BBC, retaining
Bernard Miles as narrator, but now conducted by John Pritchard.
In the title-role the young Joan Sutherland gave a stunning
exhibition of her Donizetti style a good eighteen months before her
Covent Garden success in *Lucia di Lammermoor*. Many years later (on
7 June 1987) the original 1824 score was performed in Liverpool
with its dialogue replaced by narration.
   The action of the opera takes place in a mythical Liverpool which
appears to be a village in mountainous country somewhere just
outside London. The village itself is in a valley above which, on the
brow of a hill, stands a hermitage. The plot of the revised version
differs in certain details from the original, but in broad outline they

are the same. Emilia, daughter of Claudio, Count of Liverpool, has been seduced by Federico (in the revised version Colonel Villars alias Tomson) and then deserted. This has caused her mother to die of shame, her father to disappear to foreign parts in pursuit of the seducer, and Emilia to retire to the hermitage to give comfort and help to weary travellers and alms to the village poor. The action of the opera takes place many years later when three travellers seek shelter, their carriage having been overturned in a storm. One of the three turns out to be Federico, the seducer of many years ago. Emilia's father, Claudio, also makes an unexpected reappearance, 'dressed as a slave, with a heavy beard', and challenges Federico to a duel. But Federico has repented of his heartless behaviour, he and Emilia declare their love for each other, and Emilia's father blesses their union. The opera's spoken dialogue is as ludicruous as its plot, especially the dreadful jokes in Neapolitan dialect for the character of Don Romualdo (Asdrubale in the revised version), written for the Teatro Nuovo's resident comic bass.

The score of *Emilia di Liverpool* is attractive, but with one or two exceptions no piece stands out as being at all individual or memorable, and the influence of Rossini is easily discernible. A tenor–bass duet for Federico and Romualdo, 'A n'ommo, che allancato', which is in the 1824 version of the opera only, works well in its blending of lyrical and *buffo* elements, and a quintet in Act I (which in 1828 is transferred to the finale of the act) is lively. The duet, 'Delle mie pene, o stelle', for Emilia and Claudio is dramatically apt, and the Act II duet for Claudio and Federico/Villars is effective in context. In general, the more concise second version of the opera is to be preferred. The numbers deleted are no great loss, and the four new numbers are among the most attractive in the score, especially a trio for Villars, Claudio and Asdrubale (who is Don Romualdo renamed). Best of all is the solo finale for Emilia, the pensive 'Confusa è l'alma mia', with its joyous cabaletta, 'Non intende il mio contento'. This gives the prima donna a chance to show off her vocal virtuosity, and makes a much more satisfactory end to the opera than the French vaudeville-type finale of 1824 in which each character contributes a verse before the perfunctory final chorus. Emilia's 1828 solo finale, however, was not composed specifically for the revised version. Donizetti lifted it from *Alahor in Granata*, an opera he wrote in 1825. Curiously, although in both versions of the finale the orchestra plays on quietly for a few bars after the ensemble (1824) or the soprano (1828) has finished, in 1828 it then reverts to two loud chords at the very end.

All things considered, it seems unlikely that there will be many future performances of *Emilia di Liverpool*, even in Liverpool.

Alahor in Granata

opera seria in two acts

Principal characters:
Alahor   (baritone)
Zobeida   (soprano)
Muley-Hassem   (contralto)
Alamor   (tenor)

LIBRETTO by M.A.

TIME: The middle ages
PLACE: Granada

FIRST PERFORMED at the Teatro Carolino, Palermo, 7 January 1826, with Antonio Tamburini (Alahor); Elisabetta Ferron (Zobeida); Marietta Gioia-Tamburini (Muley-Hassem); Berardo Calvari Winter (Alamor)

The period following the unsuccessful première of *Emilia di Liverpool* in Naples in the summer of 1824 was one of the least productive of Donizetti's early professional career. Discussions with the Teatro Argentina in Rome concerning a new opera were interrupted when the composer became ill with what he referred to as 'the fever'. Later in the year he composed a cantata for voice and piano and a *Credo* for the celebration of Saint Cecilia's Day (22 November) in Bergamo. Early in 1825 he wrote a rondo for piano and one or two other occasional pieces. At the beginning of April he travelled to Sicily, having accepted the post of musical director of the Teatro Carolino in Palermo for the 1825–1826 season. He was required to teach at the local Conservatorium – 'Ragged boys, terrible voices, no teachers of bel canto; in short, a synagogue, a perfect synagogue,' he wrote to his old teacher, Mayr – as well as stage the operas which, during the summer, included Mayr's *Che originali!* as well as his own *Ajo nell'imbarazzo*. He had also to compose a new opera for production in December. This was *Alahor di Granata* whose première had to be postponed until early in the new year because of the advanced pregnancy of the prima donna, Elisabetta Ferron.

'They don't want to hear Ferron,' Donizetti told Mayr, adding that the other leading soprano, Marietta Gioia-Tamburini, 'is a dog'. The première of *Alahor di Granata* on 6 January 1826 went reasonably well, but was followed by no more than a few performances of the opera. By the end of the month, Elisabetta Ferron had left Palermo with her baby. On 19 February, the season at the Teatro Carolino ended and Donizetti sailed back to Naples.

The libretto of *Alahor* is signed merely with the initials M.A., but it is actually an adaptation of a libretto written by Felice Romani for Meyerbeer's *L'Esule di Granata* (produced at La Scala in March 1821), which in turn is derived from Étienne de Jouy's libretto for Cherubini's *Les Abencérages* (Paris Opéra, 1813), which is based on the play *Gonzalve de Cordove* by the eighteenth-century French dramatist Jean-Pierre-Claris de Florian, first staged in Paris in 1793.

Curiously, Florian's play had also been the ultimate source of Bartolomeo Merelli's libretto for Donizetti's *Zoraida di Granata* of 1822. In *Alahor in Granata*, Zobeida is in love with Muley-Hassem who has succeeded his brother Aly as leader of the Abencerrages. Her brother Alahor returns in disguise to avenge the murder of their father by Aly. Alahor intends to kill Muley-Hassem who, learning of this, forgives him. The two men combine to fight off an attack by a rival leader, and the opera ends with Zobeida rejoicing at the state of amity now existing between her brother and her lover.

Until recent years the score of *Alahor in Granata* was thought to have been lost. However, a copy (not in the composer's hand) was found in Boston in 1970, and a few years later the autograph score was discovered to be in a private collection in Palermo. Donizetti plundered his score at least twice, using its solo finale for the finale of the revised *Emilia di Liverpool* in 1828, and turning a Moorish march into the entrance music for Sergeant Belcore and his troops in *L'Elisir d'amore* in 1832. *Alahor in Granata* has not been staged anywhere since its 1826 performances in Palermo and, some months later, in Naples.

In his *Donizetti*, published in Bergamo in 1948, Guido Zavadini includes in a list of the composer's operas a work entitled *Il Castello degli invalidi* (The Castle of Invalids), which he describes as a one-act farce performed at the Teatro Carolino, Palermo, in the spring of 1826. He did not know who had sung in it, nor the whereabouts of the score. In 1841 Donizetti mentioned *Il Castello degli invalidi* in a letter to his brother-in-law as having been staged in Palermo, without giving a date or even a year. Modern researchers have failed to find any mention of the opera in archives or libraries in Palermo. Perhaps it was performed, either in Palermo or elsewhere, under another title, but in any case its score remains lost.

Another lost *farsa* from 1826, which may never have been completed, is *La Bella prigioniera* (The Beautiful Prisoner). Two duets with piano accompaniment from this piece, which Donizetti referred to as having not been performed, are preserved in the Donizetti Museum in Bergamo.

Elvida

opera seria in one act

Principal characters:
Elvida   (soprano)
Zeidar   (contralto)
Alfonso   (tenor)
Amur   (bass)

LIBRETTO by Giovanni Federico Schmidt

TIME: The middle ages
PLACE: Spain

FIRST PERFORMED at the Teatro San Carlo, Naples, 6 July 1826, with Henriette Méric-Lalande (Elvida); Brigida Lorenzani (Zeidar); Giovanni Battista Rubini (Alfonso); Luigi Lablache (Amur)

Back in Naples, Donizetti's next commission was to write a one-act *opera seria*, *Elvida*, to a libretto by Giovanni Federico Schmidt, for the Teatro San Carlo to stage as part of a mixed programme on 6 July

1826, the birthday of Queen Maria Clementina. In mid-June the composer told his old teacher, Mayr, 'On Monday we shall rehearse the one-act *Elvida*. To tell you the truth, it's not up to much, but if I impress them with Rubini's cavatina and the quartet, I shall be satisfied. On gala evenings no one pays much attention.' His cynicism was justified. Despite the presence in the cast of three of the most famous singers of the time, the soprano Henriette Méric-Lalande, the tenor Giovanni Battista Rubini, and the bass Luigi Lablache, *Elvida* made little impression on its audience. It was given a further three performances and then forgotten.

The source of Schmidt's plot has not been identified. It tells a trite story concerning a Spanish noblewoman, Elvida, who is captured by a Moorish chieftain, Amur. She resists the advances of Amur's son, Zeidar, and is eventually rescued by her fiancé, Alfonso, a Spanish prince. The best numbers are those which Donizetti mentioned in his letter to Mayr, an extremely florid tenor aria, 'Atra nube al sole intorno', written with Rubini's particular capabilities in mind, and an *adagio* quartet. The rest of the score is of little interest, blandly undramatic and, in the words of the musicologist Guglielmo Barblan, imbued with an 'atmosphere of abstract musicality'.

Gabriella di Vergy

opera seria in three acts

Principal characters:

Gabriella   (soprano)
Almeide   (soprano)
Fayel   (baritone)
Raoul   (tenor)
Filippo II   (bass)

LIBRETTO by Andrea Leone Tottola

TIME: The Crusades
PLACE: Burgundy

FIRST PERFORMED as *Gabriella* (in a version made after the composer's death) at the Teatro San Carlo, Naples, 29 November

1869, with Marcellina Lotti della Santa (Gabriella); Carolina Certone (Almeide); Giuseppe Villani (Fayel); Gottardo Aldighieri (Raoul); Marco Arati (Filippo II)

In the letter he wrote to Mayr in mid-June 1826, in which he mentioned the forthcoming rehearsals of *Elvida*, Donizetti also announced to his old teacher that he was at work on the composition of another opera, not for a specific theatre but purely for his own pleasure. This was *Gabriella di Vergy*, and the libretto he used was that written by Andrea Leone Tottola for Michele Carafa's opera of the same title which had been staged in Naples at the Teatro del Fondo in 1816. Tottola's libretto was based on the play *Gabriella di Vergy* by Dormont de Belloy, produced in Paris in 1771, its ultimate source a fourteenth-century romance, *Le Chastelain de Couci*.

That Donizetti should have composed a work which no one had commissioned him to write is highly unusual, for he was a busy working composer who, throughout his entire professional life, was geared to providing operas on commission. But it is clear that at this stage of his career he was dissatisfied with many of the current operatic conventions and with the kind of opera he was expected to write, and keen to indulge his own artistic impulses. No theatre staged *Gabriella di Vergy* during Donizetti's lifetime, and it is not even certain whether the composer ever made any serious attempt to have his opera produced. As early as 1827 he lifted at least one number from it for *Otto mesi in due ore*, in 1828 a chorus from it was used in *L'Esule di Roma*, in 1829 a cabaletta found its way into *Il Paria* and in 1830 three numbers turned up in *Anna Bolena*. Indeed, the tracing of music by Donizetti from one opera to another could provide a lifetime's occupation for any under-employed musicologist.

In 1838 Donizetti returned to *Gabriella di Vergy*, revising his score thoroughly, recasting its two acts into three and changing the *travesti* part of Raoul into a tenor role. He may have done this with the intention of staging it at the Teatro San Carlo, whose impresario had commissioned an opera from him. However, for some reason he put *Gabriella di Vergy* aside, proceeded instead to write *Poliuto* for the San Carlo, and used some of *Gabriella*'s music three years later in *Adelia*. It was not until 1869, twenty-one years after Donizetti's death, that a version of his opera, now called simply *Gabriella* (no doubt to avoid confusion with an 1834 Donizetti opera, *Gemma di Vergy*), reached the stage.

Recent research has revealed this 1869 *Gabriella* to have been little more than a pastiche, put together by Giuseppe Puzone and Paolo Serrao, the co-directors of the Teatro San Carlo, utilising seven numbers from the 1826 score but adding music from other works by Donizetti. The first performance of the opera as its composer left it in 1838 seems to have been that given in concert form in Belfast on 9 November 1978, conducted by Alun Francis, with La Verne Williams as Gabriella. The first, and to date the only, stage performance was given in Sherborne, Dorset (at Sherborne School), by Dorset Opera on 31 August 1985, conducted by Patrick Shelley, with Marie Slorach as Gabriella.

The action of the opera takes place in thirteenth-century Burgundy. Believing that her beloved Raoul has died in the Crusades, Gabriella has married Fayel, Count of Vergy. However, Raoul returns and, as a reward for having saved the life of King Filippo II, is offered the hand in marriage of Fayel's sister, Almeida. Finding Raoul kneeling at Gabriella's feet, Fayel has Gabriella imprisoned in a tower and challenges Raoul to a duel. The opera ends as Gabriella dies of shock when Fayel presents her with an urn containing Raoul's heart.

The 1838 *Gabriella di Vergy* is an opera well worth reviving, for its score is dramatically strong enough to carry its overwrought plot. Donizetti's writing for the orchestra is confident throughout, terse in the prelude to Act I and moving in the Act III finale, and some of the arias are very fine, especially Fayel's graceful 'Giovin, leggiadra, amabile' with its exciting cabaletta in which the orchestra's jaunty contribution is notable; Gabriella's 'Delle nostr'anime', its cabaletta a gentler one; Filippo's graceful 'O miei fidi' and its rousing cabaletta; and Raoul's 'Io l'amai', almost Verdian in its forward movement, its cabaletta engaging and energetic. Cabalette play a major role in *Gabriella di Vergy*.

There is a splendidly vigorous duet for Gabriella and Fayel to end Act I, a magnificent ensemble finale to Act II, and in Act III an impressive duet for the confrontation between Raoul and Fayel with, as the opera's finale, a long solo for Gabriella in the form of a cavatina ('L'amai, si, come un angelo') followed by a cabaletta whose restraint makes it all the more affecting.

Olivo e Pasquale

opera buffa in two acts

Principal characters:

Olivo   (baritone)
Pasquale   (bass)
Isabella   (soprano)
Camillo   (tenor)
Le Bross   (tenor)
Columella   (bass)

LIBRETTO by Jacopo Ferretti

TIME: The eighteenth century
PLACE: Lisbon

FIRST PERFORMED at the Teatro Valle, Rome, 7 January 1827,
with Emilia Bonini (Isabella); Anna Scudellari-Cosselli (Camillo);
Domenico Cosselli (Olivo); Giuseppe Frezzolini (Pasquale);
Giovanni Battista Verger (Le Bross); Luigi Garofolo (Columella)

In the summer of 1826 Donizetti was in Rome, composing *Olivo e
Pasquale*, a comic opera, for the Teatro Valle. Its libretto by Jacopo
Ferretti was based on a play of the same title by Antonio Simone
Sografi, first staged in Venice in 1794, though one incident, the
mock suicide near the end, comes from another play by Sografi, *Il
più bel giorno della Westfalia. Olivo e Pasquale* was well enough received
at its première on 7 January 1827 to be performed several more
times during the month, and to be accepted for production in a
number of other Italian cities and also abroad. For its first
performance in Naples at the Teatro Nuovo in September 1827,
Donizetti made several changes, the most important of which
involved the role of Camillo. A mezzo-soprano *travesti* part in Rome,
Camillo became a tenor as from the Naples production.

Olivo e Pasquale was first performed in London on 31 March 1832,
but has yet to reach the USA. The opera continued to be staged in
Italy and abroad until around 1870, after which it disappeared until
it was revived in Barga at the Teatro dei Differenti on 27 July 1980.
Its inconsequential plot concerns two brothers, Olivo and Pasquale,

who are merchants in Lisbon. In their employ is Camillo, in love with Olivo's daughter, Isabella. Olivo, however, intends to marry Isabella off to Le Bross, a wealthy merchant from Cadiz who, apprised of her true feelings, sympathises with Isabella and promises to help her to marry Camillo. But it is only after the young lovers have threatened to kill themselves, and a shot has actually been fired, that Olivo consents to their marriage.

Donizetti's score, given that he had already demonstrated his flair for comic opera, is disappointing. It shows signs of having been hastily written, and lacks any indication that his attention was ever really engaged by Ferretti's text. After a frisky overture, there is little in Act I that is not either dull or mechanical, with the exception of Isabella's mildly appealing aria, 'Come vuoi che freni il pianto', until near the end of the act when a quartet for male voices (Olivo, Pasquale, Columella and Le Bross) somewhat enlivens the action. At the beginning of Act II, the Olivo–Pasquale duet ('Siete un asino calzato') utilises very ordinary *buffo* material and, although the duet for Isabella and Le Bross which follows ('Isabella! Voi scherzate?') is both fresher and indeed quite affecting, the rest of the act fails to rise above a level of amiable mediocrity.

Otto mesi in due ore
(Eight Months in Two Hours)

opera romantica in three acts

Principal characters:

Elisabetta	(soprano)
Potoski	(tenor)
Gran Maresciallo	(baritone)
Ivano	(bass)

LIBRETTO by Domenico Gilardoni

TIME: The seventeenth century
PLACE: Russia

FIRST PERFORMED at the Teatro Nuovo, Naples, 13 May 1827, with Caterina Lipparini (Elisabetta); Servoli (Potoski); Vincenzo Galli (Gran Maresciallo); Giuseppe Fioravanti (Ivano)

The opera which Donizetti wrote immediately after the Rome première of *Olivo e Pasquale* is one known under several titles. The composer had signed a new contract with Barbaja, the impresario who controlled, at various times, three theatres in Naples: the San Carlo, the Fondo and the Nuovo. Under the terms of his contract, Donizetti was required to provide four new operas a year for a period of three years and also to act as the Teatro Nuovo's musical director. The first opera, composed in the early spring and performed at the Teatro Nuovo on 13 May 1827, was *Otto mesi in due ore* (Eight Months in Two Hours), with a libretto by Domenico Gilardoni who had provided Bellini the previous year with the text for *Bianca e Gernando*, and who would supply Donizetti with ten further libretti during the next four years.

Gilardoni's libretto for *Otto mesi in due ore*, whose sub-title was *Gli Esiliati in Siberia* (The Exiles in Siberia), was based on the play, *La Fille de l'exilé, ou Huit mois en deux heures*, by René-Charles-Guilbert de Pixérécourt, which in turn had been derived from *Élisabeth, ou Les exilés de Sibérie*, a novel by Sophie Cottin, published in Paris in 1806. Gilardoni probably made use of an existing Italian stage adaptation of the novel made by Luigi Marchionni and performed in Rome in 1820 as *La Figlia dell'esiliato*.

At its Naples première, Donizetti's opera was an immense success, and was performed fifty times during the season. When it was staged in Milan in 1831, where it was called *Gli Esiliati in Siberia*, it achieved only eight performances. Donizetti revised the opera for its production in Livorno in 1833, and made further and more drastic changes for a proposed production in Paris in 1838, for which he composed much new music. When the Paris performances failed to take place, he offered the opera, unsuccessfully, to Benjamin Lumley, the impresario of Her Majesty's Theatre, London, this time with an Italian text and entitled *Elisabetta*. After Donizetti's death, a version arranged by Uranio Fontana (described on the title-page of the French score as Donizetti's pupil) was staged in Paris in 1853 as *Élisabeth ou La Fille du Proscrit*, its French text by Adolphe de Leuven and Léon Lévy Brunswick. In the following year, this version was produced at the Teatro Santa Radegonda in Milan in an Italian translation. The opera has still to be performed in Britain or America.

In 1984 an American music critic and conductor, Will Crutchfield, found a nearly complete copy of the first and third acts of

Elisabetta, in Donizetti's handwriting, in London; not at the rebuilt Her Majesty's Theatre, however, but in a dusty basement at the Royal Opera House, Covent Garden. (The Italian translation and some of the changes are written in a hand which is not Donizetti's.) Four years later, in the same basement, the conductor Richard Bonynge discovered the missing Act II. At the time of writing, the newly found *Elisabetta* has not been performed, nor has the work been staged in any version since the middle of the nineteenth century. (This *Elisabetta* is not to be confused with the Donizetti opera first staged in 1829 as *Elisabetta al castello di Kenilworth*, and more widely known as *Il Castello di Kenilworth*.)

Otto mesi in due ore describes Elisabetta's (Élisabeth's) journey on foot from Siberia to Moscow in an attempt to gain freedom for her father who had been unjustly exiled to Siberia. Though harried by floods and by Tartar hordes, she eventually reaches Moscow and gains access to the Tsar who grants a pardon to her father. The score includes, in Act II, an orchestral *andante* to accompany the stage picture of Elisabetta making her way across Siberia. According to the stage directions, 'she weeps ... she stops ... she begins to walk again ... she stumbles and almost falls ... she raises her hands to heaven ... she walks' and so on. The vocal writing in general is florid, and the opera ends with an aria for Elisabetta, for which Donizetti used again the music he had composed some years earlier for the aria-finale of *Le Nozze in villa*.

Il Borgomastro di Saardam
(The Burgomaster of Saardam)

opera buffa in two acts

Principal characters:

Marietta	(soprano)
Tsar Pietro	(baritone)
Pietro Flimann	(tenor)
Wambett, Il Borgomastro	(bass)

LIBRETTO by Domenico Gilardoni

TIME: The late-seventeenth century

PLACE: The Netherlands

FIRST PERFORMED at the Teatro del Fondo, Naples, 19 August 1827, with Caroline Unger (Marietta); Celestino Salvatori (Tsar Pietro); Berardo Calvari Winter (Pietro Flimann); Raffaele Casaccia (Il Borgomastro)

At about the time of the première in Naples of *Otto mesi in due ore*, Donizetti became engaged to marry Virginia Vasselli, the sister of a friend of his in Rome. Within three months of that première, his next opera was staged in Naples. This was *Il Borgomastro di Saardam*, its plot not dissimilar to the story about Peter the Great which had been the basis of his 1819 opera, *Il Falegname di Livonia*, though this time the plot derived immediately from a play, *Le Bourgmestre de Sardam*, by Anne-Honoré-Joseph Mélesville, Jean-Toussaint Merle and Eugène Cantiran de Boirie, staged in Paris in 1818.

At its first performance in Naples on 19 August 1827, Donizetti's opera was accorded no better than a lukewarm reception, but its popularity increased as the year progressed. By the following February the composer was able to report to his old teacher, Mayr, that *Il Borgomastro di Saardam* had achieved more than thirty-five performances and was still in the repertoire. It reached La Scala, Milan, in the following January, and Rome five months later, but on each occasion only for a single, unsuccessful performance. There were productions abroad, in Barcelona in 1829, Vienna in 1836, Berlin in 1837, and Budapest in 1839, after which *Il Borgomastro di Saardam* was neglected until 1973 when it was staged in the Netherlands town (now called Zaandam) in which its action takes place. The nine performances in Zaandam in May 1973 were conducted by Jan Schaap, and the cast included Ans Philippo (Marietta), Pieter van den Berg (Tsar Pietro), Philip Langridge (Pietro Flimann) and Renato Capecchi (Il Borgomastro).

The plot (also used by Lortzing, ten years later, for his *Zar und Zimmermann*, and by several other composers) has the disguised Peter the Great working in the shipyards of Saardam under an assumed name. He befriends a young colleague who is also named Peter (Pietro), a deserter from the Russian army who is in love with Marietta, the ward of Wambett, the Burgomaster. Having been alerted to the fact that the Tsar is working as a shipwright in Saardam, the Burgomaster identifies the wrong Peter. Eventually the opera ends with the Tsar sailing off to Russia, having pardoned the other Peter who is now free to marry Marietta.

After a rather meandering overture, the score of *Il Borgomastro di Saardam*, consisting of musical numbers separated by *recitativo secco*, is genial but for the most part conventional and undistinguished, betraying occasional signs of the haste with which it must have been composed. In Act I, Marietta's cavatina ('Lungi da te, mio bene') and cabaletta ('In seno al contento') are attractive; the Burgomaster's entrance aria ('Fate largo al Borgomastro') utilises routine *buffo* material; a trio for Wambett, the Tsar and Pietro is quite lively; and the finale to the act at least compensates in pace for what it lacks in melodic freshness.

The brief orchestral introduction to Act II is a blatant example of plagiarism, for it was first heard eleven years earlier when Rossini composed it to accompany the entrance of Almaviva disguised as an inebriated soldier in the finale to Act I of *Il Barbiere di Siviglia*. The duet for the young lovers ('Allor che tutto tace') is so formularistic that Donizetti might have written it in his sleep, but the Tsar's aria ('Va, e la nave, in un baleno') which follows it is more individual, and Marietta's duet with her guardian after he has made an unwelcome proposal of marriage to her is delightfully appropriate to the situation, its melodic interest often to be found in the orchestra beneath the bickering *parlando* phrases of Marietta and Wambett. The opera's finale consists of a hardly memorable aria and cabaletta for Marietta, topped and tailed by perfunctory comments from the ensemble.

Vincenzo Bellini, whose first three operas had already been staged, was in Milan when *Il Borgomastro di Saardam* was given its first and last public performance there in January 1828, and wrote to a friend after its dress rehearsal: 'In the first act there is nothing, in the second a duet that might please, but as a whole the work will be a fiasco.' His appraisal, though ungenerous, is not too seriously inaccurate.

Le Convenienze ed inconvenienze teatrali
(Theatrical Seemliness and Unseemliness)

farsa in two acts

Principal characters:

Corilla	(soprano)
Procolo, her husband	(bass)
Luigia	(soprano)
Mamma Agata, her mother	(bass)
Guglielmo, a German tenor	(tenor)
Biscroma, a music master	(bass)
Prospero, a poet and librettist	(baritone)

LIBRETTO by Gaetano Donizetti

TIME: The eighteenth century
PLACE: A provincial Italian theatre

FIRST PERFORMED at the Teatro Nuovo, Naples, 21 November 1827, as *Le Convenienze teatrali*, in one act, with Gennaro Luzio (Mamma Agata)
FIRST PERFORMED in its revised version as *Le Convenienze ed inconvenienze teatrali*, in two acts, at the Teatro Canobbiana, Milan, 20 April 1831, with Fanny Corri-Paltoni (Corilla); Giuseppe Giordano (Guglielmo); Giuseppe Frezzolini (Mamma Agata)

Writing to his father in October 1827, two months after the première of *Il Borgomastro di Saardam*, Donizetti said that he was busy composing a farce to be performed for his benefit evening the following month at the Teatro Nuovo. Probably with the aid of Domenico Gilardoni (who was later to provide libretti for several operas by Donizetti), the composer wrote his own libretto, based on a comedy, *Le Convenienze teatrali* by Antonio Simone Sografi, staged in Venice in 1794. Donizetti's one-act opera of the same title, a satirical view of the difficulties besetting a provincial company's attempt to stage an *opera seria*, was a huge success at its première in Naples, with the bass Gennaro Luzio especially admired for his hilarious portrayal, *en travesti*, of Mamma Agata, the mother of the company's second soprano. Four years later, for a production in

Milan, Donizetti expanded his opera into two acts, utilising new material from *Le Inconvenienze teatrali*, Sografi's sequel to his earlier play, performed in Padua in 1800. The revised opera was staged as *Le Convenienze ed inconvenienze teatrali*, under which title it was revived in 1963 in Siena, having languished forgotten for well over a century. In 1969 a German adaptation of the opera was staged in Munich as *Viva la Mamma*; later in the same year the BBC broadcast an English translation as *Upstage and Downstage*; and at the Collegiate Theatre, London, in 1972 Opera Rara produced the one-act version in English as *The Prima Donna's Mother is a Drag*. The first British stage performance of *Le Convenienze ed inconvenienze teatrali*, the two-act version, was given in London (in English) by Harrow Opera Workshop, an amateur company, on 9 April 1976. The first American performance was staged on 5 May 1977 in San Francisco by that city's Opera Theater. In 1988 the first twentieth-century revival in Italy of the one-act *Convenienze* took place in Lugo di Romagna.

The opera's plot centres upon the determination of Mamma Agata (played by a bass or baritone in female attire but using his natural male voice) to protect the interests of her daughter, the second soprano in a provincial opera company whose members include a female singer of male roles 'dell' Accademia del Mississippi' (from the Mississippi Academy). Mamma Agata disrupts a rehearsal, harrowing the composer and insulting Corilla, the prima donna. When Corilla finally storms out, Mamma Agata assures the impresario that she herself is perfectly capable of taking over the prima donna's role, and indeed does so at the dress rehearsal, after which everyone predicts a fiasco though Mamma Agata remains serenely confident of success.

Donizetti's score engagingly parodies operatic conventions, singers' and composers' egos, and theatrical tantrums in general. The opera's bustling overture, though good-humoured, is of no great musical interest. Mamma Agata's entrance aria ('Mascalzoni! sfaccendati!') in which, imitating various instruments of the orchestra, she tells the composer how best to write for her daughter's voice, noisily sets the tone for her contribution to the proceedings. Though the material of the *allegro* duet, 'Ch'io canti un duetto?', for Corilla and Mamma Agata is undistinguished, the action on stage makes it enjoyable in performance, and the same could be said of most other numbers in the score. A trio ('Per me non trovo calma') for

Guglielmo, Mamma Agata and Biscroma, the music master, is genuinely amusing; more so than the Act I finale.

Act II begins more promisingly with a duet for Prospero and Mamma Agata ('Senza tanti complimenti') which is permeated by a quirkily attractive figure in the orchestra of an individuality too rare elsewhere in the opera. Thereafter the action maintains Act I's level of theatrical liveliness accompanied by no more than competence in Donizetti's score. At one point the leading soprano is instructed to sing a bravura aria of her own choice: this could easily prove to be the musical highlight of any performance.

L'Esule di Roma
(The Roman Exile)

opera seria in two acts

Principal characters:
Argelia   (soprano)
Leontina   (soprano)
Settimio   (tenor)
Murena   (bass)
Publio   (baritone)
Lucio   (bass)

LIBRETTO by Domenico Gilardoni

TIME: *c.* 35 A.D.
PLACE: Rome

FIRST PERFORMED at the Teatro San Carlo, Naples, 1 January 1828, with Adelaide Tosi (Argelia); Edvige Ricci (Leontina); Berardo Calvari Winter (Settimio); Luigi Lablache (Murena); Giovanni Campagnoli (Publio); Gaetano Chizzola (Lucio)

In less than a month after the première of *Le Convenienze teatrali*, Donizetti's next opera was already in rehearsal. This was *L'Esule di Roma*, sub-titled *Il Proscritto* (The Outlaw) and based by its librettist Domenico Gilardoni on *Il Proscritto romano, ossia Il Leone del Caucaso* (The Roman Outlaw, or the Lion of the Caucasus) by Luigi

Marchionni, a play staged in Naples in 1820 which was itself derived from an earlier play, *Androclès, ou Le Lion reconnaissant* (Paris, 1804). Gilardoni's libretto, like most of the others he was to provide for Donizetti, is very clumsily written.

The action takes place in Rome at the time of the Emperor Tiberius (who reigned from A.D. 14 to 37), and the exile of the title is Settimio, a former tribune who, banished from Rome by Tiberius, has returned secretly to visit his beloved Argelia, the daughter of a senator, Murena, whose false testimony was the cause of Settimio's banishment. When Settimio is again arrested and sentenced to death, Murena suffers pangs of conscience and resolves to die in the arena with him. However, a lion whom Settimio had befriended during his banishment in the desert saves him from the other beasts, at which Tiberius is moved to free Settimio and forgive the treacherous Murena. The lion seems to have disappeared by the time of the final (1840) version of the opera, his function now undertaken by Murena.

At its première at the Teatro San Carlo on New Year's Day, 1828, *L'Esule di Roma* was greeted with such wild enthusiasm that the theatre's impresario, Domenico Barbaja, immediately commissioned two more operas from Donizetti. Especially admired was the Act I finale, a trio which Rossini, upon hearing it, declared would suffice to make its composer famous. The opera was staged in several other Italian towns, and within five years had reached Madrid, Corfu, Vienna, Graz, and London where it was first performed on 3 February 1832, causing the critic Henry Chorley to remark that it 'made a certain mark in favour of Donizetti because of a trio, which was found new; but the other novelties from the south fell dead in the hour of their appearance'. After 1869, the opera disappeared until it was given a concert performance at the Queen Elizabeth Hall, London, on 18 July 1982, with Katia Ricciarelli as Argelia and Bruce Brewer as Settimio. It returned to Italy after more than a hundred years' absence on 14 October 1986, with Cecilia Gasdia (Argelia) and Ernesto Palacio (Settimio).

Donizetti revised the score of *L'Esule di Roma* on several occasions: for its production in July 1828 at La Scala, Milan, where it was well received and given ten performances; for its revival at the San Carlo, Naples, in December of the same year; for various other Italian stagings; and finally in August, 1840, for its production at the Teatro Riccardi in his home town of Bergamo. It is a well-crafted score but for the most part lacking in individuality. A short prelude leads to a dignified opening chorus of tenors and basses and to Murena's aria ('Per lui nel mentre avea lustro, splendor, Senato!') and cabaletta which immediately characterise him as by no means villainous beyond redemption. In the duet ('A quel Dio') for Murena and the returning hero Publio, the former's bass and the latter's high baritone contrast effectively, but Settimio's cavatina ('Tacqui allor') and cabaletta ('Se ad altri il core t'avvinse amore') are disappointingly nondescript. However, the duet ('Fia ver? Oh ciel!') of the lovers Settimio and Argelia is lively, and the trio ('Murena! Il genitor!') which ends Act I, and which Donizetti's audiences admired so greatly, is certainly both melodious and full of dramatic movement, though it necessarily sounds less striking now in the light of the composer's later achievements.

At the beginning of Act II, Murena's mad scene is formalised into aria ('Entra nel circo') and cabaletta ('Di Stige il flutto ancor') with interjections from a chorus of his understandably concerned relatives. Settimio's aria ('S'io finor, bell' idol mio') and cabaletta ('Si scenda alla tomba'), in the third and final version which Donizetti composed for the opera's 1840 Bergamo première, are simple and forthright in feeling, and the father–daughter duet ('Vagiva Emilia ancora') for Murena and Argelia is almost Verdian in mood and movement. The opera's finale consists of a graceful F major aria ('Morte! Ah, pria che l'una uccidi') and joyous bravura cabaletta ('Ah, che nulla a tanta gioia') for Argelia, with the necessary interjections from other characters to wind up the plot.

Alina, regina di Golconda
(Alina, Queen of Golconda)

opera semiseria in two acts

Principal characters:

Alina, Queen of Golconda	(soprano)
Fiorina, her confidante	(soprano)
Seide, a princely suitor	(tenor)
Volmar, French Ambassador	(baritone)
Belfiore, his aide	(bass)

LIBRETTO by Felice Romani

TIME: The mythical past
PLACE: India

FIRST PERFORMED at the Teatro Carlo Felice, Genoa, 12 May 1828, with Serafina Rubini (Alina); De Vincenti (Fiorina); Giovanni Battista Verger (Seide); Antonio Tamburini (Volmar); Giuseppe Frezzolini (Belfiore)

Within weeks of the première of *L'Esule di Roma*, Donizetti was involved in preparations for his next operatic project. The city of Genoa had built a new opera house, the Teatro Carlo Felice, named after the reigning King of Sardinia and Piedmont, and operas had been commissioned from Rossini, Donizetti, Bellini and Francesco Morlacchi to inaugurate the new theatre. Morlacchi (1784–1841), an Italian composer who lived in Saxony where he was musical director of the Italian Opera in Dresden, composed for the occasion *Il Colombo* in praise of the Genoese Christopher Columbus, its text written by the leading librettist of the day, Felice Romani. Bellini's contribution was *Bianca e Fernando*, a reworking of his 1826 *Bianca e Gernando*, with its original Domenico Gilardoni libretto revised by Romani. Rossini, who by this time was living in Paris, did not write a new work but allowed performances of two existing operas, *Il Barbiere di Siviglia* (1816) and *L'Assedio di Corinto*, an Italian translation of *Le Siège de Corinthe* (1826) which in turn had been a revision of *Maometto II* (1820).

In addition to his work with Morlacchi and Bellini, Felice Romani also provided the libretto for Donizetti's opera. This was *Alina, regina di Golconda*, sometimes called simply *La Regina di Golconda*. Romani was known to be dilatory, and Donizetti, who had collaborated with the librettist previously on *Chiara e Serafina* in 1822, was no more successful than most other composers in extracting a libretto from him speedily. Writing to his old teacher, Mayr, in February 1828, Donizetti complained, 'That Romani, who promises everything, keeps his word about nothing! I have written to him, but he doesn't answer. He chose the subject, and I am not very pleased with it.'

The subject had already been used for at least four operas, the earliest of which was Pierre-Alexandre Monsigny's *Aline, reine de Golconde*, staged in Paris in 1766, its libretto by Michel-Jean Sedaine.

Romani based his libretto for Donizetti on Sedaine's, which in turn had been derived from a story, *La Reine de Golconde* by Stanislas-Jean de Boufflers, published in Paris in 1761.

Donizetti arrived in Genoa at the end of February 1828. The Teatro Carlo Felice opened on 7 April with Bellini's opera, though the first music to be heard in the theatre that evening was by Donizetti: an *Inno reale* (Royal Hymn) for voices and orchestra which he had dashed off for the occasion, to a text by Romani. While in Genoa, Donizetti also composed a cabaletta ('Pietosa all' amor mio') to conclude the Maometto–Pamira duet in Act II of Rossini's *L'Assedio di Corinto*, which was performed during April. His cabaletta was so enthusiastically received by its audiences in Genoa that for some time thereafter it became an integral part of Rossini's opera.

Donizetti's own opera, *Alina, regina di Golconda*, did not reach the stage until 12 May, but at least it had the distinction of being the first completely new opera to be performed in the Teatro Carlo Felice. Though it was received warmly, Donizetti was by no means entirely happy with it. Because Romani had kept him waiting for the libretto, he had been forced to compose the opera in even greater haste than usual, and was left with no more than seven days in which to rehearse it. When *Alina* was staged the following year in Rome, Donizetti took the opportunity to revise it thoroughly.

Alina was successful enough to be performed in other Italian cities, and in due course was staged abroad in Madrid, Lisbon, Cagliari (Sardinia), Vienna, Nice, Barcelona and St Petersburg. It was revived in Rome as late as 1890, after which it was neglected until produced in Ravenna on 10 July 1987, with Daniela Dessi in the title-role, Rockwell Blake as Seide and Paolo Coni as Volmar, conducted by Antonello Allemandi. *Alina* has not yet been performed in Britain or America.

Golconda is a mythical realm in India whose Queen, Alina, is a young woman from Provence who, together with her friend Fiorina, had been kidnapped by pirates and brought to Golconda where she married the King who, soon afterwards, died. Alina is now being urged by the populace to stabilise the country by marrying again, and it seems likely that she will be forced to choose Seide, the handsome Vizier. However, a French warship arrives just in time with the new Ambassador, who turns out to be none other than Ernesto Volmar, the youth to whom Alina had been betrothed in Provence. (His aide Belfiore, coincidentally, is Fiorina's long-lost husband.) Alina submits Volmar to three tests to make sure he really loves her, a jealous Seide has Alina imprisoned, and the French led by Volmar attack the palace to free her. The opera, of course, ends happily for the two pairs of lovers, but not for Seide.

It is surprising that *Alina, regina di Golconda* should have had to wait until 1987 to be rediscovered, for it is one of the more attractive and briskly paced of Donizetti's earlier non- or semi-serious operas in his lighter, still somewhat Rossinian style. The cheerful, bustling overture is highly engaging and, though its score may display only intermittently the individuality of his later comic operas, *L'Elisir d'amore* and *Don Pasquale*, *Alina* is thoroughly enjoyable. It is an opera for the prima donna, and its heroine is able to charm the audience early in the piece with her *andantino* cavatina, 'Che val ricchezza e trono', and delightful *allegro moderato* cabaletta, 'Perchè non trovo'. Seide's graceful cavatina ('Se valor, rispeto e fede') and the entrance duet for the two French diplomats ('Bel paese, ciel ridente') with its exilarating stretta are other highlights of Act I whose finest number, however, is the exquisitely crafted quartet, 'Ho inteso, ho sentito', in which the two women, in disguise, confront their confused lovers. Seide's second aria ('Dunque invano mi lusingai') and cabaletta ('Vi leggo, o magnanimi') afford the tenor splendid opportunities to display his heroic style, and the large-scale dramatic finale to Act I is magnificent, especially its *largo* ensemble ('Tace sorpreso e attonito') which is launched by Alina after she has startled Seide with the information that she is already betrothed to Volmar.

In Act II, the scene in which Volmar awakens to find himself, as he thinks, in Provence – actually a Provence created by Alina – is delightful, and equally so is his duet with Alina ('Sei pur tu che ancor rivedo?'). It is in this opera that one begins to hear Donizetti's melodic gift most confidently freeing itself from Rossini to assert its individuality. The second pair of lovers, Fiorina and Belfiore, are allowed their reunion scene too, a comical counterpart to that of Alina and Volmar, containing a *buffo* aria ('Ah! un malanno a costei che mi ha svegliato') for Belfiore whose *parlando* phrases are matched more lyrically in the orchestra. The lengthy duet ('Io t'amo, Alina') in which Seide declares his love for the woman whom he has now taken prisoner, and in which she scornfully rejects his 'vile amor', possesses a dramatic weight which would not sound out of place in *Lucia di Lammermoor*, while the opera's finale, though formally conventional – a *larghetto* aria ('Se il valor vostro, o prodi') and *vivace* cabaletta ('Sull' ali dei sospiri') for the prima donna – is appropriately joyful. *Alina* is one of the most attractive of Donizetti's pre-*L'Elisir* comic, or at least not too serious, operas.

Gianni di Calais

opera semiseria in three acts

Principal characters:

Princess Metilde	(soprano)
Gianni di Calais, her husband	(tenor)
Duchess Adelina	(mezzo-soprano)
Rustano, a sailor	(baritone)
Ruggero	(bass)
The King	(bass)

LIBRETTO by Domenico Gilardoni

TIME: The past
PLACE: Portugal

FIRST PERFORMED at the Teatro del Fondo, Naples, 2 August 1828, with Adelaide Comelli-Rubini (Metilde); Giovanni Battista Rubini (Gianni); Maria Carraro (Adelina); Antonio Tamburini (Rustano); Filippo Tati (Ruggero); Michele Benedetti (The King)

A week after the première of *Alina, regina di Golconda,* Donizetti left Genoa to go to Rome where, on 1 June 1828, he married Virginia Vasselli. He and his bride then proceeded to Naples where they moved into an apartment not far from the Teatro San Carlo. Almost immediately Donizetti began work on his next opera, *Gianni di Calais,* which was staged in Naples at the Teatro del Fondo on 2 August 1828 with great success. It also did well in Milan two years later, and at the Théâtre-Italien in Paris in 1834, after which it fell into neglect. The opera has not been revived in modern times.

Based on the play *Jean de Calais* by Louis-Charles Caigniez, produced in Paris in 1810, Gilardoni's libretto tells the story of the Portuguese Princess Metilde who, when she was captured by pirates, was rescued by a sea-faring adventurer, Gianni of Calais, whom she subsequently married. Her attempt to have Gianni recognised by her father, the King of Portugal, is opposed by the courtier Ruggero who himself desires her. However, with the help of Rustano, Gianni's lieutenant, Metilde succeeds. The opera ends with the King acknowledging Gianni, Metilde and their son as his heirs.

Donizetti's score contains at least two attractive numbers, Rustano's 'Una barchetta in mar', a barcarolle in which he warns the elderly of the dangers of sea travel, and Gianni's Act II aria, 'Fasti? Pompe? Omaggi? Onori?' which Donizetti recycled twelve years later as Tonio's entrance aria in *La Figlia del regimento*, the Italian version of *La Fille du régiment*.

Il Giovedì grasso
(Carnival Thursday)

farsa in one act

Principal characters:

The Colonel	(bass)
Nina, his daughter	(soprano)
Teodoro	(tenor)
Sigismondo	(bass)
Camilla	(mezzo-soprano)
Stefanina, a maid	(soprano)
Ernesto Roustignac	(tenor)

LIBRETTO (probably) by Domenico Gilardoni

TIME: The seventeenth century
PLACE: A house in the country, outside Paris

FIRST PERFORMED at the Teatro del Fondo, Naples, in 1828 or early 1829, with Adelaide Comelli-Rubini (Nina); Maria Carraro (Camilla); Cecilia Grassi (Stefanina); Giovanni Battista Rubini (Ernesto); Luigi Lablache (Sigismondo); Giovanni Arrigotti (Teodoro); Giovanni Campagnoli (The Colonel)

It must have been immediately after the première of *Gianni di Calais* in August 1828 that Donizetti dashed off the one-act farce, *Il Giovedì grasso* (Carnival Thursday). The exact date of its première at the

Teatro del Fondo is not known, but it was probably during the late summer or autumn, for three of its principal roles were sung by Adelaide Comelli-Rubini, her husband Giovanni Battista Rubini, and Maria Carraro, all of whom appeared in *Gianni di Calais* at the same theatre. However, it may have been as late as February 1829.

The libretto is generally thought to be by Domenico Gilardoni, though a copy bearing the name of another of Donizetti's librettists, Andrea Leone Tottola, has been found. Whoever wrote the libretto, it is derived from *Le Nouveau Pourceaugnac*, a comedy by Eugène Scribe and Charles-Gaspard Delestre-Poirson, produced in Paris in 1817. The opera is set in the country outside Paris. Nina, the Colonel's daughter, loves Teodoro but her father has arranged for her to marry Ernesto, a wealthy country squire. Sigismondo and his wife Camilla, friends of Nina and sympathetic to her plight, attempt to trick the intended bridegroom by making use of a device from Molière's *Monsieur de Pourceaugnac* in which an unwanted suitor is outwitted. The plot misfires, but Ernesto graciously withdraws, persuading the Colonel to allow Nina to marry the man she loves.

Il Giovedì grasso, a farce with spoken dialogue separating the musical numbers, contains a comic role for the bass in Neapolitan dialect. Though one of the most entertaining of Donizetti's one-act comedies, it seems to have had few performances after its Naples première, and to have disappeared from the stage until it was revived in Siena in 1959, Bergamo in 1968, and Wexford in 1970. In 1971 it was performed in Milan by the Piccola Scala. *Il Giovedì grasso* has yet to be staged in Great Britain or the United States.

After twenty-seven bars of a graceful *larghetto* orchestral introduction, the curtain rises on the lovers Nina and Teodoro singing a plaintive duet of farewell, 'E sia vero, amato bene', which soon turns into a lively quintet as the plot to rescue them from their difficulties is hatched. Ernesto's entrance aria, 'Servi, gente', begins ploddingly but acquires charm as it quickens pace. The Colonel's aria ('Taci! Io voglio') which follows is routine stuff, but the trio ('Piano, piano') for Ernesto, Sigismondo and Camilla is full of melodic ideas, and the duet ('Che intesi quali accenti?') for Nina and Ernesto is delightful. Sigismondo's lively aria ('Mo' che discopierto avimmo') in Neapolitan dialect precedes the finale, a *maestoso* aria ('Or che l'amor da l'imene sperar') for Nina which leads into an *allegretto* to which Sigismondo and Ernesto each contribute a verse, and all combine to sing in praise of the season of carnival.

10

From *Il Paria* to *Ugo, Conte di Parigi*

Il Paria
(The Outcast)

opera seria in two acts

Principal characters:

Neala	(soprano)
Idamore, her lover	(tenor)
Zarete, his father	(bass)
Akebare, Neala's father	(bass)

LIBRETTO by Domenico Gilardoni

TIME: The distant past

PLACE: India

FIRST PERFORMED at the Teatro San Carlo, Naples, 12 January 1829, with Adelaide Tosi (Neala); Giovanni Battista Rubini (Idamore); Luigi Lablache (Zarete); Giovanni Campagnoli (Akebare)

In October 1828, only two months after the première of *Gianni di Calais*, Donizetti in a letter to his father mentioned that he was already at work on another opera, but that he did not yet know the date of the première, which he thought would probably be at the end of December. The opera was *Il Paria*, which he was still composing in December and which was not staged until early in the new year.

The first-night audience at the Teatro San Carlo received the opera with moderate enthusiasm, but the composer himself was not entirely happy with it. To his father he wrote, 'I have performed the opera, and was called out [to acknowledge applause], but I think I made a few mistakes in parts of the score, and I'll try to rectify this.' However, the occasion to do so never arose, for there were no further stagings of *Il Paria* after its initial six performances in Naples, and Donizetti withdrew his score which he later plundered for use in four operas: *Anna Bolena* (1830), *La Romanziera e l'uomo nero* (1831), *Torquato Tasso* (1833) and *Le Duc d'Albe* (1839). *Il Paria* has so far not benefited from the twentieth-century revival of interest in Donizetti.

Domenico Gilardoni's libretto is based on the tragedy, *Le Paria* by Casimir Delavigne, first performed in Paris in 1821, but Gilardoni no doubt used as a crib Gaetano Rossi's libretto (derived from the same source) for Carafa's opera, *Il Paria*, staged in Venice in 1826. Donizetti's opera is set in India, with a typically complicated and overwrought plot concerning Neala, the daughter of Akebare, High Priest of the Brahmins, who is in love with Idamore, the son of her father's enemy, the outcast Zarete. At the climax of the opera, as the lovers are about to marry, the fanatical Akebare orders the execution not only of Zarete and Idamore, but of his own daughter Neala as well. Neala and Idamore go to their death swearing that their love will survive, while Zarete dies, understandably cursing the Brahmins.

The score of *Il Paria* (now reposing in the library of the Naples Conservatorium) hardly deserves its total neglect, but its best numbers were to turn up in later Donizetti operas, and it is not a likely candidate for revival. From its introductory scene containing a two-part aria for Neala to its quartet-finale it maintains a reasonably consistent level of achievement.

Il Castello di Kenilworth
(Kenilworth Castle)

opera seria in three acts

Principal characters:
Elisabetta (Queen Elizabeth I)   (soprano)

Leicester	(tenor)
Amelia, Leicester's wife	(soprano)
Warney	(baritone)
Lambourne	(bass)

LIBRETTO by Andrea Leone Tottola

TIME: The late-sixteenth century

PLACE: In and near Kenilworth Castle, Warwickshire

FIRST PERFORMED at the Teatro San Carlo, Naples, 6 July 1829, with Adelaide Tosi (Elisabetta); Luigia Boccabadati-Gazzuoli (Amelia); Giovanni David (Leicester); Berardo Calvari Winter (Warney); Gennaro Ambrosini (Lambourne)

While he was at work on his next opera for the San Carlo, within weeks of the première of *Il Paria*, Donizetti became seriously ill with what he described to his father as 'convulsions, bilious attacks and internal haemorrhoids'. His medical treatment included 'bleedings, baths, purgatives', after which he suffered a relapse. This illness was probably the primary stage of the syphilis which was eventually to be the cause of his death. By the beginning of May, however, Donizetti seems to have recovered sufficiently to resume work on his opera, the date of whose première had to be postponed from 30 May 1829 to 6 July.

The opera was *Elisabetta al castello di Kenilworth* (Elizabeth at Kenilworth Castle), Donizetti's second encounter with a subject from English history. (*Alfredo il Grande*, six years earlier, had been his first.) Tottola's libretto can be traced back to Sir Walter Scott's novel, *Kenilworth*, which had been translated into Italian in 1821 within months of its initial publication, but it is most likely that Tottola's immediate source was a play, *Elisabetta al castello di Kenilworth* by Gaetano Barbieri, performed in 1824, and itself based on Eugène Scribe's libretto for the opera *Leicester, ou Le Château de Kenilworth*, staged in Paris in 1823. Scribe's source was, of course, the novel by Sir Walter Scott.

The première on 6 July 1829 was a royal gala in honour of Isabella Maria, the Queen of Naples, and audience enthusiasm was contained within bounds of decorum which were not normally observed at opera performances in Naples. A second performance on 12 July went better with, according to Donizetti in a letter to Mayr, 'the theatre crowded and the singers happy – I alone trembled.' The Queen was present again, this time with the King, and the audience also included the King and Queen of Sardinia and Piedmont, and Prince Leopoldo of Salerno. The performers, Donizetti told Mayr, were animated, the audience let itself go, and the result was continuous applause. 'But', said the composer to his old teacher, 'between you and me, I wouldn't give one number from *Il Paria* for the whole of *Il Castello di Kenilworth.*'

Critics having complained of the lack of vocal contrast between the two leading male roles of Leicester and Warney, both written for the tenor voice, for the opera's revival in Naples the following year (when its title formally became *Il Castello di Kenilworth*) Donizetti re-cast the role of Warney for baritone, and made some minor revisions. Apart from a production in Madrid in 1835, the work was not performed again anywhere until its revival in London by Opera Rara at the Collegiate Theatre on 29 March 1977 as part of the Camden Festival. The conductor was Alun Francis, and the cast included Janet Price as Elisabetta and Yvonne Kenny as Amelia. *Il Castello di Kenilworth* has yet to be performed in the United States.

The plot, concerning Leicester's attempts to keep his marriage a secret from the Queen, is a formalised and simplified version of that of Scott's novel, with the important exception that, whereas in the novel Leicester's wife, Amy Robsart, suffers neglect, insult and finally death at her husband's hands, in the opera a happy ending is achieved when Amy (now Amelia) is saved by Leicester from swallowing poison adminstered by Warney; and Queen Elizabeth, though she is in love with Leicester, behaves magnanimously to him and to Amelia. 'How fortunate is England', observes the chorus of courtiers, 'to have such a Queen, the splendour of the century.'

There is no overture. In Act I, Leicester's entrance aria ('Veggo, ahimè, l'ingenua sposa') and cabaletta ('Oh affetti tiranni') are no more than adequate, but Amelia's duet with Warney, 'Non mentir!', though in its florid passages it is not entirely free either of Rossini or of formula, possesses great dramatic energy, especially in its cabaletta, 'Ebben, de' tuoi rifiuti ti pentirai'. Elizabeth's aria ('Sì, miei figli') and cabaletta ('In estasi soave') are attractive. The opera's finest numbers, however, are to be found in Act II, in the forward movement of the duet, 'Dal genitor', for Leicester and Amelia, in the fascinating tension between words and music in Warney's aria, 'Taci, amor!', which speaks of ferocity but sings of tenderness, in the confrontation between Elizabeth and Amelia ('Perchè ti affanni, e piangi?') which prefigures the meeting of the rival queens in *Maria Stuarda*, and in the quartet finale which is arguably the most impressive number in the entire score.

Act III, which opens with a fine duet ('Ah! Sospira!') in which Elizabeth tricks Leicester into revealing that he is Amelia's husband, contains Amelia's aria, 'Par, che mi dica ancora', with its delicate harp and glass harmonica obbligato, and ends with a highly Rossinian aria ('Tu potesti un solo istante') and florid cabaletta ('È parga appien quest' alma') for the Queen.

Il Castello di Kenilworth is an opera which occasionally rises above the limitations imposed by its formulaic, uninspired libretto. Though hardly one of Donizetti's more successful works, it does at least reveal intermittent signs of its composer's emerging individuality.

I Pazzi per progetto
(Lunatics by Design)

farsa in one act

Principal characters:

Darlemont, director of an insane asylum	(bass)
Norina, his niece	(soprano)
Blinval, a Colonel married to Norina	(bass)
Cristina, a young French woman in love with Blinval	(mezzo-soprano)
Eustachio, a trumpeter in Blinval's regiment	(bass)
Venanzio, an old miser and Cristina's guardian	(bass)
Frank, a servant	(bass)

LIBRETTO by Domenico Gilardoni

TIME: The early-nineteenth century
PLACE: A lunatic asylum in Paris

FIRST PERFORMED at the Teatro del Fondo, Naples, 6 February 1830, with Luigia Boccabadati-Gazzuoli (Norina); Maria Carraro

(Cristina); Luigi Lablache (Darlemont); Gennaro Luzio
(Venanzio)

After the première of *Elisabetta al castello di Kenilworth* on 6 July 1829,
the year did not continue happily or productively for Donizetti. In
order to recuperate fully from the illness he had suffered in the
spring, he obtained a six-week leave of absence and departed for
Rome with his now pregnant wife Virginia. On 29 July Virginia
gave birth prematurely to a boy who lived for no more than two
weeks. It was not until the end of the year that Donizetti began work
on his next opera for Naples, a three-act *azione tragico-sacra* or sacred
tragedy, *Il Diluvio universale*, on the Old Testament subject of Noah
and the flood. He turned aside from this, however, to compose a
one-act farce, *I Pazzi per progetto* (Lunatics by Design), which was
performed at the Teatro del Fondo on Donizetti's benefit night, 6
February 1830. The theatre was only half full because a ball was
being given on the same evening by the Russian Minister, but the
farce 'went off very brilliantly', its composer told his father.

I Pazzi per progetto continued to be performed in Naples for a few
seasons, after which it was forgotten until revived at the Teatro dei
Differenti, Barga, on 8 September 1977, in a double-bill with
Donizetti's *Pigmalione*. There have since been productions in
Lucerne and Lugo di Romagna, both in 1988, and the opera was
given its American première at Mannes College, New York, in
March 1992. It has not yet been staged in Great Britain.

Gilardoni's libretto for *I Pazzi per progetto* was based on a play of
the same title by Giovanni Carlo di Cosenza, staged in Naples in
1824, which had also served as the basis of a libretto for *Una Visita
in Bedlam* by a composer named Bertini, performed in Naples in the
same year. The ultimate source was a comedy by Eugène Scribe
and Charles-Gaspard Delestre-Poirson, *Une Visite à Bedlam*, performed in Paris in 1818. The plot of Donizetti's farce, whose action
takes place in a lunatic asylum in Paris, is a mindlessly complicated
affair hardly worth unravelling. The director of the asylum is
Darlemont whose niece, Norina, pretends to be mad in order to test
the love of her husband, Blinval, a Colonel. He, in turn, pretends to
be mad for a similar reason. An old miser, Venanzio, wants to have
his ward, Cristina, declared insane so that he can get his hands on
her fortune. (Cristina, whose utterances are liberally sprinkled with
French words and phrases, is in love with Blinval, who has

apparently promised to marry her as soon as his wife is dead.) A trumpeter, Eustachio, who has deserted from Blinval's regiment, turns up at the asylum, posing, for no apparent reason, as a psychiatrist. By the end of the opera most of the characters have achieved a degree of happiness and have admitted – or perhaps pretended – to sanity.

An unusual feature of Donizetti's score – perhaps its only unusual feature – is that there is no tenor role: all five male parts (the four already mentioned, and Frank, a servant) are written for basses. Might this have been Donizetti's sly method of commenting on the standard of the Teatro del Fondo's tenors at the time? The plot of *I Pazzi per progetto* is, for the most part, carried on in sloppily written dialogue delivered in lengthy stretches of dull *recitativo secco*. The musical content, thin in terms of quantity, is uneven in quality. Norina's lyric coloratura has the chance to display itself in two arias, the affecting 'All' udir che il mio tesoro' (a tune first heard in Rossini's *Semiramide*) with which she introduces herself, and the charming aria ('Piacer si nuovo e grato') and sparkling cabaletta ('Donne care qui fra noi') which end the opera. Norina also precedes her jaunty duet with Blinval ('Ehi! sergente') with a graceful solo ('Tirsi lontan da Clori'), its contrabass obbligato played by Blinval. Eustachio's patter song ('Per me vi parlino') and a *buffo* duet ('Io son pazzo e non son pazzo') for Eustachio and Blinval are the kind of thing that Donizetti ought to have been able to write in his sleep, but the ensemble, 'Che figura graziosa', is a delight. All in all, *I Pazzi per progetto* is capable of making an innocuous and undemanding start to an operatic double-bill.

Il Diluvio universale
(The Great Flood)

azione tragica-sacra in three acts

Principal characters:

Noè (Noah)   (bass)
Sela, wife of Cadmo   (soprano)
Ada, Sela's servant   (mezzo-soprano)
Cadmo, Satrap of Senaar   (tenor)

Iafet		(bass)
Sem	sons of Noè	(tenor)
Cam		(bass)

LIBRETTO by Domenico Gilardoni

TIME: The period of the Biblical Great Flood
PLACE: Asia Minor

FIRST PERFORMED at the Teatro San Carlo, Naples, 28 February 1830, with Luigia Boccabadati-Gazzuoli (Sela); Maria Carraro (Ada); Luigi Lablache (Noè); Berardo Calvari Winter (Cadmo); Gennaro Ambrosini (Iafet); Giovanni Arrigotti (Sem); Lorenzo Salvi (Cam)

Having begun work on his next opera for the Teatro San Carlo at the end of 1829, Donizetti broke off to write the one-act farce *I Pazzi per progetto* in a hurry. After it was staged on 7 February 1830, he returned to the composition of *Il Diluvio universale*, which was to have its première during Lent. Described as an *azione tragica-sacra*, or tragic sacred play, the new opera told its own version of the biblical story of Noah and the flood. Gilardoni's libretto, written under Donizetti's guidance, was based primarily upon the tragedy *Il Diluvio* by Francesco Ringhini, first performed in Venice in 1788, though it also took some details from Lord Byron's play, *Heaven and Earth* (1822), and Thomas Moore's narrative poem, *Loves of the Angels* (1823). Donizetti had read not only Ringhini's play but also the two English authors in Italian translation, in order to shape a synopsis for his librettist Gilardoni to versify. 'This time', the composer told his father, 'I want to reveal myself as the inventor of the plan of the drama as well as the music.'

At its première on 28 February 1830, *Il Diluvio universale* was reasonably well received, except for the inadequate staging of the final scene, the great flood itself, which was greeted with derisive whistling. Performances continued to be given throughout the Lenten season, but the work was never revived in Naples. Donizetti took the opportunity to revise it extensively for its production at the Teatro Carlo Felice, Genoa, in January 1834, when it was given thirteen performances. It was produced in Paris in 1837, and then not staged again until 22 January 1985 when it was performed at the Teatro Margherita in Genoa, conducted by Jan Latham-

Koenig, with Bonaldo Giaiotti as Noè and Yasuko Hayashi as Sela.

Because they have built an ark to save themselves from the flood threatened by Jehovah, Noah and his sons and daughters-in-law – Noah's wife and the animals are missing from this version of the story – have incurred the enmity of Cadmo, Chief Satrap of the nearby city of Senaar. The action of the opera takes place at the site of the ark and in Cadmo's palace in Senaar. Cadmo's wife Sela, banished by her husband, takes refuge with Noah, and the Satraps led by Cadmo attack Noah who warns them of the coming flood. The wedding of Cadmo to Ada, Sela's handmaiden, is being celebrated when Sela rushes in, begging to be allowed to embrace her son. Cadmo offers to take her back if she renounces the God of Noah, and she reluctantly does so. As she utters a curse on Jehovah, there is a great clap of thunder and she falls dead. Many are drowned in the flood, but the ark is seen to float safely away.

Il Diluvio universale suffers by comparison with Rossini's *azione tragica-sacra* of 1818, *Mosè*, whose best features it attempts to emulate, not only in the solemn utterances of Noah but also in the opera's final tableau of the safely floating ark. But the contrast between Noah's devout family in their ark and the one-dimensional operatic hedonists in the city of Senaar is crudely presented. The introductory quintet with chorus, 'Dio di pietà', led by Noah, is a dignified piece, and Noah's solemn Act II prayer, 'Dio tremendo onnipossente', if not the equal of Moses' 'Dal tuo stellato soglio', is affecting in its context, and enhanced by its accompaniment of wind instruments and harp arpeggios. But the music given to Sela, Cadmo and Ada, though not unattractive, is conventional, and when Noah finds himself in duet with Sela ('Qual che del ciel su i cardini') he too becomes less individual. (His 'Si quell' arca nell' ira de' venti' in Act I, inappropriately jaunty in this context, was to find its proper home ten years later as the hoydenish heroine's 'Chacun le sait' in *La Fille du régiment*.)

Though they add little to the opera's dramatic content, Ada's Act II aria ('Ah, non tacermi in core') and cabaletta are entertaining examples of the bel canto style, and the ensemble, 'Gli empii'l circondano', sung by Noah and his family, is impressive. The finales to Acts I and II are engagingly energetic, Sela's last desperate plea to Cadmo ('Senza colpi mi scacciasi') is dramatically effective, and, though its effect will depend largely on the staging, the music of the final tableau is graphic. Much of the score of *Il Diluvio universale* may not be appropriate for its subject, but the work is at least as stageworthy as many another flawed piece of pre-*Anna Bolena* Donizetti.

Imelda de' Lambertazzi

opera seria in two acts

Principal characters:

Imelda	(soprano)
Lamberto, her brother	(tenor)
Orlando, their father	(tenor)
Bonifacio	(baritone)

LIBRETTO by Andrea Leone Tottola

TIME: The sixteenth century
PLACE: Bologna

FIRST PERFORMED at the Teatro San Carlo, Naples, 5 September 1830, with Antonietta Galzerani (Imelda); Berardo Calvari Winter (Lamberto); Giovanni Basadonna (Orlando); Antonio Tamburini (Bonifacio)

A month or two after the première of *Il Diluvio universale*, Donizetti began work on his next opera for the San Carlo, *Imelda de' Lambertazzi*, which he completed within a few weeks. Its première on 5 September 1830 was reasonably successful but only one further performance was given, three days later. The opera was revived for four performances in the following season and also given in Venice, but after being produced twice in Spain in 1840 and once in Senigallia in 1856 it disappeared until given a concert performance in Lugano on 19 February 1989. It has not been staged either in Great Britain or in the USA.

Tottola's libretto is based on the tragedy *Imelda* by Gabriele Sperduti, which was performed in Naples in 1825, and from which Tottola had already derived his libretto for the opera *Imelda* by Sgricci, staged in Naples in 1827. The ultimate source of Sperduti's play was Bombaci's *Historia dei fatti d'Antonio Lambertazzi* (Bologna, 1532). The story is similar to that of *Romeo and Juliet*, the warring families in this tale of sixteenth-century Bologna being those of

Lambertazzi (of the Ghibelline faction) and Geremei (supporters of the Guelphs). The lovers are Imelda Lambertazzi and Bonifacio Geremei, and Bonifacio's attempt to make peace with the Lambertazzis leads to tragedy. He is killed by Imelda's fanatical brother, Lamberto, with a sword dipped in poison, and Imelda dies after she has sucked the poison from Bonifacio's wound.

There is more of war than of love in Tottola's libretto and in Donizetti's score which, in its pace and energy, looks ahead to Verdi rather than back to Rossini. Could this sound have been too new, too raw, for Donizetti's audience in 1830? It is difficult to explain, otherwise, why *Imelda* achieved only two performances. From its brief orchestral introduction and its opening chorus to the finale in which, shunned by her father and brother, Imelda dies, the opera moves swiftly and with confidence. The opening scene contains a splendidly martial trio, 'Ah! s'oda lo squillo', for Lamberto, his father Orlando, and their henchman Ubaldo, and it is soon followed by Imelda's opening aria ('Amarti, e nel martoro fido serbarti il core') and cabaletta ('Ma il ciel non ode i miei lamenti') which immediately establish her as a strong musical personality, not unlike Verdi's Leonora in *Il Trovatore* of more than twenty years later.

Though Imelda is classified as a soprano role, the tessitura of her music is closer to that of a high mezzo-soprano. Her duets with Bonifacio ('Non sai qual periglio') and with Lamberto ('Geremei! Qual nome!') display a dramatic urgency which permeates the entire opera. In its confident simplicity and directness, *Imelda* has a good claim to be considered the finest of Donizetti's pre-*Anna Bolena* scores. The finale, though centred upon the prima donna, is no all-purpose florid aria and cabaletta, but a solo scene in which Imelda's dying words are set to music which is dramatically apt. *Imelda de' Lambertazzi*, last given a stage performance in 1856, is a work which opera companies would do well to consider.

Anna Bolena

opera seria in two acts

Principal characters:
Anna Bolena   (soprano)

Giovanna Seymour	(mezzo-soprano)
Smeton	(mezzo-soprano)
Lord Riccardo Percy	(tenor)
Enrico VIII	(bass)
Lord Rochefort	(bass)
Hervey	(tenor)

LIBRETTO by Felice Romani

TIME: 1536
PLACE: Windsor and London

FIRST PERFORMED at the Teatro Carcano, Milan, 26 December
1830, with Giuditta Pasta (Anna Bolena); Elisa Orlandi
(Giovanna Seymour); Enrichetta Laroche (Smeton); Giovanni
Battista Rubini (Riccardo Percy); Filippo Galli (Enrico VIII)

A few days after the two September 1830 performances of *Imelda de'*
Lambertazzi, Donizetti and Virginia left Naples. They stayed with
friends in Rome, and then Donizetti travelled on alone, his eventual
destination, after visits to Bologna and to his parents in Bergamo,
being Milan. His next opera was to be written for that city, not for
La Scala but for the Teatro Carcano, where a season of opera was
being mounted in competition with Italy's most prestigious theatre.
Donizetti's librettist was the famous Felice Romani who, this time,
did not behave in his usual dilatory manner but who produced his
libretto for the new opera, *Anna Bolena*, quite swiftly, delivering it to
the composer by 10 November. Donizetti went to stay with Giuditta
Pasta, the famous soprano who was to perform the title-role, and it
was in her villa at Blevi on Lake Como that he composed the opera,
no doubt profiting from the advice or at least obediently adopting
the suggestions of his prima donna. By 10 December he was back in
Milan, and rehearsals began.

At its première on 26 December 1830, *Anna Bolena* had a
resounding success, though Donizetti himself was not impressed by
the performance. 'I did not write to you after the first evening,' he
informed a friend on 3 January, 'because they could not have
performed my poor opera worse – which, even though it made some
effect and the audience called me out on stage, so infuriated me that
I did not want to appear.' But to his wife he wrote: 'I am pleased to
announce to you that the new opera by your beloved and famous

husband has had a reception that could not possibly be improved upon. Success, triumph, delirium – it seemed that the public had gone mad. Everyone says that they cannot remember ever having been present at such a triumph.'

During January Donizetti made some changes to the opera to strengthen its first act, and these were duly incorporated into the Milan performances. With *Anna Bolena*, his position was confirmed as one of the three leading Italian composers, together with Rossini (whose *Guillaume Tell*, which was to prove his last opera, had been staged the previous year) and Bellini (whose tragically early death was to occur five years later). *Anna Bolena* was soon being staged throughout Italy and, in due course, abroad. Its first performance outside Italy was at His Majesty's Theatre in the Haymarket, London, on 8 July 1831. In September of that year *Anna Bolena* became the first Donizetti opera to be heard in Paris, and in November 1839 it reached the United States when it was performed in New Orleans, in French. (The first New York performance, in 1843, was also in French.) In Europe, between 1831 and 1850, it was staged in at least twenty-five cities from Brussels to St Petersburg.

Anna Bolena was still being performed in Italy as late as 1881, when it was staged in Livorno, after which it suffered from the change of taste brought about by the advent of *verismo* in opera. It resurfaced in Barcelona in 1948 and in Bergamo in 1956. In 1957 it was produced at La Scala with Maria Callas (Anna), Giulietta Simionato (Giovanna Seymour) and Nicola Rossi-Lemeni (Enrico). The conductor was Gianandrea Gavazzeni. Since then, other famous Annas have included Leyla Gencer, memorable at Glyndebourne in 1965, Beverly Sills with the New York City Opera in 1973 (in the final part of a cycle of Donizetti's British history operas, in which she also sang Queen Elizabeth in *Roberto Devereux* in 1971, and the title-role in *Maria Stuarda* in 1972), Renata Scotto (Dallas, 1975) and Joan Sutherland, who came late but triumphantly to *Anna Bolena*, making her first appearance as Anna in Toronto (in May 1984), and singing the role also in San Francisco (1984), Chicago (1985), Houston (1986) and superbly at Covent Garden in 1988.

Romani based his libretto on two plays: Ippolito Pindemonte's *Enrico VIII*, performed in Turin in 1816 (a translation of *Henri VIII* by Marie-Joseph de Chénier, staged in Paris in 1791), and Alessandro Pepoli's *Anna Bolena*, performed in Venice in 1788. Tiring of his wife Anna (Anne Boleyn), Enrico (King Henry VIII) has turned his attentions upon her lady-in-waiting, Giovanna (Jane Seymour), who, though she feels remorse for her behaviour, cannot suppress her love for the King. Enrico summons back from exile Lord Riccardo Percy, a former lover of Anna to whom she was once betrothed, in order to be able to accuse Anna of infidelity. Smeton, a page, is in love with Anna, and circumstances conspire to provide Enrico with an excuse to have Anna, Percy and Smeton imprisoned, although all are innocent. Giovanna pleads with Enrico to pardon the Queen, but Anna, her brother Rochefort, and Percy are brought to trial, found guilty and condemned to death. Anna's mind wanders as she faces death, but she goes to her execution refusing to invoke vengeance upon the wicked couple responsible for her plight. She is taken to the executioner's block as the sounds of the populace acclaiming their new Queen are heard.

The overture is engaging enough, but hardly appropriate to what follows. Among the most effective numbers in Act I are Smeton's touching romanza, 'Deh! non voler costringere', interrupted by Anna's plangent cavatina, 'Come, innocente giovane', with its thoughtful, troubled cabaletta, 'Non v'ha squardo cui sia dato'; and the duet, 'Tutta in voi la luce mia', for Enrico and Giovanna, in which Donizetti employs the unusual device of having Giovanna repeat in the second section, to different words, a musical phrase she has sung in the first section, her feeling of guilt being used to connect the two parts of the duet. The quintet, 'Io sentii sulla mio mano', begun by Anna, was borrowed from *Otto mesi in due ore*, but is more impressive in this revision, in which it displays something of the dramatic impetus of the famous sextet in *Lucia di Lammermoor* (still five years away in the future). Some pieces, such as Percy's aria and cabaletta, and Smeton's cavatina in the third scene, are on a lower level of achievement, but the duet ('S'ei t'aborre, io t'amo ancora') for Anna and Percy advances the dramatic action, and the finale to Act I is magnificent, with Anna's cry of terror and outrage, 'Giudici! Ad Anna!' leading to an exciting stretta.

Act II contains not only such affecting and elegiac choruses as the introductory 'O! Dove mai ne andarono' and the choral contributions to the opera's final scene, but also a duet, 'Dio, che mi vedi in core', for Anna and Giovanna, in which the two rivals indulge in a dramatic exchange, much of it carried on in arioso or recitative, their voices not combining until the stretta. In some respects this duet scene anticipates the great confrontation between

Norma and Adalgisa in Bellini's *Norma* of the following year. The influence of the younger composer, on the other hand, is apparent in the mordant yet elegant melody with which Percy begins the fine trio, 'Fin dall' età più tenera', which ends in an exciting and florid stretta. Giovanna's aria, 'Per questa fiamma indomita', in which she pleads with the King to spare Anna's life, is affecting although not highly individual (and not effective, for Enrico's answer is an abrupt 'Stolta!' [fool]). Even when the chorus adds its collective voice to the gently persuasive tone of Giovanna's cabaletta, ('Ah! pensate'), Enrico remains obdurate. The spirit of Bellini hovers over Percy's exquisite aria, 'Vivi tu', with its brave cabaletta, 'Nel veder la tua costanza', but in the opera's finale Donizetti's individuality asserts itself. Anna's aria, 'Al dolce guidami castel natio', preceded by an arioso in which music associated with her happier days is recalled, is followed by her gentle 'Cielo, a' miei lunghi spasimi', whose debt to the opening strains of Sir Henry Bishop's 'Home, Sweet Home' (from his *Clari, or The Maid of Milan*, staged in London in 1823) has often been recognised. Donizetti embellishes the tune delicately, then swiftly moves on to an impassioned cabaletta, 'Coppia iniqua', in which Anna contrives both to inveigh against her accusers and to pardon them.

Anna Bolena represents both the culmination of Donizetti's earlier experience and the beginning of a highly productive period in which he would create a number of superb romantic tragedies, among them *Torquato Tasso*, *Lucrezia Borgia* and *Lucia di Lammermoor*.

Gianni di Parigi

opera comica in two acts

Principal characters:

Gianni di Parigi	(tenor)
La Principessa di Navarra	(soprano)
Oliviero, a page	(mezzo-soprano)
Pedrigo	(bass)
Il Siniscalco (The Steward)	(bass)

LIBRETTO by Felice Romani

TIME: The fourteenth century

PLACE: An inn in the country, outside Paris

FIRST PERFORMED at the Teatro alla Scala, Milan, 10 September 1839, with Antonietta Raineri-Marini (La Principessa di Navarra); Felicità Baillou-Hillaret (Oliviero); Lorenzo Salvi (Gianni); Agostino Rovere (Pedrigo); Ignazio Marini (Il Siniscalco)

On his return to Naples after the Milan première of *Anna Bolena*, Donizetti occupied himself with completing the composition of an opera, *Gianni di Parigi*, which had not been commissioned by any theatre but which he intended as a vehicle for the famous tenor Giovanni Battista Rubini, who had sung the role of Percy in *Anna Bolena*. Rubini, at this time in his mid-thirties and at the height of his career, was the most famous Italian tenor of his day, excelling in the operas of Rossini, Bellini and Donizetti. During 1831 he was to appear in the London and Paris productions of *Anna Bolena*, and it was Donizetti's hope that the tenor would also perform *Gianni di Parigi* in those cities. But it was not to be. Rubini appears not to have made any serious attempt to interest managements in the opera, which finally reached the stage in 1839 in Italy, at La Scala, without his participation, and indeed without Donizetti's permission. The score had somehow found its way into the hands of Bartolomeo Merelli, who had once written libretti for Donizetti but who had become the impresario of La Scala.

Recent research by a Swedish musicologist, Anders Wiklund, has suggested that parts of *Gianni di Parigi* may have been composed by Donizetti between 1828 and 1830 for a performance in Naples which failed to materialise. What is certain, however, is that the composer presented the opera to Rubini in 1831, and that Rubini did nothing with it. Eight years later, early in September 1839, Donizetti heard of the imminent première of *Gianni di Parigi*. He immediately wrote a letter of protest to Duke Carlo Visconti (who, as director of La Scala, was Merelli's employer), but to no avail. On 10 September the opera was performed, with Lorenzo Salvi in the role Donizetti had written for Rubini. Twelve performances were given during the season, after which *Gianni di Parigi* disappeared until it was revived at the Teatro San Carlo, Naples, in 1846. After that, it was not performed again until December 1985 when it was staged by a small opera company, the Vineyard Opera Shop, in New York, its score arranged for a reduced ensemble of piano, flute, clarinet and bassoon. In 1988 and 1991 it was produced at the Donizetti Festival in Bergamo.

Donizetti, probably without even consulting Felice Romani, had made use of a libretto which Romani had written for Francesco Morlacchi's opera of the same title, performed at La Scala in 1818 and subsequently in Naples (1820) and Rome (1826) as well as in cities abroad. Boieldieu's *Jean de Paris*, on the same subject, had been staged in Paris in 1812 and was still popular. The opera's extremely slight plot involves the Dauphin disguising himself as a commoner, Gianni di Parigi (Johnny of Paris), in order to make the acquaintance of the Princess of Navarre, his prearranged spouse, without her being aware of his real identity. The Princess sees through his disguise, but plays along with him until she is ready to reveal that she knows who he is. The opera ends with the royal couple happily agreeing to marry.

A full-scale overture makes the most of one or two elegant wisps of melody. After an introductory ensemble, Gianni makes his entrance with a cavatina ('Questo albergo, o locandiere') and cabaletta ('Tutto qui spiri gioia e allegria') which are a gift to any tenor with an agile voice and a lively personality. The cabaletta, transposed down a fifth, was to appear again, four years later, in *Don Pasquale*. The Princess's cavatina ('Ah, quanto e qual diletto') and cabaletta ('È pur dolce a propria stima') compensate in vocal virtuosity for what they lack in musical substance; a scene for Gianni and the two *buffo* basses, the innkeeper and the steward, trots along at a lively pace; and the Act I finale works up a fine momentum, with the Steward discomfited, the innkeeper terrified, Gianni composed, and the Princess enjoying herself.

Act II begins with an amusing duet, 'Eccellenza, se sapesse', for the two comic basses, and contains a suave aria ('Il mio destin') and engaging cabaletta ('Ah! Presso ad essere') for Gianni; a rather dull and unnecessary song ('Mira, o bela, il trovatore') for the page Oliviero, inserted presumably because the singer insisted on a solo; a quite beautiful romantic duet ('Nulla di più perfetto') for Gianni and the Princess; and of course a rondo finale ('Tutto vorrei presente') for the soprano to display her virtuoso technique. *Gianni di Parigi*, though no masterpiece, is a highly agreeable trifle which well deserves an occasional hearing.

Francesca di Foix

opera semiseria in one act

Principal characters:

Francesca	(soprano)
The King of France	(baritone)
The Count, Francesca's husband	(bass)
The Duke	(tenor)
Edmondo, a page	(mezzo-soprano)

LIBRETTO by Domenico Gilardoni

TIME: The middle ages
PLACE: France

FIRST PERFORMED at the Teatro San Carlo, Naples, 30 May 1831, with Luigia Boccabadati-Gazzuoli (Francesca); Marietta Gioia-Tamburini (Edmondo); Antonio Tamburini (The King); Giovanni Campagnoli (The Couı t); Lorenzo Bonfigli (The Duke)

After *Anna Bolena*, which had been given its première on 26 December 1830, Donizetti's next operas to be staged in Naples were two one-act pieces, *Francesca di Foix*, an *opera semiseria* which was performed at the San Carlo on 30 May 1831, and *La Romanziera e l'uomo nero*, a farce, staged some weeks later, on 18 June, at the Teatro del Fondo. Neither work made much impression on its audiences. *Francesca di Foix* disappeared immediately, and *La Romanziera*, after being produced in Palermo, followed *Francesca* into obscurity. Both operas were next performed, as a double-bill, by Opera Rara at the Collegiate Theatre, London, on 20 March 1982. So far, they have not been staged anywhere else.

Gilardoni's libretto for *Francesca di Foix* was based on an earlier libretto by Jean-Nicolas Bouilly and Emanuel Mercier-Dupaty for the opera *Françoise de Foix* by Henri-Montan Berton, staged in Paris in 1809. Though classified as *semiseria*, the plot is really that of a comedy. A jealous Count keeps his beautiful wife, Francesca, in seclusion, away from the court, and has spread the rumour that she is extremely ugly. At the instigation of the King of France, a certain

Duke manages to entice Francesca to court where she is presented under an assumed name. Her husband the Count is at first unwilling to acknowledge that the beautiful woman is the wife he has maligned, but when the King offers her hand in marriage to the winner of a tournament, he can control himself no longer. He confesses, and is rebuked for his excessive jealousy.

Though it serves its purpose well enough, the score of *Francesca di Foix* is disappointingly inconsequential when one considers that Donizetti composed it immediately after *Anna Bolena*. Francesca is given an attractive entrance aria, and the page Edmondo has a jaunty song, 'È una giovane straniera', but this is an opera which will be revived only very rarely.

La Romanziera e l'uomo nero
(The Lady Novelist and the Man in Black)

opera buffa in one act

Principal characters:

Antonina, a novelist	(soprano)
The Count, her father	(bass)
Carlino	(baritone)
Fedele	(bass)

LIBRETTO by Domenico Gilardoni

TIME: The nineteenth century
PLACE: France

FIRST PERFORMED at the Teatro del Fondo, Naples, 18 June 1831, with Luigia Boccabadati-Gazzuoli (Antonina); Antonio Tamburini (Carlino); Gennaro Luzio (Fedele); Gennaro Ambrosini (The Count)

La Romanziera e l'uomo nero, Donizetti's second opera in 1831, is another very slight piece of work. Its libretto by Gilardoni, which is lost, was probably based on the play *L'Homme noir* by Eugène Scribe and Jean-Henri Dupin, staged in Paris in 1820. From the seven musical numbers in the score it is clear that the plot was a satire on the newly fashionable literary genre of romanticism, with the opera's heroine a young woman set on becoming a romantic novelist. In her rondo finale she at last assures her father that she will give up the trappings of romanticism, and indulge in healthier pursuits such as dancing and going to the opera. The music, some of it borrowed from earlier Donizetti scores, is amiable but hardly memorable.

Fausta

opera seria in two acts

Principal characters:

Fausta	(soprano)
The Emperor Constantine (Costantino)	(baritone)
Crispo, his son	(tenor)
Massimiano, Fausta's father	(bass)
Irella	(mezzo-soprano)

LIBRETTO by Domenico Gilardoni (completed by Gaetano Donizetti)

TIME: 326 A.D.
PLACE: Rome

FIRST PERFORMED at the Teatro San Carlo, Naples, 12 January 1832, with Giuseppina Ronzi de Begnis (Fausta); Antonio Tamburini (Costantino); Giovanni Basadonna (Crispo); Giovanni Campagnoli (Massimiano)

In the spring of 1831, while Donizetti was busy composing his two one-act operas, *Francesca di Foix* and *La Romanziera e l'uomo nero*, the German composer Felix Mendelssohn arrived in Naples for a stay of several weeks. Contemptuous of Italian composers in general and of Donizetti in particular, Mendelssohn wrote: '... Donizetti finishes an opera in ten days. Of course it may be hissed, but that is no matter, as it is paid for just the same, and he can then go about enjoying himself ... but he sometimes spends as long as three weeks on an opera, taking considerable care with a couple of the arias, so that they will please the public and he can then afford to enjoy himself once again, and go back to writing rubbish.'

The last of the operas Donizetti composed during 1831 was *Fausta*, which he worked on in the autumn, and which was staged at the San Carlo on 12 January 1832. Domenico Gilardoni, his usual Naples librettist, died at the early age of thirty-three while at work on *Fausta* (whose provenance, probably an Italian play, is unknown), and Donizetti himself completed the libretto, possibly with help from Andrea Leone Tottola.

Fausta was a success at its première in Naples, and in December 1832 it was staged in Milan to open the carnival season at La Scala, where it was performed thirty-one times during the season. For these Milan performances Donizetti composed an overture, and later added other numbers to the score for the opera's production in 1833 in Venice, in 1834 in Turin, and for a revival at La Scala in 1841. *Fausta* was also staged in Madrid, Lisbon and Havana during the 1830s, and in Vienna in 1841. It was first performed in London on 29 May 1841, and was unfavourably received in Bergamo in 1843. After being revived again at La Scala in 1859, it disappeared from the world's stages until 27 November 1981 when it was produced at the Rome Opera with a cast headed by Raina Kabaivanska (Fausta), Renato Bruson (Costantino) and Giuseppe Giacomini (Crispo). Though it has not been staged since then, *Fausta* was given a concert performance during the 1987 Donizetti Festival in Bergamo. It has not yet been performed in the United States.

The tragic plot of *Fausta* is strong in dramatic situations. Fausta, married to the Emperor Constantine (Costantino), is in love with her stepson Crispo, who in turn is in love with Irella (called Beroe in early editions of the score), a Gallic princess whom he has captured in his war against the Gauls and brought to Rome. When Fausta confesses her feelings to Crispo he expresses his horror, at which she threatens to kill Irella if he does not accede to her desires. Pleading for the life of his beloved, Crispo falls on his knees before Fausta, at which point Costantino enters. Thinking quickly, Fausta tells her husband that his son is in the process of declaring his incestuous love for her, to which information the Emperor responds by condemning his son to exile. Fausta's father, the former Emperor Massimiano, is delighted at this turn of events, for he plans to murder both father and son in order to regain the throne. Later, attempting to foil

Massimiano and his fellow conspirators, Crispo attacks Costantino by mistake, and is arrested and condemned to death. Fausta attempts to persuade Crispo to flee with her, but again he rejects her. In despair, Fausta swallows poison, and Crispo is led away to execution. Costantino learns too late that his son was innocent of attempting to kill him, but at least has the satisfaction of ordering the execution of Massimiano. When Fausta, now dying, confesses all to Costantino, he orders her to be executed as well. She insists, however, on dying where she is and, as she breathes her last, the chorus informs her that she is the greatest monster the world has ever seen.

There is a reasonable degree of truth embedded in Gilardoni's overwrought libretto. In the year 310 A.D., Maximian, the father of Fausta, attempted to revolt and was put to death by Constantine the Great who, sixteen years later, had Fausta and Crispus, his son by his first wife, executed for adultery. It is in 326 A.D. that, according to the libretto, the action of the opera takes place, at a time when one of its principal characters had, as a matter of historical fact, been dead for sixteen years.

The score of *Fausta* is disappointingly uneven, and much of it is commonplace. The heroine herself, whose situation is not unlike that of Racine's Phèdre, is given some fine dramatic opportunities, but the characters of her husband, Costantino, and her stepson, Crispo, come to life only intermittently, and that of her father, Massimiano, not at all. After a nondescript overture, the introductory scene augurs well, for it is a large-scale affair containing an opening chorus, a prayer ('Dea, che siedi in terzo cielo') which is Fausta's opening utterance, a trio, and an extended reprise of the triumphal chorus. But even here some of the choral writing is singularly uninspired, and in the following scene (added to the opera in 1841 for a Milan revival, and thus the latest part of the score to be composed) there is little of interest beyond an oddly Verdian phrase – sung to the words 'Fausta non è colpevole' – in the duet ('Spinto da quella smania') for Costantino and Crispo.

That Fausta is a rewarding role for a first-rate dramatic coloratura soprano is first revealed by the cavatina, 'Ah! se d'amor potessi' (lifted from *Il Castello di Kenilworth*), which calls for a finely spun *legato* line – an aria for a Sutherland, a Gencer or a Caballé – and whose cabaletta, 'Fuggi l'immagine', is an effective piece of claptrap. But throughout the opera much of the accompanied recitative is ploddingly mundane. Fausta's Act I duet with Costantino is lacking in individuality, nor is her subsequent duet with Crispo, in which she attempts to seduce him, at all worthy of the strong dramatic situation. The Act I finale begins splendidly, but its stretta is pedestrian.

In Act II, Massimiano has a mechanically contrived solo ('Beato momento'), the aria for Crispo added to the score in Turin in 1834 is rather dull, and there is little of interest in the senate scene, though Costantino's quite conventional aria, 'T'amo ancora', is not unattractive. The duet for Fausta and Crispo, 'Per te rinunzio al soglio', which was added to the score for the Venice performances in 1833, is a sad, graceful piece, one of the opera's more impressive numbers, though its *allegro* conclusion is unsatisfactory. By far the best number is the solo finale for Fausta. Her cavatina, 'Tu che voli già spirto beato', with its emphatic cabaletta, 'No, qui morir degg'io', brings the opera to an applause-inducing end, and is much more compact than the otherwise not dissimilar finale of *Anna Bolena*. Given a really fine interpreter of the title-role, *Fausta* could prove enjoyable, though it is hardly one of Donizetti's more interesting or original scores.

Ugo, Conte di Parigi

opera seria in two acts

Principal characters:

Bianca, Princess of Aquitania	(soprano)
Adelia, her sister	(soprano)
Luigi V, King of France	(mezzo-soprano)
Emma, his mother	(soprano)
Ugo, Count of Paris	(tenor)
Folco di Angiò	(bass)

LIBRETTO by Felice Romani

TIME: The tenth century
PLACE: France

FIRST PERFORMED at the Teatro alla Scala, Milan, 13 March

1832, with Giuditta Pasta (Bianca); Giulia Grisi (Adelia); Clorinda Corradi-Pantanelli (Luigi V); Domenico Donzelli (Ugo); Vincenzo Negrini (Folco di Angiò)

Donizetti's next opera after *Fausta* had been commissioned by La Scala, Milan. Most of it was already written before the composer left Naples, but upon his arrival in Milan Donizetti discovered that the local censors had so mutilated the text of the new opera, *Ugo, Conte di Parigi*, that its librettist, Felice Romani, now refused to put his name to it. (Regicide was considered a politically undesirable subject for stage presentation, not only in Milan which was under Austrian rule, but also in the other kingdoms of a not then united Italy.) Last-minute revisions had to be made, which delayed the première until 13 March. The opera was received coldly, and withdrawn after no more than five performances. It achieved six further productions, in Pisa, Trieste (both in 1835), Prague (1837), Madrid (1839), Ferrara (1840) and Lisbon (1846), the *travesti* role of King Luigi V being sung in Madrid and Ferrara by a bass. After 1846, *Ugo, Conte di Parigi* was not performed again until it was recorded by Opera Rara in London in 1977. It still awaits its first twentieth-century stage performance.

The provenance of Romani's libretto, probably a French historical play, has not been traced. Later, Romani's text was to be used by another composer, Alberto Mazzucato, for his opera *Luigi V, Re di Francia*, staged in Milan in 1843. The action of Donizetti's opera, its occasional obscurity emphasised by the alterations demanded by the censors, takes place in Laon at the beginning of Luigi's reign, and revolves around the historical characters of Luigi (King Louis V, last of the Carolingian rulers of France), Ugo (Hugues Capet, who in 987 became the first of the Capetian Kings of France, a dynasty which was to last until the French Revolution), and Folco di Angiò (Foulques d'Anjou). The plot, shorn of much confusing and confused detail, is roughly as follows: Bianca (Blanche of Aquitaine) is betrothed to the young Luigi but is in love with Ugo who, alas, loves Bianca's sister, Adelia, who returns his love. Encouraged by the scheming Folco to suspect that Bianca and Ugo are lovers, Luigi has Ugo arrested, but later releases him. Folco tells Bianca of the imminent marriage of Ugo and Adelia. When Bianca declares she will find a way to destroy them both, Folco helpfully presents her with a poison ring. But Bianca swallows the poison herself after an encounter with Emma, the widowed mother of Luigi, who appears to be repenting a crime she committed five years previously (probably the murder of her husband: the libretto, as it now stands after mutilation by censorship, does not make this clear). The newly married couple and their attendants arrive, and Bianca tells Ugo how greatly she could have loved him but how much she now hates him. With her dying words she bequeathes to her sister both her hatred and her love ('Io, morendo, lascio a lei e quest'odio e questo amor').

Donizetti plundered some of his earlier operas in the composition of *Ugo, Conte di Parigi*, and after its failure he raided its score on several future occasions. Nevertheless *Ugo*, despite its untidy libretto, is an enjoyable opera in its own right. It is a highly melodious work, though the quality of that melody is not particularly individual, and its music never simply marks time but moves the drama forward at a brisk pace. Once past its sombre beginning, the overture (to be transferred, a year later, to *Parisina*) is deceptively light-hearted, and the opening scene gets the opera off to a lively start with a happy chorus ('No, che in ciel de' Carolingi') in praise of the new King, which Donizetti took from his 1830 opera, *Imelda de' Lambertazzi*, and which he was to use for the third time the following year in *Parisina*. Immediately after the chorus, Folco wastes no time on recitative but launches into 'Vanni voti!', with whose lilting tune he announces his villainous intentions. The vigorous final chorus of the introductory scene, 'L'orifiamma ondeggi al vento', bears a close resemblance to Warney's Act II cabaletta in *Il Castello di Kenilworth* of 1829. Bianca's Act I aria has a curiously introspective *andante* cabaletta, 'No, che infelice appieno'; the depth of Bianca's nastiness is first revealed in her duet, 'Io lo vidi', with her sister, Adelia. (Donizetti originally intended to call the opera *Bianca d'Aquitania*. Did he perhaps change his mind because he came to realise how unpleasant a character Bianca was?) Part of the Act I finale ('Quando fia sgombro e libero') was taken from the previous year's unsuccessful *Francesca di Foix*. This music was to be used yet again in *Il Furioso all'isola di San Domingo*.

The orchestral introduction to the opening scene of Act II had already been heard in *Imelda de' Lambertazzi*, its clarinet obbligato now given to the oboe. Like virtually every number in *Ugo*, the duet 'Tu lo sdegni?' for Ugo and Bianca has a brisk pace and good forward movement. It becomes an even livelier trio ('Io l'amai') with the entrance of Adelia, though there does come a point at which one

Donizetti stretta or cabaletta begins to sound very like another. Luigi's aria, 'Prova mi dai, lo sento', is graceful, and its cabaletta, 'Quanto mi costi', is equally charming. In the next scene, the orchestral introduction contains a phrase which will be familiar to many as the beginning of the hymn, 'Lead, kindly light', composed much later in the century. The phrase recurs in the accompaniment to Bianca's long recitative monologue in which she contemplates murder. Luigi's mother, Emma, is allowed a sorrowful duet with Bianca, 'Ah! tutto il mira!', in which the two women attempt to console each other, but Bianca then proceeds to her tragic solo finale, a scene truncated before the première by the composer, who deleted the first part of the *larghetto* but used it later in *Il Furioso all'isola di San Domingo*. The final section, 'Di che amor io t'abbaia amato', at the end of which the odious heroine drops dead, is identical with the final aria in *Fausta*, Donizetti's most recent opera, which had been given its first performance two months earlier in Naples but had not yet been heard in Milan. At the point where Bianca expires at the end of the opera, Donizetti drew a skull and crossbones in his score, adding the comment, 'Convulsione e morte', which perhaps suggests that his attitude to Bianca and her problems was not entirely serious.

11

From *L'Elisir d'amore*
to *Marino Faliero*

L'Elisir d'amore
(The Love Potion)

opera comica in two acts

Principal characters:

Adina	(soprano)
Nemorino	(tenor)
Belcore	(baritone)
Doctor Dulcamara	(bass)

LIBRETTO by Felice Romani

TIME: Early-nineteenth century
PLACE: An Italian village

FIRST PERFORMED at the Teatro della Canobbiana, Milan, 12 May 1832, with Sabina Heinefetter (Adina); Giambattista Genero (Nemorino); Henri-Bernard Dabadie (Belcore); Giuseppe Frezzolini (Dulcamara)

The four operas which Donizetti composed in 1831 immediately after *Anna Bolena*, the historical drama which made his name well-known outside Italy, were by and large disappointing. One of them, *Gianni di Parigi*, was not performed until several years later, two one-act pieces (*Francesca di Foix* and *La Romanziera e l'uomo nero*) came and went without leaving much trace, while the fourth, *Ugo, Conte di*

Parigi, was soon to disappear from the stage. But his next opera, which he wrote for the Teatro della Canobbiana in Milan, was Donizetti's comic masterpiece, *L'Elisir d'amore*.

The failure of *Ugo, Conte di Parigi* at its première at La Scala, Milan, in March 1832 did not deter Alessandro Lanari, the impresario of a rival Milanese theatre, the Canobbiana, from commissioning its composer to provide a comedy for the spring season at extremely short notice when another composer failed to deliver the opera he had promised. A contract was signed in mid-April, Felice Romani wrote a libretto within a week, and Donizetti composed the opera, *L'Elisir d'amore*, in no more than two weeks. After a few days' rehearsal, it opened at the Teatro della Canobbiana on 12 May 1832 to great and instantaneous success, even though, according to Romani's wife in her biography of the librettist, Donizetti had said to Romani, 'It bodes well that we have a German prima donna, a tenor who stammers, a *buffo* who has a voice like a goat, and a French bass who isn't up to much.'

The critic of the *Gazzetta privilegiata di Milano* wrote: 'The style of this score is lively, and brilliant. The shading from *buffo* to *serio* takes place with surprising gradations and the emotions are handled with musical passion. The orchestration is always brilliant and appropriate to the situation. It reveals a great master at work, accompanying a vocal line now lively, now brilliant, now impassioned.' The opinion of Johann Simon Mayr, Donizetti's old teacher, was that *L'Elisir d'amore* was 'inspired throughout with joy and happiness'.

The French composer Hector Berlioz, who was in Milan ten days after the première, left a sour description of the audience at the performance of *L'Elisir* which he attended: 'I found the theatre full of people talking in normal voices, with their backs to the stage. The singers, undeterred, gesticulated and yelled their lungs out in the strictest spirit of rivalry. At least I presumed they did, from their wide-open mouths; but the noise of the audience was such that no sound penetrated except the bass drum. People were gambling, eating supper in their boxes etc., etc. Consequently, perceiving it was useless to expect to hear anything of the score, which was then new to me, I left.'

After being given thirty-three performances during its initial season in Milan, *L'Elisir d'amore* was soon taken up by other Italian cities, and by opera houses abroad, throughout Europe and in the Americas, North Africa (Cairo, Alexandria and Algiers) and

Australia (Melbourne). Its first performance in England was given at the Lyceum Theatre, London, on 10 December 1836, and its first American performance in New York on 18 June 1838. It remains one of the most popular comic operas in the international repertory.

Romani based his *Elisir* text on the libretto written by Eugène Scribe for the opera, *Le Philtre*, by the French composer Daniel Auber, which had been produced in June of the previous year at the Paris Opéra (when Henri-Bernard Dabadie, who sang the role of Belcore in Donizetti's opera, had portrayed the same character, then named Jolicoeur). Scribe's plot had been taken from an Italian play, *Il filtro*, by Silvio Malaperta.

The action of Scribe's libretto for Auber takes place in the early nineteenth century, in a farming village in the Basque country. Though he Italianised the characters' names, with Térézine becoming Adina, Guillaume Nemorino, and Jolicoeur literally translated as Belcore, Romani seems not to have bothered to move the locale, which, however, should be assumed to be an Italian village. He did, however, humanise Scribe's farce by adding elements of tenderness which inspired Donizetti to compose some of his most attractive music.

Nemorino – his very name suggests a nobody – is a poor young farm labourer in love with Adina, a wealthy landowner who seems not to reciprocate his love. When he overhears Adina recounting to her companions a confused version of the story of Tristan, Isolde and their love potion, the gullible Nemorino allows an itinerant quack, Dr Dulcamara, to sell him an elixir (actually a cheap red wine) which, he is assured, will win Adina for him if he, Nemorino, partakes of it. But when Adina announces that she is about to marry the dashing Sergeant Belcore, Nemorino is persuaded by Dulcamara to purchase some more of the magic potion, which he is able to pay for only by allowing Belcore to enlist him in the army. Meanwhile, news of the death of Nemorino's rich uncle has reached the village. This makes his heir, Nemorino, suddenly popular with the village girls, a state of affairs which he attributes to the elixir. When Adina learns that Nemorino has enlisted in order to win her, she realises that she really loves him. All ends happily, even for Belcore who tells himself that there are plenty of other women in the world.

From the first high-spirited bars of its prelude to the end of its equally happy finale, there is hardly a dull moment in the

miraculous score of this most engaging of all comic operas which is
not only free of the mechanical plot manipulation of the majority of
Donizetti's earlier comedies and farces but also breaks free of the old
formal musical structures. The opening ensemble is interrupted by
Nemorino's charming cavatina, 'Quanto è bella', which is followed
not by a cabaletta but by Adina's cavatina, 'Della crudele Isotta', in
which she reads aloud, and derisively comments upon, the story of
Tristan and Isolde. A comical march brings on Sergeant Belcore
and his platoon. (At least, it is comical in intent in this context: when
it was first heard in *Alahor in Granata*, six years earlier, the march was
used to accompany some distinctly ungenial Moorish troops.)
Belcore's cavatina is not at all comical but surprisingly graceful,
though his pompousness – he is, after all, a stock comedy character,
as is Dr Dulcamara – is allowed to reveal itself in the lively ensemble
which follows. Adina rejects Nemorino very gently in their first
duet, 'Chiedi all'aura lusinghiera', in which the ostensibly illiterate
youth shows himself to be adept in the use of poetic metaphor.
Donizetti's melodic gift is profusely employed throughout the opera,
even in the *buffo* patter of Dulcamara's 'Udite, udite, o rustici',
introduced by solo trumpet, and in his delightful duet with
Nemorino, 'Voglio dire lo stupendo elisir', in which Dulcamara
passes off a bottle of cheap Bordeaux as Isolde's love potion. The
scene in which Adina discovers Nemorino imbibing his potion is
sheer delight, and their duet, 'Esulti pur la barbara', is quite
irresistible. The depth of feeling in Nemorino's 'Adina, credimi'
which launches the *larghetto* of the Act I finale is affecting: the opera
here is at its most seriously, and beautifully, romantic.

   The chorus, 'Cantiamo, facciam brindisi', gets Act II off to a
rollicking start. For the duet, 'Io son ricco e tu sei bella', which
Adina and Dulcamara sing at the party to celebrate her betrothal to
Belcore, and whose rather stilted tune will be heard again in the
opera's finale, Donizetti made use of a song he had already written,
his setting of a poem in Milanese dialect. Nemorino's duet with
Belcore contrasts and combines the yearning *legato* of the tenor's 'Ai
perigli della guerra' with the self-satisfied patter of the baritone's
'Del tamburo al suon vivace', while in her duet with Dulcamara
('Quanto amore!') Adina at last acknowledges that she loves
Nemorino, and her tone for the first time adopts that same air of
romantic yearning that has characterised the lovesick youth's
utterance throughout the opera.

L'Elisir d'amore is really the tenor's opera, and its great moment of pure sentiment comes with Nemorino's romanza, 'Una furtiva lagrima', a two-stanza aria of great beauty in which, preceded by an introduction on solo bassoon (not normally a romantic instrument), Nemorino pours out his love. This, the opera's most popular number and a *locus classicus* of the bel canto style, was inserted at Donizetti's insistence, Romani having complained that it would hold up the action. In the scene following Adina's touching 'Prendi, per me sei libero', all is resolved, and her joyous cabaletta, 'Il mio rigor dimentica', is followed by the brisk withdrawal of Belcore, and an equally brisk finale begun by Dulcamara to the tune of 'Io son ricco e tu sei bella' and rounded off by the assembled company.

Its masterly blend of sparkling gaiety and warm sentiment has made *L'Elisir d'amore* one of the most popular of operatic comedies. Its superiority to Donizetti's earlier comic operas lies not only in the wealth and quality of its melody but also in its musical characterisation. Though Belcore and Dulcamara are, in essence, figures from farcical stock, they have been given individuality by Donizetti and Romani. The opera's hero and heroine, too, are real characters, despite being placed in the milieu of a somewhat unreal plot. Is Adina's sudden realisation that she loves Nemorino really convincing? Will the marriage of the illiterate labourer to the cultivated lady farmer who reads about Tristan and Isolde be likely to endure? What a pity that Donizetti and Romani never collaborated on a sequel.

Sancia di Castiglia

opera seria in two acts

Principal characters:

Sancia	(soprano)
Garzia, her son	(mezzo-soprano)
Ircano	(bass)
Rodrigo	(tenor)

LIBRETTO by Pietro Salatino

TIME: The middle ages

PLACE: Castile, Spain

FIRST PERFORMED at the Teatro San Carlo, Naples, 4 November 1832, with Giuseppina Ronzi de Begnis (Sancia); Diomilla Santolini (Garzia); Giovanni Basadonna (Rodrigo); Luigi Lablache (Ircano)

Soon after the première of *L'Elisir d'amore*, Donizetti agreed to compose two more operas for Alessandro Lanari, one for production at the Teatro della Pergola in Florence and the other for La Fenice in Venice, both to have libretti by Romani. (But the Venice opera seems never to have been written.) In Rome, he signed another contract to write an opera for the Teatro Valle. He had already begun work on the Rome opera, *Il Furioso all'isola di San Domingo*, when he broke off to compose yet another opera, this time for the forthcoming season at the San Carlo in Naples. This was *Sancia di Castiglia*, its text provided by a Sicilian, Pietro Salatino, who was writing his first (and almost only) libretto, Romani having refused the assignment claiming that the fee offered was insufficient. Composed quickly in September and rehearsed during October, *Sancia di Castiglia* was given its first performance at the Teatro San Carlo on 4 November 1832 with, according to *La Rivista teatrale*, 'decided and fanatical success, repeated plaudits, and the composer and singers called out on to the stage by tumultuous acclamation.'

Donizetti himself was pleased with the performance and reception of his opera, but the work failed to hold the stage, and disappeared from view until it was revived in Bergamo at the Teatro Donizetti on 2 October 1984. There have been no subsequent productions, and *Sancia di Castiglia* has yet to be staged in Great Britain or the United States.

The provenance of the plot is not known. Writing to his brother-in-law Antonio Vasselli nine years after the première of *Sancia*, Donizetti casually referred to the opera as Bianca *di Castiglia*. This is either a slip of the pen – *Bianca d'Aquitania* was the title he had originally intended to give to *Ugo, Conte di Parigi* – or a clue. In 1835, a ballet, *Bianca di Castiglia*, was staged at La Scala. Perhaps its source, also not known, was the same as that of *Sancia di Castiglia*.

Salatino's dully written libretto tells the story of Sancia, Queen of Castile, whose husband, the King, has been killed in battle. Believing that their son, Garzia, has also been killed, Sancia plans to marry the Saracen prince, Ircano, against the advice of her minister, Rodrigo. When Garzia, having survived an assassination attempt instigated by Ircano, reappears to claim the throne, Ircano tells Sancia that he will marry her only if she administers poison to her son. In the opera's final scene, Garzia is about to drink from the poisoned goblet when a suddenly repentant Sancia snatches it from him and drains it herself. Ircano confesses that his interest was not in Sancia but in acquiring the throne for himself, while the dying Queen with her last breath pleads for her son's forgiveness.

Sancia di Castiglia is a throw-back to Donizetti's earlier *opera seria* style. Though no less stageworthy than some of those operas which have been successfully revived, it relies on a conventional formulaic structure, and on its composer's skill in the composition of arias and ensembles which have an immediate surface attractiveness but which are lacking in individuality. Neither Ircano's aria and cabaletta in the opening scene nor Sancia's in the scene which follows manages to rise above routine. The jaunty beginning of Sancia's duet with Rodrigo is attractive, likewise its moderato section, 'Cessa, Rodrigo, ah lasciami', part of whose material is borrowed from *Ugo, Conte di Parigi*. Music from that opera also makes an appearance in *Sancia*'s lively Act I finale. The opera's final scene, preceded by an elaborate orchestral introduction with clarinet solo, is by far its most enjoyable, with Sancia's aria ('Al figlio tuo') and cabaletta ('Il tuo perdona allora') making an affecting and effective conclusion to an opera which, though it is not one of its composer's more original creations, could surely still work on stage, given performers of sufficient calibre.

Il Furioso all'isola di San Domingo
(The Madman on the Island of San Domingo)

opera semiseria in three acts

Principal characters:

Eleonora	(soprano)
Marcella	(soprano)
Cardenio	(baritone)
Fernando	(tenor)

Bartolomeo   (bass)
Kaidamà   (bass)

LIBRETTO by Jacopo Ferretti

TIME: The sixteenth century
PLACE: An island in the West Indies

FIRST PERFORMED at the Teatro Valle, Rome, 2 January 1833, with Elisa Orlandi (Eleonora); Marianna Franceschini (Marcella); Giorgio Ronconi (Cardenio); Lorenzo Salvi (Fernando); Filippo Valentini (Bartolomeo); Ferdinando Lauretti (Kaidamà)

In September 1832, Donizetti was already at work on his opera for Rome, *Il Furioso all'isola di San Domingo*, when he broke off to write *Sancia di Castiglia* quickly for Naples. On 10 November, only a few days after the première of *Sancia*, he left Naples for Rome, taking with him his wife Virginia and his unfinished score of *Il Furioso*, whose composition he completed in Rome in time for rehearsals to begin in December. At its première on 2 January 1833 the opera was an immediate success, and during its composer's lifetime it was to be revived frequently in Rome, staged in at least seventy other Italian opera houses, and performed abroad in Vienna, Lisbon, Mexico City, Havana, Brussels, Constantinople (now Istanbul), Alexandria, Bucharest, Buenos Aires, Berlin, St Petersburg and several other cities. Its first London performance was at the Lyceum Theatre on 17 December 1836.

After a production in Trieste in 1889, *Il Furioso all'isola di San Domingo* was not seen again until its revival in 1958 in Siena, at the Teatro dei Rinnovati. Since then the opera has been performed in Spoleto (1967), Charleston, South Carolina (4 June 1978, its American première), New York (its first performance in that city, at the Helen Carey Playhouse in the Brooklyn Academy of Music, on 22 February 1979), Washington DC (1979), London (a concert performance, 1979), Philadelphia (1982) and Savona (1987).

Ferretti's libretto for *Il Furioso all'isola di San Domingo* is based on a play of the same title whose authorship is unknown, staged at the Teatro Valle in 1820. The ultimate derivation of both play and libretto is an episode in Part I (Chapters 23 to 27) of *Don Quixote* by Miguel Cervantes, published in Madrid in 1605. In the opera,

Cardenio, driven out of his senses by his wife's infidelity, has fled to the island of San Domingo in the West Indies, where he is looked after by Bartolomeo and his daughter Marcella whose black servant Kaidamà is terrified by the madman's behaviour. A shipwreck brings to the island Cardenio's wife Eleonora and his brother Fernando who have been searching for him. When Cardenio recognises Eleonora he first tries to stab her, and later rushes off to leap into the sea. He is rescued by his brother, but is still convinced that his sufferings can be eased only by death. Eleonora confesses her guilt, Cardenio hands her a pistol and tells her they will shoot each other, but when he sees Eleonora aiming the gun at herself he realises that she really loves him and forgives her.

After a brief orchestral introduction the opera begins, rather unusually, with a duet, 'Freme il mar lontan lontano', for Marcella and Bartolomeo, which imparts a certain amount of background information before discussing the behaviour of Cardenio. Kaidamà arrives fleeing in terror from the madman, and recounts his experience in a lively aria, 'Scelsi la via brevissima', with amused interjections from the assembled islanders. The noble, expressive melody of Cardenio's *andante* entrance aria, 'Raggio d'amor parea', establishes him as a sympathetic if not entirely rational character; its *allegro* cabaletta, 'A quale squillido ferale aspetto', is sung not by Cardenio who has rushed off in suicidal mood, but by everyone else.

Eleonora's turbulent cavatina, 'Ah lasciatemi, tiranni', Cardenio's eloquent, almost Verdian recitatives and his duet with Kaidamà ('Di begli occhi i lampi ardenti') are all lively and original. Fernando's aria and cabaletta are more conventional, but the finale to Act I is superb, especially its emotionally powerful *largo* sextet, 'Ah! un mar di lagrime', begun by Cardenio. The Act II Eleonora–Cardenio duet, 'Apri il ciglio', the chorus, 'Oh sciagura!', and Eleonora's final rondo are other fine numbers in a score which, though not consistently of the highest quality, can still prove extremely effective in performance. Parts of it, for example a cabaletta for Eleonora and Marcella, the beginning of the Act I finale, and the orchestral introduction to the Cardenio–Kaidamà duet, were taken from Donizetti's failure of the previous year, *Ugo, Conte di Parigi*.

Parisina

opera seria in three acts

Principal characters:

Parisina	(soprano)
Azzo, Lord of Ferrara, her husband	(baritone)
Ugo, her stepson	(tenor)
Ernesto, Azzo's Minister	(bass)

LIBRETTO by Felice Romani

TIME: 1425
PLACE: In and near Ferrara, Northern Italy

FIRST PERFORMED at the Teatro della Pergola, Florence, 17 March 1833, with Caroline Unger (Parisina); Domenico Cosselli (Azzo); Gilbert-Louis Duprez (Ugo); Carlo Porto (Ernesto)

Immediately after the première of *Il Furioso*, Donizetti left Rome for Florence with the intention of beginning work on *Parisina*, the first of the two operas he had promised the impresario Alessandro Lanari. An overworked Romani was extremely late with his libretto, but in due course it arrived and the composer set it to music with his customary celerity. At its première at the Teatro della Pergola on 17 March 1833 *Parisina* was warmly applauded, but it had opened so late that it could be performed only nine times before the season came to an end. When Lanari complained to Donizetti that this had involved him in financial loss, the composer's indignant reply was that Lanari ought to have addressed his comment to Romani, 'and not to Donizetti, who finished the opera for you in so very few days, who staged it, and who even corrected the printing of the libretto.'

Parisina was produced in other Italian theatres and in a number of cities abroad, among them Madrid, Paris, Dresden, Vienna, Budapest and Rio de Janeiro. It was first performed in London on 1 June 1838, and in New York on 22 October 1850. (On 4 June 1837, at the St Charles Theatre in New Orleans, it had become the first opera by Donizetti to be staged in the United States.) By the end of the nineteenth century, however, it had ceased to be staged until it was revived in Siena at the Teatro dei Rinnovati, on 17 September

1964, in a production which was seen the following year in Bologna and Parma. Since then *Parisina* has been performed in Bergamo (1972), New York (a concert performance in Carnegie Hall, with Montserrat Caballé in the title-role, in 1974), Nice and Barcelona (both in 1977, again with Caballé), Basle (1988), and in its original home, the Teatro della Pergola, Florence, in 1990. (Most of these modern productions called the opera *Parisina d'Este*, perhaps to distinguish it from Mascagni's *Parisina*, an unsuccessful work of 1913 with a libretto by Gabriele D'Annunzio.)

Romani's libretto was based on Lord Byron's poem, *Parisina* (1816), which describes the illicit love of Parisina and her husband's natural son, Hugo. The action of Byron's poem, taken from Gibbon's *Antiquities of the House of Brunswick*, is founded on fact, occurring in the life of Niccola III of Ferrara who had the lovers beheaded. Romani's libretto legitimises Hugo (Ugo), making him Azzo's son by an earlier marriage. Already suspecting that his wife and Ugo love each other, Azzo hears Parisina murmur Ugo's name in her sleep, and swears vengeance. It is only after he has condemned Ugo to death that Azzo discovers the young man to be his son. Nevertheless he allows the sentence to stand. Ugo is executed and Parisina immediately dies of grief.

For some years, *Parisina* remained Donizetti's own favourite among his operas, and it is indeed one of the more impressive of his pre-*Lucia di Lammermoor* serious operas. After an overture, lifted intact from the previous year's *Ugo, Conte di Parigi*, the opening scene introduces the leading male characters with a romantic aria ('Per veder su quel bel viso') and belligerent cabaletta ('Dall' Eridano si stende') for Azzo, and an attractive duet ('Io l'amai') for Ugo and Ernesto, Azzo's Minister whom Ugo looks upon as his father. The beginning of Azzo's cabaletta makes use of a theme from *Ugo, Conte di Parigi*, whose score was further raided elsewhere in *Parisina* for a few bars here, a few bars there. In the second scene, Parisina's opening cavatina, 'Forse un destin', exudes a certain melancholy which persists even in her cabalatta, 'V'era un dì', and in her exquisite love duet with Ugo, 'Dillo, ah dillo tel chieggo in merito', with its elegantly sad cabaletta, 'Quando più grave'.

The Act I finale begins well but becomes somewhat diffuse, and is redeemed by its lively stretta. Among the highlights of Act II is Parisina's delicate *larghetto* aria, 'Sogno talor di correre', followed not by a cabaletta but by a theatrically effective scene in which Azzo hears his wife murmuring Ugo's name in her sleep. Their subsequent duet of confrontation ('Tu, signore?') has a fine quasi-Verdian dramatic energy, firmly sustained in the stretta, 'Non pentirti'. Ugo's *larghetto* cavatina, 'Io sentii tremar la mano', is dull, but its jaunty cabaletta, 'Quest' amor', at least allows the tenor to display his high C and even a D flat. In the Act II finale which takes the form of a quartet for the four principals, the *larghetto* section ('Per sempre') launched by Parisina builds into an impressive and affecting ensemble. The brief third act consists of an imposing chorus and a double aria for Parisina, its sorrowful yet elegant *andante* ('Ciel, sei tu che in tal momento') followed, when Parisina is shown Ugo's corpse, by a highly dramatic cabaletta, 'Ugo! è spento'.

Torquato Tasso

opera semiseria in three acts

Principal characters:

Torquato Tasso	(baritone)
Eleonora d'Este	(soprano)
Eleonora di Scandiano	(mezzo-soprano)
Roberto	(tenor)
Don Gherardo	(bass)

LIBRETTO by Jacopo Ferretti

TIME: The sixteenth century
PLACE: Ferrara, Northern Italy

FIRST PERFORMED at the Teatro Valle, Rome, 9 September 1833, with Adelina Spech (Eleonora d'Este); Angiolina Carocci (Eleonora di Scandiano); Giorgio Ronconi (Torquato Tasso); Antonio Poggi (Roberto); Ferdinando Lauretti (Don Gherardo)

After the first performances of *Parisina* in Florence, Donizetti made his way to Rome to discuss terms for an opera he had, in principle, agreed to write for the Teatro Valle. By early June a contract had been signed, and the composer, with his Rome librettist Jacopo

Ferretti, was at work on an opera based on incidents in the life of the sixteenth-century Italian poet, Torquato Tasso. For years, Donizetti had wanted to compose an opera about Tasso, and now, he told Simone Mayr, 'I am forming a plan, and from that an opera.' Although composer and librettist indulged in a great deal of background reading about their subject – among the authors Donizetti mentions to Mayr are Goethe, Goldoni (both of whom wrote plays about Tasso), Giovanni Rosini, Antonio Serassi and Alexandre Duval – Ferretti's libretto, which also incorporated actual lines from Tasso, was not derived from any one play or book. Rosini's *Torquato Tasso* (1832), Carlo Goldoni's *Tasso* (1755), Byron's poem *The Lament of Tasso* (1817) and Goethe's *Tasso* (published in 1790 but not performed until 1809) were all drawn upon.

Beginning work on the score early in June, Donizetti had completed *Torquato Tasso* by 11 July, which was rather more time than he normally spent composing an opera. At the end of his score he wrote a dedication which refers to Tasso: 'To Bergamo, Sorrento and Rome – the city that conceived him, the one in which he saw the light, and the one that has his body.' Rehearsals began on August 22, and on 9 September 1833 *Torquato Tasso* was given its première in Rome at the Teatro Valle.

The opera was liked well enough for more than fifteen performances to be given during a period of three weeks, after which it was revived in Rome every few years until quite late in the century. It was produced in more than a score of other Italian cities, and abroad in several countries from Ireland (Dublin) to Turkey (Smyrna now called Izmir). The first London performance was on 3 March 1840, but although it was staged in Santiago, Cuba (1841), Rio de Janeiro (1843), Montevideo (1855) and Buenos Aires (1857), *Torquato Tasso* has not yet reached North America. It disappeared from the stage after 1881 until performed by Opera Rara at the Collegiate Theatre, London, on 27 February 1974 (and again in 1975). A production mounted in Savona was performed there and in other Northern Italian towns during the 1985–1986 season, and the opera was staged at the Opera House in Buxton, Derbyshire, as part of the 1988 Buxton Festival.

Torquato Tasso (1544–1595) was born in Sorrento and educated by the Jesuits in Naples. He later studied law and philosophy in Padua. At the age of twenty-one he went to Ferrara to serve the Este family, and there began to write his masterpiece, *Gerusalemme liberata*

(Jerusalem Liberated). Some years later his mental health began seriously to decline, and in 1579 the Duke of Ferrara had him placed in an asylum where he remained for seven years. The quality of Tasso's writing during his incarceration led writers such as Goethe to see him as the victim of a forbidden attachment to the Duke's sister. After his release, though in poor health, he continued to write. Pope Clement VIII planned to honour him, but Tasso died before the ceremony could take place.

In Ferretti's libretto, Tasso is characterised as a poet sick with love. He has two rivals at the Ferrarese court: Roberto, the Duke's secretary, who is simply envious of Tasso's fame, and Don Gherardo who believes that Tasso loves Eleonora di Scandiano, the woman with whom Gherardo himself is in love. However, the object of Tasso's affections is another Eleonora, sister of the Duke. Through the machinations of Gherardo and Roberto, the Duke is led to spy on Tasso as the poet is in the act of urging Eleonora to flee with him. Declaring that Tasso has taken leave of his senses, the Duke has the poet committed to an asylum.

The opera's last act takes place seven years later in Tasso's cell in the asylum. Courtiers arrive to announce that he is to be set free and is to be crowned Poet Laureate in Rome. When Tasso declares he will fly to Eleonora's side, he is informed that she is no longer living, and is urged to turn his thoughts to his future glory. The curtain falls on Tasso contemplating the honour that is to be bestowed upon him, while the courtiers exclaim that at last his barbarous destiny has changed for the better.

Torquato Tasso is an odd work in its blend of comic and serious elements which ultimately fail to cohere. Donizetti's attempt to write a serious role, that of Don Gherardo, for the Teatro Valle's *buffo* bass is unsuccessful, and Ferretti's patchwork libretto, frequently bogged down in insignificant detail, does not help matters. The opera's uncertainty of tone is apparent from the very beginning. There is no overture, merely a few bars of the kind of music one might expect from Sergeant Belcore's platoon in *L'Elisir d'amore*, after which the curtain rises on a chorus of courtiers describing, in all-purpose melodic phrases, the bitter and jealous Gherardo who, when he appears, is frustrated by being made to utter serious dramatic statements in the musical language of conventional comic opera.

Stretches of *recitativo secco*, which Donizetti had not used for some time, add to the opera's confusion about its genre. It contains some pleasing numbers, for instance the tenor's Act I double aria, but even here one finds murderous sentiments and blithe expression of them at odds with one another. Tasso's opening arioso ('Alma dell' alma mia'), repeating a yearning violin phrase from its orchestral introduction, falls pleasantly on the ear, and Eleonora's aria ('Io l'udia ne' suoi bei carmi'), in which she muses upon Tasso's beautiful poetry, is equally attractive. The duet, 'Colei Sofronia', in which the poet reads to Eleonora from Canto II of his *Gerusalemme liberata*, is unusual and can prove immensely effective in performance. Eleonora's melody is taken from the beginning of the final quartet in *Il Paria* (which Donizetti had composed four years previously).

Act II is disappointing until its concerted finale which also utilises material from the final quartet of *Il Paria*, but the brief third act (which is sometimes described, not very accurately, as a 'mad scene' for baritone) is both interesting and immensely enjoyable. It consists entirely of an aria with cabaletta for Tasso (his only solo aria in the entire work), interrupted by the chorus of courtiers. After an orchestral introduction, Tasso begins his moving recitative and aria ('Perchè dell' aure in sen') with colourful flute solo. The courtiers arrive to tell him of his release and impending honour, greeting him with a reminiscence of the Act I prelude, and Tasso reacts in a troubled cabaletta ('Parlera'). The opera ends on a note of incautious optimism. This final act survived *Torquato Tasso* for some years as a concert item for baritones. The English baritone Sir Charles Santley is known to have sung it, and Mattia Battistini was still doing so as late as 1925 when he was in his seventieth year.

Lucrezia Borgia

opera seria in a prologue and two acts

Principal characters:

Lucrezia Borgia, Duchess of Ferrara	(soprano)
Maffio Orsini, a young nobleman	(mezzo-soprano)
Gennaro, a young soldier	(tenor)
Don Alfonso, Duke of Ferrara	(bass)

LIBRETTO by Felice Romani

TIME: The early-sixteenth century
PLACE: Venice and Ferrara

FIRST PERFORMED at the Teatro alla Scala, Milan, 26 December 1833, with Henriette Méric-Lalande (Lucrezia); Marietta Brambilla (Maffio Orsini); Francesco Pedrazzi (Gennaro); Luciano Mariani (Alfonso)

After the third performance of *Torquato Tasso*, Donizetti left Rome for Milan where *Il Furioso all'isola di San Domingo* was to be staged at La Scala. The first performance there on 1 October 1833 of this opera which Roman audiences had received warmly at its première at the beginning of the year was a huge success, and a further thirty-five performances were given at La Scala during the season. In October its composer signed a contract to write two new operas for La Scala, the first of which he was to embark upon almost immediately.

Felice Romani had been at work for at least several weeks on a libretto based on Victor Hugo's play, *Lucrèce Borgia* (first staged in Paris earlier in the year), but had put it aside to work on a text about the ancient Greek poetess Sappho for an opera by Mercadante. When La Scala's prima donna, Henriette Méric-Lalande, announced her disapproval of Sappho as a subject, the impresario of La Scala, Duke Carlo Visconti, turned to Donizetti, who agreed to compose two operas, the first of which would be *Lucrezia Borgia*, its libretto by Felice Romani. Somewhat confused by the train of events, Romani wrote to Visconti asking, in effect, what he was supposed to be writing and for whom. Given the assurances he required, Romani completed his *Lucrezia Borgia* libretto by the end of November, and Donizetti, composing at his usual manic pace, finished the opera in time for it to be rehearsed and to open at La Scala on 26 December 1833.

Though its critical reception was mixed – the *Gazzetta privilegiata di Milano* summed up the new score as 'little better than mediocre' – *Lucrezia Borgia* proved popular with audiences, was performed at La Scala thirty-three times during the season, and was soon being produced throughout Italy and abroad. When the opera was staged in Paris in 1840, Victor Hugo, author of the play on which Romani's libretto had been based, objected not to the performance of the opera itself but to the French translation which he considered plagiarised his play. He won his suit against the translator and his publisher, as a result of which the opera was subsequently performed in France with changes to its plot and characters. In Versailles in 1842 it was *Nizza de Grenade*, and when it returned to Paris in 1845 it was as *La Rinnegata*. To appease various Italian censorship authorities, the opera was called *Eustorgia da Romano* in Florence, *Alfonso, Duca di Ferrara* in Trieste, *Giovanna I di Napoli* in Ferrara, and *Elisa da Fosco* in Rome.

The first performance of *Lucrezia Borgia* in London was given at Her Majesty's Theatre on 6 June 1839. Its first American performance took place in New Orleans on 11 May 1843, and on 25 November 1844 the opera reached New York. Its fame was such that it was staged not only in the usual European and American operatic centres but also further afield in, for example, Christiana, Sydney, Bogotá, Tiflis and Cape Town. Though performances in the first half of the twentieth century were rare outside Italy. *Lucrezia Borgia* has never completely disappeared from the repertoire. Famous interpreters of the title-role in recent years have included Montserrat Caballé (concert performances in London and New York, stage productions in Marseilles, Philadelphia, Milan and Barcelona), Leyla Gencer (in Naples, Rome, Bergamo, Dallas and Florence), Beverly Sills (in New York), Katia Ricciarelli (in Florence), and Joan Sutherland (in Vancouver, Houston, and in 1980 in London where *Lucrezia Borgia* had not been staged since 1888).

The action of the opera takes place in Venice and Ferrara in the early sixteenth century. The interest shown by Lucrezia Borgia in a youth named Gennaro is misunderstood by her husband, Duke Alfonso, who suspects that she is having an affair with him. Actually Gennaro is Lucrezia's son whose identity is known only to her. When Gennaro is arrested on Alfonso's orders for having insulted the Borgia family, Lucrezia arranges his escape. Later, at a banquet, Lucrezia poisons a number of her enemies, and is shocked when she finds that Gennaro was among them. He refuses the antidote she offers him, because the amount is insufficient to save the lives of his companions as well, and is horrified when she confesses she is his mother. Gennaro dies, and Lucrezia, distraught, also collapses and dies.

A drum-roll precedes a brief, sombre orchestral introduction leading into a scene of festivity, which Verdi (who saw the opera when he was a twenty-year-old music student in Milan) must have remembered when he came to compose the opening scene of *Rigoletto* eighteen years later. Much more than in any earlier serious opera by Donizetti, the drama is impelled forward by the music. Orsini's romanza, 'Nella fatal di Rimini', is a dramatic narrative in which the youth describes how he and his friend Gennaro had once encountered an old man dressed in black, clearly the personification of death, who had warned them to keep their distance from the Borgias. In this scene, and throughout the opera, male voices predominate, even the chorus usually consisting either of male revellers or spies in the employ of Lucrezia's husband, with only the young Orsini (mezzo-soprano) and the soprano voice of Lucrezia as contrast. Lucrezia's exquisite *larghetto* romanza, 'Com' è bello', is followed by her duet with Gennaro, embedded in which is Gennaro's solo, 'Di pescatore ignobile', with its popular Neapolitan flavouring. The *moderato* section of the duet, 'Ama tua madre', leads into the exciting finale of the Prologue in which Lucrezia is denounced by Gennaro's companions, one by one, not unlike the Act I finale of *Don Giovanni*.

In Act I, Alfonso's cavatina ('Vieni, la mia vendetta') and cabaletta ('Qualunque sia l'evento') both have a positively Verdian energy, as does the jauntily conspiratorial chorus of the Duke's henchmen. The remainder of the act is musically thin, though the duet stretta ('Infelice!') of the finale which had begun as a trio is lively in its conventional way. The brief opening scene of Act II consists of an awkwardly shaped duet ('Minacciata è la mia vita') for Orsini and Gennaro which never manages to get into its stride, sandwiched between two quite attractive conspiratorial choruses. The opera's final scene begins in unconvincing concerted jollity, relieved by Orsini's cheerful song, 'Il segreto per esser felici', the opera's most famous number and one widely performed out of its context. Orsini's two strophes are separated by the distant tolling of a bell and a solemn chorus warning of the transitory nature of happiness. This is the beginning of the end for the revellers, who have been poisoned by the wine whose praises they were singing. Lucrezia's *largo* aria, 'M'odi, ah m'odi', is a superb piece of writing, its vocal *fioriture* dramatically expressive.

At the Milan première, after Gennaro died Henriette Méric-Lalande as Lucrezia launched into a bravura cabaletta, 'Era desso il figlio mio', which the singer had inisted upon, and which Donizetti dutifully provided for her. To Méric-Lalande it was inconceivable that an opera might end any other way than with a brilliant cabaletta for the soprano. Seven years later, however, for a revival at La Scala, Donizetti revised the finale, deleting Lucrezia's cabaletta and adding a moving arioso, 'Madre, se ognor lontano', for the dying Gennaro. It is this 1840 version of the finale which is most commonly used in modern performances, though Joan Sutherland, both in the opera house and on a recording of the opera, has demonstrated that the cabaletta, 'Era desso il figlio mio', can be highly effective when performed by a great dramatic coloratura soprano. Indeed *Lucrezia Borgia*, though uneven, is an opera which succeeds in the theatre whenever it is given performers of sufficient stature.

Rosmonda d'Inghilterra

opera seria in two acts

Principal characters:

Rosmonda Clifford   (soprano)
Leonora   (soprano)
Arturo, a page   (mezzo-soprano)
Enrico II   (tenor)
Clifford   (bass)

LIBRETTO by Felice Romani

TIME: The second half of the twelfth century
PLACE: In and near Woodstock Castle, Oxfordshire

FIRST PERFORMED at the Teatro della Pergola, Florence, 27 February 1834, with Fanny Tacchinardi-Persiani (Rosmonda); Anna del Serre (Leonora); Giuseppina Merola (Arturo); Gilbert-Louis Duprez (Enrico II); Carlo Porto (Clifford)

Leaving Milan at the end of December 1833 after the première of *Lucrezia Borgia*, Donizetti proceeded first to Turin to supervise a staging of his *Fausta*, then to Genoa to visit his nephew, Andrea, who was studying law there, and finally to Florence to fulfil his obligation to write an opera for performance at the Teatro della Pergola. This was *Rosmonda d'Inghilterra*, Rosmonda being Rosamond Clifford who may have been the mistress of Henry II of England. The libretto by Felice Romani had originally been written for Carlo Coccia's opera of the same title, performed in Venice in 1829. Romani made some changes to it at Donizetti's request, and the work was composed at Donizetti's usual speed.

At its première on 27 February 1834, *Rosmonda d'Inghilterra* was liked well enough, but seems to have had only two other stagings: in Naples in 1837, partly revised, as *Eleanora di Gujenna*, and in Livorno in 1846, after which it was not heard again until given a concert performance by Opera Rara at the Queen Elizabeth Hall, London, on 11 October 1975, with Yvonne Kenny in the title-role. The opera still awaits its first stage performance since 1846.

The action takes place in and around Woodstock Castle in Oxfordshire, in the second half of the twelfth century. Enrico (King Henry II) has returned from the wars hoping to find peace in the arms of his mistress, Rosmonda, who knows him only as Edegardo. When her father, Clifford, informs her that her lover is the King, Rosmonda is horrified. Enrico promises to make Rosmonda his queen, but his jealous wife, Leonora (Eleanor of Aquitaine), kills her.

Often, when Donizetti had composed a really first-rate opera, his next was something of a disappointment. *Anna Bolena* was followed by *Gianni di Parigi*, *L'Elisir d'amore* by *Sancia di Castiglia*, and now *Lucrezia Borgia* is followed by *Rosmonda d'Inghilterra* whose score, though pleasant, is, with the exception of one number, hardly memorable. Romani's libretto is oddly confused and formless, and Donizetti's mind seems not to have been fully occupied by the task in hand, for most of his score sounds like music that he had already written, though there is little, if any, actual self-borrowing.

After a lively, tuneful, but inappropriately light-hearted overture, the first act begins with a conventional chorus of welcome to the returning King Henry, and a quite agreeable duet ('Invan sopir tu tenti') for Leonora and the page, Arturo. But the dramatic situation at this point is not clear, nor do the characters emerge with any clarity throughout the opera. Enrico's entrance aria, 'Dopo i lauri di vittoria', is nondescript, though its cabaletta, 'Potessi vivere com' io vorrei', is vigorous. The duet for Clifford and Rosmonda ('Era, ahi lasso!') is unmemorable, and the ensemble finale to the act lacks individuality.

The most successful numbers in Act II are an exciting cabaletta ('Senza pace e senza speme') for Rosmonda, and an attractive duet ('Tu morrai, tu m'hai costretta') for Rosmonda and Leonora shortly before the opera's dramatic finale with its effective ensemble and solo cabaletta for Leonora. The finest number in the entire score, Rosmonda's Act I aria ('Perchè non ho del vento') and cabaletta ('Torna, ah, torna, o caro oggetto'), was later salvaged by Donizetti and inserted into the 1839 French version of his 1835 opera, *Lucia di Lammermoor*.

Maria Stuarda

opera seria in three acts

Principal characters:

Maria Stuarda (Mary, Queen of Scots)	(soprano)
Elisabetta (Elizabeth I)	(soprano)
Leicester	(tenor)
Talbot	(bass)
Cecil	(bass)

LIBRETTO by Giuseppe Bardari

TIME: 1587
PLACE: London and Fotheringhay Castle, Northamptonshire

FIRST PERFORMED (as *Buondelmonte*) at the Teatro San Carlo, Naples, 18 October 1834, with Giuseppina Ronzi de Begnis (Bianca); Anna del Serre (Irene); Francesco Pedrazzi (Buondelmonte); Federico Crespi (Lamberto)
PERFORMED (as *Maria Stuarda*) at La Scala, Milan, 30 December 1835, with Maria Malibran (Maria Stuarda); Giacinta Puzzi-Tosi (Elisabetta); Domenico Reina (Leicester); Ignazio Marini (Talbot)

After the third performance of *Rosmonda d'Inghilterra* in Florence, Donizetti made his way via Rome (where he rejoined his wife, Virginia) to Naples where, on 12 April 1834, he signed a contract to compose a new opera for the Teatro San Carlo. He had also been invited by Rossini, now in charge at the Théâtre-Italien in Paris, to write an opera for that theatre; and in June, by command of the King of Naples, he was appointed professor of counterpoint and composition at the Royal College of Music in Naples.

The opera for the San Carlo was to be *Maria Stuarda*, based on Schiller's play, *Maria Stuart* (first produced in Weimar in 1800), which Donizetti had seen in Milan in Andrea Maffei's Italian translation. The composer wanted Romani to write the libretto, and also to provide a libretto for his Paris opera, but when the celebrated librettist failed to reply to his communications, Donizetti turned to a seventeen-year-old law student in Naples, Giuseppe Bardari, who wrote his first libretto under the composer's guidance. (It turned out also to be his last: Bardari later became a magistrate.) Donizetti composed *Maria Stuarda* during the summer, and it went into rehearsal in September.

Unfortunately, after a successful dress rehearsal, the opera was banned by order of the King, perhaps because his Queen, Maria Cristina, was a direct descendant of Mary Stuart (Mary, Queen of Scots). News may have reached the court of the opera's famous scene of confrontation between Mary and Elizabeth I, in which Mary calls the English Queen a vile bastard (*vil bastarda*). At the first orchestral rehearsal, the soprano (Giuseppina Ronzi de Begnis) playing Maria delivered this line with such conviction that the Elizabeth (Anna del Serre) attacked her physically, tearing her hair and beating her with her fists. Ronzi de Begnis retaliated so ably that Anna del Serre fainted and had to be carried home. Donizetti later wrote to Ferretti, his Roman librettist:

> You've heard about the battle between the women, but I don't know if you're aware that, thinking I was out of earshot, Ronzi said of me, 'Donizetti protects that whore of a del Serre.' To her surprise I answered, 'I do not protect either of you. Those two queens were whores, and you two are whores.' I convinced her. Either she was ashamed or decided to keep quiet. She said no more, the rehearsal continued, and after that the opera was not performed.

Donizetti reluctantly agreed to adapt the music of *Maria Stuarda* to another text. Lady Jane Grey was first suggested as a subject, perhaps so as not to waste the Tudor sets and costumes already prepared, but permission for this was denied by the censors, and the subject finally chosen was a story of strife between Guelphs and Ghibellines in mid-thirteenth-century Florence. As *Buondelmonte*, with some additional music provided by Donizetti and a libretto by Pietro Salatino (the librettist of *Sancia di Castiglia* in 1832) put together in a few days, virtually syllable by syllable to fit the existing music, the revised opera had its première, after eleven days' rehearsal, on 18 October 1834. Its plot concerned the Florentine Buondelmonte – he features in Dante's *Paradiso* – who apparently caused a local war between the Guelphs and the Ghibellines by going back on his promise to marry Bianca degl'Amadei. Giuseppina Ronzi de Begnis switched roles from Maria Stuart to Bianca, and Anna del Serre (Elizabeth I) became her rival, Irene. As Donizetti had already told Jacopo Ferretti:

> ... the big prayer in *Stuarda* has turned into a fine, full conspiracy in *Buondelmonte*. The leading female character went to her death? Now it is the tenor Pedrazzi who dies. It was Del Serre who signed the death sentence? Now she suffers ill-treatment. There used to be six characters in all? Now there are ten or more. You can imagine what the opera has become. The same scenery, appropriate or not, will be used. I haven't been able to bring myself to ask whether it works or not.

Buondelmonte was received coolly, and Donizetti withdrew the opera immediately after its Naples performances, determined to have *Maria Stuarda* produced somewhere as he had originally planned it. Fourteen months were to elapse before he achieved this, during which time he composed three more operas, *Gemma di Vergy* for Milan, *Marino Faliero* for Paris, and *Lucia di Lammermoor* for Naples. *Maria Stuarda* finally reached the stage in Milan at La Scala, on 30 December 1835, in its original form with the addition of one new number (a duet Donizetti had written for *Buondelmonte*, now given to Maria and Leicester) and an overture. The famous Maria Malibran, in the title-role, was unwell, not in good voice – the première was postponed from 28 December because of her indisposition – and also annoyed because of the various cuts and alterations demanded by the censorship. '*Vil bastarda*', for example, had been softened to '*donna vile*', but Malibran insisted on using the original text. After six performances, some of them only of Act I in which Maria Stuarda does not appear (in a double-bill with two acts of Rossini's *Otello* in which Malibran sang Desdemona), the authorities forbade any future stagings of *Maria Stuarda*.

There were a few productions at other Italian opera houses, and two abroad, in Oporto and Lisbon, but it was not until 1865 that the opera reached Naples (the city of the *Buondelmonte* première) in its original form as *Maria Stuarda*. It then disappeared until its revival on 12 October 1958 at the Teatro Donizetti, Bergamo, conducted by Oliviero de Fabritiis. The first English performance of *Maria Stuarda* was given at the St Pancras Town Hall, London, on 1 March 1966. New York heard a concert performance on 16 November 1964, but the first American stage performance was on 12 November 1971 at the San Francisco Opera House, with Joan Sutherland as Maria Stuarda, conducted by Richard Bonynge. Sutherland, Montserrat Caballé, Leyla Gencer and Beverly Sills have all sung the title-role with great success in opera houses throughout the world, and *Maria Stuarda* is now among the more popular of Donizetti's serious operas.

Bardari's libretto is a travesty of Schiller's *Maria Stuart*, eliminating almost all of the play's political and religious references and reducing the number of characters from twenty-one to six. However, it retains the chief emotional situations of the play, and is compact and structurally sound, in other words an excellent text for opera. The leading characters are Elizabeth I and Mary, Queen of Scots. Elizabeth, in love with the Earl of Leicester, is persuaded by him to visit Mary who is being held prisoner at Fotheringhay. During the visit, Mary insults Elizabeth, and in due course Elizabeth signs Mary's death warrant. Leicester, in love with Mary, is ordered to witness her execution.

The overture which Donizetti wrote for the Milan première of *Maria Stuarda* is an imposing, large-scale piece. (*Buondelmonte* had a much shorter prelude containing a fascinating clarinet part in recitative.) The opera's opening chorus and Elisabetta's graceful entrance aria ('Ah! quando all'ara scorgemi'), with its attractive cabaletta ('Ah! dal ciel discenda un raggio'), are all quite conventional in form and content, but Leicester's cavatina ('Ah! rimiro il bel sembiante') and cabaletta ('Se fida tanto colei mi amò') are more interesting, the baritone, Talbot, joining the tenor, Leicester, in the second stanzas of both cavatina and cabaletta. A duet for Elisabetta and Leicester, its opening arioso leading into a melodious *larghetto* ('Era d'amor l'immagine'), a smooth reworking of material initially composed for a revival of *Fausta*, and its *vivace* ('Sul crin la rivale') fiercely urgent, makes a strong and distinctly unconventional conclusion to Act I.

Act II introduces Maria Stuarda in a *larghetto* aria, 'Oh! nube che lieve per l'aria ti aggiri', whose elegant, yearning vocal line perfectly reflects Maria's mood and situation, her longing for freedom and her native France. Her cabaletta, 'Nella pace del mesto riposo', after Maria hears the approach of the English Queen and her party, is made to sound all the more determined by its deliberately moderate pace. Just as affecting as the aria is Maria's duet with Leicester, 'Da tutti abbandonata', which leads to a brief sextet whose opening phrase ('È sempre la stessa') sung by Elisabetta may have been in Verdi's mind seventeen years later when he came to write Leonora's opening phrase in *Il Trovatore*'s 'Miserere' duet. The scene in which Elisabetta and Maria (the two rivals who in real life never met) confront each other, described in Donizetti's score as 'Dialogo delle due regine' (Dialogue of the two Queens), subordinates music to the demands of the dramatic situation. However, music takes precedence over drama in the finale of the act, with pent-up emotions finding release in a fast and furious stretta.

After a brooding, restless orchestral prelude, Act III begins poorly with a carelessly written duettino for Elisabetta and Cecil which becomes a very ordinary trio with the entrance of Leicester. But this last act improves as it progresses. Its second scene is that of Maria's 'Duetto della Confessione' with Talbot, a beautifully written scene in which the sacrament of confession is administered to the Catholic Queen who comes to terms with her conscience in a moving *larghetto* ('Quando di luce rosea') ushering in a duet of a scale, intensity, and inexorable forward movement that one has come to think of as essentially Verdian.

The opera's finest scene is its last, with an ominous prelude, an elegiac, grief-laden 'Inno della morte' for a chorus of Maria's friends (surely the inspiration for more than one of Verdi's great choruses), and Maria's solo finale. Her voice rises to sustain a high note (G above the stave) for several bars above the chorus in the prayer ('Deh! Tu di un umile preghiera il suono odi') which is preceded by recitative prominently featuring a melancholy clarinet solo together with a muted comment from the chorus. This extremely moving number is based on a melody from *Il Paria* which was to be used yet again by Donizetti, with modifications, in both *Linda di Chamounix* and *Le Duc d'Albe*. Maria's sad yet serene final *larghetto* ('Di un cor che more'), called in the score *Aria del supplizio* or Execution aria, is followed, as she prepares to mount the scaffold, by a simple, dignified, and intensely moving cabaletta, 'Ah! se un giorno de queste ritorte'.

Though not all of its score is on the same high level, the

confrontation of the two queens in Act II and the gripping final scenes of *Maria Stuarda* will ensure that the opera remains alive in the repertoire.

Gemma di Vergy

opera seria in two acts

Principal characters:

Gemma, ex-wife of Count Vergy	(soprano)
Ida, the Count's fiancée	(mezzo-soprano)
Tamas, an Arab slave	(tenor)
Count Vergy	(baritone)
Guido, the Count's Chief Officer	(bass)
Rolando, the Count's equerry	(bass)

LIBRETTO by Emanuele Bidera

TIME: 1428

PLACE: The château of Vergy, in the French province of Berry

FIRST PERFORMED at the Teatro alla Scala, Milan, 26 December 1834, with Giuseppina Ronzi de Begnis (Gemma); Felicità Baillou Hillaret (Ida); Domenico Reina (Tamas); Orazio Cartagenova (Il Conte di Vergy); Ignazio Marini (Guido); Domenico Spiaggi (Rolando)

After seeing *Buondelmonte* staged at the San Carlo Theatre in October 1834, Donizetti plunged into a flurry of operatic activity, first of all dividing his attention between his next two operas which had been promised to Milan and to Paris. Having failed to engage Romani as librettist for either of them, he turned to Emanuele Bidera, a fifty-year-old Sicilian who was then active in Naples as a purveyor of libretti to composers such as Carlo Coccia, Giuseppe Balducci and Francesco Chiaromonte. Bidera provided Donizetti with the texts for both operas, and the composer began immediately to write *Marino Faliero* for Paris, turning aside in November to dash off *Gemma di Vergy* for Milan.

At its première at La Scala on 26 December 1834, *Gemma di Vergy* was well received, and was performed twenty-six times during the season. (The twenty-one-year-old Giuseppe Verdi, who was at the beginning of his professional career but had not yet had an opera produced, attended the première and, though not disappointed by the work, felt that he himself would have done something different with the Dumas play on which the libretto was based.) Donizetti's opera was staged not only in a number of Italian towns but also throughout Europe, and further afield in Algiers, Havana, Trinidad, Mexico City and Buenos Aires. After the first London performance on 12 March 1842, one critic described the music as 'amongst the feeblest' and the plot as 'one of the most sickly and improbable that ever came out of the brain of an enervated librettist'.

The opera reached New York on 2 October 1843. It continued to be staged until the end of the century, after which it languished until its revival in Naples at the Teatro San Carlo in December 1975 with Montserrat Caballé in the title-role. Caballé also sang the role at the Gran Teatre del Liceu in Barcelona in January 1976, and in a concert performance at Carnegie Hall, New York, later in the same year. *Gemma di Vergy* was subsequently staged at the Donizetti Festival in Bergamo in October 1987.

Bidera's libretto was based on the play *Charles VII chez ses Grands Vassaux* by Alexandre Dumas *père*, staged in Paris in 1831. Gemma, Countess of Vergy, discovers that her husband has had their marriage annulled because of her inability to produce an heir. Tamas, an Arab slave secretly in love with Gemma, kills Rolando who has come to announce the arrival of the Count with his new bride, Ida. The Count sentences Tamas to death, but Gemma successfully pleads for his life. Gemma attempts to kill Ida, but is prevented from doing so by Tamas, who kills the Count during the wedding ceremony, only to be cursed by Gemma who has now decided to enter a convent. Tamas kills himself, and Gemma looks forward to death as a release from her suffering.

After an episodic, highly engaging overture which has little in common with the bloodthirsty plot it prefaces, the opera begins with an elegantly tuneful opening scene for Guido and chorus which is far superior to some of Donizetti's earlier and more routine opening ensembles. The double arias for Tamas and Gemma, and Gemma's duet with Guido (except for its beautiful *larghetto* section), are disappointing. When, fourteen years later in Palermo, Tamas' cabaletta ('Mi togliesti e core e mente') incited the entire audience to wave handkerchiefs and shout 'Long live the Pope, the King and the Italian league', it was surely the sentiment ('You took away my heart, my soul, country, gods and liberty') which moved them, rather than the music.

Act I improves as it progresses towards its splendid concerted finale. But it is the second act which contains the opera's finest music. The Count's aria is mundane, but the scene in which Gemma threatens Ida, leading to a trio with the arrival of the Count and then a quartet when Tamas intervenes, has a fierce dramatic energy. A female chorus, 'Vieni, o bella', is charming, and the duet for Gemma and Tamas ('Non è ver'), introduced by an attractive oboe solo, at least begins well. The finest number in the entire score is Gemma's solo finale. Dramatic *maestoso* recitative ('Eccomi sola alfine') ushers in a beautiful *larghetto* prayer, 'Un altare ed una benda'. Tamas' confession and suicide are squeezed into a few lines of recitative between Gemma's prayer and her cabaletta, 'Chi m'accusa', whose moderate tempo is maintained almost to the end.

Gemma di Vergy's eponymous heroine is an unappealing character, and although the opera is intermittently entertaining, it would doubtless have been much better had Donizetti not composed it while his mind was also occupied with the still unfinished *Marino Faliero*.

Marino Faliero

opera seria in three acts

Principal characters:

Elena   (soprano)
Fernando   (tenor)
Israele Bertucci (baritone)
Marino Faliero   (bass)
Michele Steno   (bass)

LIBRETTO by Emanuele Bidera, with revisions by Agostino Ruffini

TIME: 1355
PLACE: Venice

FIRST PERFORMED at the Théâtre-Italien, Paris, 12 March 1835, with Giulia Grisi (Elena); Giovanni Battista Rubini (Fernando); Antonio Tamburini (Israele Bertucci); Luigi Lablache (Marino Faliero)

After the première of *Buondelmonte* in October 1834, Donizetti set to work on his next opera, *Marino Faliero*, for the Théâtre-Italien in Paris, breaking off to compose *Gemma di Vergy* quickly for La Scala, Milan, where it was staged on 26 December. On New Year's Eve he left Milan for Paris, taking with him the not yet completed score of *Marino Faliero*. Dissatisfied with parts of Emanuele Bidera's libretto, he asked Agostino Ruffini, a young Italian poet and revolutionary living in exile in Paris, to make a few alterations. (Eight years later, Ruffini's elder brother, Giovanni, was to provide Donizetti with the libretto for *Don Pasquale*.)

Donizetti was in the audience at the Théâtre-Italien on 24 January for the première of Bellini's final opera *I Puritani*, which enjoyed a great success. Its leading roles were played by four great singers, Giulia Grisi, Giovanni Battista Rubini, Antonio Tamburini and Luigi Lablache, who were also to appear in *Marino Faliero*. Donizetti's opera had its première on 12 March 1835 before a fashionable audience which included the composers Adolphe Adam, Giacomo Meyerbeer and Vincenzo Bellini. Although, or perhaps because, *Marino Faliero* was received favourably, the envious Bellini wrote on the following morning to his uncle: 'Donizetti's new opera staged last night, *Marino Faliero*, has had a semi-fiasco. The newspapers will perhaps be favourable to him, but the public has been left discontented, and the proof will be the imminent reappearance of *I Puritani*.' In a subsequent letter Bellini described *Marino Faliero* as 'deprived of novelty, most commonplace, and most ordinarily orchestrated'.

Marino Faliero (called *Marin Faliero* on some early playbills) reached London on 14 May 1835, only two months after its première, with the singers who had performed the opera in Paris. A week later, Bellini's *I Puritani* was staged in London. The critic Henry Chorley wrote: 'The production of these two new operas was the event of the season. On such occasions there is always a success and a failure. The public will not endure two favourites. In spite of the grandeur of Lablache as the Doge of Venice, in spite of the beauty of the duet of the two basses in the first act of *Marino*, in spite of the second act containing a beautiful moonlight scene with a barcarolle sung to perfection by Ivanoff, and one of Rubini's most incomparable and superb vocal displays, *Marino Faliero* languished, in part from want of interest in the female character – a fault fatal to an opera's popularity.'

The first Italian performance of *Marino Faliero* was given in Florence, at the Teatro Alfieri, in April 1836. At La Scala, Milan, in 1837, the opera achieved thirty-nine performances, and was revived several times in subsequent seasons. It went on the usual international rounds, reaching New York on 15 December 1843, and it continued to be revived in Italy until 1892 (in Florence), after which it lay dormant until performed for the first time in the twentieth century at the Teatro Donizetti, Bergamo, on 12 October 1966 (with a second performance on 15 October). Since then, *Marino Faliero* has been staged only once, by Opera Viva at the Camden Town Hall, London, for three performances beginning on 21 February 1967.

A tragedy of adultery, intrigue and honour, *Marino Faliero* tells of the love of Elena, wife of the Doge, for the Doge's nephew Fernando. The Doge is arrested for having conspired against the Council. Before his execution, he forgives Elena. Bidera's libretto was drawn both from Lord Byron's 1820 verse tragedy, *Marino Faliero* (possibly the finest of Byron's works for the theatre), and from a play of the same title by Casimir Delavigne, partly based on Byron and produced in Paris in 1829.

Marino Faliero was the forty-ninth Doge of Venice, who joined an unsuccessful conspiracy to overthrow the republic and was beheaded upon the Giant's Staircase, where Doges traditionally took their oath of fidelity to the city-state. The historical Faliero acted from political motives, but the opera follows Byron and Delavigne whose Faliero decides to overthrow the government because the Council of Forty passed, in his view, an insufficiently severe sentence upon Michele Steno, a young patrician who had publicly lampooned Faliero's wife, Elena.

Marino Faliero does not represent Donizetti at his best. Its overture is tuneful and, unlike the opera itself, well constructed, and the chorus of artisans, 'Issa, issa, issa, là', is rousing. But thereafter much of the score is mediocre. In Act I, the confident *cantabile* of Israele's aria, 'Ero anch'io', and the energy of its cabaletta with chorus ('Orgogliosi, scellerati') are welcome, but Fernando's solo scene is rather ordinary, and the duet for him and Elena is competently but dully written. A duet for Faliero and Israele begins well, though it develops disappointingly, and the finale of the act is nondescript. The gondolier's barcarolle near the beginning of Act II is musically characterless, though it can make an effect in the context of a stage performance. Fernando's aria ('Io ti veggio') and cabaletta ('Mi tornano presenti') are noteworthy more for the opportunities they provide for the tenor to indulge in vocal display (and to demonstrate his high D in the cabaletta) than for their intrinsic musical quality.

In the Act II finale, Faliero's 'Fosca notte, notte orrenda' uses an endearingly jolly tune to articulate violent sentiments. Elena's expressive recitative, aria ('Dio clemente') and cabaletta ('Fra due tombe') enliven the third act, and the opera's final scene for Faliero and Elena is affecting. The *larghetto* of their duet, 'Santa voce', begins as though it is going to recycle a number from *Il Paria*, but soon develops along its own lines. There is no cabaletta, the opera ending with the off-stage execution of the Doge, and Elena's half-spoken words of grief and guilt.

This is an opera worthy of occasional revival, despite its awkwardness of construction and the ordinariness of parts of its score.

12

From *Lucia di Lammermoor* to *Les Martyrs*

Lucia di Lammermoor

opera seria in three acts

Principal characters:

Lucia	(soprano)
Edgardo	(tenor)
Enrico, Lucia's brother	(baritone)
Raimondo Bidebent, Lucia's tutor	(bass)
Arturo	(tenor)

LIBRETTO by Salvatore Cammarano

TIME: The late-seventeenth century
PLACE: Scotland

FIRST PERFORMED at the Teatro San Carlo, Naples, 26 September 1835, with Fanny Tacchinardi-Persiani (Lucia); Gilbert-Luis Duprez (Edgardo); Domenico Cosselli (Enrico); Carlo Porto (Raimondo)

While Donizetti was in Paris for the première of *Marino Faliero*, he was made a Chevalier of the Legion of Honour. By the end of April he and Virginia were back in Naples, where he returned to his duties as musical director of the royal theatres and as a professor at the Conservatorium. His next opera was to be composed for the Teatro San Carlo, and on 18 May he wrote to a friend that its subject would be derived from Sir Walter Scott's novel, *The Bride of Lammermoor*. Donizetti's new librettist was Salvatore Cammarano, who was to provide the composer with a further seven libretti before going on to write *Alzira*, *La Battaglia di Legnano*, *Luisa Miller* and *Il Trovatore* for Verdi.

Rehearsals for Donizetti's *Lucia di Lammermoor*, delayed by financial and administrative crises at the Teatro San Carlo, began in mid-August, and the opera was given its première at the San Carlo on 26 September 1835. It was a huge and immediate success. As its composer told his publisher, Giovanni Ricordi, 'It pleased, and it pleased greatly, if I am to believe the applause and the compliments I received ... every piece was listened to in religious silence and honoured with spontaneous *vivas*.'

Lucia di Lammermoor to this day remains Donizetti's most famous and most popular opera. During its composer's lifetime it was produced all over the civilised world, London first hearing it at Her Majesty's Theatre on 5 April 1838. The first performance in the United States was given in New Orleans on 28 December 1841 (in French), and a New York production (in Italian) followed on 15 September 1843. Unlike so many popular bel canto operas, *Lucia di Lammermoor* survived changes in fashion and never completely disappeared from the international operatic repertoire. Around the turn of the century, famous Lucias included the Australian soprano Nellie Melba, the Viennese Selma Kurz and the Italian Luisa Tetrazzini. Toti dal Monte in Italy and Lily Pons in America were popular Lucias in the thirties, and a Covent Garden production in 1959 launched the international career of another great Australian soprano, Joan Sutherland.

There is, of course, much more to Walter Scott's *The Bride of Lammermoor* than is communicated in Cammarano's libretto for Donizetti's opera. The novel, published in 1819, was inspired by an occurrence in 1668 involving Janet Dalrymple, the daughter of a Scottish noble family, who was forced to marry a man she did not love while already secretly betrothed to another. On the wedding night, her screams brought members of the household rushing into her chamber to find her cowering insane in a corner with her husband lying stretched out on the bed and covered in blood.

Scott changed the characters' names, shifted the locale from one part of the Scottish borderlands to another, and invented a complex plot. In *The Bride of Lammermoor*, set in the late-seventeenth century, the heroine is Lucy Ashton, daughter of the unscrupulous Sir William Ashton who has brought about, through legal trickery, the financial ruin of Lord Ravenswood. Lucy Ashton and Ravenswood's son Edgar fall in love, and plight their troth at the Mermaid's Fountain. However, while Edgar is away, Lucy is forced by her parents to marry the dissolute Laird of Bucklaw. On her wedding night she stabs and critically wounds her bridegroom, and dies in convulsions on the following day. On his way to fight a duel with her brother, Edgar is lost in the quicksands of Kelpies Flow. Other characters in the novel include the Reverend Mr Bide-the-Bent, a kindly clergyman (who survives in the opera as Raimondo Bidebent, Lucia's tutor), and Caleb Balderstone, a loyal old family retainer who, along with the cowardly Craigengelt, provides a certain amount of comic relief. Donizetti and Cammarano concentrated on the bare bones of the tragic plot, and made one or two major changes. Arturo now dies when stabbed by Lucia on their wedding night, and Edgardo, heart-broken when he learns of Lucia's death, kills himself.

The qualities which distinguish *Lucia di Lammermoor* from even the finest of Donizetti's pre-*Lucia* operas are its tautness of construction, the manner in which the music consistently serves the drama, and the sheer prodigality of the composer's melodic invention. A brief orchestral prelude, horns and woodwind providing its sombre colouring, sets a mood of romantic foreboding, and in the opening scene Enrico's cavatina, 'Cruda, funesta smania', with its furious cabaletta, 'La pietade in suo favore', immediately display the quality of Donizetti's writing for the voice. The role of Enrico is written for a high baritone, and the top of the singer's range is exploited in a manner which was to be developed and emphasised by Verdi.

The second scene of Act I, which takes place in the park of Ravenswood Castle by moonlight, is introduced by a charming harp solo, which sets the romantic mood for Lucia's assignation with Edgardo. Lucia's *larghetto* aria ('Regnava nel silenzio'), as she awaits his arrival, is reflective in tone, but nevertheless finds opportunities for coloratura display which are even more abundant in the cabaletta, 'Quando rapita in estasi'. Here, and in virtually every number throughout the opera, Donizetti's melody has moved on to a more exalted plane than in the past, as though he were now unselfconsciously pouring into his music the very soul of Italian bel canto. Lucia's two-part duet with Edgardo, its *larghetto* opening section, 'Sulla tomba', leading to the flowing legato of 'Verranno a te', constitutes the first act finale.

(The first Lucia, Fanny Tacchinardi-Persiani, seems not to have liked her Act I aria and cabaletta. Once free of the première and the supervision of the composer, she was in the habit of substituting the aria 'Perchè non ho del vento' and its cabaletta, 'Torna, torna, o caro oggetto', from Donizetti's *Rosmonda d'Inghilterra*, an opera whose title-role she had created in 1834. The words fitted the dramatic situation quite well, for they tell of Rosmonda's impatience for the return of her lover whom she knows as 'Edegardo' – only a syllable removed from Lucia's Edgardo. Most Lucias of the nineteenth century followed Persiani in substituting the *Rosmonda* aria for 'Regnava nel silenzio'.)

The scene for Lucia and Enrico which begins Act II takes the form of a superb three-part duet, the orchestra contributing to the drama as distinctly as the singers. A plaintive oboe tune accompanies Lucia's entrance, and the strings call attention to her plight at the beginning of the duet's *moderato* ('Il pallor funesto'). The *larghetto*, 'Soffriva nel pianto', leads to a fraught *vivace* concluding section, 'Se tradirmi tu potrai', in which her brother bullies Lucia into a marriage which will be advantageous to him. (In all printed scores, the duet begins and ends in G major. On the second of her two recordings of the opera, Joan Sutherland – with Sherrill Milnes – sings it a tone higher in A, the key in which it is written in Donizetti's autograph score.)

Raimondo, Lucia's spiritual adviser, is allowed a fine double aria ('Ah! cedi, cedi') before the second act finale which opens with a joyously tuneful chorus, 'Per te d'immenso giubilo' (admired by both Bernard Shaw and the Salvation Army, as is revealed in Shaw's *Major Barbara*). Sandwiched between the two stanzas of the chorus is the hapless Arturo's elegant cavatina, 'Per poco fra le tenebre'. The great sextet, 'Chi mi frena in tal momento', the most famous ensemble in all opera, is begun by Edgardo and Enrico, who are joined first by Lucia and Raimondo and then by Arturo and Alisa, Lucia's maid. After the sextet, the action is borne swiftly along until it culminates in a fierce stretta ('Esci, fuggi').

Act III contains three scenes. The first, involving only Edgardo and Enrico, is more often than not omitted from performances; the second is the *raison d'être* of a good many productions, the celebrated mad scene for Lucia; the opera's final scene, for Edgardo, used until comparatively recent (pre-Sutherland) times to be omitted as a matter of course, presumably on the unwarranted assumption that the opera is over when the fat lady sings. The author can remember attending more than one such performance in the 1950s.

The scene for Edgardo and Enrico is labelled in the score, '*Uragano, scena e duetto*'. The '*uragano*' (hurricane) consists of thirty-six bars of a magnificently violent *allegro vivace* which then dies away between Edgardo's outbursts of recitative. Edgardo's short and sharp exchanges with Enrico lead to their virile and not over-long duet, 'Qui del padre ancor respira'. Directors and conductors should resist the temptation to cut this scene, for it makes a much more suitable beginning to Act III than is provided by an immediate plunge into the Mad Scene.

The short-lived joyousness of the chorus, 'D'immenso giubilo', which begins the second scene of Act III is suddenly interrupted by Raimondo whose sad *larghetto*, 'Dalle stanze ove Lucia tratta', leads to the moving choral lament, 'Oh! qual funesto avvenimento!' and to the entrance of the deranged Lucia. Her mad scene is an extended scena for the soprano, with flute obbligato. (Donizetti had at first intended to use a glass harmonica here.) The recitative is highly expressive, and a quotation from the Act I love duet, 'Verranno a te', brings to mind that line from Dante's *Inferno*: 'There is no greater sorrow than to recall a time of happiness in misery.' The *larghetto* ('Ardon gl'incensi') of what is in effect a double aria introduces a nostalgic melody, 'Alfin son tua', and the *moderato*, 'Spargi d'amaro pianto', plunges Lucia deeper into an ecstasy of despair, her insanity characterised by frantic coloratura, trills and chromatic runs. Sopranos find it difficult to resist the temptation to end on the E flat *in alt*, an octave above the note in Donizetti's score.

Edgardo is given his equivalent of Lucia's mad scene in his double aria in the final scene of the opera. 'Fra poco a me ricovero', preceded by a portentous orchestral introduction and by somewhat formal recitative, is dignified in its grief, but the second part of the aria, 'Tu che a Dio spiegasti l'ali' – separated from the first by the villagers' moving chorus of lament – gives way to emotion in a melody which wears its heart, sentimentally but beautifully, on its sleeve.

For *Lucie de Lammermoor*, a French version of the opera which was staged in Paris in 1839, Donizetti made a number of changes to his score. It is the original Italian version, however, which has survived in the international repertoire, an opera as popular now as when it first reached the stage.

Belisario

opera seria in three acts

Principal characters:

Belisario, a Byzantine General	(baritone)
Antonina, his wife	(soprano)
Giustiniano, Emperor of Byzantium	(bass)
Alamiro	(tenor)
Irene, Belisario's daughter	(mezzo-soprano)

LIBRETTO by Salvatore Cammarano

TIME: The sixth century
PLACE: Byzantium

FIRST PERFORMED at the Teatro La Fenice, Venice, 4 February 1836, with Caroline Unger (Antonina); Antonietta Vial (Irene); Celestino Salvatori (Belisario); Ignazio Pasini (Alamiro)

On 23 September 1835, three days before the première of Donizetti's *Lucia di Lammermoor* in Naples, its composer's young rival, Vincenzo Bellini, died in France in his thirty-fourth year. On 20 October, Donizetti told his publisher Ricordi that he wanted to honour Bellini's memory by composing a Mass. However, he had already signed a contract to produce a new opera for Venice, to be staged early in the new year, so instead he turned his attention to *Belisario*, whose libretto had been provided by Salvatore Cammarano. In December, Donizetti's father died in Bergamo. The composer paid for his funeral, but was unable to be present as he was detained in Milan where his *Buondelmonte* was about to be performed under its proper title of *Maria Stuarda* for the first time. A few days after its première on 30 December, Donizetti made his way to Venice to begin rehearsals of his new opera.

Belisario was received with great enthusiasm at its première at the

Teatro La Fenice on 4 February 1836, and was given a further seventeen performances during the season. The *Gazzetta privilegiata di Venezia* said: 'A new masterwork has been added to Italian music ... *Belisario* not only pleased and delighted, but also conquered, enflamed and ravished the full auditorium.' However, writing to a French publisher in April, its composer said that he knew *Belisario* was effective in the theatre but that he himself placed it below *Lucia*. It went the rounds of the Italian theatres and was also staged in thirty-one cities abroad, in Europe and in the Americas. Its first London performance was on 1 April 1837. It reached the United States first in Philadelphia, on 29 July 1843, and was heard in New York on 14 February 1844. After a production in Coblenz in 1899, *Belisario* disappeared until its first twentieth-century revival on 6 May 1969 when it returned to the Teatro La Fenice in Venice for the first time since 1841, with Leyla Gencer as Antonina and Giuseppe Taddei as Belisario, conducted by Gianandrea Gavazzeni. There have been subsequent performances in Bergamo in 1970 with Leyla Gencer and Renato Bruson, in London in 1972 (at Sadler's Wells Theatre, with students of the Royal Academy of Music), in Naples in 1973 with Gencer and Taddei, in Buenos Aires in 1981 with Mara Zampieri and Bruson, in London in 1981 (the Royal Academy of Music again), and in New Brunswick, New Jersey, in 1990, at Rutgers University.

Grove's *Dictionary* lists Cammarano's libretto as being 'after Marmontel'. However, Cammarano's primary source was not Jean-François Marmontel's 1766 novel, *Bélisaire*, a plea for religious tolerance, but a play, *Belisarius*, by Eduard von Schenk, which was first staged in Munich in 1820, and produced in Naples in 1826 in an Italian adaptation by Luigi Marchionni. Belisarius is an historical character, a general in the army of the sixth-century Byzantine Emperor Justinian. In the opera, Belisario, having defeated the Bulgarians, returns in triumph to Byzantium with prisoners all of whom he releases, except one, Alamiro, who chooses to remain with him as a kind of foster-son. Belisario's wife, Antonina, believing her husband to have been responsible for the death of their own son, denounces him to the Emperor Giustiniano as a traitor. Belisario is blinded and sentenced to exile, but is later reunited with his son who is revealed to be Alamiro. After another battle in which Belisario is fatally wounded, a remorseful Antonina confesses her guilt to her dying husband.

The opera's three acts are each given titles: *Il Trionfo* (Triumph), *L'Esilio* (Exile), and *La Morte* (Death). Act I, *Il Trionfo*, is preceded by a highly engaging, if dramatically inappropriate, overture. The double arias for Irene and for Antonina are characterless and awkwardly written, and the jaunty chorus which both precedes and follows Giustiniano's dull arioso would be more suitable accompanying a quick two-step than the ceremonial appearance of an Emperor. The duet, 'Quando di sangue tinto', in which Belisario and Alamiro, unaware that they are father and son, swear to remain united forever, is the nearest approach to a love duet in this opera in which romantic love never rears its fascinating head. The duet is, however, an oddly crude piece to have come from the composer who had only some months previously written *Lucia di Lammermoor*. The Act I finale of *Belisario* is, for the most part, stiffly formal, though a *larghetto* ensemble, 'Non ti nascondi, o sol', brings it momentarily to life.

A very brief Act II (*L'Esilio*) consists of no more than an introductory chorus, an aria and cabaletta for Alamiro, and a duet for Belisario and Irene, none of which, with the possible exception of the *moderato* section of the duet ('Dunque andiam'), reveals Donizetti at anywhere near his best. Alamiro's vigorous cabaletta, 'Trema Bisanzio!', has been compared to the famous 'Di quella pira' from Verdi's *Il Trovatore* to which it bears a superficial resemblance, though it lacks Verdi's elemental fury. The Belisario–Irene duet, too, has been described by at least one writer on Donizetti as a prototype of Verdi's great father–daughter duets, but in this instance the comparison seems rather far-fetched.

After an orchestral introduction imbued with an almost Bellinian melancholy, the main features of Act III (*La Morte*) are a trio for Irene, Alamiro and Belisario with a moving *larghetto* ('Se il fratel stringere m'è dato al seno'), followed by the obligatory final aria and cabaletta for a remorseful Antonina who has not been heard from since Act I. The aria, 'Da quel dì', is not particularly remarkable, although it can be made to sound effective by a soprano with a secure Donizetti style. Likewise, the cabaletta ('Egli è spento').

No opera stands or falls by its libretto, and if Donizetti had poured music of the calibre of his *Lucia di Lammermoor* into the score of *Belisario* the shortcomings of its wayward plot and clumsy dramatic structure would matter less. However, its characters remain ciphers mainly because their music rarely rises above that workaday level of competence which Donizetti had so often proved capable of surmounting. As he himself realised, *Belisario* is able to make an effect in the theatre, but it is a disappointment after *Lucia*.

Il Campanello di notte
(The Night Bell)

farsa in one act

Principal characters:

Serafina	(soprano)
Don Annibale Pistacchio, her husband	(bass)
Enrico, her cousin	(baritone)
Madama Rosa, her mother	(mezzo-soprano)
Spiridione, a servant	(tenor)

LIBRETTO by Gaetano Donizetti

TIME: The early-nineteenth century
PLACE: Naples

FIRST PERFORMED at the Teatro Nuovo, Naples, 1 June 1836, with Amalia Schütz-Oldosi (Serafina); Giorgio Ronconi (Enrico); Raffaele Casaccia (Don Annibale Pistacchio)

The days following the première of *Belisario* were unhappy ones for Donizetti. On his way back to Naples he learned that his wife Virginia had given birth to a still-born child and was herself very weak and unwell, and that his mother had died in Bergamo at the age of seventy. Arriving in Naples, which was at the time under a threat of cholera, he found himself involved in negotiations with the Teatro La Fenice, in Venice, over a new opera (*Pia de' Tolomei*), during the course of which he composed a one-act farce for the Teatro Nuovo in Naples, for which he provided the libretto himself. Choosing a French one-act sketch or vaudeville, *La Sonnette de Nuit* by Léon Lévy Brunswick, Mathieu-Barthélemy Troin and Victor Lhérie, which had been recommended to him and which he may well have seen performed in Paris the previous year, Donizetti wrote his libretto quickly and set it to music with his customary celerity. *Il Campanello di notte* was so well received at its first performance at the Teatro Nuovo on 1 June 1836 that Donizetti immediately felt encouraged to compose another farce (*Betly*), once again acting as his own librettist.

Sometimes given as *Il Campanello dello speziale* (for instance, in Venice in 1853), Donizetti's new farce proved popular in a number of cities in Italy and abroad. It was first performed in London at the Lyceum Theatre on 30 November 1837, but took its time to reach the United States where it was staged for the first time in Philadelphia on 25 October 1861, and in New York three days later. Though *Il Campanello di notte* disappeared from the stage for a time in the first half of the twentieth century, there have been productions since 1950 in London, Rome, Berlin, Milan, Naples, Bregenz, Rio de Janeiro, Vienna, Barcelona, Lucca and elsewhere. It lends itself well to student performances and small-scale workshop productions, though ideally it requires supreme professional assurance and style in performance.

Donizetti's libretto is capably written, his versification in the sung numbers – there is also a great deal of prose recitative – being at least as good as that provided by most of the professional librettists he used. There is more situation than plot to this comedy. When Don Annibale Pistacchio, an elderly pharmacist, marries the young Serafina, her cousin and former fiancé Enrico constantly interrupts their wedding-night by ringing the night-bell and presenting himself in various disguises with prescriptions for the bridegroom to dispense. Since a Naples statute required pharmacists to fill prescriptions at any hour of the day or night upon pain of imprisonment, Don Annibale is effectively prevented from consummating his marriage.

Enrico first appears as a French dandy suffering from a surfeit of food and drink, next an opera singer who is about to make his debut in a new opera, *Il Campanello*, but has developed a sore throat, and finally an eccentric old man with an impossibly long prescription to be filled for his wife who appears to suffer from every possible ailment. When Don Annibale thinks he has got rid of his last customer, he steps on some fire-crackers which he has left outside his bedroom door to scare off intruders, thus rousing everyone in the vicinity. He then has to leave home immediately to attend to urgent business in Rome, and is merrily cheered on his way by all as he anxiously instructs his wife to open her door to no one before his return.

A few bars of *allegretto* orchestral introduction featuring the eponymous night-bell lead directly to an opening chorus which strikes exactly the right light-hearted tone for this slight but highly amusing piece. Don Annibale's amiable cavatina, 'Bella cosa, amici cari', is followed by a scene in *recitativo secco* and a galop which the bride dances with her cousin Enrico, the object of Annibale's quite justified suspicion. The duet, 'Non fuggir', for Serafina and Enrico is an engaging parody which avoids sentiment in its concentration on the ex-lovers' comical expressions of mutual recrimination. Discovered kneeling at Serafina's feet by the bridegroom, Enrico glibly and extravagantly talks his way out of an awkward situation, and then leads the chorus in a lilting brindisi, 'Mesci, mesci', for which Donizetti made use of a song he had composed recently (to words by Leopoldo Tarantini) as part of a collection, *Notti d'estate a Posilippo* (Summer Nights at Posilippo).

The episode of Enrico's first visit in disguise as the French dandy is conducted entirely in unaccompanied recitative, but his return as an ailing opera singer results in an amusing duet with Don Annibale, 'Ho una bella', in which Enrico demonstrates what is wrong with his voice, is miraculously cured by the chemist's lozenges, and then proceeds to become hoarse again. To test his improvement at one stage he begins to sing the Gondolier's song from Donizetti's *Marino Faliero*. Don Annibale's encounter with his final customer of the night is conducted in a typical patter duet, 'Mio signore venerato', after which the final ensemble, 'Da me lungi ancor vivendo', launched by Serafina with the opera's sole expression of real sentiment, charmingly rounds off one of Donizetti's most delightful one-act farces.

Betly, o La Capanna Svizzera
(Betly, or The Swiss Chalet)

opera giocosa in one act (later revised in two acts)

Principal characters:
Betly   (soprano)

Daniele   (tenor)
Max   (baritone)

LIBRETTO by Gaetano Donizetti

TIME: The eighteenth century
PLACE: A Swiss mountain chalet

FIRST PERFORMED at the Teatro Nuovo, Naples, 24 August 1836, with Adelaide Toldi (Betly); Lorenzo Salvi (Daniele); Giuseppe Fioravanti (Max)

Encouraged by the success of *Il Campanello*, Donizetti immediately set to work on another comedy, again writing the libretto himself. This time, he derived his subject from the libretto written by Eugène Scribe and Anne-Honoré-Joseph Mélesville for Adolphe Adam's opera *Le Chalet*, which was first performed in 1834 at the Opéra-Comique in Paris where Donizetti had seen it. (The ultimate source of the French libretto was *Jerry und Bätely*, a 1780 Singspiel by Goethe.)

Donizetti's one-act comic opera, *Betly*, subtitled *La Capanna Svizzera* (The Swiss Chalet), reached the stage of the Teatro Nuovo, Naples, on 24 August 1836, less than three months after the première at the same theatre of *Il Campanello*. The new piece proved so popular that the composer expanded it into two acts for a production in Palermo in autumn of the following year. It was staged in other Italian towns and abroad, the first London performance taking place at the Lyceum Theatre on 9 January 1838. It was not until 25 October 1861, however, that *Betly* reached America, when it was performed in Philadelphia and, three days later, in New York. Its first reappearance in the twentieth century was in Lugano, in May 1933, since when it has been seen in Bergamo (1948 and 1968), Rome (1952), London (1954), and several other places. It was staged as recently as January 1990 in Lugo, in a double bill with the original one-act *Convenienze ed inconvenienze teatrali*.

In mood, though not in detail, the plot of *Betly* is reminiscent of that of *L'Elisir d'amore*. Daniele arrives at Betly's chalet in the Swiss Alps expecting to marry her, but she rejects him as she prefers to remain independent. Her brother Max, returning home from service in the army, comes to Daniele's aid which involves turning a platoon of soldiers loose in the chalet, and, in disguise, challenging

Daniele to a duel. Eventually all ends happily with Betly agreeing to marry Daniele.

Though it is uncertain in style, the opera contains several delightful numbers, among them the opening chorus, 'Già l'aurora in ciel appar', preceded by a brief pastoral prelude; Daniele's exuberant opening solo, 'È fia ver!'; and Betly's carefree aria, 'In questo semplice modesto asilo', with its quasi-yodelling refrain. The entrance of Max and his soldiers is strongly reminiscent of that of Sergeant Belcore in *L'Elisir d'amore*. However, Max's graceful love song, 'Ti vedo, ti bacio', is addressed not to a woman but to Switzerland, on his return to his beloved native land, and in its harmlessly boastful martial cabaletta he sings of the glory of being allowed to die for his country. The scene in which Max's soldiers run amok in Betly's chalet is suitably high-spirited, but the duet for Betly and Daniele, 'Dolce istante inaspettato', is less satisfactory. A tenor–baritone duet, 'O la bella immantinente', in which Max pretends to challenge Daniele to a duel, is unexpectedly engaging, and its stretta, 'Mi sprona la gloria', is robust and reliably applause-inducing. Betly's aria, 'Se crudele il cor mostrai', and cabaletta, 'Ah no, non posso esprimere', end the opera winningly. The two-act version which Donizetti produced for Palermo in October 1837 spreads his melodic material rather thinly: the original piece in one act is to be preferred.

L'Assedio di Calais
(The Siege of Calais)

opera seria in three acts

Principal characters:

Eustachio de Saint-Pierre, Mayor of Calais	(baritone)
Aurelio, his son	(mezzo-soprano)
Eleonora, Aurelio's wife	(soprano)
Edoardo III, King of England	(bass)
Isabella, Queen of England	(soprano)

LIBRETTO by Salvatore Cammarano

TIME: 1347

PLACE: Calais

FIRST PERFORMED at the Teatro San Carlo, Naples, 19 November 1836, with Almerinda Manzocchi (Aurelio); Caterina Barili-Patti (Eleonora); Paul Barroilhet (Eustachio de Saint-Pierre); Federico Lablache (Enrico III)

The cholera epidemic which had been threatening Naples finally erupted there in October 1836. By the following March it had caused over six thousand deaths and had spread south into Sicily where, by September 1837, about a tenth of the population had died of the disease. In the early days of the epidemic in Naples, Donizetti was busy with *L'Assedio di Calais*, his next commission for the Teatro San Carlo, and was already giving thought to another opera, *Pia de' Tolomei*, which he was to write for Venice. *L'Assedio di Calais*, its libretto by Salvatore Cammarano, was completed by the end of September, and was given its première at the Teatro San Carlo on 19 November 1836, at a royal gala performance. After the second night, Donizetti wrote to his publisher Ricordi to say that the opera

> went well. I was called out six times (the evening after the gala). The third act is the least felicitous (note my honesty). Who knows? I may revise it ... It is my most carefully worked-out score. Barroilhet, la Manzocchi, la Barili, Gianni, they were all applauded. But the cholera keeps everyone in the country.

L'Assedio di Calais was performed sixteen times during the season. Donizetti was unhappy with the third act which, after the initial performances, he revised but not to his satisfaction. Therefore, when the opera was revived at the San Carlo on 6 July of the following year only its first two acts were performed, the evening ending with another composer's ballet. The next three performances were of Act I only! In all, *L'Assedio di Calais* was given thirty-eight performances in Naples, only some of them complete, after the last of which, on 4 February 1840 (two acts only), it remained unstaged until produced by the Donizetti Festival at the Teatro Donizetti in Bergamo in September 1990, and in Ireland at the 1991 Wexford Festival (in Wexford's Theatre Royal) for six performances beginning on 24 October. (It had, however, been recorded in London in 1988 by Opera Rara.) The British stage première of *L'Assedio di Calais* was given by students at the Guildhall School of Music in London on 3 March 1993.

The subject of the opera is a famous incident in the One Hundred Years' War: the siege of Calais in 1347 by the army of the English King Edward III, the heroic resistance of the burghers of Calais, and the intervention of Queen Philippa (here called Isabella) on behalf of the hostages. Cammarano took as his chief sources a play, *Edoardo III, ossia L'Assedio di Calais* by Luigi Marchionni, performed frequently in Naples between 1825 and 1835, and a ballet, *L'Assedio di Calais*, choreographed by Luigi Henry and performed in Naples in 1828. Both play and ballet are derived from a 1765 play, *Le Siège de Calais* by Dormont de Belloy, via *Eustache de Saint-Pierre, ou Le Siège de Calais* by Hubert, first performed in Paris in 1822.

Calais is under siege. In Act I, a stranger attempting to arouse the citizens against their mayor, Eustachio de Saint-Pierre, is unmasked as an English spy. In Act II, Edoardo (Edward III) announces that he will spare Calais in return for the lives of six of its leading citizens. Six, among them Eustachio and his son Aurelio, offer themselves. In Act III, the hostages are about to be put to death when Edward's Queen, who has arrived from a victory in Scotland, persuades him to spare their lives. The opera ends in general rejoicing.

Many opera directors today, unable to bear leaving the curtain down during an opera's overture, frequently inflict scenes of sometimes irrelevant or incomprehensible mime on audiences before the legitimate action begins. *L'Assedio di Calais* actually calls for mime during its *larghetto* prelude for woodwind. After a few bars of orchestral flurry have engaged the audience's attention, the curtain rises to show Aurelio, son of the Mayor of Calais, stealing bread from the English camp. It is only as he is seen to be making a successful escape that the opening chorus of English soldiers ('All' armi') is allowed to burst forth.

The frequently derided closed forms of early nineteenth-century Italian opera, from which Verdi over a long period was eventually to deliver the art-form, can work magnificently when used by a musical dramatist of genius as Donizetti certainly was, albeit intermittently. The structure of slow aria followed by fast cabaletta, imaginatively handled, is no more a bar to creativity than were the rules of rhythm, metre and rhyme in the days when poetry used to be easily distinguishable from prose; Donizetti and Cammarano use the dramatic conventions in masterly fashion throughout *L'Assedio di Calais*, as they had in *Lucia di Lammermoor*. (If *Lucia* is Donizetti's most popular opera while *L'Assedio* remains one of his least performed, the reason must surely be sought in the greater profusion of memorable tunes in the earlier opera, and perhaps a falling-off of invention in the final act of the later one.) The sorrowful duet, 'Le fibre, oh Dio, m'investe!', for Eustachio and Eleonora, with its joyous cabaletta ('Un instante i mali obblio') after the arrival of the news that Aurelio is not dead, is a fine example of the confidently established form of Italian *ottocento* music drama.

Having failed to find a satisfactory tenor for Aurelio, Donizetti wrote the role for mezzo-soprano, or *musico* (his term for the female singer of a male role). Aurelio's heartfelt *larghetto* aria ('Al mio core, oggetti amati') is followed by a vigorous cabaletta ('Giammai del forte') which ends as an ensemble. The first act finale, one of Donizetti's finest, introduces the figure of *Un Incognito* (an unknown man), soon revealed to be an English spy. The *largo* of the finale ('Che s'indugia?'), begun by Eustachio, develops into an impressive ensemble whose stretta ('Come tigri di strage anelanti') ends the act with a vehement energy of the kind one associates with early Verdi.

The first scene of Act II consists mainly of a duet ('La spada ostil') for the two female voices of Aurelio and Eleonora, a vocal combination which Donizetti uses less frequently than Rossini and Bellini, but which here produces a charming *larghetto* and, in the cabaletta, 'La speme un dolce palpito', an exhilarating *allegretto*. The second scene opens with a chorus of the citizens of Calais, after which a scene in recitative, in which an English soldier (Edmondo) delivers King Edward's demand for six hostages, leads to the act finale, its shocked *largo*, 'In sen mi corse un brivido', followed by a dramatic section in which the demand is at first indignantly rejected and then sorrowfully accepted, the brave citizens vying with each other to volunteer. The act's concluding ensemble is, unusually, not a fierce stretta, but a moving prayer, 'O sacra polve', as the chosen six say farewell to their fellow-citizens.

A brisk march begins Act III which thereafter proves, until its finale, to be the opera's weakest act. King Edoardo's triumphal aria, 'L'avvenir per me fia tutto', is oddly trivial, the jovial music accompanying the arrival of his Queen unsuitably flippant, and Edoardo's cabaletta, 'Il suon di tanto plauso', dull and characterless. The Queen having just come from conquering Scotland, the dramatic action breaks off for a celebration in her honour, with four dances for two of which Donizetti has provided instantly forgettable music. (All four movements are engagingly noisy: the music for the other two was composed by Antonio Vaccari.) Donizetti included a ballet in his opera only because he had composed it with one eye on Paris, where operas were expected to contain ballets. However, although its composer wrote to the tenor Gilbert-Louis Duprez, the creator of the role of Edgardo in *Lucia di Lammermoor*, that the work he 'would most like to see performed at the Paris Opéra would be *L'Assedio di Calais*', the opera was never staged in Paris.

Matters improve in the finale with a funeral march accompanying the entrance of the hostages; an emotional *adagio* ensemble, 'Raddopia i baci tuoi', begun by Aurelio; the English Queen's brief intervention; and a concluding joyous *allegro* ensemble, 'Fin che i secoli vivranno'. By far the best of *L'Assedio* is to be found in the ensemble finales to all three acts. Donizetti's revision of Act III, eliminating the ballet and adding a cabaletta for Eleonora, is not an improvement upon his first thoughts.

Pia de' Tolomei

opera seria in two acts

Principal characters:

Pia   (soprano)
Rodrigo   (mezzo-soprano)
Ghino   (tenor)
Nello   (baritone)
Ubaldo   (tenor)
Piero   (bass)

LIBRETTO by Salvatore Cammarano

TIME: 1260
PLACE: In and around Siena

FIRST PERFORMED at the Teatro Apollo, Venice, 18 February 1837, with Fanny Tacchinardi-Persiani (Pia); Rosina Mazzarelli (Rodrigo); Antonio Poggi (Ghino); Giorgio Ronconi (Nello); Alessandro Giacchini (Ubaldo); Alessandro Meloni (Piero)

Even before the première in Naples of *L'Assedio di Calais* in November 1836, Donizetti was at work on *Pia de' Tolomei*, the opera he had agreed to write for the Teatro La Fenice in Venice. Having completed it, he left Naples by ship for Genoa *en route* to Venice, but had to remain in Genoa for eighteen days because of the cholera quarantine regulations. While there, he received news that the Teatro La Fenice had been destroyed by fire on the night of 12 December. Nevertheless he proceeded overland to Venice, where he agreed that his opera could be performed at another Venetian theatre, the Apollo, to which the Fenice's season had been transferred. *Pia de' Tolomei* was given its first performance at the Teatro Apollo on 18 February 1837, and two days later its composer wrote to a friend simply that '*Pia* pleased altogether, except for the first act finale'.

The finale to the first act had, indeed, been greeted with whistles of disapproval, and Donizetti revised it for performances of the opera in the Adriatic resort of Sinigaglia in July. Further revisions were made for a production at the Teatro Argentina in Rome, in May of the following year when Giuseppina Strepponi (who many years later was to become the wife of Giuseppe Verdi) sang the title-role. Even more changes were made, this time at the demand of the censors, when *Pia* was staged in Naples in September 1838. After performances in Milan and Florence in 1839, productions abroad in Barcelona (1844), Lisbon (1847) and Malta (1854–1855), and a few other stagings in Italian towns, *Pia de' Tolomei* disappeared from the repertoire for over a hundred years until it was revived on 3 September 1967 at the Teatro dei Rinnovati in Siena, in a production which was seen in Bologna in March 1968. The opera finally reached London in a concert performance at the Queen Elizabeth Hall on 26 February 1978, but has yet to be performed in the United States.

Salvatore Cammarano's libretto derives from one, or perhaps both, of two plays. The playwrights were Giacinto Bianco, whose *Pia de' Tolomei* was staged in Naples in April 1836, and Carlo Marenco, whose play of the same title was produced in May. Both plays were based on a novella, also of the same title, by Bartolomeo Sestini, published in 1822. (The ultimate source is Canto V of Dante's *Purgatorio*.) The action of the opera takes place in and around Siena in 1260. Pia, married to Nello, is loved by her husband's cousin, Ghino, whose advances she firmly rejects. Ghino accuses Pia of adultery with an unknown man, as a result of which Pia is imprisoned by her husband in his castle. The unknown man, however, is not a lover but Pia's brother, Rodrigo, whose freedom from prison she has purchased. Although Ghino is stricken with remorse, he confesses to Nello too late to save Pia from being poisoned on Nello's instructions. The dying Pia begs her husband (a Ghibelline) and her brother (a Guelph) to end their feuding.

The recitative leading to Ghino's *larghetto* cavatina, 'Non puo dirti la parola', in Act I scene i contains four bars of arioso sung to the words, 'O Pia mendace! ov'è, ov'è il rigore?' which sixteen years later, with a change of key, would become Violetta's 'Amami, Alfredo, amami quant' io t'amo' in Act II scene i of Verdi's *La Traviata*. The aria and its cabaletta ('Mi volesti sventurato?') possess a splendid energy of the kind usually associated with early Verdi, but Pia's entrance aria, 'O tu che desti il fulmine', and its cabaletta, 'Di pura gioia in estasi', are rather pallid, as is most of this dully passive heroine's music. The duet for Ghino and Nello in the second scene has a disappointingly crude opening section ('È men fero, è meno ferrendo'), but its cabaletta, 'Del ciel che non punisce', is splendidly fierce. A scene in the dungeon in which Pia's brother is incarcerated contains only a mundane aria and cabaletta for the mezzo-soprano Rodrigo, and the final scene of Act I in Pia's apartments is also musically undistinguished, except for the Bellinian *cantabile*, 'Fra queste braccia', shared by Pia and Rodrigo.

Near the beginning of Act II, a duet ('Ti muova il gemito dell' innocente') for Pia and Ghino is intermittently effective. The second scene begins with an orchestral thunderstorm and a fine prayer sung by Piero and his chorus of fellow-hermits. (Italian operatic hermits are curiously gregarious creatures.) The scene continues with Nello's sorrowful aria ('Lei perduta') and urgent cabaletta ('Ciel pietoso'), with aria separated from cabaletta by the arioso of Ghino's eloquent and affecting death scene. A solemn orchestral introduction precedes the opera's final scene in which the dying Pia's aria ('Sposo, ah! tronca ogni dimora') and cabaletta ('Ah! di Pia . . . che muore . . . e geme') fail to be as moving as they should be, though the disjointed vocal line of her cabaletta's second verse is dramatically effective.

Pia de' Tolomei is too uneven an opera to be likely to achieve frequent performance, but it is fascinating enough not to disappear entirely from the repertoire.

Roberto Devereux

opera seria in three acts

Principal characters:

Elisabetta, Queen of England	(soprano)
Roberto Devereux, Count of Essex	(tenor)
Duke of Nottingham	(baritone)
Sara, Duchess of Nottingham	(mezzo-soprano)
Lord Cecil	(tenor)
Sir Gualtiero Raleigh	(bass)

LIBRETTO by Salvatore Cammarano

TIME: 1598
PLACE: London

FIRST PERFORMED at the Teatro San Carlo, Naples, 29 October 1837, with Giuseppina Ronzi de Begnis (Elisabetta); Giovanni Basadonna (Roberto Devereux); Almerinda Granchi (Sara); Paul Barroilhet (Nottingham)

Soon after the Venice première of *Pia de' Tolomei* on 18 February 1837, Donizetti was back in Naples, teaching at the Conservatorium, and composing various orchestral and choral pieces to commemorate deaths and anniversaries of prominent musicians and royal personages. In June his wife Virginia gave birth to a second son, who died within an hour, and on 30 July Virginia herself died at the age of twenty-nine, perhaps of the cholera which was still sweeping the city, perhaps of complications following a bout of measles, but most probably of syphilis caught from her husband. That Donizetti had contracted the disease some time before he married Virginia is virtually certain. 'Oh, my Toto,' he wrote to Virginia's brother Antonio, 'let my grief find an echo in yours ... I shall be unhappy forever.'

In a state of acute depression and physical weakness, Donizetti turned to work for consolation. His next commission was for an opera to be staged at the Teatro San Carlo in the autumn, and the subject he chose was from English history: the relationship of Queen Elizabeth I and the Earl of Essex. Salvatore Cammarano wrote a libretto derived from the play *Élisabeth d'Angleterre* by François

Ancelot, staged in Paris in 1832, and also from Felice Romani's libretto for the opera *Il Conte d'Essex* by Saverio Mercadante, which had been given an unsuccessful première in Milan in 1833. Donizetti's *Roberto Devereux* was given its first performance at the Teatro San Carlo on 29 October 1837, and two days later its composer told a friend that 'the results could not have been more flattering'.

Roberto Devereux proved to be one of Donizetti's most successful operas, with productions throughout Italy and in a number of cities in Europe and further afield. In its first five years of life it was staged in Lisbon, Barcelona, Paris, Havana, Brussels, Corfu, Malta, Odessa, Berlin, London (on 24 June 1841), Lugano, Copenhagen, Mexico City and Athens. Its New York première was on 15 January 1849. After 1882 there appear to have been no performances of *Roberto Devereux* until 2 May 1964 when it was revived in Naples at the San Carlo, the theatre of its première, with Leyla Gencer as Queen Elizabeth. Montserrat Caballé assumed the role in a concert performance at Carnegie Hall, New York, on 14 December 1965, and subsequently sang it in stage productions in Barcelona (1968) and Venice (1972), and in concert performances in London (1970) and Hamburg (1978). Beverly Sills was the Elizabeth in a New York City Opera production first seen in 1970, Katia Ricciarelli sang the role in Naples in 1987, and Edita Gruberova (with Richard Bonynge conducting) sang Elizabeth in Barcelona in 1990. There have also been productions of the opera in Bergamo (1967), Bonn (1969), Usti, Czechoslovakia (1976), Bregenz (1977), Valle d'Itria (1985), Lisbon (1986), Bielefeld (1987), Rome (1988), Monte Carlo and Bologna (both 1992), so *Roberto Devereux* can be said to have firmly re-established itself in the repertoire.

Cammarano's libretto makes no claims to historical accuracy. His Elisabetta is in love with Roberto, Earl of Essex, who in turn loves Sara, wife of Roberto's close friend the Duke of Nottingham. (The historical Earl of Nottingham, whose wife was named Catherine, was not a close friend of Essex.) When Essex is accused of treason, the Queen at first refuses to sign his death sentence, but eventually does so when she suspects that he has been unfaithful to her. A message that would have saved Essex arrives too late, for which the jealous Queen blames Sara. The Nottinghams are led away to prison, while a distraught Elisabetta expresses her wish for death and for the accession of James VI of Scotland to the English throne.

The overture, not heard at the opera's première but composed a year later for Paris, has two main themes, an anachronistic but engaging use of 'God Save the Queen' and a livelier tune which occurs again in Roberto's cabaletta in Act III. From the very beginning of Act I with its sympathetic female chorus introducing Sara's elegantly melancholy romanza, 'All' afflitto è dolce il pianto', it is clear that this will be one of Donizetti's most confident and original scores. Elisabetta's expressive *larghetto*, 'L'amor suo mi fè beata', is followed by a sprightly *allegro* cabaletta, 'Ah! ritorna qual ti spero', when she is told of Essex's imminent arrival. Her duet with Roberto ('Un tenero core') is fine, especially the new cabaletta ('Un lampo, un lampo orribile') which Donizetti provided shortly after the first performances to replace the less adventurous one performed at the première. Nottingham's suave *larghetto* cavatina, 'Forse in quel cor sensibile', with its almost comically ardent protestations of friendship in the cabaletta, 'Qui ribelle ognun ti chiama', is one of the weaker numbers in the score, but the duet for Sara and Roberto which ends Act I, its *larghetto* first section ('Dacchè tornasti, ahi misera') followed by an urgent cabaletta ('Ah! questo addio fatale, estremo'), is first-rate. The cabaletta, although it was originally composed for the Paris production of *Marino Faliero*, makes an apt conclusion to the scene, and also somewhat resembles another duet of parting, that of Gilda and the Duke of Mantua in Act I scene ii of Verdi's *Rigoletto*.

The brief second act, consisting of no more than three numbers, is superb, its dramatic tension sustained throughout from its opening chorus with the voices commenting over a broad Verdian melody in the orchestra, through Elisabetta's duet ('Non venni mai sì mesto') with Nottingham, to Roberto's entrance and the trio 'Alma infida, ingrato core', again an anticipation of Verdi in its sheer energy. In the stretta ('Va, va, la morte sul capo ti pende') Elisabetta's fury is expressed in wide vocal leaps.

Act III consists of three short scenes and, effectively, of three numbers, the first of which, a dramatic duet for Sara and Nottingham, culminates in a powerful cabaletta, 'All' ambascia ond' io mi struggo'. Roberto's affecting aria ('Come uno spirto angelico') in his prison cell in the Tower of London is preceded by a solemn orchestral introduction which looks back to the prelude of Florestan's aria in Beethoven's *Fidelio*, and forward to that of Ulrica's aria in Verdi's *Un Ballo in maschera*, while his perhaps unsuitably jaunty cabaletta ('Bagnato è il sen di lagrime') uses a melody already heard as the second subject of the overture. The final scene, with Elisabetta's beautiful aria, 'Vivi, ingrato', and its fierce, heartfelt cabaletta, 'Quel sangue versato', makes a powerful end to one of Donizetti's finest and most affecting operas.

Maria de Rudenz

opera seria in three acts

Principal characters:

Maria de Rudenz	(soprano)
Matilde	(soprano)
Corrado	(baritone)
Enrico	(tenor)

LIBRETTO by Salvatore Cammarano

TIME: 1400
PLACE: Switzerland

FIRST PERFORMED at the Teatro La Fenice, Venice, 30 January 1838, with Caroline Unger (Maria); Napoleone Moriani (Enrico); Giorgio Ronconi (Corrado)

Some time before the October 1837 première of *Roberto Devereux* in Naples, Donizetti had agreed to compose another opera for the Teatro La Fenice in Venice. Salvatore Cammarano was again the librettist, and the subject Donizetti eventually chose, after considering at least two others, was a French play, *La Nonne Sanglante* by Anicet-Bourgeois, Cuvelier and Mallian, a piece of Gothic horror derived from an episode in Matthew G. Lewis's 1795 novel, *The Monk*, and staged in Paris in 1835.

Composition of the opera, *Maria de Rudenz*, proceeded slowly, for the bereaved and grieving Donizetti found it difficult to concentrate on the task. 'I keep asking for whom do I work, and why?' he told his brother-in-law, Antonio Vasselli. In November he wrote that he was making headway with the opera but was not pleased with it and expected the Venetian audience to share his opinion. They did. At its première on 30 January 1838 *Maria de Rudenz* was unfavourably received, and was withdrawn after its second performance to be replaced by Donizetti's *Parisina*.

Though it was produced in a few other Italian towns, and abroad in Madrid, Corfu, Lisbon, Malta, Alexandria, Barcelona, Rio de Janeiro and Buenos Aires during the following twenty years, *Maria de Rudenz* did not reach London or New York. When it was staged in Ancona in 1841, Donizetti wrote to a friend that he was happy to hear of its success there, but 'I still bleed for the severity with which it was treated in Venice'.

London eventually heard the opera in a concert performance by Opera Rara at the Queen Elizabeth Hall on 27 October 1974, but its first staging in the twentieth century was at the Teatro La Fenice in a series of performances beginning on 21 December 1980, with Katia Ricciarelli as Maria. The production, with a change of cast, was revived in Venice in the autumn of 1981 and toured to Dresden in 1982.

The opera's complex, overwrought and grisly plot, set in the year 1400 in Switzerland, concerns two brothers, Corrado and Enrico, one of whom, Corrado, had abducted and subsequently abandoned a woman, Maria, some years earlier. The brothers are now both in love with Matilde, whom Corrado is about to marry. Maria, whom Corrado had left to die in the catacombs of Rome, has survived and now wanders about the castle grounds, still in love with Corrado who she has discovered is really the son of a murderer. When she threatens to kill Matilde, Corrado stabs Maria. However, she survives to murder Matilde before dying, still protesting that she loves Corrado who, meanwhile, has killed Enrico in a duel.

Though Donizetti's score is disappointingly uneven, the opera does contain some first-rate numbers. In Act I, entitled *Il Testamento* (The Testament), after an opening off-stage chorus for female voices, Corrado makes his entrance with a suave romanza, 'Ah! non avea più lagrime', followed, not by the expected solo cabaletta but, after a lengthy passage of recitative, by a lively duet with his brother, Enrico. In the second scene Maria's expressive cavatina, 'Sì, del chiostro penitente', is followed by a cabaletta, 'Sulla mia tomba gelida', whose jaunty vocal line belies its dramatic content. (An amiable tenor aria and cabaletta which Donizetti wrote after the première, but which was never performed, was first heard at this point in the 1974 London concert performance.) The expansive Act I finale, the *larghetto* of which Donizetti later used in *Poliuto*, is both musically and dramatically the most satisfactory scene in the opera.

After a brief but impressive orchestral prelude featuring a solo bass clarinet, Act II (*Un Delitto*: A Crime) begins with a lively chorus, followed by a disappointingly nondescript aria ('Talor del mio delirio') and cabaletta ('La parola che dicesti') for Enrico. The only other number in the act, a dramatic duet ('Fonte d'amare lagrime') for Maria and Corrado, is of a much higher standard. Its cabaletta ('E' d'altra il cor'), occasioned by Maria's threat to murder Matilde, leads to a gloriously frenetic finale to the act as a desperate Corrado stabs Maria and she falls, apparently dead.

After the opening chorus of Act III (*Lo Spettro*: The Spectre), the duet ('A me, cui financo la speme togliesti') for Corrado and Enrico is undistinguished, though its cabaletta ('O tremenda gelosia') can prove exciting in performance. A dance with chorus, described by Donizetti as a Swiss waltz, opens the last scene with its final aria for Maria who had not been killed outright by Corrado but seriously wounded. Off-stage, she now stabs Matilde who shrieks and dies on the spot, allowing the prima donna to enter, confront Corrado, and expire more slowly after a double aria. Its affecting *larghetto*, 'Mostro iniquo', is followed, not by a conventional cabaletta in a fast tempo, but by an *andante*, 'Al misfatto enorme e rio', in which Maria claims she was forced to behave monstrously because of her love for Corrado whom she now forgives. Thus ends an opera whose dramatic content it is difficult to take with total seriousness, but which, musically, at least begins and ends splendidly.

Poliuto

opera seria in three acts

Principal characters:

Poliuto, Magistrate of Mytilene	(tenor)
Paolina, his wife	(soprano)
Severo, the Roman Proconsul	(baritone)
Nearco, leader of the Armenian Christians	(bass)
Felice, Paolina's father, and Governor of Mytilene	(tenor)
Callistene, High Priest of Jupiter	(bass)

LIBRETTO by Salvatore Cammarano

TIME: 257 A.D.
PLACE: Mytilene, capital of Armenia

FIRST PERFORMED at the Teatro San Carlo, Naples, 30 November 1848, with Carlo Baucardé (Poliuto); Eugenia Tadolini (Paolina); Filippo Colini (Severo); Domenico Ceci (Nearco); Anafesto Rossi (Felice); Marco Arati (Callistene)

After the failure of *Maria de Rudenz* in Venice at the end of January 1838, Donizetti returned to Naples to work on his next opera, *Poliuto*, whose libretto by Cammarano was based on the play *Polyeucte* by Pierre Corneille, first performed in Paris in 1642. He also began negotiations with the Paris Opéra, whose Director had invited him to compose two works. In July he was able to inform his brother-in-law that he was still working on *Poliuto* but that 'the censorship is making sour faces, saying that it is too sacred', its offence being that it dealt with Christian martyrdom in Roman times.

After *Poliuto* was completed, Donizetti was informed that, by express command of the King who was a very religious man, its performance would not be allowed. The Naples impresario staged *Pia de' Tolomei* in its place, and a furious Donizetti decided to leave Naples permanently. He had composed the title-role of *Poliuto* for the famous French tenor, Adolphe Nourrit, who had in fact suggested the subject of the opera. Nourrit, who suffered from bouts of severe depression, had to make his Naples debut in another opera, and six months later committed suicide by leaping out of a window.

In 1840, Donizetti adapted most of the music of *Poliuto* to a French text, and the opera was staged in Paris as *Les Martyrs* (see pp 267–269). The original *Poliuto* had to wait until 30 November 1848 (some months after its composer's death) to be staged, when it was performed at the theatre for which it had been written, the San Carlo in Naples, the political climate there being for a brief period more liberal. The opera's performance history since then has been complicated, for it was staged in Rome in 1849 as *Paolina e Severo*, and in other Italian cities either as *Poliuto* or *I Martiri*, an Italian translation of the French version. It was first heard in London as *I Martiri* at Covent Garden on 20 April 1852, and first staged in the United States in New York as *Poliuto* on 25 May 1859. (It had, however, been given a concert performance in Boston on 16

December 1849.) In Vienna in 1853 the opera was performed as *Paolina e Poliuto*. Often staged in a conflation of the Italian and French versions, it never entirely disappeared from the repertoire. Productions in the last half-century have included those in Rome (in the open air at the Terme di Caracalla) with Giacomo Lauri-Volpi and Maria Caniglia in 1955, at La Scala with Franco Corelli and Maria Callas in 1960 (in the hybrid version), in Bergamo in 1975 as *Les Martyrs*, and, as *Poliuto*, in Rome in 1988 and Ravenna in 1992.

The plot differs only in detail from version to version. Poliuto, the Magistrate of Mytilene in Armenia who has secretly embraced Christianity, is followed to a hidden sanctuary by his wife, Paolina, who witnesses his baptism. Severo, the Roman Proconsul with whom Paolina was once in love and whom she has believed dead, arrives in Armenia to liberate the country from the scourge of Christianity. When, in order to save the life of the Christian leader Nearco, Poliuto reveals that he too has become a Christian, he is condemned to death. Paolina, though she still loves Severo, visits Poliuto in prison and, moved by his refusal to renounce his new faith, decides to embrace the Christian religion. Husband and wife go forth to martyrdom together.

The overture is unusual, not only in its solemn opening *larghetto* scored for four bassoons, but also in its interruption of the subsequent *allegro vivace* by an off-stage chorus of prayer. In the score, the overture is followed by a separate, much shorter prelude, which repeats the *allegro vivace* of the overture. Presumably Donizetti wrote the prelude to supplant the overture, or perhaps *vice versa*. The introductory male chorus of Christians ('Scendiam, scendiam') immediately puts one in mind of Verdi, a greater composer but one whose debt to Donizetti is apparent throughout this opera. Poliuto's *larghetto* prayer, 'D'un' alma troppo fervida', is not one of Donizetti's more individual tenor arias, but Paolina's cavatina, 'Di quai soavi lagrime', preceded by a lengthy clarinet solo and a scene in which she hears in the distance the voices of her husband and his fellow-Christians at prayer, is an arrestingly individual piece. The coloratura brilliance of its *allegro giusto* cabaletta, 'Perchè di stolto giubilo', is more conventional. The second scene of Act I consists of a rousing march and chorus followed by Severo's fairly ordinary aria ('Di tua beltade immagine') and cabaletta ('No, l'acciar non fu spietato').

In the first scene of Act II the *allegretto* duet for Paolina and

Severo, 'Il più lieto dei viventi', is persuasive, and its cabaletta ('Quest' alma è troppo debole'), a slower *andante*, is both attractive and unusual. Poliuto's aria ('Fu macchiato l'onor mio'), a vigorous *allegro giusto*, is exciting, and its cabaletta ('Sfolgorò divino raggio') even more so. Act II, scene ii, like the triumphal Act II, scene ii in Verdi's *Aida* of more than thirty years later which it undoubtedly influenced, is a magnificent achievement. Set in a Temple of Jupiter, it begins with a hymn to the god, sung first in unison by the male priests 'in a tone of fanatical zeal' and then, more gently, by the women's chorus. The *larghetto* ensemble, 'La sacrilega parola', taken from the Act I finale of *Maria de Rudenz*, is followed by an exciting and entirely new stretta. This is one of the finest scenes in any Donizetti opera, and a clear indication of the composer's relationship to the operas of his great successor, Giuseppe Verdi.

Callistene's aria ('Alimento alla fiamma si porga') at the beginning of Act III is unremarkable, but the duet for Poliuto and Paolina ('Ah! fuggi da morte orribil cotanto') in Poliuto's prison cell is both dramatic and moving in his serene acceptance of martyrdom and her newly found faith. The cabaletta, 'Il suon dell' arpe angeliche', uses the tune already heard as the second subject of the overture, a melody which was to become one of Donizetti's most popular. The finale is both eloquent and affecting, with the crowd in the arena calling for blood, the Christians' hymn heard in the distance, and husband and wife walking out confidently into the arena to face death together. So ends one of Donizetti's finest operas, and one which deserves to be staged whenever a tenor and a soprano can be found who are capable of doing justice to the roles of Poliuto and Paolina.

Les Martyrs
(The Martyrs)

grand opéra in four acts

Principal characters:

Polyeucte	(tenor)
Pauline	(soprano)
Sévère	(baritone)

Néarque   (bass)
Félix   (bass)
Callisthènes   (bass)

LIBRETTO by Eugène Scribe

TIME: 257 A.D.
PLACE: Mytilene, capital of Armenia

FIRST PERFORMED at the Paris Opéra, 10 April 1840, with
Gilbert Duprez (Polyeucte); Julie Dorus-Gras (Pauline); Jean-
Étienne Massol (Sévère); Pierre-François Wartel (Néarque);
Prosper Dérivis (Félix); Émile Serda (Callisthènes)

After the suppression of his *Poliuto* by royal decree, Donizetti left
Naples in October 1838, and proceeded to Paris. In November he
wrote to a friend: 'I have been in Paris for more than three weeks. I
can tell you quickly what I am doing. I am staging *Roberto Devereux* at
the Théâtre-Italien. As for what I shall do after that, here it is. I
shall give the opera (*Poliuto*) that was forbidden in Naples, at the
great French theatre, the Académie Royale de Musique, in French.'

He had agreed to compose two operas to French texts for
performance at the Académie Royale (the Paris Opéra). For the
first, he turned to *Poliuto*, and engaged Eugène Scribe to produce a
text based, as was Cammarano's Italian libretto, on the Corneille
play, *Polyeucte*. (Scribe's text stayed closer to Corneille than Cammarano's had done.) There were delays, caused mainly by Scribe's
tardiness in delivering his libretto. In April 1839, Donizetti wrote to
his old teacher, Mayr, that *Poliuto* was being turned into a French
grand opera, with four acts instead of its original three, and

> translated and adjusted for the French theatre by Scribe. For that
> reason, I have had to redo the recitatives, write a new finale for Act I,
> and add arias, trios, and the appropriate ballets which they require here
> ... This *Poliuto*, changed into *Les Martyrs*, will be given within the year.

By the middle of May Donizetti had finished *Les Martyrs*, and had
begun to compose his second work for the Opéra, *Le Duc d'Albe*. 'Oh,
my maestro,' he wrote to Mayr, 'I shall bid the theatre a bitter
farewell as soon as possible. I say "bitter" even though it makes me
rich, but I say it from the bottom of my heart because that will
remove me from so much suffering.'

During the summer of 1839 Donizetti also supervised the French-language production of the opera which was now called *Lucie de Lammermoor*, and by the autumn he had 'written, scored and delivered a little opera to the Opéra-Comique'. This 'little opera' was *La Fille du régiment*, which was staged in February 1840. It was not until 10 April 1840 that *Les Martyrs* was performed at the Opéra. Though its reception by critics was mixed, Berlioz describing it as 'a credo in four acts', *Les Martyrs* proved popular with audiences, and was performed twenty times over two seasons.

Donizetti achieved the extension of the opera from three to four acts by dividing the first act of *Poliuto* into two, and adding music for the ballet which Paris audiences would have expected. There are several musical changes throughout the work, as well as some new numbers. For example, the vocal line of Pauline's Act I aria (formerly Paolina's 'Di quai soave lagrime', now 'Qu'ici ta main glacée') has undergone some alteration, and the act now ends with a new and beautiful trio, 'Objet de ma constance'. In Act II Félix (Felice), no longer a comprimario tenor but a principal bass, is given an aria ('Dieux des Romains') and cabaletta ('Mort, mort à ces infâmes'), and the second scene of the act contains three numbers for the ballet. Act III of *Les Martyrs* is virtually the same as Act II of *Poliuto*, except that Poliuto's aria and cabaletta have been replaced by a new aria ('Mon seul trésor') and cabaletta ('Oui, j'irai dans leur temples') for Polyeucte, with a higher tessitura to suit the new tenor, Gilbert Duprez, famous for his high C sung in full voice from the chest. Callisthènes' dull aria at the beginning of Act IV is replaced by a trio, and there are further changes in the opera's remaining two scenes.

Les Martyrs is undoubtedly an impressive achievement. However, despite the fact that much of the finest music in the two scores appears in both versions, this French adaptation lacks something of the southern warmth and energy of *Poliuto*.

13

From *Le Duc d'Albe* to *Ne m'oubliez pas*

Il Duca d'Alba (Le Duc d'Albe)

grand opéra in four acts

Principal characters:

Il Duca d'Alba	(baritone)
Amelia di Egmont	(soprano)
Marcello di Bruges	(tenor)
Daniele	(bass)

LIBRETTO by Eugène Scribe and Charles Duvéyrier, translated and revised by Angelo Zanardini

TIME: 1573
PLACE: Brussels

FIRST PERFORMED at the Teatro Apollo, Rome, 22 March 1882, with Leone Giraldoni (Il Duca d'Alba); Abigaille Bruschi-Chiatti (Amelia di Egmont); Julian Gayarré (Marcello di Bruges); Alessandro Silvestri (Daniele)

Donizetti began to write *Le Duc d'Albe* in Paris in May 1839, for performance at the Opéra. He had finished *Les Martyrs*, which was staged in April 1840, and he also found time, in the autumn of 1839, to dash off *La Fille du Régiment* for the Opéra-Comique. For various reasons, however, among them a change of management at the Opéra and the whims of a prima donna, the production of *Le Duc d'Albe* was delayed. When, some years later, it seemed as though the Opéra was ready to stage the work, Donizetti objected because he considered that appropriate singers for the principal roles were not available. When its composer died in 1848, *Le Duc d'Albe* had still not been staged. The manuscript score was examined and reported to be incomplete and unorchestrated.

It was not until 1875, when Donizetti's body was exhumed from the public cemetery in Bergamo for ceremonial reburial in the church of Santa Maria Maggiore, that the possibility of staging *Le Duc d'Albe* was considered again. The decision was still negative, but the score was subsequently acquired by the publishing firm of Lucca, and a version of the opera in Italian, edited by Matteo Salvi, was announced for publication and performance.

Donizetti had left the third and fourth acts unorchestrated, and the fourth act incomplete. Salvi set to work to complete the opera in accordance with its composer's intentions, to the extent that they were known, and *Il Duca d'Alba* was revealed to the world thirty-four years after Donizetti's death. On 22 March 1882 Queen Margherita attended the enormously successful première at the Teatro Apollo, Rome. But a production in Naples the following month was a failure. After performances in Bergamo in August, Barcelona in December, Malta in 1884 and Turin in 1886, *Il Duca d'Alba* lapsed until revived by the Spoleto Festival at the Teatro Nuovo, Spoleto, on 11 June 1959, directed by Luchino Visconti in the 1882 sets which had been found in a Rome warehouse. Thomas Schippers, the conductor of the Spoleto performances, prepared a new performing edition of the score, reshaping it in three acts. It was this version, again conducted by Schippers, which introduced the opera to the United States in a concert performance in Carnegie Hall, New York, in October 1959.

To commemorate the four hundredth anniversary of the Treaty of Ghent, *Il Duca d'Alba*, whose subject stems from Belgian history, was staged at the Royal Opera in Ghent in September 1976. The millennium of Brussels was similarly celebrated in September 1979 at the Théâtre-Royale de la Monnaie. In December 1979, the opera again met with a cool reception in Naples, and in 1981 it fared little better in Florence. The Spoleto Festival returned to *Il Duca d'Alba* in June 1992, this time using Matteo Salvi's edition as staged in Rome in 1882. The opera has yet to be performed in Britain.

The libretto by Eugène Scribe and Charles Duvéyrier sets most of the opera's action in Brussels in 1573, with the Flemish suffering under Spanish tyranny. Amelia (Hélène in the French original) is in love with Marcello (Henri), who is revealed to be the missing son of their oppressor, the Duke of Alba. When Amelia attempts to kill the Duke, Marcello throws himself between them and receives the blow. As he dies, he begs the Duke, his father, to forgive Amelia. (Since the opera was not staged, Scribe took the opportunity to use his libretto again fourteen years later, changing the locale to thirteenth-century Sicily and making a few minor adjustments, in order to sell it to Verdi as *Les Vêpres Siciliennes*.)

Donizetti's score is remarkable more for the dramatic energy of its lengthy passages of recitative and for its skilful orchestration than for any melodic richness. (Verdi's setting of virtually the same libretto is consistently superior in its masterly blend of dramatic strength and eloquent melody.) Act I of *Il Duca d'Alba*, after an orchestral prelude which, for Donizetti, is unusual in its relevance to the dramatic content of the opera, contains Amelia's fine solo, 'In seno ai mar', and, as finale, a rousing tenor–baritone duet ('Un vil io non son') for Marcello and the Duke of Alba. Amelia's romanza in Act II, 'Ombra paterna', is both graceful and affecting, and her duet with Marcello ('Ah! si, l'ardente affanno'), which begins lyrically and develops dramatically, is highly effective. The ensembles and scenes of dramatic confrontation in the latter part of the act are especially impressive.

The Duke's aria, 'Nei miei superbi gaudi' (lifted by Donizetti from *Il Paria*), at the beginning of Act III and his duet, 'Ne volea sfidar lo sdegno', are fine, but the glory of the act is its dramatic ensemble finale. Marcello's gentle *andante* aria, 'Angelo casto e bel', which opens Act IV is not by Donizetti but by Matteo Salvi who prepared the score for its 1882 première. (Donizetti had removed 'Spirto gentil', the aria which he had composed at this point, to transfer it to *La Favorite*.) The duet for Marcello and Amelia which follows is stolid, both in its *moderato* opening section and its *marziale* conclusion, but the opera returns to form in the concerted numbers of its final scene, especially the finale for the three principals and ensemble.

La Fille du régiment
(The Daughter of the Regiment)

opéra comique in two acts

Principal characters:

Marie	(soprano)
Tonio	(tenor)
Sulpice	(bass)
La Marquise de Birkenfeld	(mezzo-soprano)

LIBRETTO by Jules-Henri Vernoy de Saint-Georges and Jean-François-Alfred Bayard

TIME: Early-nineteenth century
PLACE: The Swiss Tyrol

FIRST PERFORMED at the Opéra-Comique, Paris, 11 February 1840, with Juliette Bourgeois (Marie); Mécène Marié de l'Isle (Tonio); M. Henry (Sulpice); Marie-Julienne Boulanger (La Marquise de Birkenfeld)

It was in Paris during the summer of 1839 that Donizetti, having completed the task of fashioning *Les Martyrs* from his Italian opera *Poliuto*, and having begun *Le Duc d'Albe* (which was fated not to be staged during his lifetime), turned aside to compose a work for the Opéra-Comique. To a libretto provided by the prolific team of Vernoy de Saint-Georges and Bayard he wrote one of his most popular comic operas, *La Fille du régiment*. When it was staged at the Opéra-Comique on 11 February 1840, its success at first was only moderate. Several critics, among them Berlioz, accused Donizetti of having inserted into an ostensibly new opera music which had already been heard in Italy, to which charge the composer replied indignantly and truthfully that the score of *La Fille du régiment* was entirely new, having been composed expressly for the Opéra-Comique.

Over the months, the new opera began to attract Parisian audiences. By the beginning of the following year it had achieved fifty performances, and in due course it became highly popular throughout France. It remained in the repertoire of the Opéra-

Comique in Paris, reaching its thousandth performance in 1914, and it is still to be encountered there. Abroad, it soon became popular in Italy in a translation by Calisto Bassi as *La Figlia del reggimento*, and was staged in the vernacular in such countries as Denmark, Germany, Spain, Hungary, Sweden, Poland, Russia, Croatia, Slovenia and Estonia. Though its first performance in Great Britain, at Her Majesty's Theatre, London, on 27 May 1847, was in Italian (with Jenny Lind in the title-role), an English translation followed at the Surrey Theatre on 21 December 1847. New Orleans was the first American city to hear the opera (in its original French) on 6 March 1843, with New York following on 19 July 1843 (also in French), 5 June 1844 (in English) and 15 May 1855 (in German). Lily Pons was a greatly loved Marie at the Metropolitan Opera during the Second World War, and in more recent times the role has belonged, in London, New York, Sydney and elsewhere, to Joan Sutherland.

Set in the Swiss Tyrol during the period of the Napoleonic wars, the action centres around Marie, who has been brought up since childhood by Sergeant Sulpice and his regiment, who regard her as their mascot. She and Tonio, a mountaineer, are in love and, in order to be near Marie, Tonio enlists in the regiment. When it is discovered that Marie is the niece of the Marquise de Birkenfeld, she is made to leave her friends of the regiment, take up residence with the Marquise, and receive an education more in keeping with her new station in life. In the palace of the Marquise, Marie pines for Tonio and for her other friends. Suddenly the regiment arrives at the palace. Sulpice learns from the Marquise that Marie is really her daughter. He passes this information on to Marie, who had intended to elope with Tonio but who now feels she cannot defy her mother who wishes her to marry a nobleman. Finally, however, Marie's obvious misery touches the Marquise's heart, and she consents to the marriage of her daughter to Tonio.

The opera consists of an engaging overture, which makes good use of Marie's Act I aria, 'Chacun le sait'; an elegant entr'acte; and twelve musical numbers separated by spoken dialogue (replaced in the Italian version by *recitativo secco*). It is clear from the very first number, which incorporates a comic strophic song for the Marquise, that Donizetti has not simply composed an Italian *opera buffa* to a French text but has succeeded in mastering the style and form of French *opéra comique*. Indeed, *La Fille du régiment* is the link between the comic operas of Grétry and Adam and the operettas of Offenbach. The hoydenish Marie makes her entrance in a scene with Sulpice which leads into a duet, 'Au bruit de la guerre', ending with a brisk military Rataplan which Verdi must have remembered many years later when he was composing the Rataplan chorus in *La Forza del destino*.

Marie's regimental song, 'Chacun le sait', makes use of a cheeky tune already heard ten years earlier in *Il Diluvio universale*. Her love duet with Tonio, 'Depuis l'instant', is similarly light-hearted, and Tonio's double aria, 'Ah! mes amis', in which he succeeds in gaining the regiment's consent to his marrying Marie, is a gloriously ebullient piece in whose second section, the *allegro* 'Pour mon âme', he exultantly emits eight high Cs. Most tenors cannot resist adding a ninth in the aria's final bars. In the Act I finale Marie's touching romance, 'Il faut partir', develops into a splendid ensemble.

After the entr'acte, Act II begins with a farcical scene in which the Marquise's attempt to teach Marie a respectable song is undermined by her pupil and Sulpice, who eventually break into their Rataplan, but only after Marie has ended one of her coloratura outbursts with a scream on high C. The sadness of Marie's aria, 'Par le rang', turns to joy with the arrival of Tonio and the regiment who support her in a lively patriotic cabaletta, 'Salut à la France'. An *allegro* trio, 'Tous les trois réunis', for Marie, Tonio and Sulpice, positively Offenbachian in its *joie de vivre*, is followed by a tender *larghetto* aria for Tonio, 'Pour me rapprocher de Marie' and by the brisk Act II finale which features a reprise of 'Salut à la France'.

The changes that Donizetti made some months later for the Italian version, *La Figlia del reggimento*, are not improvements, nor do they succeed in turning the work into an Italian *opera buffa*. Tonio loses his two arias and is given a new one (borrowed from *Gianni di Calais*), the Marquise loses her couplets at the beginning of the opera, and at the end a duet for Maria and Tonio ('In questo sen riposati') replaces the reprise of 'Salut à la France'. *La Figlia del reggimento* is a stylistic hybrid, but *La Fille du régiment* remains a delightful example of authentic French *opéra comique*.

La Favorite
(The Favourite)

grand opéra in four acts

Principal characters:

Alphonse XI, King of Castile	(baritone)
Léonore de Guzman	(mezzo-soprano)
Fernand	(tenor)
Balthasar	(bass)
Inès	(soprano)

LIBRETTO by Alphonse Royer and Gustave Vaëz

TIME: 1340
PLACE: Santiago de Compostela and Seville

FIRST PERFORMED at the Paris Opéra, 2 December 1840, with Rosine Stolz (Léonore); Gilbert-Louis Duprez (Fernand); Paul Barroilhet (Alphonse XI); Nicholas-Prosper Levasseur (Balthasar)

After the première of *La Fille du régiment* in February 1840, Donizetti's *Les Martyrs*, his adaptation of *Poliuto*, finally reached the stage of the Paris Opéra in April. The composer, now firmly resident in Paris, travelled in the summer to Italy where he attended a performance in Bergamo of his opera *L'Esule di Roma* on 14 August in the company of his old teacher, Mayr. Arriving back in Paris in September, Donizetti resumed work on an opera he had begun to compose the previous year as *L'Ange de Nisida* (The Angel of Nisida) for the Théâtre de la Renaissance, a theatre which had, however, been forced to close. Donizetti now, with the aid of Alphonse Royer and Gustave Vaëz, the librettists of *L'Ange de Nisida*, proceeded to transform into four acts that three-act opera (which itself contained music he had written five years earlier for an opera, *Adelaide*, which he abandoned incomplete). The new four-act opera was *La Favorite*. According to Alphonse Royer, Donizetti composed the music of the fourth act in a single night, though this seems highly unlikely.

The première of *La Favorite* at the Opéra on 2 December 1840 was only moderately successful, but after a few performances its audiences began to grow in size and in enthusiasm, and the new opera soon became popular in French provincial towns. In 1841, its French publisher commissioned the young Richard Wagner to produce a reduction of the score for voice and piano and to make a number of arrangements of pieces from the opera for various instruments. When it was first performed in Italy, in June 1842 in Padua, *La Favorite* was known as *Leonora di Guzman*. In what has become the standard Italian translation by Calisto Bassi, it was staged as *La Favorita* at La Scala, Milan, in 1843. On 18 October 1843 it was performed at the Drury Lane Theatre, London, in English, and at Covent Garden on 9 June 1845 in its original French. New Orleans heard *La Favorite* on 9 February 1843, and the opera reached New York on 25 June 1845. It has never completely disappeared from French and Italian stages. Distinguished inter-preters of the title-role in the present century have included Ebe Stignani in the thirties and forties, and Giulietta Simionato in the fifties and sixties. After an absence from London since 1903, when its last act alone was given at Covent Garden as part of a triple-bill, the opera was heard again, in its Italian version, at the now demolished Scala Theatre in Charlotte Street, on 7 June 1960, when it was performed by the Revival Opera Company. *La Favorite* was performed in French in Bergamo in 1991 and Madrid in 1992. In 1993 it was staged by Welsh National Opera (in Italian) in a number of Welsh and English cities.

The provenance of the libretto by Royer and Vaëz is somewhat complex. Part of their libretto for the abandoned *L'Ange de Nisida* was based on a play, *Le Comte de Comminges*, by François-Thomas Baculard d'Arnaud, staged in Paris in 1790, but it also derived from other sources, and was altered considerably for *La Favorite* (perhaps with the assistance of Scribe) to incorporate the story of Léonore de Guzman. Set in fourteenth-century Spain, the opera tells of the love of Fernand, a young novice at the Monastery of Santiago de Compostela, for Léonore, mistress of Alphonse, King of Castile. Fernand becomes an officer in the King's forces. He is not aware of Léonore's identity or situation until Alphonse, under threat of excommunication unless he abandons his mistress, bestows Léonore on Fernand. A disillusioned Fernand returns to his monastery, but Léonore follows him in male disguise, only to die in his arms.

More than one other commentator has detected a similarity, not only in mood but also in thematic material, between the overture to *La Favorite* and that to Verdi's *La Forza del destino*, composed more than twenty years later. That Verdi may have remembered Donizetti's overture when he wrote Leonora's fate motif is possible, but the overture to *La Favorite* does not aspire to the stature and dramatic energy of Verdi's overture. In the opening scene of *La Favorite* Fernand's *larghetto* aria, 'Un ange, une femme inconnue', freely adapted from an aria composed for *L'Ange de Nisida*, requires the tenor to produce a high C in his first few minutes on stage. His duet with Balthasar, Father Superior of the monastery Fernand is about to leave, does indeed put one in mind of *La Forza del destino* which also has a Father Superior and a tenor with a troubled conscience.

After a first scene consisting entirely of the male voices of Fernand, Balthasar and a chorus of monks, the contrast offered by the second scene, with its graceful and serene double aria ('Rayons dorés') for Léonore's confidante Inès and a chorus of young ladies, is welcome. (Taken over from *L'Ange de Nisida*, it had first been heard three years earlier in *Pia de' Tolomei*.) The Fernand–Léonore duet (also from *L'Ange de Nisida*) is mediocre, but Fernand's newly composed martial aria, 'Oui, ta voix m'inspire', makes a lively end to Act I.

The recitative preceding his aria at the beginning of Act II reveals King Alphonse to be a fascinating and complex character, and his *larghetto* aria, 'Léonore, viens', is both elegant and sensuous, though saddled with a mundane cabaletta. His dull duet with Léonore, 'Quand j'ai quitté', part of which had been composed for *L'Ange de Nisida*, is followed by the obligatory ballet (to banal music) and a highly effective quartet finale to the act, expanded from a trio composed for *L'Ange de Nisida*.

The brief orchestral prelude to Act III quotes from Fernand's Act I aria, 'Un ange, une femme inconnue'. Though described in the score as a trio, 'Pour tant d'amour, ne soyez pas ingrate' is really an elegantly suave *andante* aria for Alphonse, with muted comments from Léonore and Fernand. It is followed immediately by one of the opera's two best-known numbers, Léonore's melodically generous 'O mon Fernand', with its splendid bravura cabaletta, 'Mon arrêt descend du ciel'. The wedding chorus, 'Déjà dans la chapelle', and the Act III finale were composed for *L'Ange de Nisida*, as were the orchestral prelude and opening chorus of Act IV, musically and dramatically the finest act of the opera. The solemn prelude, with prominent solos for organ and cello, leads into the chorus which includes Balthasar's dignified solo, 'Les cieux s'emplissent d'étincelles'. Fernand's celebrated *larghetto* aria, 'Ange si pur' (recorded by countless Italian tenors as 'Spirto gentil'), is one of Donizetti's most exquisitely crafted melodies, originally intended for *Le Duc d'Albe*. The chorus, 'Que de très-haut' and most of the final duet, 'Viens, viens, je cède éperdu', for Léonore and Fernand, were both composed for *L'Ange de Nisida*, but the lengthy duet makes an appropriate and effective end to *La Favorite*, an opera which, while not one of its composer's most finely wrought scores, can still prove successful if performed with a proper appreciation of its French grand opera style. Toscanini admired it greatly (in its Italian version) and said that, in the last act, 'every note is a masterpiece'.

Adelia

opera seria in three acts

Principal characters:
Adelia   (soprano)
Oliviero   (tenor)
Arnoldo   (bass)

LIBRETTO by Felice Romani (Acts I and II) and Girolamo Marini (Act III)

TIME: The past
PLACE: Burgundy

FIRST PERFORMED at the Teatro Apollo, Rome, 11 February 1841, with Giuseppina Strepponi (Adelia); Lorenzo Salvi (Oliviero); Ignazio Marini (Arnoldo)

While still at work on *La Favorite*, Donizetti had concluded an agreement with the Teatro Apollo in Rome to compose a new opera, *Adelia*, to an existing libretto by Felice Romani which, based on an unidentified French play, had originally been written for Michele Carafa's *Adele di Lusignano*, staged in Milan in 1817, and had later been used for *La Figlia dell'arciere*, an opera by Carlo Coccia performed in Naples in 1834. The management of the Teatro Apollo, unhappy with the last act of Romani's text, called in another writer, Girolamo Marini, to provide a new Act III which, when he received it, Donizetti found unsatisfactory. However, he accepted it and, immediately after the Paris première of *La Favorite*, began to compose *Adelia*. By the end of November he had completed Acts I and II, and on 28 December he arrived in Rome with the finished opera, rehearsals for which began in mid-January. The singer of the title-role was a twenty-five-year-old soprano, Giuseppina Strepponi, later to become the mistress, and in due course the wife, of Giuseppe Verdi.

The first night of *Adelia* at the Teatro Apollo on 11 February 1841 was a stormy occasion. The theatre had contrived to sell many more tickets than it had seats, and the performance was disrupted by angry ticket holders demanding either seats or refunds. The singers were unable to finish the opera, and the impresario was arrested and had to be bailed out by Strepponi and others the following day. *Adelia* was performed eight more times during the season, but thereafter was staged only in a few other Italian towns, and abroad in Lisbon, Malta, Madrid and, on 11 March 1843, in London. It still awaits modern revival. Donizetti himself accepted that *Adelia* was a failure, and blamed himself for having accepted a libretto which he felt lacked dramatic situations, passion, or even verses capable of inspiring him.

Adelia's father, Arnoldo, captain of the Duke of Burgundy's guards, resolves to kill the man who has been seen climbing out of the window of Adelia's room. However the man turns out to be Oliviero, a nobleman whom Arnoldo, as a mere commoner, is unable to challenge. Knowing that any nobleman who marries a commoner will, by decree of the Duke, be beheaded, Arnoldo persuades the Duke to permit the marriage of Adelia and Oliviero. Adelia attempts to postpone the ceremony, but her father insists on its proceeding. The wedding takes place, but the Duke spares Oliviero's life by presenting Arnoldo with a patent of nobility.

Some of the music of *Adelia* was borrowed from earlier Donizetti operas, most notably *Gabriella di Vergy*. Act I is distinguished by a well-crafted finale, Act II by a *larghetto* duet, 'Ah, non posso, o figlia mia', for Adelia and Arnoldo, and Act III by Adelia's aria-finale. Its affecting *larghetto*, 'Chi le nostr'anime', in which she laments her husband's imminent fate, is followed swiftly by a joyous cabaletta,

'Vivi! ah, non m'inganno', when she learns of her father's ennoble-
ment. Some of the remainder of the score is workaday Donizetti,
which of course does not mean that, in an age starved of melody, a
revival of *Adelia* would be anything other than welcome.

Rita

opéra comique in one act

Principal characters:
Rita   (soprano)
Beppe   (tenor)
Gaspar   (baritone)

LIBRETTO by Gustave Vaëz

TIME: The eighteenth century
PLACE: A country inn in Switzerland

FIRST PERFORMED at the Opéra-Comique, Paris, 7 May 1860,
with Caroline Lefebvre-Faure (Rita); Warot (Beppe); Barielle
(Gaspar)

Leaving Rome in February 1841 after the *Adelia* première, Donizetti
made his way back to Paris. In the summer he signed a contract for
an opera to open the carnival season at La Scala, Milan. While he
was waiting for suggestions from the Scala impresario, Merelli,
regarding a libretto, the composer busied himself by writing a one-
act comic opera, *Rita*. Gustave Vaëz, Donizetti's friend and collaborator on *La Favorite*, obligingly wrote the text, and Donizetti
proceeded to amuse himself by setting it to music, even though there
was no immediate possibility of it being performed. Vaëz later
recalled how Donizetti would take the manuscript from him page by
page, draw five stave lines on it, and note down ideas for the
melodies which had come to him while Vaëz had been reading the
words aloud. According to the librettist, the opera was composed in
eight days.
    The libretto for *Maria Padilla*, the new opera for Milan, now
arrived, and Donizetti began to set it. *Rita* was forgotten, and in fact

did not reach the stage until several years after its composer's death when it was performed at the Opéra-Comique, Paris, on 7 May 1860, and in Brussels in December of that year. Its first performance in Italy was given at the Palazzo Cassano, Naples, on 18 May 1876. *Rita* has survived in its Italian version, and is still quite often performed as part of a double-bill in Italian theatres. The opera's London première appears to have been the performance given by the London Opera Club on 14 December 1958. In the summer of 1960 *Rita* was staged in Vienna for the first time by the Wiener Kammeroper. If there have been any performances in the United States, they have been fugitive ones.

Vaëz's libretto deals with a sado-masochistic threesome. Rita, a Swiss innkeeper, is married to the unassertive Beppe whom she delights in treating brusquely. Her first husband, Gaspar, who used to beat her occasionally and whom she believed to have been drowned at sea, arrives unexpectedly. Beppe sees this as his opportunity to escape from Rita, but Gaspar has plans to marry a Canadian girl. The two men play a game, the loser having to accept Rita. Both cheat in order to be free of her, but finally it is Beppe who makes the best of a bad lot and remains with Rita, while Gaspar is free to marry his Canadian. Before he leaves, Gaspar offers some helpful advice to Beppe: 'A man must do what a man must do', which is to beat his wife whenever the occasion appears to call for it.

The opera, slight but charming, consists of eight numbers separated by spoken dialogue. After a brief prelude, Rita makes her entrance with a lively aria about the delights of her present existence, the hapless Beppe joins her in a duet in which he gets beaten for having broken a china cup, and Gaspar sings in a boisterous *allegro* of the joys of wife-spanking. The most enjoyable number in the score is a duet, 'Il me vient une idée', in which the two men play their game. Beppe's ebullient *allegro* aria, 'Je suis joyeux', is worthy of Nemorino in *L'Elisir d'amore*. A duet for Rita and Gaspar is rather more mundane, but the trio, 'Je suis manchot', and the opera's brief finale are both delightful.

Maria Padilla

opera seria in three acts

Principal characters:

Maria Padilla	(soprano)
Ines Padilla	(soprano)
Don Ruiz di Padilla	(tenor)
Don Pedro di Castillo	(baritone)
Don Ramiro	(bass)
Don Luigi	(tenor)
Don Alfonso di Pardo	(bass)

LIBRETTO by Gaetano Rossi

TIME: The fourteenth century
PLACE: Castile

FIRST PERFORMED at the Teatro alla Scala, Milan, 26 December 1841, with Sophie Loewe (Maria Padilla); Luigia Abbadia (Ines Padilla); Domenico Donzelli (Don Ruiz di Padilla); Giorgio Ronconi (Don Pedro di Castillo)

Having finished composing *Rita* which he then set aside, Donizetti began work on *Maria Padilla*, his opera for La Scala. In September he made his way to Milan where he completed the opera which was staged on 26 December 1841, to open the carnival season. The first night went well, and a further twenty-three performances were given during the season. A production at the Teatro La Fenice, Venice, in 1843 was withdrawn after only two performances, but abroad *Maria Padilla* was heard in a number of cities in Spain and Portugal, as well as in Malta, Vienna, Odessa and Corfu. A French translation was staged in Versailles, Nantes and Marseilles, and there were performances as far afield as Lima and Rio de Janeiro. After 1869 the opera languished until 1973 when a concert performance was given by Opera Rara at the Queen Elizabeth Hall, London, on 8 April 1973. The North American première appears to have been a concert performance given by the Long Island Opera Society at Stony Brook, NY, on 23 April 1983. The first British stage performance was that of Dorset Opera at Sherborne School, Dorset, on 19 August 1988, and the first stage performance in the USA was given by Opera Omaha in the Joslyn Arts Museum, Omaha, Nebraska, on 15 September 1990.

Donizetti himself had chosen the subject for his new opera, a play, *Maria Padilla* by François Ancelot, which had been staged in Paris in 1838. As librettist, the Scala impresario chose the sixty-seven-year-old Gaetano Rossi, who had provided the libretti of *Tancredi* and *Semiramide* for Rossini. When Donizetti arrived in Milan, he collaborated actively with Rossi in the writing of the libretto, to such an extent that, in a letter to his brother-in-law, the composer described the text as being 'by Rossi and Donizetti'. Though the plot can only be described as operatic, the characters are historical. King Pedro the Cruel, ruler of Castile between 1350 and 1369, has, under an assumed name, been having an affair with Maria Padilla. Discovering his true identity, she extracts from him a promise that he will marry her. They elope, but circumstances force Pedro to negotiate a marriage with Blanche, a Bourbon princess. Don Ruiz, Maria's father, arriving at court to discover that his daughter is regarded as the King's mistress, challenges Pedro to a duel. Blanche is hailed as Queen by Maria's enemies, but Pedro rejects her and acknowledges Maria as his Queen, at which Maria, overcome with joy, dies. (The ending originally had Maria snatching the crown from her rival's head, asserting her rights and then killing herself. This, however, was considered by the censors in Milan to be unedifying.)

After a brief prelude and a conventional opening chorus celebrating the wedding of Maria's sister Ines Padilla and Don Luigi, Ines is given a *larghetto* aria, 'Eran già create in cielo', and *allegro* cabaletta, 'Sorridi, o sposo amato', whose floridity, evident even in the recitative preceding the aria, is somewhat extravagant for a mere *seconda donna*. Maria's entrance aria, 'Il più tenero suon', and cabaletta, 'Ah, non sai', are flexible enough in form to advance the action, and Pedro's aria, 'Lieto fra voi ritorno', develops into an impressive sextet. The final scene of Act I, a dramatic extended duet ('Core innocente e giovane') for Maria and Pedro, is an example of Donizetti at his most imaginative, the music faithfully serving the requirements of the plot without being made subservient to them.

After the chorus of courtiers ('Nella reggia dell' amore') at the beginning of Act II, a piece which is functional as well as decorative, Don Ruiz, the heroine's father, contributes an embittered tenor aria, 'Il sentiero di mia vita', and a rhythmically energetic cabaletta, 'Una gioia ancor mi resta'. The duet, 'A figlia incauta', for the sisters Maria and Ines, a worthy successor to the great soprano–mezzo duet scenes of Rossini and Bellini, actually calls to mind 'Mira, o Norma' in Bellini's 1831 opera, *Norma*. The Ruiz–Pedro duet, 'Io lo vedo', less noteworthy, leads directly to the Act II finale which, dispensing with the expected *larghetto* ensemble, rushes urgently to its exciting conclusion.

The *andante* prelude to Act III introduces a melody for cello and bassoon which will be heard again in Don Ruiz's romanza. The lengthy father–daughter duet, 'Padre, padre, oh rio dolore', for Ruiz and Maria is positively Verdian in its intensity, its affecting pathos, and its freedom of form. Pedro's shapely aria of repentance, 'Ah! quello fu per me di paradiso un dì' is saddled with a cabaletta, 'Lasciar Maria', whose insouciant vocal line belies its sentiments, but the opera's elaborate finale in its uncensored form is superb, from its celebratory chorus, through its dramatic episode of Maria snatching the crown, to its traditional double aria for the heroine, its two parts here separated by Ruiz's plaintive solo and the ensemble which develops from it. Maria's brilliant cabaletta, 'O padre, tu l'odi?' brings the curtain down and the audience, cheering, to its feet. This is an opera which deserves to be heard more often.

Linda di Chamounix

opera semiseria in three acts

Principal characters:

Linda	(soprano)
Pierotto	(mezzo-soprano)
Carlo	(tenor)
Antonio	(baritone)
The Prefect	(bass)
Marchese di Boisfleury	(bass)

LIBRETTO by Gaetano Rossi

TIME: 1760

PLACE: Chamonix in the French Alps, and Paris

FIRST PERFORMED at the Kärntnertor Theater, Vienna, 19 May 1842, with Eugenia Tadolini (Linda); Marietta Brambilla (Pierotto); Napoleone Moriani (Carlo); Felice Varesi (Antonio); Prosper Dérivis (The Prefect); Agostino Rovere (Marchese)

After the première of *Maria Padilla* in December 1841, Donizetti remained in Milan, staying at the home of his friends Andrea and Giuseppina Appiani. Bartolomeo Merelli, the impresario who had commissioned *Maria Padilla* for La Scala, was also responsible for the Kärntnertor Theater in Vienna, and had asked Donizetti to compose an opera for performance there. To a libretto provided by Gaetano Rossi, Donizetti began to write the opera, *Linda di Chamounix*, which he completed by the beginning of March when he sent the score to Vienna. He himself stayed in Milan long enough to hear the first performance of the young Giuseppe Verdi's *Nabucco* at La Scala on 9 March 1842. The following day he left for Bologna, where he conducted three performances of Rossini's *Stabat Mater* at the invitation of the composer whose ill health prevented him from conducting it himself. After the third performance, Rossini embraced and kissed Donizetti as the two men were cheered by the audience. Rossini later referred to Donizetti as 'the only maestro in Italy who knows how to perform my *Stabat* as I want it done.'

Armed with a letter to Metternich, the Austrian Minister of Foreign Affairs, Donizetti arrived in Vienna on 27 March, and three days later wrote to a friend, 'Vienna is beautiful, beautiful, beautiful'. On 4 May he conducted Rossini's *Stabat Mater* in the presence of the Emperor and Empress and the Dowager Empress, Maria Theresa. *Linda di Chamounix* had its première on 19 May 1842, and a few days later Donizetti wrote to his brother-in-law: 'The maestro was called out seventeen times, alone and with the singers. The theatre packed. At the second performance, an enormous bouquet of flowers tossed at the maestro.' The theatre continued to be packed at subsequent performances – there were seventeen in all – and the enthusiasm of the Viennese audiences was overwhelming. After the première, the Empress Maria Carolina presented the composer with a scarf on which she herself had embroidered in gold, 'The Empress of Austria to Donizetti on the evening of 19 May 1842 for the opera *Linda*.' In June, Donizetti was appointed Composer to the Austrian Court, a position which had once been held by Mozart.

The first performance of *Linda di Chamounix* in Italy was given in

Turin, three months after the Vienna première. During the next ten years the opera was staged all over Europe and the Americas, and later reached Melbourne (in 1861), Calcutta (1867) and Batavia (1892). The first London performance was at Her Majesty's Theatre, on 1 June 1843, and the first New York performance took place on 4 January 1847 at Palmo's Opera House. *Linda di Chamounix* never completely disappeared from the international repertoire. There were prestigious revivals at the Metropolitan Opera, New York, in 1934 with Lily Pons as Linda, and at La Scala, Milan, in 1939 with Toti dal Monte, while in the second half of the twentieth century the opera has been performed in Barcelona (1954 and 1977), Palermo (1957), Naples (1958), Lisbon (1963), London (for the first time since 1887, at the St Pancras Town Hall in 1963), Milan (1972), Genoa (1975), Wexford (1983), Trieste (1989), and Boston (1993, in concert performance).

Rossi's libretto, based on the play, *La Grâce de Dieu*, by Adolphe-Philippe d'Ennery and Gustave Lemoine (staged in Paris in 1841), tells the story of Linda, a maiden in the village of Chamonix (as it is spelt today) in the Savoie Alps, who, to escape the unwelcome attentions of the Marquis of Boisfleury, flees to Paris where she lives in an apartment belonging to Carlo, with whom she is in love, and who is really the Viscount of Sirval, nephew of the Marquis. Linda's father finds her and refuses to believe that she is not living in sin. Linda loses her reason, but regains it when she returns to Chamonix where Carlo sings to her a song of their happier days together. The opera ends joyously with Linda and Carlo reunited.

The overture, one of Donizetti's finest, was composed during the rehearsal period in Vienna, when Donizetti was made aware that the classically-minded Viennese expected a full-scale overture, and not merely a few bars of prelude. For the main *allegro* section of the overture, he orchestrated the opening movement of a string quartet (his eighteenth) in E minor which he had written in 1836 in Naples. The opening chorus of Swiss villagers, 'Presti! al tempio', establishes from the outset the opera's predominantly pastoral mood or *tinta*, and the gentle entrance aria ('Ambo nati') for Antonio, Linda's father, is in similar vein. The villain of the piece, the elderly Marquis who presses his unwelcome attentions upon Linda, is given in his aria ('Buona gente') and cabaletta ('Oh, già in collera non sono') music more suitable to a comic bass than to a rather nasty old rake; however, since the Marquis transforms himself at the end of the opera into a genial old uncle, presumably he could not earlier be characterised as irredeemably horrid.

At the première in Vienna, when Linda made her first entrance she sang only a passage of recitative. Her brilliant coloratura aria, 'O luce di quest'anima', now the best known number in the score, was composed by Donizetti for the Paris production six months later, when Linda was sung by Fanny Tacchinardi-Persiani (who had created the title-role in *Lucia di Lammermoor* in Naples in 1835). Pierotto, the itinerant musician, is a mezzo-soprano *travesti* role. In Act I, instead of the expected *larghetto* aria and *allegro* cabaletta, he sings two simple songs which share a slow tempo, accompanying the first, 'Cari luoghi', on his hurdy-gurdy, but being given the support of the orchestra in his second song, 'Per sua madre'. The Linda–Carlo love duet, 'Da quel dì che t'incontrai', is delightful, especially its *allegro moderato* cabaletta, 'A consolarmi affrettisi', whose joyous theme, first stated by Carlo and then repeated by Linda, is heard three more times in the course of the opera, during Linda's mind-wandering scenes in Acts II and III and at the end when Carlo's singing of it restores her to sanity. The musical style and indeed the sentiments of Verdi are heard in the baritone–bass duet, 'Quella pietà si provvida', for Antonio and the Prefect, in which both men express their concern for Antonio's daughter. Act I ends with an impressive prayer, 'O tu che regoli gli umani eventi', begun by the Prefect and developed by Antonio and the ensemble. Its music had already been heard in *Maria Stuarda*, and could also have been heard in *Le Duc d'Albe* if that opera, composed in 1839, had reached the stage instead of having had to wait until 1882 for its première.

Structurally, *Linda di Chamounix* is paradoxically both a return to the traditional forms of Italian opera and a negation of them. Some of its arias are shorn of their cabalettas, and occasionally a cabaletta will appear without an antecedent aria. Linda's 'O luce di quest' anima' in Act I is such a cabaletta; the Linda–Pierotto duet near the beginning of Act II, 'Al bel destin che attendevi', in which the hurdy-gurdy man demonstrates that he is capable of a more sophisticated musical utterance than he had revealed in his folk-like songs in Act I, can be heard either as a duet without its stretta or a cabaletta in a moderate tempo without its first section. The action has moved to Paris for Act II. Linda rejects the old Marquis's advances for the second time in their duet, 'Io vi dico che partiate', in which she maintains a serious and dignified air in the face of his seemingly harmless comical style of patter. (The ambiguous role of the Marchese di Boisfleury cannot be easy to interpret convincingly or consistently.) Carlo's 'Se tanto in ira' is one of Donizetti's most charmingly elegant arias for tenor, and the moving father–daughter duet, 'Ah! che il ciel vi benedica', finds the composer at his most Verdian (although, in these post-*Nabucco* operas of Donizetti, who is influencing whom is a moot point). Act II ends with Linda's collapse into dementia, in her pathetic recollection of 'A consolarmi affrettisi', and her forceful cabaletta, 'No, non è ver, mentirono', whose high tragic style makes her sound like Anna Bolena or Maria Stuarda facing execution.

The action returns to Chamonix in Act III, which opens with another delightful chorus for the villagers, after which the Marquis's aria in praise of Linda serves to assist him in his transition from dirty old man to avuncular charmer. The still deranged heroine herself enters with Pierotto who plays his hurdy-gurdy as she makes her way into the village square. In the highly effective finale Linda's senses fully return only when Carlo quotes 'A consolarmi affrettisi'. Her joyous duet with Carlo, 'Ah! di tue pene sparve il sogno', ends an opera which, though less consistently inspired, has much of the charm of *L'Elisir d'amore*.

Don Pasquale

opera buffa in three acts

Principal characters:

Don Pasquale   (bass)
Ernesto   (tenor)
Dr Malatesta   (baritone)
Norina   (soprano)

LIBRETTO by Giovanni Ruffini

TIME: Early-nineteenth century
PLACE: Rome

FIRST PERFORMED at the Théâtre-Italien, Paris, 3 January 1843, with Giulia Grisi (Norina); Mario (Ernesto); Antonio Tamburini (Dr Malatesta); Luigi Lablache (Don Pasquale)

After the highly successful première of *Linda di Chamounix*, Donizetti stayed in Vienna to conduct two performances of Rossini's *Stabat Mater*. At the beginning of July he made his way to Milan. From there he wrote to Vernoy de Saint-Georges, one of the two librettists of *La Fille du Régiment*, about a new comic opera intended for Paris in December. He actually began to compose the opera, which was to be called *Ne m'oubliez pas* (Don't Forget Me), but for some unknown reason abandoned it (see pp 304–306). By October he was in Paris, where he began work on what was meant to be his next opera for Vienna, *Caterina Cornaro*. However, this too he was forced, for the time being, to abandon (see pp 300–304). He had by this time been asked to compose a new opera for the Théâtre-Italien in Paris, and the subject he chose was one which had been used by the librettist Angelo Anelli for Stefano Pavesi's opera, *Ser Marcantonio*, first performed in Milan in 1810. Giovanni Ruffini, an Italian political exile living in Paris, wrote a new libretto based on Anelli's text, and Donizetti set to work on the opera, *Don Pasquale*, which he claimed took him no more than eleven days to complete. It was staged at the Théâtre-Italien on 3 January 1843.

Don Pasquale's period of gestation had not been untroubled. Donizetti, dissatisfied with some of Ruffini's verses, made suggestions and changes of his own, and one of the singers, the baritone Antonio Tamburini, insisted on his role being enlarged at the expense of the title-role, which was being undertaken by Luigi Lablache. Ruffini refused to attach his name to the printed libretto which was issued as being by 'M.A.'. This has led countless writers on Donizetti to assert that the libretto was the work of Michaele Accursi, a pseudonym of Giovanni Ruffini. Accursi, however, was no pseudonym, but another Italian political exile and Donizetti's theatrical agent in Paris. Accursi was instrumental in persuading Ruffini to undertake the task of providing a libretto for Donizetti, but had no hand in the writing of it.

At its première, *Don Pasquale* was enthusiastically received. 'I was called out at the end of the second and third acts,' Donizetti wrote to Giovanni Ricordi, 'and there was not one piece, from the overture on, that was not applauded to a greater or lesser extent. I am very happy.' Within months the opera began to be produced all over

Europe, beginning with Milan in April, Vienna in May, London (Her Majesty's Theatre) on 29 June and Brussels in August. The first performance in the United States took place in New Orleans on 7 January 1845; the first New York performance followed on 9 March 1846. In due course the opera reached the southern hemisphere (Santiago, Buenos Aires, Lima, Rio de Janeiro, Melbourne), and it is still frequently produced all over the world. *Don Pasquale* and *L'Elisir d'amore* remain Donizetti's two most popular comic operas, and two of the three most popular of all Italian comic operas, the third being Rossini's *Il Barbiere di Siviglia*.

Don Pasquale is set in Rome in the early-nineteenth century, and its plot is, as comic opera plots go, relatively uncomplicated. When the crusty old bachelor Don Pasquale decides to marry in order to spite his nephew Ernesto, of whose fiancée Norina he disapproves, Ernesto and Norina concoct a plot, with the aid of Dr Malatesta, by which Pasquale is tricked into a mock marriage with one Sofronia, a demure maid fresh from a convent. She is, of course, Norina in disguise. After the wedding ceremony, Sofronia begins to behave so shrewishly that Pasquale is only too anxious to be rid of her. He is made to admit he acted foolishly, and agrees to the marriage of Ernesto and Norina.

If the plot of *Don Pasquale* seems very similar to that of Richard Strauss's *Die schweigsame Frau*, there is every reason why it should, for ultimately they derive from the same source, Ben Jonson's 1609 play, *Epicoene or The Silent Woman*. Jonson's play was used as the basis of an opera, *Angiolina*, by Salieri in 1800. With its female impersonation aspect removed (for Jonson's old bachelor is married off to a boy dressed as a young woman), it served as the basis of Angelo Anelli's libretto for Pavesi's *Ser Marcantoniuo* in 1810, which in turn was plundered by Ruffini for Donizetti's opera. For Strauss's *Die schweigsame Frau* (The Silent Woman) in 1935, the librettist Stefan Zweig adapted Jonson's play.

The tuneful overture makes use of two themes which will be heard later in the opera, its *andante* drawn from Ernesto's Act III serenade, 'Com' è gentil', and its *moderato* section from the cabaletta of Norina's aria at the beginning of Act II. *Don Pasquale* is an opera which moves at an engagingly brisk pace from beginning to end, with only one or two moments in Acts II and III where tender sentiment is allowed to slow it down. In its opening scene, Pasquale and Malatesta plan the former's marriage, with Malatesta singing the praises of the young maiden from the convent in a graceful *larghetto*, 'Bella siccome un angelo', whose cabaletta is provided not by himself but by Pasquale's delighted reaction in the sprightly *vivace* 'Ah! un foco insolito'. Ernesto's duet scene with Pasquale ('Prender moglie?') is actually a beautifully nostalgic aria, 'Sogno soave e casto', sung by Ernesto, with comic asides from Pasquale who also contributes virtually non-stop patter to Ernesto's desperate cabaletta, 'Mi fa il destin mendico'. Norina's *andante* aria, 'Quel guardo il cavaliere', in which she reads from a romantic novel, and her sprightly cabaletta, 'So anch'io la virtù magica', in which she comments satirically upon it, are followed by her tunefully prodigal duet with Malatesta, 'Pronta io son', which makes a delightful, if unusual, finale to Act I, its *maestoso* and *allegro* sections sharing melodic material and cleverly welded into a single structure.

A version of the melody of Ernesto's sad *larghetto* farewell to his home at the beginning of Act II ('Cercherò lontana terra') is heard first in the orchestral prelude with its trumpet solo. Ernesto's cabaletta, 'E se fia che ad altro oggetto', follows in the same vein without any intervening material and with only a moderate increase in tempo. The scheme to trick Pasquale is advanced in the lively trio, 'Sta a vedere', in which the old bachelor is introduced by Malatesta to his apparently shy and retiring bride-to-be. The arrival of Ernesto leads to a delightful prolonged quartet of confusion, 'Pria di partir, signore', with which the act ends, but only after the bride has shown her true colours in some sparkling coloratura.

The chorus, which has so far not made an appearance, opens Act III as a flock of servants who, engaged by Pasquale's bride, rush hither and thither to do her bidding. Norina continues to torment Pasquale in their duet, 'Signorina, in tanta fretta', and a note of seriousness is struck when she gets carried away with her impersonation of a shrew, and slaps the old man's face. The tempo changes suddenly from *allegro* to *larghetto* as Donizetti allows a cloud of real feeling to pass momentarily across the sunny insouciance of his score. After a chorus of gossiping servants, Don Pasquale and Dr Malatesta confer in a comical duet, 'Cheti, cheti, immantinente', whose irrepressible high spirits have made it a great favourite with audiences, who expect, and are usually given, an encore of its hectic stretta ('Aspetta, aspetta, cara sposina'). The final scene opens with Ernesto's famous serenade, 'Com' è gentil', a graceful piece whose elegant solo line is punctuated by helpful comments from an off-stage chorus. Ernesto's beautiful duet with Norina, 'Tornami a dir', was adapted by Donizetti from music he had already written for *Caterina Cornaro*, and the opera's *rondo* finale, 'La morale in tutto questo', an exhilarating cabaletta for Norina and the ensemble, is another piece of self-borrowing, having begun its life as a song, 'La bohémienne'.

Maria di Rohan

opera seria in three acts

Principal characters:

Maria di Rohan	(soprano)
Armando di Gondi	(mezzo-soprano)
Riccardo, Conte di Chalais	(tenor)
Enrico, Duca di Chevreuse	(baritone)

LIBRETTO by Salvatore Cammarano

TIME: Early-seventeenth century
PLACE: Paris

FIRST PERFORMED at the Kärntnertor Theater, Vienna, 5 June 1843, with Eugenia Tadolini (Maria di Rohan); Michele Novaro (Armando di Gondi); Carlo Guasco (Riccardo, Conte di Chalais); Giorgio Ronconi (Enrico, Duca di Chevreuse)

It was in the autumn of 1837 that Donizetti first considered writing an opera based on the play, *Un Duel sous le Cardinal de Richelieu*, by Édouard Lockroy (the pseudonym of a French comic actor and dramatist, Joseph-Philippe Simon), which had been staged in Paris five years earlier. However, he and the librettist Salvatore Cammarano finally decided upon a different subject, which became the opera *Maria de Rudenz*. It was for another composer, Giuseppe Lillo, that Cammarano completed his libretto based on Lockroy's play, and Lillo's opera, *Il Conte di Calais*, was staged unsuccessfully in Naples in 1839. Another opera on the same subject, *Un Duello sotto Richelieu* by Federico Ricci, was produced at La Scala, Milan, also in 1839, but with a libretto by Federico dall' Ongaro. In June 1840, asked to compose an opera for the Teatro Apollo in Rome, Donizetti again considered setting Cammarano's libretto, but instead wrote *Adelia*.

After the huge success of *Linda di Chamounix* in Vienna in May 1842, Donizetti was asked to compose another opera for performance there. In Paris in the autumn of 1842, he began work on an opera to be called *La Regina di Cipro* (The Queen of Cyprus), with a libretto by Giacomo Sacchèro. After he had composed the first act, Donizetti learned that an opera on the same subject by the German composer Franz Lachner, which had been given its première in Munich the previous December, was to be staged in Vienna in November. Lachner's opera was called *Catharina Cornaro, Königin von Cypern*. Its libretto was a German translation of a text by Jules-Henri Vernoy de Saint-Georges, who had written it for Halévy, whose *La Reine de Chypre* had been staged at the Paris Opéra in December 1841. Donizetti would not have been inhibited from composing his *Caterina Cornaro* for Vienna merely because two operas on the same subject had been performed the previous December in Munich and Paris, but the fact that Lachner's *Catharina Cornaro* was about to be staged in Vienna (on 19 November) made him decide to choose another subject for that city. Putting *Caterina Cornaro* aside, he recalled the play, *Un Duel sous le Cardinal de Richelieu*, which he had considered in 1837, and began to set Salvatore Cammarano's libretto, unconcerned that, since he had abandoned it, the libretto had been used by two other composers, Lillo and Ricci.

On 27 November 1842, having already completed *Don Pasquale* which was to be staged at the Théâtre-Italien on 3 January 1843, Donizetti told a friend that it had taken him no more than twenty-four hours to compose two acts of his new opera, based by Cammarano on Lockroy's play, and now entitled *Maria di Rohan*. 'When the subject is pleasing,' Donizetti wrote, 'the heart speaks, the head soars, and the hand writes.' Four days after the *Don Pasquale* première in January, he left Paris, by way of Strasbourg, Munich and Linz, for Vienna. Here he finished composing *Maria di Rohan* whose orchestration he completed by mid-February, began to write 'a five-act Portuguese subject' (which would become *Dom Sébastien*) for the Paris Opéra, composed a *Miserere* for the Austrian Emperor and conducted its performance, supervised a Viennese revival of *Linda di Chamounix* and the first Viennese production of *Don Pasquale*, as well as that of his young rival Verdi's *Nabucco*, and finally began to rehearse *Maria di Rohan* which was given its première at the Kärntnertor Theater on 15 June.

The Austrian imperial family attended the first performance of *Maria di Rohan* which was greeted with what Donizetti called, in a letter to his brother-in-law, 'a sea of applause'. Both critical response and audience reaction were highly enthusiastic, and the opera was soon being staged in other European cities. For its Paris première in November, the composer changed the relatively unimportant tenor role of Armando di Gondi into a major contralto or mezzo *travesti* role for Marietta Brambilla, for whom he added two arias. He made further changes to the score for the opera's first Italian performance in Parma in 1844, and for its Viennese revival in the same year. *Maria di Rohan* then made its way to Naples, Brussels, Budapest, Malta, St Petersburg, Rome, Corfu, Barcelona, London (where it was staged at Covent Garden on 8 May 1847), Berlin, New York (on 10 December 1849), Lisbon, Constantinople (now Instanbul), Lemberg (now Lvov), Prague, Agram (now Zagreb), Graz, Mexico City, Lima, Buenos Aires, Bucharest and elsewhere. The role of Enrico became a favourite of the great Italian baritone Mattia Battistini who sang it for the first time in Florence in 1885, and continued to perform it in Italy and abroad until well into the twentieth century.

Although the opera fell from favour for several decades, it has been revived in the latter half of the twentieth century in Bergamo (1957), Naples (1962), New York (in concert performance, 1963), Lisbon (1968, with Renata Scotto in the title-role), Venice (1974, again with Scotto), London (a concert performance at the Queen Elizabeth Hall, 1976), and at the Festival della Valle d'Itria in Martina Franca, 1988.

In Cammarano's libretto, whose action takes place in Paris during the reign of Louis XIII, Maria di Rohan is secretly married to the Duke of Chevreuse. When her husband kills the nephew of Cardinal Richelieu in a duel, she begs an ex-lover, Riccardo, Count of Chalais, to intercede for him. Her love for Riccardo is reawakened, and Chevreuse, led to believe that Maria has been unfaithful to him, challenges Riccardo to a duel. Rather than kill Maria's husband, Riccardo turns his pistol upon himself. Maria begs her husband to kill her, but he condemns her instead to a life of disgrace.

Both the overture and the introductory chorus of courtiers are unmemorable, but a generous melodic vein is struck in Riccardo's two-part tenor aria, the *larghetto* 'Quando il cor da lei piagato' followed without any intervening material by its cabaletta, 'A te, divina immagine'. Maria's double aria is fiercely dramatic, its *andante mosso* ('Cupa, fatal mestizia') quite stark in its vocal line, with an expressive, insistent accompaniment, and its *allegro giusto* cabaletta ('Ben fu il giorno avventurato') equally urgent and comparatively unadorned. Armando di Gondi's eccentric little ballata, 'Per non istare all' ozio', was no doubt shaped to the requirements of Marietta Brambilla (who, ten years earlier, had created another male role in a Donizetti opera, that of Orsini in *Lucrezia Borgia*). Enrico's *moderato* cavatina, 'Geme a di tetro carcere', an original piece well attuned to the dramatic situation, exploits the upper fifth of the baritone range; its cabaletta, 'Se ancor m'è dato stringerti', does so even more insistently. The Act I finale is a splendid ensemble begun in a flowing *andante* by Enrico ('D'un anno il giro') and ending in a lively stretta.

Perhaps as a consequence of Donizetti's exposure to Verdi's *Nabucco* both in Milan and in Vienna, the orchestra plays an unusually prominent role throughout *Maria di Rohan*. It contributes strongly to the eloquent recitative preceding Riccardo's splendid aria, 'Alma soave e cara', at the beginning of Act II, though it reverts to being more subservient in Armando's florid cavatina, 'Son leggero è ver'. A dramatic duet for Riccardo and Enrico leads to the Act II finale, which also takes the form of a duet, a confrontation between Maria and Riccardo, with an affecting *larghetto*, 'Ah, e s'io pur mi disonoro', and an exciting stretta, 'A morire incomminciai'.

The *larghetto* duet, 'Ah, così santo affetto', for Maria and Riccardo at the beginning of Act III is preceded by a brief orchestral prelude whose melancholy tune played by the horns suddenly gives way to an *allegro crescendo*. Maria's *larghetto* prayer, 'Havvi un Dio', introduced and supported by cor anglais, is an individual and, in context, highly effective piece, as is the feverish cabaletta, 'Benigno il cielo arridere', which follows it. Enrico's aria ('Bella e di sol vestita') and cabaletta ('Ogni mio bene') are magnificent depictions of a gnawing jealousy, and from here to the end of the opera Donizetti's score possesses a dramatic intensity and momentum that are positively Verdian. The *larghetto* duet, 'So, per prova il tuo bel core', for Maria and Enrico leads directly to a trio finale in which musical form is sacrificed to the demands of the drama with a freedom that Donizetti was beginning to use confidently just at a time when his health and career were about to collapse around him.

Maria di Rohan is an opera perhaps to be admired as much for its forward-looking structure as for the quality of its musical invention.

Dom Sébastien, Roi de Portugal

grand opéra in five acts

Principal characters:

Zaïda	(mezzo-soprano)
Dom Sébastien	(tenor)
Camoëns	(baritone)
Dom Juan de Silva	(bass)
Abayaldos	(baritone)
Dom Henrique	(bass)

LIBRETTO by Eugène Scribe

TIME: The sixteenth century
PLACE: Lisbon and Morocco

FIRST PERFORMED at the Paris Opéra, 13 November 1843, with Rosina Stolz (Zaïda); Gilbert-Louis Duprez (Dom Sébastien); Paul Barroilhet (Camoëns); Nicholas-Prosper Levasseur (Dom Juan de Silva); Jean-Étienne Massol (Abayaldos); Ferdinand Prévost (Dom Henrique)

It was during the months he spent in Vienna in 1843 that Donizetti's health began seriously to decline. He himself believed that he had caught a new venereal infection in Paris, but it is likely that he had been suffering from syphilis for a considerable period. While he was still in Vienna he began thinking about *Dom Sébastien, Roi de Portugal*, the five-act grand opera he had agreed to write for the Paris Opéra. Leaving Vienna on 11 July, he arrived in Paris about ten days later and immersed himself in the composition of the new opera which occupied him until the end of August. In October he wrote to a friend in Naples: 'My five-act opera will be given a month from now. You can imagine what a staggering spectacle it will be – Portuguese, Arabs, an Inquisition auto-da-fé, a royal procession with a cata-falque – the underground dungeons of the Inquisition. The poor

King of Portugal is dragged everywhere until they kill him, and Philip II takes possession of Lisbon ... I am terribly wearied by this enormous five-act opera which contains loads of music for singing and dancing.'

Dom Sébastien was given its première at the Paris Opéra on 13 November 1843. (The first Paris performance of Maria di Rohan took place at the Théâtre-Italien on the following evening.) The new opera proved immensely popular with audiences, though less so with the Paris critics. It was soon being staged in the French provinces and in several European cities. In Vienna on 6 February 1845 Donizetti himself conducted the first three performances of a German-language version, and an Italian translation, Don Sebastiano, was first heard in Lisbon on 4 May 1845. In due course it reached the Americas, the first New York performance taking place on 25 November 1864. The opera has still to be performed in Britain. Its only production in recent times was at the Florence Maggio Musicale in May 1955, conducted by Carlo Maria Giulini.

Scribe's libretto, based on the play, Dom Sébastien de Portugal, staged in Paris in 1838 and itself derived from John Dryden's 1691 drama, Don Sebastian, tells a complicated story involving the sixteenth-century Portuguese King, the famous poet Camoëns who accompanies him to Morocco on a crusade against the Moors, and Zaïda, an Arab maiden whom Sébastien has rescued from a sentence of death. At the end of the opera, Sébastien and Zaïda are killed while attempting to escape from their captivity at the hands of the King's enemies who have, during his absence abroad, been plotting to betray Portugal to Philip II of Spain.

Dom Sébastien, especially in its original full version as performed in Paris, is a lengthy and highly sombre work, not unlike Verdi's Don Carlos of twenty-five years later, though at a lower level of inspiration. After an orchestral prelude which makes use of the theme of a funeral march to be heard later in the opera, the opening chorus of sailors, 'Nautoniers, mettez à la voile', is compensatingly lively, and Camoëns's first aria, 'Soldat, j'ai rêvé la victoire', cabaletta-like in its tempo, is an effective piece of musical characterisation. The solemn chorus of judges ('Céleste justice'), sung as Zaïda is being led to the stake, is interrupted by the King who commutes her sentence to one of banishment. Zaïda's gratitude is expressed in a cantabile aria, 'O mon Dieu, sur la terre', which, unremarkable in itself, leads into an expansive ensemble. Camoëns's prophecy, 'Oui, le ciel m'enflamme', alternates declamation with a rousing refrain in which he is joined by the chorus. The act ends in a stirring *vivace* ensemble.

Act II, which takes place in Morocco, opens with a colourful and appropriately oriental-sounding orchestral prelude, and a graceful chorus, 'Les délices de nos campagnes', sung by Zaïda's hand-maidens. Zaïda's attractive *larghetto* aria, 'Sol adoré de la patrie', had a superb cabaletta ('So mög denn Gott die Sünde') added to it by Donizetti for the Viennese production. In Paris, Zaïda's *larghetto* was followed by the obligatory ballet sequence for which Donizetti provided three delightful and colourfully orchestrated movements, a *pas de trois*, a *pas de deux* and a lively, somewhat Rossinian *galop* finale. Abayaldos' martial 'Levez-vous' is undistinguished, as is the fierce chorus of Arabs at the beginning of Act II, scene ii. However, the two-part duet, 'Grand Dieu! sa misère est si grande', for Zaïda and Sébastien, is superb, its *larghetto* opening section quite moving in its simplicity, and its *allegro* conclusion exhilarating. After a second lively chorus of Arabs ('Du sang! du sang!') and a brief ensemble passage, the act comes to a quiet and unusual conclusion with Sébastien's sad, graceful *larghetto*, 'Seul sur la terre'. The aria's exposed vocal line with its three high Cs and one D flat made it a popular tenor item in the early days of recording, especially in its Italian translation, 'Deserto in terra'.

In Act III the action has moved back to Lisbon where it remains for the remainder of the opera. After a brief orchestral prelude, the only number in the first scene is an effective two-part duet for Zaïda and Abayaldos, 'C'est qu'en tous lieux', with cabaletta ('En vain pour te soustraire'). The second scene contains Camoëns's tuneful *larghetto*, 'O Lisbonne', in praise of his homeland, an aria quite well known outside the context of the opera through recordings by several baritones. It is followed by Camoëns's duet with Sébastien, 'C'est un soldat qui revient de la guerre', with its perfunctory cabaletta, 'O jour de joie', and by the grim funeral march already heard as the opera's prelude. (Liszt made a transcription for piano of the funeral march, which prompted Donizetti to instruct his brother-in-law, 'Buy the march as arranged by Liszt. It will scare you.') Act III ends with a chorus of inquisitors, a later substitution by Donizetti for the conventional stretta performed at the première.

Act IV is set in the court of the Inquisition. After a solemn prelude for the brass playing in unison, and a grim chorus of judges ('O voûtes souterraines'), the trial of Sébastien proceeds, interrupted by the sudden appearance of Zaïda who begins the magnificent septet ('D'espoir et de terreur') which leads into the ensemble finale of the act. The last act begins with a prelude whose theme will be heard later in the barcarolle sung by Camoëns. Zaïda's 'Mourir pour ce qu'on aime', a cabaletta without its preceding aria, is followed by a duet, 'Du moins dans ma misère', which is for the most part so disturbingly trite that one cannot help wondering whether Donizetti's ability to concentrate had already been weakened by disease when he wrote it. Camoëns's dull barcarolle leads to a trio, 'De la prudence', which ends the first scene of the act. There is a change of scene for the brutally swift finale, for which, as Donizetti wrote to a Viennese colleague, 'music can do nothing'. Its fifty bars of music which he seems to have produced absent-mindedly certainly do nothing to enhance the reputation of *Dom Sébastien*, an opera which Donizetti hoped would prove to be his masterpiece.

After the first Vienna performance of the opera in its German translation, the composer wrote to friends in Paris, reporting a warmer reception than the work had received at its Paris première. In Vienna, 'three numbers were repeated, and the applause is still resounding in my head . . . Believe me, my dear friends, in Paris they will change their minds about *Dom Sébastien*, an opera with which I took great pains and which I think a capital work. I don't like to talk about myself, but I assure you that I was greatly hurt by the way in which your newspapers treated my opera . . . In time, justice will be rendered regarding all of that, and *Dom Sébastien* will be found bearable.'

In its shorter German version, it may well be more stageworthy than in its original form as a French *grand opéra*. When it was produced in Florence in 1955 as *Don Sebastiano*, the opera was poorly sung, its score was hacked about, and a new finale, lifted from *Belisario*, was inserted. *Dom Sébastien* still awaits a decent modern revival.

Caterina Cornaro

opera seria in a prologue and two acts

Principal characters:

Caterina	(soprano)
Gerardo	(tenor)

Andrea Cornaro   (bass)
Lusignano   (baritone)
Mocenigo   (bass)

LIBRETTO by Giacomo Sacchèro

TIME: 1472
PLACE: Venice and Cyprus

FIRST PERFORMED at the Teatro San Carlo, Naples, 12 January 1844, with Fanny Goldberg (Caterina); Gaetano Fraschini (Gerardo); Marco Arati (Andrea Cornaro); Filippo Coletti (Lusignano)

It was while *Dom Sébastien* was being rehearsed at the Paris Opéra in the autumn of 1843 that Donizetti, now approaching his forty-seventh birthday, began to be very seriously affected by the symptoms of his disease. The normally amiable composer was irritable at rehearsals, and an argument over whether the prima donna should remain on stage while the baritone was singing his off-stage barcarolle led to his angrily leaving the theatre. The Parisian music publisher Léon Escudier and two other friends followed him home where, according to Escudier, Donizetti 'gave vent to rattling sounds of rage, his mind confused'. From that day, Escudier wrote later, 'little by little the frightful sickness that undermined his faculties' made its inexorable progress. However, at first the symptoms revealed themselves only intermittently, and Donizetti was able to go on working for a further two years. On 20 December, he left Paris for Vienna where, as court composer, he was required to compose and conduct a new piece for the Imperial Chapel. He was still in Vienna when his opera, *Caterina Cornaro*, which he had begun to compose in Paris in the autumn of 1842, was given its première in Naples on 12 January 1844.

Donizetti had abandoned *Caterina Cornaro* (initially called *La Regina di Cipro*) after completing Act I, because, having intended the opera to be performed in Vienna, he had then learned that another opera on the same subject was about to be performed there. Instead, he wrote *Maria di Rohan* for Vienna, and returned to the composition of *Caterina Cornaro* in March 1843, since he had agreed to provide an opera for the Teatro San Carlo in Naples. By the end of May he had completed his score and sent it off to Naples, having come to an agreement with the management of the San Carlo that, due to his poor health, he would not himself be required to come to Naples to direct the first performances. He requested the Neapolitan composer, Mercadante, to keep an eye on the rehearsals and make any changes he thought necessary.

Caterina Cornaro was given its première in Naples on 12 January 1844 while its composer, in Vienna, was having gloomy forebodings about it. 'I am waiting with anxiety the news of the fiasco of *Caterina Cornaro* at Naples,' he wrote to his brother-in-law some days before the première: 'La Goldberg as the prima donna is my first disaster. I wrote for a soprano, and they give me a mezzo! God knows whether Coletti [the baritone] or Fraschini [the tenor] understand the roles as I intended them. God knows what a slaughterhouse the censorship may have created.' His fears were justified, for neither audiences nor critics liked the opera, which survived for only six performances. To the Neapolitan friend who informed him of this, Donizetti replied:

> A fiasco? Then so be it, a fiasco! But who says that this music is not by me, or that I wrote it in my sleep, or in revenge against the management? No. I assume all the responsibility, the blame and the punishment. Why would I have had it composed by others? Did I perhaps not have the time? Why in my sleep? Don't I, perhaps, work with facility? Why for revenge? Could I be so ungrateful to a public that has suffered me for so many years? ... As for the reminiscences of other music? Eh, *mon Dieu*, who doesn't make them? As for stealing (and, what is worse, without meaning to), who doesn't?

A year after its Naples première, *Caterina Cornaro* was given five performances in Parma, for which Donizetti made a few changes to his score. The opera was not staged again until 28 May 1972 when it returned to Naples and the San Carlo with Leyla Gencer as Caterina, on which occasion it was more generally admired than it had been in 1844. On 10 July 1972 Montserrat Caballé sang the title-role in a concert performance of the opera at the Royal Festival Hall, London. This was the work's London première. It was first heard in New York on 15 April 1973 in a concert performance at Carnegie Hall, again with Caballé who, later that year, sang the role in a concert performance at the Salle Pleyel, Paris. A stage production at the Teatro Colón, Buenos Aires, in 1982 was only moderately successful; the likelihood of *Caterina Cornaro* being found on any list of Donizetti's most popular operas is remote.

Giacomo Sacchèro's libretto was based on that of Jules-Henri Vernoy de Saint-Georges, written for Halévy's opera, *La Reine de Chypre*, which was staged in Paris in 1841. Caterina Cornaro was an historical character, born in Venice in 1454, who married James de Lusignan, the illegitimate son of King John II of Cyprus. In 1472 she became Queen of Cyprus, but her husband died within the year (not, as in the opera, in battle, but from natural causes). The action of the opera, which takes great liberties with historical fact, is set in Venice and Cyprus in 1472. The wedding of Caterina to a French knight, Gerardo, is postponed when Mocenigo brings word that Lusignano, King of Cyprus, wishes to marry her. Gerardo and Lusignano later meet, and Gerardo helps Lusignano defend Cyprus against the Venetians. Lusignano is killed in battle but before he dies he entrusts his people to Caterina's care.

The opera consists of a prologue, set in Venice, and two acts, set in Cyprus. After a brief orchestral prelude, the prologue begins with a conventional introductory chorus of wedding guests, followed, via a passage for solo flute above sustained string chords, by a pleasant love duet, 'Tu l'amor mio', for Caterina and Gerardo. The *larghetto* cavatina, 'Dell' empia Cipro il popolo', in which Mocenigo prohibits the wedding, has a splendidly menacing swiftness, and the scene ends with a forceful ensemble stretta of disconcerted guests. The second scene, in Caterina's bedroom, begins with an off-stage chorus of gondoliers singing a barcarolle whose melody has already been heard in the opera's prelude. Caterina, after being informed that Gerardo intends to elope with her, sings an exquisite *larghetto* romanza, 'Vieni, o tu che ognor io chiamo', followed without any intervening material by a cabaletta of joyous anticipation ('Deh! vieni, t'affretta'). But, warned by her father and Mocenigo that her beloved will be killed unless she dismisses him, she is forced to tell Gerardo that she no longer loves him. This she does in the disappointingly mundane two-part duet ('Spera in me, della tua vita') which ends the prologue.

The orchestra at the begining of Act I makes it clear that the action has moved in an easterly direction to Cyprus. Mocenigo's nondescript *andante* cavatina, 'Credi che dorma, o incauto?' is followed by Lusignano's cabaletta-like entrance aria, 'Da che sposa Caterina' and by a fierce chorus of hired ruffians ('Core e pugnale'). An attractive friendship duet ('Vedi, io piango!') and cabaletta ('Si, dell' ardir degl'empi') for Gerardo and Lusignano ends the first scene of the act. A typical chorus of ladies-in-waiting ('Gemmata il serto, giovine') begins the second scene, set in Caterina's apartment in the royal palace. Lusignano's graceful *andante* romanza, 'Ah, non turbarti a questi accenti', one of the opera's most attractive numbers, leads to a not very individual *larghetto* duet ('Da quel dì che lacerato') and cabaletta ('T'amo ancora') for Caterina and Gerardo, in which he informs her that he has entered a religious order, and the former lovers agree to sublimate their passion. The act ends in an exciting dramatic quartet, begun by Lusignano ('Indietro! Io, vil carnefice').

An orchestral prelude to Act II describes the war which is now being waged in Lusignano's kingdom. Gerardo's dull *larghetto* aria, 'Io trar non voglio campi ed onori', is followed by a martial cabaletta ('Morte! morte!') in which he rallies the troops. A vigorous female chorus, 'O ciel! che tumulto!', precedes the opera's finale which exists in two forms. What was heard in Naples was a *larghetto* aria ('Pietà, o Signor') for Caterina, separated from its forceful and effective cabaletta ('Non più affani, mie genti, preghiere') by the dying Lusignano's affecting *larghetto*, 'Orsù della vittoria'. For Parma in 1845 Donizetti expanded Lusignano's role in the finale. His first thoughts are to be preferred.

Ne m'oubliez pas
(Do Not Forget Me)

opéra comique in three acts (incomplete)

Principal characters:
Henriette   (soprano)
André   (tenor)
Franz   (baritone)

LIBRETTO by Jules-Henri Vernoy de Saint-Georges

TIME: Unspecified
PLACE: A cottage in the middle of a forest

FIRST PERFORMED on a long-playing gramophone record made at

the Henry Wood Hall, London, in January 1979, with Margreta Elkins (Henriette); Alexander Oliver (André); Christian du Plessis (Franz)

During the course of his career, Donizetti abandoned a few projected operas. *Ne m'oubliez pas* is singled out for inclusion here because he completed more of it than of the others and also because it is a late work which he might well have finished composing had his final illness not overtaken him.

The opera is first mentioned in a letter Donizetti wrote from Milan to Jules-Henri Vernoy de Saint-Georges (the co-librettist of *La Fille du Régiment*) in Paris in the summer of 1842, agreeing to work with him on a comic opera and asking for an interesting libretto with not too many characters. Intending to compose the opera in time for it to be performed in Paris in December, Donizetti signed a contract with the Opéra-Comique at the end of September. However, by February of the following year he had still not received the libretto, and wrote from Vienna to a colleague in Paris requesting him to instruct Saint-Georges ('Is he sleeping?') to send the completed libretto no later than the beginning of May.

No libretto has been discovered; but presumably it arrived in Vienna, for it was in that city, in the summer of 1843, that Donizetti began to work on *Ne m'oubliez pas*, composing and orchestrating six numbers and beginning a seventh. However, for some reason he abandoned it, perhaps to concentrate on *Dom Sébastien*. Thereafter, the contract with the Opéra-Comique was allowed to lapse. It is unlikely that, after the première of *Dom Sébastien* in Paris in November 1843, Donizetti was any longer capable of sustained creative effort.

From the words of the existing numbers, as recorded in London in 1979, it would seem that Vernoy de Saint-Georges's story, set in a cottage in the middle of a forest, concerns two young lovers, Henriette and André, and that in Act II Henriette is abducted by the villainous Franz. Presumably Act III brings a happy ending. What follows is a brief description of the six numbers completed by Donizetti:

1. A bucolic duet for horns, to be played off-stage (Act I).
2. A simple romance, 'Oh! la belle campagne', for Henriette (Act I).

3. A dull strophic ballade, 'Heinach disait', for Henriette, with the help of André and a chorus of huntsmen (Act I.).

4. A duet, 'Belle Henriette', for Henriette and Franz, which is oddly staid, given that, in the course of it, he carries her off under the nose of the sleeping André (Act II).

5. A tuneful romance, 'Ah, faudrait-il qu'elle appartient', for André (Act III).

6. A gentle duet, 'Adieu, ma paupière est lassée', for Henriette and André (Act III).

Though Donizetti continued working for a time, conducting in Vienna as late as the spring of 1845, his physical and mental condition went on deteriorating until his collapse into paralysis and insanity, the last stages of his venereal disease. His final two years were spent in a sanatorium outside Paris in an almost comatose condition, until he was taken home to Bergamo to die in 1848.

III

Vincenzo Bellini

1801–1835

14

From *Adelson e Salvini* to *I Capuleti e i Montecchi*

Adelson e Salvini

dramma semiserio in two acts

Principal characters:

Nelly	(soprano)
Madama Rivers	(mezzo-soprano)
Fanny	(contralto)
Salvini	(tenor)
Lord Adelson	(baritone)
Bonifacio	(bass)
Struley	(bass)

LIBRETTO by Andrea Leone Tottola

TIME: The eighteenth century
PLACE: Naples

FIRST PERFORMED (in a three-act version) at the Real Collegio di Musica di San Sebastiano, Naples, in February (probably 12 February) 1825, with an all-male student cast including Giacinto Marras (Nelly), Luigi Rotellini (Madama Rivers), Leonardo Porugini (Salvini), Antonio Manzi (Lord Adelson). The revised two-act opera was first performed at the Teatro Massimo Bellini, Catania, 23 September 1992, with Fabio Previati (Adelson), Bradley Williams (Salvini), Alicia Nafè (Nelly), Aurio Tomicich (Bonifacio), Roberto Coviello (Struley).

Although Vincenzo Bellini was born into a musical family – his father was an organist in the Sicilian town of Catania where Vincenzo was born on 2 November 1801 – he took up music as a profession only in the face of severe opposition from his family. Eventually the child's musical ability simply forced itself on his father's attention, and a number of friends of the family exerted pressure as well. Bellini senior gave in and allowed Vincenzo to study at the Real Collegio di Musica in Naples, the costs being met by a Sicilian nobleman who was struck by Vincenzo's talent. At the conservatorium where Donizetti had studied only a few years earlier, the young composer proved a diligent student and produced his first work for the stage, *Adelson e Salvini*, as a graduation exercise while he was still in his final year.

The first performance of *Adelson e Salvini* at the college, with an all-male student cast, was an overwhelming success, and several further performances had to be given. Nicola Zingarelli, Bellini's teacher, and the Duke of Noja, governor of the college and superintendent of the Naples theatres, were so impressed that they arranged for Bellini to be commissioned to write an opera for the following season at the Teatro San Carlo. *Adelson e Salvini*, however, was not performed outside the Real Collegio di Musica, although Bellini revised it two years later, reshaping it into two acts and substituting *recitativo secco* for the spoken dialogue of the three-act version, in the hope of its being produced professionally. It was not staged again until 6 November 1985, when it was performed in its original three-act version at the Teatro Metropolitan in Catania, on the occasion of a Bellini conference organised by the University of Catania. Bellini's two-act revision remained unstaged until it was produced at the Teatro Massimo Bellini in Catania in 1992.

The opera's libretto by Andrea Leone Tottola (librettist of several operas by Rossini and Donizetti) may have been based on a comedy performed at Esterháza in 1778, though it seems to have derived ultimately from a story by François-Thomas de Baculard d'Arnaud, published in Paris in the 1770s. Tottola's libretto was not written for the student Bellini, but for an opera by Valentino Fioravanti which was performed in Florence in 1816. Set in seventeenth-century Ireland at the castle of Lord Adelson, Bellini's *Adelson e Salvini* tells a story of friendship, love and jealousy. A Roman painter, Salvini, the house-guest of his friend Lord Adelson, falls in love with his host's fiancée, Nelly. Torn between his love for her and his affection for his friend, he contemplates suicide. A melodramatic plot, involving Nelly's villainous uncle, Colonel Struley, who attempts to abduct her as an act of revenge upon his enemy Adelson, ends with Salvini transferring his affections to his pupil Fanny, and with the marriage of Adelson to Nelly.

After a well constructed though not very interesting overture, the opera begins in dull imitation of Rossini with Fanny's aria, 'Immagine gradita' and the ensemble which follows. Struley's *andante sostenuto* aria, 'Tu provi un palpito per tal dimora', is hardly livelier, though at least one discerns momentarily in its opening phrase the young Bellini's original voice attempting to assert itself. Bonifacio's *buffo* scena, 'Bonifacio Beccheria qui presente', is routine stuff as is his subsequent *allegro moderato* duet with the love-stricken Salvini ('Speranza seduttrice') in which Bellini expects remarkable range and flexibility from his tenor. By far the finest number in the score is Nelly's F minor romanza, 'Dopo l'oscuro nembo', a gently flowing *andante* which would not, and indeed does not, sound out of place in one of Bellini's more mature operas, for five years later it was to become Giulietta's romanza, 'Oh, quante volte', in *I Capuleti e i Montecchi*. The duet, 'Felice istante', for Nelly and Salvini is competently written but not highly individual; the *allegro* trio, 'Questa buona signorina', in which they are joined by Bonifacio is trivial; and the Act I finale ('Noi, qui l'attenderemo'), with Adelson making a belated first appearance in an elegant *andante*, 'Obliarti! abbandonarti!', is for the most part melodically threadbare.

Struley's *allegro moderato* aria, 'Ehi! Geronio', with contributions from his henchman Geronio and the chorus, begins Act II, followed by a featureless duet, 'Poni l'esca a contatto del fuoco', for Nelly and Bonifacio. The *allegro* duet, 'Torna, o caro, a questo seno', for the two friends Adelson and Salvini, its words perhaps more suitable to a love duet, is a robust extended number in two parts, but Bonifacio's aria, 'Taci, attendi, e allor vedrai', is a tedious *buffo* piece which long outstays its welcome. Much more enjoyable are the ensemble, 'Si, venite, miei cari', involving all the principals, and the lively finale, 'Lieti facciam ritorno', with its graceful solo passage, 'Ecco signor la sposa', in which Salvini relinquishes Nelly to his friend Adelson.

If *Adelson e Salvini* now seems less impressive than it did to Bellini's friends, colleagues and teachers in 1825, it nevertheless intermittently reveals clear signs of its composer's individuality, not only in the aria, 'Dopo l'oscuro nembo', but also in a number of isolated passages which were in due course to find their way into *Bianca e Fernando, Il Pirata, La Straniera, I Capuleti e i Montecchi* and *Norma*. And, especially in its earlier version in which the role of Bonifacio is in Neapolitan dialect, it is the only opera by Bellini in which elements of Rossinian *opera buffa* are to be found.

Bianca e Fernando

melodramma in two acts

Principal characters:
Bianca   (soprano)
Fernando   (tenor)
Filippo   (bass)
Carlo   (bass)

LIBRETTO by Domenico Gilardoni, revised by Felice Romani

TIME: The thirteenth century
PLACE: Agrigento, Sicily

FIRST PERFORMED as *Bianca e Gernando*, at the Teatro San Carlo, Naples, 30 May 1826, with Henriette Méric-Lalande (Bianca); Giovanni Battista Rubini (Gernando); Luigi Lablache (Filippo) Revised version, *Bianca e Fernando*, first performed at the Teatro Carlo Felice, Genoa, 7 April 1828, with Adelaide Tosi (Bianca); Giovanni David (Fernando); Antonio Tamburini (Filippo)

For the opera he had been commissioned to compose as a result of the success of *Adelson e Salvini*, Bellini chose a new young librettist, Domenico Gilardoni (who was later to write several libretti for Donizetti). The subject, probably also chosen by the young composer, was taken from a play, *Bianca e Fernando alla tomba di Carlo IV, Duca d'Agrigento* by Carlo Roti, which had been staged in 1820. Later, at least three other composers used the same subject: Campiuti's *Bianca e Fernando* was performed in Venice in 1827,

Berio's opera of the same title in Treviso, also in 1827, and Vaccai's *Bianca di Messina* in Turin in 1828.

The cast of Bellini's opera was to be headed by Adelaide Tosi, Giovanni David and Luigi Lablache, three of the finest singers of the time. However, when the première was postponed for several months to suit the convenience of the King of Naples, the soprano and tenor became unavailable, and their places were taken by Henriette Méric-Lalande and Giovanni Battista Rubini. When it was finally staged on 30 May 1826, *Bianca e Gernando* was an immediate success. Donizetti wrote that it was 'beautiful, beautiful, beautiful, especially for someone who is writing his first opera'. The twenty-four-year-old composer from Sicily became the talk of Naples and was immediately offered a contract by the impresario Domenico Barbaja to write an opera for Italy's most prestigious theatre, La Scala, in Milan.

It was as a result of the success of *Il Pirata*, his opera for La Scala (discussed on pp 315–318), that Bellini was invited by another impresario, Bartolomeo Merelli, to provide an opera for the opening of a new theatre in Genoa. As time was pressing, Bellini's suggestion that he revise his *Bianca e Gernando* was accepted, and the composer immediately set to work, with the help of Felice Romani who provided what new text was required. The 1826 opera's short introduction was replaced by a full-scale overture, four new numbers were added, and changes were made to all but two numbers of the original score. 'Everything else is altered, and about half is new,' Bellini wrote to his friend and fellow student Francesco Florimo in Naples.

The character of Fernando had been called Gernando in the original Naples version of the opera, as Fernando was the name of the heir apparent to the King and thus could not be used on royal stages within the kingdom. In Genoa the title of the opera became *Bianca e Fernando*. Tosi and David, the soprano and tenor for whom the work was initially conceived, sang the title-roles, but Luigi Lablache, the bass of the première, was not available. His place was taken by Antonio Tamburini, a young baritone who had distinguished himself in *Il Pirata* the previous year.

Although *Bianca e Fernando* was greeted enthusiastically at its Genoa première, it received few performances elsewhere. It was produced in Messina in 1828, Milan, Naples and Reggio Calabria in 1829, and at one or two other Italian theatres, but outside Italy it was staged only in Barcelona in 1830 and Madrid in 1831. After its production at the Teatro Valle, Rome, in 1837, it was not heard of again until 30 April 1976 when a concert performance was given in the RAI auditorium, Turin, with Yasuko Hayashi as Bianca, Antonio Savastano as Fernando and Enrico Fissore as Filippo, conducted by Gabrielle Ferro. Cristina Deutekom sang the title-role in the first modern stage production of the opera in Genoa in 1978, since when it has been staged only once, in Catania in 1991. It was given in concert performance at the Queen Elizabeth Hall, London, on 15 March 1981, but has yet to be staged either in Britain or America.

The action takes place in Agrigento in the thirteenth century. The dukedom of Carlo IV has been usurped by Filippo, who has imprisoned the Duke and spread a rumour that he has died. Fernando, the Duke's son, has returned from exile in disguise to avenge his father's death. Fernando's sister, Bianca, a widow with a baby son, prepares to marry Filippo, but is persuaded by Fernando that Filippo was responsible for the disappearance of their father. The opera ends with Duke Carlo being rescued by Fernando and his followers, and Filippo overthrown.

In the overture a charming *andante* is followed by an overlong and uninteresting *allegro*, but at least the overture sounds as though it has some connection with the mood of the opera which it precedes. The orchestral introduction to Fernando's accompanied recitative – there is no *recitativo secco* in Bellini's operas after *Adelson e Salvini* – is banal, but the chorus of Fernando's followers ('Sgombra quel duol, serenati') sounds what we now recognise as a Bellinian note in a work whose Act I in general is distinctly Rossinian. Fernando's graceful *larghetto* cavatina, 'A tanto duol', and its cabaletta, 'Ascolta, o padre', which requires high Cs and Ds from the tenor, lead by way of a scene in not very expressive recitative to Filippo's dull cavatina, 'Ah no, sì lieta sorte', and its livelier though perhaps excessively ornate cabaletta, 'O contento desiato!'. A trio, 'Di Fernando son le cifre', cleverly differentiates between the three characters with their conflicting thoughts and feelings, and the Act I finale, once past its overlong and overwrought chorus of welcome to Bianca ('Viva Bianca!'), is impressive, its spirited *allegro* conclusion preceded by Bianca's cavatina ('La mia scelta a voi sia grata') and its cabaletta, 'Contenta appien quest' alma'. The cabaletta is the most attractive number in the act and one whose music Bellini was to make use of again, three years later, as 'Ah! bello a me ritorna', the cabaletta to 'Casta diva' in *Norma*.

Filippo's aria ('Allor che notte avanza') and cabaletta ('Bramato momento') at the beginning of Act II are unmemorable. However, the romanza, 'Sorgi, o padre', for Bianca, in which her maid Eloisa also plays an important role, is a mature example of typically Bellinian melody in its blend of sweetness and melancholy. The duet, 'No! mia suora più non sei', for Bianca and Fernando, is disappointingly mundane. The penultimate scene of the opera opens with a chorus, 'Tutti siam?', whose theme suggests strongly that Bellini had been listening to Beethoven's 'Moonlight' sonata. He was to use this chorus twice again: in *Zaira* and, somewhat altered, in *Norma*. Neither Fernando's *larghetto* aria, 'All' udir del padre afflitto', nor its *allegro* cabaletta, 'Odo il tuo pianto, o padre', rises above the commonplace, but Carlo's recitative and *andante maestoso* cavatina, 'Da gelido sudore', are moving. A trio, 'Oh Dio! Qual voce!' leads to the opera's finale which takes the form of an aria and cabaletta for Bianca. The expressive aria, 'Deh! non ferir', benefits from the contributions of Fernando and Filippo, but the cabaletta sounds hastily put together (as, according to a contemporary account, it was).

Bianca e Fernando is an uneven work, though its finest pages show a great advance upon Bellini's first opera, especially in his writing for the orchestra. It is an opera which, fitfully, looks back to Rossini and forward to Verdi, confidently inhabiting its own Bellinian world in only one or two numbers.

Il Pirata
(The Pirate)

opera seria in two acts

Principal characters:

Ernesto, Duke of Caldora   (baritone)
Imogene, his wife   (soprano)
Gualtiero, leader of a band of pirates   (tenor)

LIBRETTO by Felice Romani

TIME: The thirteenth century
PLACE: Sicily

FIRST PERFORMED at the Teatro alla Scala, Milan, 27 October 1827, with Henriette Méric-Lalande (Imogene); Giovanni Rubini (Gualtiero); Antonio Tamburini (Ernesto)

The success of *Bianca e Gernando* at the Teatro San Carlo in Naples attracted the attention of Domenico Barbaja, the impresario whose interests extended to Milan and Vienna. Barbaja invited Bellini to compose an opera for La Scala, Milan, and on 5 April 1827 the young composer left Naples to travel to Milan. There he renewed acquaintance with the composer Saverio Mercadante who was busy rehearsing his new opera, *Il Montanaro*, but who nevertheless helped his young colleague find lodgings. Mercadante also introduced Bellini to Felice Romani, the official librettist at La Scala, and the man with whom Bellini would collaborate in the creation of all but one of his future operas. Romani, who had already provided texts for such composers as Donizetti, Mercadante, Meyerbeer and Rossini, was widely regarded as the finest librettist of the day. It was probably he who suggested the subject of Bellini's first opera for La Scala, *Il Pirata*, which was enthusiastically received at its première. By the end of the season it had been given fifteen performances, all to full houses.

Il Pirata was Bellini's first international success. In the five years following its Milan première it was performed in Vienna, Dresden, London (at Her Majesty's Theatre on 17 April 1830), Madrid, Paris and New York (on 5 December 1832), and it continued to be performed, in French and German translation as well as in Italian, throughout Europe and Latin America for a number of years. By the beginning of the twentieth century it had fallen into neglect, but it was revived in Rome in January 1935. The first post-war performances were given in Catania in 1951 and Palermo in 1958, both with Lucy Kelston as Imogene. Maria Callas assumed the role at La Scala in 1958, after which it became the property of Montserrat Caballé for some time: 1966 in concert in New York; 1967 Florence; 1968 Philadelphia; 1969 London (in concert); 1971 Barcelona. Christiane Eda-Pierre was Imogene at Wexford in 1972. In 1992 *Il Pirata* was produced in Zurich with Mara Zampieri as Imogene.

Romani's libretto is based on a five-act tragedy, *Bertram*, by

Charles Robert Maturin, an Irish clergyman who was the author of a number of Gothic romances. Maturin's *Bertram* was staged at Drury Lane in 1816 with Edmund Kean in the title-role, but Romani probably used the French translation which was performed at the Théâtre Favart in Paris and published in 1821. He shortened and simplified Maturin's extravagant plot, changing the names of most of the characters. In the opera, Gualtiero, formerly Count of Montalto but now an exile and head of a band of Aragonese pirates, returns to find that his beloved Imogene has married his enemy, Ernesto, Duke of Caldora. When Ernesto surprises his wife in a secret rendezvous with her former lover, he challenges Gualtiero to a duel. Ernesto is killed by Gualtiero, who is then arrested and condemned to death. When this is revealed to her, Imogene loses her reason.

After a charming though loosely constructed overture, part of which is borrowed from the overture to *Adelson e Salvini*, the curtain rises on an opening scene of storm, shipwreck and rescue. The extended chorus, which magnificently portrays the raging elements, is striking enough to put one in mind of the opening of Verdi's *Otello*, written sixty years later. The prayer, 'Nume che imperi', is taken from a passage in *Adelson e Salvini*. In his cavatina, 'Nel furor delle tempeste', not a conventionally slow entrance aria but an impassioned *allegro moderato* in polonaise rhythm, Gualtiero sings of his beloved Imogene. His cabaletta, 'Per te di vane lagrime', is lifted from Salvini's 'Oh! quante amare lagrime' in *Adelson e Salvini*. Like virtually all of Bellini's tenor characters, Gualtiero needs to have secure high Cs, C sharps and Ds within his range.

Imogene's aria, 'Lo sognai ferito', marked *allegro moderato assai*, is a succession of fine Bellinian melodies, and its cabaletta, 'Sventurata', has a lavishly embellished vocal line. The pirates' chorus is a lively and imaginative tarantella with an echo effect of which Bellini was proud. 'It gave so much pleasure,' he wrote of its performance at the première, 'because of the novelty of my having imagined the echo so well.' The duet, 'Tu sciagurato!', for Imogene and Gualtiero is one of the finest numbers in the opera, with Gualtiero's reaction to the story of Imogene's forced marriage ('Pietosa al padre') especially affecting. A few bars have been borrowed from the overture to *Adelson e Salvini*. The brisk march and chorus ('Più temuto, più splendido nome') which accompany the entrance of Ernesto perform their function competently, but Ernesto's somewhat over-florid aria,

'Si vincemmo', and cabaletta sung to the same words as the aria are less effective. The aria, an *andante* accompanied gently by strings and three trombones, is lifted from *Adelson e Salvini*. The Act I finale consists of an elaborate quintet (marked *largo agitato*) with chorus, based on one of those long-breathed melodies in the creation of which Bellini had already become a master, followed by an exciting ensemble stretta (*allegro molto agitato*) led by Imogene.

The gently lilting chorus of women ('Che rechi tu?') which opens Act II contains a solo part for Imogene's companion, Adele. The most attractive section of an extended duet for Imogene and Ernesto ('Tu m'apristi in cor ferita') is the *larghetto* ('Ah! lo sento'), while the following duet ('Vieni, vieni') for Imogene and Gualtiero, though it begins like *I Puritani*'s 'Vieni fra queste braccia', fails to develop interestingly. The *andante sostenuto* opening section of the trio ('Cedo al destin orribile') which follows with the entrance of Ernesto is quite masterly, but its concluding fast and furious *allegro* is almost risible. An impressive chorus, 'Lasso! perir cosi', in which the ladies of the court mourn Ernesto's death while the knights swear vengeance, is followed by Gualtiero's *larghetto* aria, 'Tu vedrai la sventurata', and its highly decorated cabaletta, 'Ma non fia sempre odiata', both effective enough in context though hardly memorable. The final scene of the opera is superb, with Imogene's moving *andante* aria, 'Col sorriso d'innocenza', preceded by a plaintive cor anglais solo and followed by a powerfully dramatic cabaletta, 'Oh sole, ti vela di tenebre oscure'.

Unven though it is, and dramatically unsatisfactory, *Il Pirata* contains some of Bellini's most affecting music, and deserves to retain its recently reacquired place in the operatic repertory.

La Straniera
(The Stranger)

opera seria in two acts

Principal characters:

Alaide (The Stranger)	(soprano)
The Signore di Montolino	(bass)
Isoletta, his daughter	(mezzo-soprano)

Arturo, Count of Ravenstel   (tenor)
Baron Valdeburgo, Alaide's brother   (baritone)

LIBRETTO by Felice Romani

TIME: The beginning of the fourteenth century
PLACE: Brittany

FIRST PERFORMED at the Teatro alla Scala, Milan, 14 February
1829, with Henriette Méric-Lalande (Alaide); Stanislao
Marcionni (Il Signore di Montolino); Caroline Unger (Isoletta);
Domenico Reina (Arturo); Antonio Tamburini (Baron
Valdeburgo)

Immediately after the première of *Il Pirata*, Bellini was approached
by the impresario Bartolomeo Merelli and invited to write an opera
for the opening of a new theatre in Genoa. What he in fact provided
for the occasion was a revision of his *Bianca e Gernando* (see pp 312–
315). While in Genoa he met Giuditta Turina, the young wife of a
wealthy silk merchant, and embarked upon a clandestine love affair
with her which lasted for five years until Bellini's departure for
England in 1833. The success in Genoa of *Bianca e Fernando*, as it was
now called, led to Bellini being offered another contract by La Scala,
for an opera to open the next carnival season in December 1828.

   The new opera was *La Straniera*, whose libretto by Felice Romani
was derived from *L'Étrangère*, a novel by Victor-Charles Prévôt,
Vicomte d'Arlincourt, and from *La Straniera*, an Italian dramatised
version of the novel made by the Baron Giovan Carlo Cosenza and
performed in Naples in 1827. 'The subject Romani has found',
Bellini wrote to his friend Francesco Florimo, 'is more susceptible
than all the others I suggested.' The opera should have had its
première on 26 December, the traditional date for the opening of the
carnival season, but Romani's illness in the autumn made him more
than usually dilatory. For a time Bellini feared that he might have to
use another librettist, Gaetano Rossi. But Rossi, he told Florimo,
would 'never, never be able to write verses like Romani, and
especially not for me, since I am so dependent on good words. Just
notice in *Il Pirata* how it is the verses, not the situations, that inspire
my talent ... that's why I must have Romani.'

   Romani recovered, but not soon enough for the opera to be
composed in time for the opening of the season. Rossini's *L'Assedio di*

Corinto, an Italian version of *Le Siège de Corinthe*, was performed in its place on 26 December, and the première of Bellini's opera was postponed to 14 February 1829. On 16 February the *Gazzetta privilegiata di Milano* was able to write of *La Straniera*: 'The new opera of Maestro Bellini had a clamorous success. The poet served the composer well, and the composer could not have served his singers better. Everyone competed to make themselves pleasing to the public, and succeeded to such an extent that they were applauded greatly during the course of the opera and at its conclusion.' Three days later the same journal described the new opera as having recalled the days of Jommelli, Marcello and Pergolesi with its 'beautiful song, and its splendidly elegant and pleasing instrumentation'.

To Romani, who had left for Venice some weeks before the première, Bellini wrote: '*La Straniera* outdid *Il Pirata* by more than a little. Without exception, all the pieces were applauded ... the enthusiasm of the Milanese is beyond belief. I was called on to the stage seven times, and the singers even more ... We were in seventh heaven. Your libretto provides poetry and effective *coups de théâtre* that one cannot imagine improved ... Burn this letter, as we should not be seen detailing our triumphs now. But with it, accept my gratitude more than ever, as I owe half of my success to you. Never change, my good friend, and we shall be able to share a really glorious career.'

La Straniera was staged in several other Italian cities, and its popularity continued for several decades. Its first performances abroad were in Dresden and Madrid in 1830, Graz and Vienna (in German) in 1831, London at His Majesty's Theatre on 23 June 1832, Paris in 1832, in German in Prague, Berlin and Budapest in 1832, New York at the Park Theatre on 10 November 1834, Lisbon and Vienna (this time in Italian) in 1835. After the Second World War the opera was revived at the Teatro Massimo Bellini in Catania, on 18 March 1954, with Adriana Guerrini in the title-role, since when it has had several productions in Italy, the United States and elsewhere. Notable modern interpreters of the role of Alaide have included Renata Scotto (Palermo, 1968; Venice and Rome, 1970; Edinburgh, 1972), Montserrat Caballé (Carnegie Hall, New York, 1969) and Carol Neblett (Charleston, South Carolina, 1989).

The opera is set in Brittany at the beginning of the fourteenth century, with a plot which borders on absurdity. Arturo, betrothed to Isoletta, falls in love with Alaide, a stranger in the locality who is suspected by the local inhabitants of being a witch. Seeing her embracing Valdeburgo, who he does not realise is her brother, Arturo challenges his supposed rival to a duel, and Valdeburgo falls, wounded, into the lake. Thinking him dead, Alaide reveals to Arturo that Valdeburgo was her brother. When she is accused of his murder, Arturo confesses that he is the guilty one, but both are saved from execution only by the sudden appearance of Valdeburgo. Arturo and Isoletta, apparently reconciled to each other, are about to marry when Arturo discovers that Alaide, with whom he is still in love, is in fact Agnese, whom the King of France had bigamously married. (The King, threatened with excommunication unless he returned to his wife, Isamberga, Princess of Denmark, had sent Agnese to Brittany in the care of her brother.) Isamberga having died, Agnese is now Queen of France. All this proves too much for Arturo, who kills himself. Agnese prays that she, too, may die, and swoons as the curtain falls.

There is no overture, merely a brief orchestral introduction leading to an opening chorus, 'Voga, voga, il vento tace', in the rhythm of a barcarolle. The *allegro moderato* duet, 'Io la vidi', for Valdeburgo and Isoletta is colourless until the distant chorus warning of 'la straniera', and the ensuing lively stretta. Preceded by Arturo's expressive recitative and punctuated by his cries of adoration, Alaide's *andante* romanza, 'Sventurato il cor che fida', is one of the earliest examples of those exquisitely sad melodies which epitomise Bellini. It leads without pause into the Alaide–Arturo *allegro moderato* love duet, 'Serba, serba i tuoi segreti'. The chorus of hunters is rather ordinary, but the air of elegant melancholy which pervades the *andante* trio, 'No, non ti son rivale', reveals Bellini at his finest and most characteristic, and the chorus, 'La straniera a cui fè tu presti', in which the seeds of doubt and suspicion are implanted in Arturo's mind is simple but effective. A brief trio for Alaide, Arturo and Valdeburgo, 'Ah! non partir', leads to an intensely dramatic Act I finale of almost Verdian pace and intensity with the duel of the two men, Valdeburgo's fall into the lake (accompanied graphically by a descending scale in the orchestra), the accusations of the villagers, and Alaide's guilt-racked aria, 'Un grido io sento'.

The second part of Valdeburgo's aria, 'Sì, li scogliete, o giudici', at the beginning of Act II is the simple and touching 'Meco tu vieni, o misera' (an adaptation of music already heard in *Adelson e Salvini*), one of the most affecting melodies in *La Straniera*. Berlioz, not noted for generous assessment of Italian composers, described it as a tune which would 'move the indifferent to tears'. The lengthy and restless duet, 'Si! Sulla salma del fratello', for Arturo and Valdeburgo undergoes a number of tempo changes to advance the plot but, except for its *andante mosso* section ('Tu togliesti alla dolente'), is of little musical interest. Isoletta's sad aria, 'Ah! se non m'ami più', with its Mozartian flute obbligato and its mood of gentle resignation, is attractive, and its joyous *allegro moderato* cabaletta, 'Ah! al mio sguardo!', even more so. A graceful wedding chorus, 'È dolce la vergine', is followed by the fraught scene with its splendid quartet ('Si! si, tu il sei') in the porch of the church where Arturo and Isoletta are to be married, and by the opera's final scene which is dominated by Alaide's beautiful and moving prayer, 'Ciel pietoso', and her tremendous, intensely dramatic, almost Verdian cabaletta, 'Or sei pago, o ciel tremendo'. It was this final number that gave Bellini and Romani the most trouble, the composer making his librettist rewrite the words three times before finding himself stirred by them.

Even more than *Il Pirata*, *La Straniera* is an opera which, with its wealth of melody, its expressive recitative and its sensitive instrumentation, could easily regain the popularity it enjoyed when it was first staged at La Scala.

Zaira

opera seria in two acts

Principal characters:

Zaira, a slave of the Sultan	(soprano)
Nerestano, a French knight	(mezzo-soprano)
Corasmino, Vizier	(tenor)
Orosmane, Sultan of Jerusalem	(bass)
Lusignano	(bass)

LIBRETTO by Felice Romani

TIME: The Crusades
PLACE: Jerusalem

FIRST PERFORMED at the Teatro Ducale, Parma, 16 May 1829, with Henriette Méric-Lalande (Zaira); Teresa Cecconi (Nerestano); Carlo Trezzini (Corasmino); Luigi Lablache (Orosmane); Mario Rinaudo (Lusignano)

The contract to compose an opera to open the new Teatro Ducale in Parma was offered first to Rossini, who declined as he was at work on *Le Comte Ory* in Paris. After a certain amount of intrigue, during the course of which the names of such other composers as Pacini, Generali, Coccia and Mercadante were considered and passed over, the committee entrusted to manage the new theatre (which is now called the Teatro Regio) made an approach to Bellini in August 1828. Late in November a contract was signed, and Bellini wrote to his friend Florimo: 'The impresario would like me to compose *Cesare in Egitto*. But, as I have made it a condition in the contract that the libretto must satisfy me in general and in detail, I have refused, although it is the work of the Parma lawyer Torrigiani, for the subject is as old as Noah ... I shall be presenting my opera *La Straniera* not later than early February, and so I shall then have almost three months to compose the new one for Parma. I think that's long enough, as the contract obliges them to deliver a complete libretto by mid-January. Having it all, I shall easily be able to finish the opera without rushing.'

Luigi Torrigiani, the writer of the *Cesare in Egitto* libretto, did not give up without a struggle. He travelled to Milan to talk to Bellini and Henriette Méric-Lalande, who was to be the opera's prima donna. But Bellini stood his ground. He wanted, in any case, to collaborate again with Felice Romani, who now suggested to him at least two subjects, one concerning Charles the Bold, and another based on *Le Solitaire*, a novel by D'Arlincourt, from whose novel *L'Étrangère* the libretto of *La Straniera* had been derived. It was not until after the Milan première of *La Straniera* in February 1829 that, at Bellini's suggestion, Romani agreed to provide an Italian libretto, *Zaira*, derived from Voltaire's French tragedy, *Zaïre*. Voltaire's play had already been used by several other composers, among them Sebastiano Nasolini (Venice, 1797), Francesco Federici (Palermo, 1799) and Peter Winter (London, 1805).

Though *Zaïre* (1732) was for many years generally considered Voltaire's greatest play, it does not read very convincingly today. Set in Jerusalem at the time of the Crusades, its plot, which

Romani followed with reasonable fidelity, tells of the Sultan Orosmane who has fallen in love with his captive Zaïre (Zaira), a Christian girl who, as a child, had been kidnapped and brought up in Jerusalem. Zaïre returns Orosmane's love, and a wedding is planned. Shortly before the marriage, Zaïre's childhood companion and fellow-captive, Nérestan (Nerestano in the opera), returns from France with the ransom for ten French knights. The ransom, however, has exhausted his fortune and, unable to buy his own freedom, Nérestan surrenders himself. Orosmane magnanimously refuses the ransom and frees everyone with the exception of Zaïre and another captive, the elderly Lusignan (Lusignano).

When Zaïre begs him to show mercy, Orosmane frees Lusignan who recognises Zaïre and Nérestan as his own lost son and daughter. Horrified that Zaïre is now a Muslim, Lusignan asks as a dying wish that she be baptised. Zaïre postpones her wedding to accomplish this. Intercepting a letter from brother to sister, and mistakenly thinking it a love letter, Orosmane goes to the place where Zaïre is to be baptised. Seeing Nérestan there, he considers his suspicions confirmed, and he stabs Zaïre. When Nérestan tells him the truth, Orosmane kills himself. (Voltaire is said to have derived the motif of Orosmane's jealousy from Shakespeare's *Othello*.)

Bellini and Romani travelled together on 17 March 1829 to Parma to work on *Zaira*, which Bellini had not yet started to compose, but Romani (or, to be precise, his moustache) almost immediately fell foul of the Parma police. Moustaches, considered at the time to be symbols of liberalism, were outlawed in Parma, and foreigners were given only three days' grace to shave them off. Romani refused to comply and threatened to leave Parma. It was only after the Court Chamberlain had sought the intervention of the Grand Duchess Marie-Louise (Napoleon's widow) that Romani was allowed to remain hirsute.

For some reason, work on *Zaira* proceeded very slowly, due this time not only to Romani's well-known propensity for dilatoriness but also to a curious lethargy on Bellini's part. The première of *Zaira* had to be postponed, and the opera-lovers of Parma began to wonder why, since composer and librettist had been resident in the city for several weeks, they had not progressed further with the task in hand. It was noted that Bellini was only rarely to be found at work, but instead was frequently to be seen wandering through the streets of Parma by day and socialising till all hours in the evenings. Some people were only too ready to accuse the composer of caring nothing for Parma and its new theatre. When members of the audience assembled for the première on 16 May 1829, they cannot have been pleased to read Romani's foreword to the printed libretto in which he wrote: 'I realise that more care should have been taken with the style, and that here and there certain repetitions of phrases should have been corrected. But the verse was written in bits and pieces while the music was being composed, in such a way that I was not permitted to revise what had already been written. The poetry and the music were completed in less than a month.'

Either because they genuinely disliked the opera itself, or because they were offended by what they discerned to be the *de haut en bas* attitude to Parma of both composer and librettist, the audience greeted *Zaira* coldly. The theatre's official report of the première stated that 'the music in the opera seems not to have given pleasure, except for a trio in Act I, but the singers were warmly applauded'. A local wit distributed handbills after the first night, which read, 'Anyone who finds the musical inspiration of Signor Bellini is asked to take it to the box office of Signor Bandini, the impresario, where he will be rewarded.'

Zaira was Bellini's first and only failure, and his reaction seems to have been to distance himself from it. He withdrew the score, but was to plunder it later, principally for his next opera, *I Capuleti e i Montecchi. Zaira* was given eight performances in Parma, but was never performed again during its composer's lifetime, and was not published. (Two numbers from the opera were published separately, with piano accompaniment.)

Nine months after Bellini's death, *Zaira* was staged at the Teatro della Pergola, Florence, in the spring of 1836, after which it was not seen again until revived at the Teatro Massimo Bellini in the composer's home town of Catania on 1 April 1976, with Renata Scotto as Zaira. Since then it seems to have been staged only once, again in Catania, on 23 September 1990, with Katia Ricciarelli in the title-role.

There is no overture. The opening chorus of slaves, 'Gemma, splendor di Solima', in praise of Zaira is undistinguished. Nor are the *larghetto* aria ('Perchè mai, perchè pugnasti') and *allegro marziale* cabaletta ('Sì, d'un furor colpevole') of the vizier, Corasmino, at all memorable, though Bellini thought sufficiently highly of the aria to use it again in *I Capuleti e i Montecchi* as Tebaldo's cavatina, 'E serbato a questo acciaro'. Zaira's *allegro* cavatina, 'Amo ed amata io sono' is inappropriately, indeed mindlessly, florid. The middle section of its amiable cabaletta, 'Non è, non è tormento', was to surface again in *I Capuleti e i Montecchi* where it became Romeo's aria, 'Deh tu, deh tu, bell' anima'. That the music is used to express feelings of great joy in *Zaira* and the depths of sorrow in *I Capuleti e i Montecchi* is perhaps a trifle disconcerting. The ensemble, 'Prezzo non v'ha che basti', and its stretta, 'Ritorni al tuo sembiante', sung by Orosmane are nondescript.

At this point one might be forgiven for concluding that Bellini's heart was not really in this opera. However, it improves as it progresses. The *allegro moderato* chorus of French prisoners, 'Chi ci toglie ai ceppi nostri', is weak, but the trio, 'Cari oggetti', in which Lusignano recognises Zaira and Nerestano as his children, though preceded by plodding and lengthy recitative, is effective, especially its moving second section, 'Qui, crudele, in questa terra'. The stretta, 'Non si pianga', is even finer. Its main theme was to surface again in *I Capuleti* as the ensemble, 'Se ogni speme', in that opera's Act I finale. (This trio was one of the two pieces from *Zaira* to be published.) Parts of 'Oh! qual vibrasti orribile', a splendid duet for Zaira and Nerestano, were used again in the Romeo–Giulietta duet in Act I of *I Capuleti*. The quartet, 'Io saprò di qual deriva', makes a quite strong dramatic ending to *Zaira*'s Act I.

At the beginning of Act II, the *allegro moderato* duet, 'Io troverò nell' Asia', for Orosmane and Zaira (the second piece from the opera to be published) has an affecting middle section ('Ma se tu m'ami, o barbara') which was to find its way later into *Beatrice di Tenda* as the trio, 'Angiol di pace'. The solemnly beautiful chorus of knights ('Più non è') was used again by Bellini in Act II of *Norma* for the male chorus, 'Non partì?'. Nerestano's *larghetto* aria, 'O Zaira! in qual momento', and his *allegro* cabaletta, 'Sì, mi vedrà la barbara', were rightly considered by their composer good enough to be used again in *I Capuleti e i Montecchi*. The aria became Romeo's cavatina, 'Se Romeo t'uccise un figlio', and the cabaletta Giulietta's 'Ah, non poss'io partire'. However, in the next scene the equally fine *andante mosso* duet, 'E pur ora al mio cospetto', for Orosmane and Corasmino, with its frantic cabaletta, 'Vieni meco; a me t'affida', remains buried in the relative obscurity of *Zaira*'s score.

Zaira's *andante* aria, 'Che non tentai per vincere', with Lusignano's funeral chorus providing a bridge to her *allegro agitato* cabaletta, 'Ah! crudeli', is the finest number in the opera, worthy of insertion into any later Bellini score. Not surprisingly, it was made use of in *I Capuleti*. The aria became Giulietta's 'Morte io non temo', and the cabaletta Romeo's 'La tremenda ultrice spada'. Even Lusignano's funeral chorus, 'Poni il fedel tuo martire', was pressed into service as Giulietta's funeral dirge, 'Pace alla tua bell'anima'. Preceded by a lengthy *andante* orchestral introduction with solo cor anglais, the final scene of *Zaira* opens with an unimpressive quintet, 'Lieto ci mira adesso' (taken from Bianca's 'Contenta appien quest'alma' in *Bianca e Fernando*, and to be heard a third time, improved by a quicker tempo, as the heroine's cabaletta, 'Ah, bello a me ritorna', in *Norma*). At the end of the quintet, Orosmane kills Zaira, sings his remorseful but dull cabaletta, 'Un grido d'orrore', and then stabs himself while the assembled onlookers utter a brief but supereroga- tory comment, 'Spirò' (He is dead).

Nearly half of *Zaira*'s score was to be used again by Bellini, most of it in his next opera, *I Capuleti e i Montecchi*. '*Zaira* was avenged in *I Capuleti*,' he remarked after the hugely successful première of the latter work. But a case can be made for the occasional exhumation of the admittedly uneven *Zaira*. Its undeserved failure in Parma seems to have been due mainly to a determinedly hostile audience, and if Bellini had not suppressed the score to plunder it for his next opera it would probably have been performed in a number of other cities in Italy and abroad.

I Capuleti e i Montecchi
(The Capulets and the Montagues)

tragedia lirica in two acts

Principal characters:

Giulietta (Juliet), a Capulet	(soprano)
Romeo, a Montague	(mezzo-soprano)
Tebaldo (Tybalt), a Capulet	(tenor)
Capellio (Capulet), Juliet's father	(bass)
Lorenzo, a physician	(baritone)

LIBRETTO by Felice Romani

TIME: The thirteenth century
PLACE: Verona

FIRST PERFORMED at the Teatro La Fenice, Venice, 11 March
1830, with Rosalbina Caradori-Allan (Giulietta); Giuditta Grisi
(Romeo); Lorenzo Bonfigli (Tebaldo); Gaetano Antoldi
(Capellio); Rainieri Pocchini Cavalieri (Lorenzo)

Invited to supervise a production of *Il Pirata* at the Teatro La Fenice
in January 1830, Bellini left Milan for Venice on 12 December 1829.
The carnival season in Venice, which opened on 26 December with
a new opera, *Costantino in Arles* by Giuseppe Persiani, was also
expected to include a new opera by Giovanni Pacini. Pacini was ill
and unable to complete his opera, but his librettist, Felice Romani,
was available, so Alessandro Lanari, the impresario of the Fenice,
having alerted Bellini and Romani early in January, engaged them
later in the month to provide a new opera. (Bellini's *Il Pirata* had
opened on 16 January and was proving popular.)

As time was short, Romani made no attempt to write a new
libretto but instead adapted one that he had written for Nicola
Vaccai's *Giulietta e Romeo* which had been staged in Milan in 1825
and subsequently in Barcelona, Paris and Lisbon. Romani's
changes to his libretto were considerable, but he and Bellini
completed their new opera, now called *I Capuleti e i Montecchi*, in six
weeks, and it was given its première on 11 March 1830. (When the
opera was produced later in the year at La Scala, its title was given
in a more pedantically correct form as *I Capuleti ed i Montecchi*. An
early vocal score, however, bears the title *I Montecchi e i Capuleti*.)

The opera was an immediate and immense success. It was
performed eight times within the ten days left before the end of the
season on 21 March, and after the third performance Bellini was
conducted to his lodgings by a huge crowd of people carrying
torches, preceded by a military band playing excerpts from his
operas. Before the end of the year *I Capuleti* had been staged in
Sinigaglia, and at La Scala, Milan, where it ran for twenty-five
performances. The following year it was produced in Palermo,
Trieste and Naples, and given its first performance abroad, in
Dresden. Soon it was being staged in a number of cities throughout
the world, and translated into German, Hungarian, Russian, Czech

and, in due course, Danish, French and Polish. Its first performance in London was on 20 July 1833. It reached Boston in May 1847, Philadelphia in August, and New York on 28 January 1848. Beginning with a performance in Bologna in 1832, Bellini's opera was for many years given with a different final scene, that of Vaccai's *Giulietta e Romeo*, a practice which persisted until near the end of the century.

I Capuleti e i Montecchi never completely disappeared from the repertory. In 1935, during the centenary commemorations of Bellini's death, it was staged in the composer's home town of Catania, with Aurora Buades (Romeo) and Ines Alfani Tellini (Giulietta). On 10 February 1954 at the Teatro Massimo, Palermo, it was revived with Giulietta Simionato (Romeo) and Rosanna Carteri (Giulietta), and in 1958 and 1964 it was given concert performances at Carnegie Hall, New York, with Simionato as Romeo. Anna Maria Rota (Romeo) and Renata Scotto (Giulietta) appeared in the opera in Lisbon in 1964, this time to commemorate the four hundredth anniversary of the birth of Shakespeare. The conductor Claudio Abbado produced an edition of Bellini's score with the mezzo-soprano *travesti* role of Romeo rewritten for tenor. His version was first staged at La Scala, Milan, on 26 March 1966 with Renata Scotto, Giacomo Aragall (Romeo) and the young Luciano Pavarotti (Tebaldo). Abbado himself conducted.

The first performances of the opera in Great Britain in the twentieth century were given in 1967 by students of the Royal Manchester College of Music, who used Bellini's version. The first American performances of the century were those of Philadelphia Grand Opera in 1968, in the Abbado version, with Renata Scotto and Giacomo Aragall. More recent performers of the roles of the young lovers have included Tatiana Troyanos (Romeo) and Beverly Sills (Giulietta) in Boston in 1975; Agnes Baltsa and Celia Gasdia in Florence in 1981; and Baltsa and Edita Gruberova in a Royal Opera production in London in 1984, which was revived in 1985 with Troyanos and Katia Ricciarelli and in 1992 with Anne Sofie von Otter and Amanda Roocroft.

Romani's taut, single-minded libretto was based not on Shakespeare but on Giuseppe Maria Foppa's libretto for Zingarelli's *Giulietta e Romeo* (Milan, 1796) whose ultimate derivation was a fifteenth-century novella by Masuccio Salernitano. (Shakespeare discovered the story through Arthur Brooke's narrative poem, *The*

Tragical History of Romeus and Juliet, published in 1562.) Set in thirteenth-century Verona, Bellini's opera tells the tragic story of Romeo, a Montague, who loves Giulietta, daughter of Capellio, the leader of the Capulets, a rival faction. Capellio intends to marry Giulietta to Tebaldo. Although she loves Romeo, Giulietta refuses to elope with him because of her duty to her father. Romeo's attempt to abduct her from Capellio's palace fails, but Capellio's adviser, the physican Lorenzo, persuades Giulietta to take a potion which will temporarily make her appear to be dead. However, he is prevented from revealing this plan to Romeo who, hearing Giulietta's funeral dirge as he is about to fight Tebaldo, hastens to her tomb and takes poison. Giulietta revives as Romeo dies, and then she, in her grief, falls dead on his body.

The bustling, somewhat Rossinian overture which conjures up images of warring factions rather than of young love, was probably written last, as it makes use of a melody from the opera's opening chorus and a motif from the Act I finale. The chorus of Capulet partisans, 'Aggiorna appena', beginning slowly and quietly but developing into a brisk *allegro*, is held together by rhythmic motifs in the orchestra. When he accepted the commission to write an opera which had to go on stage within a few weeks, Bellini must clearly have decided to use as much of his *Zaira* score as possible. His first borrowing from it comes in Tebaldo's cavatina, 'È serbato a questo acciaro', which is an altered and improved version of Corasmino's cavatina, 'Perchè mai, perchè pugnasti'. Tebaldo's graceful yet ardent cabaletta, 'L'amo, l'amo', is new. Romeo's moving *larghetto* cavatina, 'Se Romeo t'uccise un figlio', an adaptation of Nerestano's 'O Zaira, in qual momento', is typically Bellinian in its long-breathed melody, while his belligerent cabaletta, 'La tremenda ultrice spada', taken from Zaira's cabaletta, 'Ah, crudeli, chia-marmi', proves yet again that Bellini was not simply a purveyor of soulful and melancholy tunes.

For Giulietta's languid, delicate and touching romanza with harp accompaniment, 'Oh quante volte', preceded by impressively elo-quent recitative, Bellini had recourse to his first opera, *Adelson e Salvini*, reshaping and improving Nelly's 'Dopo l'oscuro nembo'. The love duet, 'Sì, fuggire', is both dramatic and fervent, the orchestra here playing no mere accompanying role but contributing signifi-cantly to the romantic atmosphere. This duet borrows from 'Oh qual vibrasti', a duet for Zaira and Nerestano in Act I of *Zaira*. A festive chorus, 'Lieta notte', leads to *I Capuleti*'s Act I finale which contains a beautiful *larghetto* quintet, 'Soccorso, sostegno accordale, oh cielo', its first twelve bars unaccompanied, and a thrilling faster section, 'Se ogni speme' (based on the cabaletta of the trio for Zaira, Nerestano and Lusignano in Act I of *Zaira*), with the voices of Romeo and Giulietta soaring in unison above ensemble and orchestra.

At the beginning of Act II, Giulietta's scene in recitative with Lorenzo, and her affecting *lento* cavatina, 'Morte io non temo' (its melody borrowed from Zaira's aria, 'Che non tentai', in Act I of *Zaira*), are preceded by a short orchestral prelude with a mournful solo part for cello. The chief melody of Giulietta's cabaletta, 'Ah! non poss'io partire', all the more effective for being given a moderate tempo until its last bars, is an adaptation of Nerestano's cabaletta, 'Sì, mi vedrà la barbara', in Act II of *Zaira*. Preceded by a hauntingly beautiful clarinet solo, the martial duet, 'Stolto! a un sol mio grido', for Romeo and Tebaldo is interrupted by a funeral dirge (alias the funeral chorus, 'Poni il fedel tuo martire', from Act II of *Zaira*), after which the two rivals launch into the duet's fierce *allegro moderato*, 'Ella è morta, o sciagurato', and begin to fight their duel.

The finale of the opera, a chorus, aria and duet (for which Vaccai's almost equally effective finale, similarly laid out as chorus, aria and duet, used to be substituted), is superb. The brief chorus of Montagues arriving at Giulietta's tomb ('Siam giunti') is perhaps a little too serene for the occasion, but Romeo's *andante* aria, 'Deh! tu, deh! tu, bell' anima' (its gentle melody taken from Zaira's 'Non è tormento' in Act I of *Zaira*), unerringly sounds the right note (though Vaccai's 'Ah! se tu dormi' is no less fine), and the final brief duet ending with the death of the two lovers is conducted in anguished recitative and arioso, broadening momentarily into melody.

Surprisingly, in view of the fact that so much of it was initially composed to fit other words and situations – eight of its ten numbers contain music first heard in other Bellini operas, notably *Zaira* – *I Capuleti e i Montecchi* succeeds in capturing the essence of the Romeo and Juliet story. The mezzo-soprano role of Bellini's adolescent Romeo can be made completely convincing if suitably cast, as Anne Sofie von Otter demonstrated at Covent Garden in 1992, and the score's blend of elegiac melancholy and martial ardour makes this one of Bellini's most fascinating and affecting operas. There is no valid reason for the existence of Claudio Abbado's edition of the opera with its tenor Romeo.

15

From *La Sonnambula*
to *I Puritani*

La Sonnambula
(The Sleepwalker)

opera semiseria in two acts

Principal characters:

Amina, an orphan raised by Teresa	(soprano)
Lisa, an innkeeper	(soprano)
Teresa, owner of the mill	(mezzo-soprano)
Elvino, a wealthy villager	(tenor)
Il Conte Rodolfo, Lord of the village	(bass)

LIBRETTO by Felice Romani

TIME: The early-nineteenth century
PLACE: A village in Switzerland

FIRST PERFORMED at the Teatro Carcano, Milan, 6 March 1831, with Giuditta Pasta (Amina); Elisa Taccani (Lisa); Giovanni Battista Rubini (Elvino); Luciano Mariani (Il Conte Rodolfo)

Shortly after the final performance of *I Capuleti e i Montecchi* in Venice in March 1830, Bellini made his way back to Milan. He was in poor health, but recuperated during the summer on Lake Como where he became friendly with the famous soprano Giuditta Pasta who had a villa in the vicinity. His friendship with Pasta, who was to create the title-roles in two out of his three future operas, lasted until the end of his brief life.

It was while he was at Como that Bellini negotiated the contract for his next opera, to be composed not for La Scala but for the 1830–1831 carnival season at another theatre in Milan, the Teatro Carcano. For the same season at the Carcano, Donizetti had also been commissioned to write a new opera, and he and Felice Romani produced *Anna Bolena* which had its première on 26 December 1830 (see pp 193–197). By mid-July Bellini and Romani had decided that their opera would be based on Victor Hugo's play, *Hernani*, which had been staged in Paris earlier in the year to enormous success. However, Romani was preoccupied with his *Anna Bolena* for Donizetti, and did not begin to write *Hernani* until November. During December, Bellini worked on the score of *Hernani*, completing four numbers and beginning a fifth before abandoning the project. (Some of this music was in due course to find its way into *Norma*.) By the end of December, Bellini and Romani had decided to substitute *La Sonnambula*.

Why *Hernani* was abandoned is still not clear. Fifty years later, Romani's widow was to claim that, envious of the success of Donizetti's *Anna Bolena* at its première on 26 December 1830, and fearful that he might not be able to equal it with *Hernani*, Bellini had asked Romani to produce a new libretto on a completely different 'pastoral subject'. Bellini himself, however, wrote on 3 January 1831 to his friend Giovanni Battista Perucchini that *Hernani* would have run into difficulties with the Austrian police and that Romani therefore thought it expedient to make a change. Whatever the reason, by early January the two men were already at work on *La Sonnambula* which they completed fairly quickly, though not in time for the original date of the première in February to be adhered to. The opera reached the stage on 6 March 1831.

The success of *La Sonnambula* was immediate, and has proved enduring. The day after its première, Bellini wrote to a friend, reporting 'the resounding success that my opera had last night', and adding that his principal singers, Rubini and Pasta, were 'two angels, who excited the public to an enthusiasm bordering on madness'. Soon the opera was being staged abroad, in numerous cities in Europe and the Americas. The first London performance was given in Italian on 28 July 1831, only some months after the Milan première. New York first heard *La Sonnambula* on 13

November 1835, in English, but had to wait until 13 May 1844 to hear it in Italian. The opera's pastoral charm and enchanting melodies have kept it popular whenever and wherever there have been singers able to do it justice.

Notable Aminas in the first half of the twentieth century included Luisa Tetrazzini, Amelita Galli-Curci, Toti dal Monte and Lily Pons. Tito Schipa was a notable Elvino. After a performance at Covent Garden with Tetrazzini and John McCormack in 1911, *La Sonnambula* was not heard again in London until Renata Scotto sang Amina at the Theatre Royal, Drury Lane, in 1958. Other highly acclaimed Aminas in the second half of the century have included Maria Callas (who first sang the role at La Scala in 1955 in a production by Luchino Visconti, conducted by Leonard Bernstein), Joan Sutherland (most notably at Covent Garden in 1960, conducted by Tullio Serafin; at the Metropolitan Opera in 1963, with Nicolai Gedda as Elvino; and again at Covent Garden in 1965 with Luciano Pavarotti), and June Anderson at La Scala in 1986.

The plot of the libretto was taken from the scenario of a ballet, *La Sonnambule, ou l'Arrivée d'un Nouveau Seigneur* by Eugène Scribe (with choreography by Jean-Pierre Aumer) which had been staged at the Paris Opéra in 1827 with music by Hérold. The ballet in turn was derived from a two-act vaudeville by Scribe and Casimir Delavigne, first performed in Paris in 1819. The story of the sleep-walking village maiden became popular in several adaptations not only in Paris but also in London. Romani transferred the action from the French Camargue to a Swiss village in the early nineteenth century, altered the names of the characters, and wrote elegant verse for them to sing.

At the beginning of the opera, Amina, the foster-daughter of Teresa who owns the village mill, is celebrating her betrothal to Elvino, a young farmer, when the ceremony on the village green is interrupted by the arrival of a handsome stranger. He is Count Rodolfo, returning to the village of his childhood after many years. He takes a room at the village inn, whose proprietress, Lisa, is in love with Elvino.

Unknown to anyone, Amina is a sleep-walker, and that evening in her sleep she walks into the Count's room at the inn. The Count discreetly withdraws, but Amina's presence there is discovered by Lisa and disclosed to Elvino, who arrives as Amina awakes, unable to explain her presence in the Count's room. Elvino, thinking the worst, denounces Amina and proposes marriage to Lisa. The Count attempts to explain matters, but the villagers have never heard of somnabulism, and do not believe him. It is only when Amina is seen sleep-walking on the roof of the mill house, along a half-rotted beam bending dangerously beneath her weight, that the truth becomes clear. Amina awakes to find Elvino asking her forgiveness.

After eighty-seven bars of a cheerful *allegro* orchestral introduction, agreeably bucolic in character, the curtain rises on an equally sparkling chorus of villagers ('Viva Amina') offering their greetings to Amina on the day of her betrothal. In her cavatina, 'Tutto è gioia', Lisa laments that she is losing Elvino to Amina. Her resentment has to contend with the chorus of happy villagers in the cabaletta, 'In Elvezia non v'ha rosa', its melody rescued from one of the sketches for the abortive *Hernani*.

Amina's entrance aria, 'Come per me sereno', marked *cantabile sostenuto*, is one of Bellini's most beguiling melodies, an expression of the innocence and unalloyed happiness of young love, while its cabaletta, 'Sovra il sen la man mi posa', sung with the enthusiastic support of the chorus, is one of Bellini's most exhilarating melodies with its spontaneous air of sheer delight, its rapid descending scale passages, and its joyously carefree coloratura.

When the Notary arrives, Bellini gives him a fussy little motif. The lovers' *andante sostenuto* duet is begun by Elvino with the gently languorous melody of 'Prendi: l'anel ti dono'. Its *allegretto* cabaletta, 'Ah! vorrei trovar parola', launched almost skittishly by Amina, takes Elvino four times to his top C. (The tessitura of Elvino's role remains high throughout the opera.) Count Rodolfo's nostalgic, smoothly flowing cavatina, 'Vi ravviso', is one of the most attractive arias ever written for the bass voice.

Romani had wanted to make Amina the Count's long-lost daughter, born out of wedlock, but Bellini vetoed the idea. A trace of Romani's suggestion, however, remains in the words of Count Rodolfo's elegant cabaletta, 'Tu non sai', in which he is moved by Amina's beauty to exclaim that she strongly resembles a young woman he loved long ago. In the dramatic chorus, 'A fosco cielo', the credulous villagers regale the sceptical Count Rodolfo with their tale of a pale ghost who is seen in the village at night, after which all disperse to allow Elvino and Amina to end the scene (after an outburst of jealousy in recitative from Elvino) with their charming *andante* duet, 'Son geloso del zeffiro errante'.

The second scene of Act I in the Count's room at the inn begins in recitative and arioso. The villagers come to pay their respects in a chorus, 'Osservate', but discover Amina there. Her moving duet with the distraught and outraged Elvino, 'D'un pensiero e d'un accento', begins the finale which develops into a swelling ensemble with Elvino carrying the melody. (It is affectionately parodied by Sir Arthur Sullivan in *Trial by Jury*'s 'A nice dilemma we have here'.) An *allegro* stretta, 'Non più nozze', brings the act to a lively conclusion.

A delightful *allegretto* chorus, 'Qui la selva è più folta', begins Act II, followed by Amina's affecting scene with Elvino, leading to his sad aria, 'Tutto è sciolto', and his intense, heartbroken *allegro moderato* cabaletta, 'Ah! perchè non posso odiarti'. The final scene contains Lisa's oddly superficial *andante* aria, 'De' lieti auguri'; a quartet ('Lisa mentrice anch' essa') in the form of a canon, initiated by Elvino; and the opera's great finale, Amina's *andante cantabile* aria sung as she sleep-walks, the exquisitely sad 'Ah! non credea mirarti' and, after her awakening, the ecstatically joyous 'Ah! non giunge', the very epitome of the brilliant cabaletta, its *fioriture* used not for mere vocal display but to express Amina's great happiness. Thus ends the enchanting *Sonnambula*, one of Bellini's finest operas, a melodically prodigious work which Kobbé describes with impressive understatement as 'a good evening's entertainment'.

Norma

opera seria in two acts

Principal characters:

Norma, High Priestess of the Druid temple	(soprano)
Adalgisa, a virgin of the temple	(mezzo-soprano)
Pollione, Roman Proconsul in Gaul	(tenor)
Oroveso, Archdruid, Norma's father	(bass)
Clotilde, Norma's confidante	(soprano)
Flavio, a Roman centurion	(tenor)

LIBRETTO by Felice Romani

TIME: Around 50 B.C., at the time of the Roman occupation
PLACE: Gaul

FIRST PERFORMED at the Teatro alla Scala, Milan, 26 December 1831, with Giuditta Pasta (Norma); Giulia Grisi (Adalgisa); Domenico Donzelli (Pollione); Vincenzo Negrini (Oroveso)

After the triumphant première of *La Sonnambula* in March 1831, Bellini left Milan to spend the spring and summer months with Giuditta Turina at Moltrasio on the west shore of Lake Como. He had agreed to provide a new opera for the next carnival season at La Scala, and by the end of July he and Romani had decided on its subject, a play, *Norma, ou L'Infanticide* by the French dramatist Alexandre Soumet, which had been presented for the first time in April at the Théâtre de l'Odéon in Paris. (Soumet was the co-librettist of Rossini's *Le Siège de Corinthe*, staged in Paris in 1826.) Unusually for him, Romani completed his libretto fairly quickly. Bellini was able to begin composing *Norma* early in September, and from his correspondence one discovers that, on this occasion at least, he began with the overture, then sketched the introductory chorus, and probably composed his score from beginning to end instead of darting from number to number in no particular order. He had finished the opera by the end of November, giving ample time for it to be rehearsed and staged on 26 December 1831, the opening night of the season.

At its première, *Norma* was greeted coldly. Immediately after the performance, Bellini reported to his friend Florimo: 'I am writing to you in a state of bitter grief which I cannot express, but which you alone will understand. I have just come from La Scala where the first performance of *Norma* was, would you believe it, a dismal fiasco!!! I tell you truly, the audience was very severe, and seemed to me to want my poor *Norma* to suffer the same fate as the Druid priestess. I no longer recognised those dear Milanese who greeted *Il Pirata*, *La Straniera* and *La Sonnambula* with joy on their faces and warmth in their hearts, although I had hoped that with *Norma* I had given them something just as worthy.' He went on to say that, whatever the audience thought, the Introduction, Norma's entrance and her 'Casta diva', the Norma–Adalgisa duet, the trio finale of Act I, the second duet for the two women and the finale to Act II were all pieces which pleased him. ('I admit I would be happy to compose pieces like that for the rest of my artistic life.')

Why the first-night audience in Milan should have failed to appreciate *Norma* is difficult to understand. Bellini suspected that it was the work of a formidable faction 'supported by lots of money from that mad woman' the Countess Samoiloff, mistress of the composer Giovanni Pacini whose opera *Il Corsaro* was about to be given its première at La Scala. But, whatever the reason, every subsequent performance of *Norma* at La Scala (and there were to be thirty-nine in all during the season) was greeted with enormous enthusiasm. The opera went on to become the most popular of Bellini's works, with productions in thirty-five countries in sixteen different languages by the end of the century. It was first performed in London on 20 June 1833 at His Majesty's Theatre, in Italian, and at Covent Garden four years later in English. It reached the United States on 11 January 1841 when it was performed in Philadelphia, in English, at two different theatres on the same night. The first New York performance of *Norma* was given in English on 25 February 1841.

Generally regarded as Bellini's masterpiece, *Norma* has retained its popularity to this day. Famous twentieth-century interpreters of the title-role have included Rosa Ponselle, Zinka Milanov, Maria Callas, Leyla Gencer, Joan Sutherland (who, early in her career, in 1952, sang Clotilde to Callas's Norma at Covent Garden), Montserrat Caballé and Renata Scotto.

Giulia Grisi, who sang Adalgisa at the opera's première in 1831, was a soprano. (Her mezzo-soprano sister, Giuditta, created the role of Romeo in Bellini's *I Capuleti e i Montecchi*.) The role of Adalgisa is, however, usually sung by a mezzo-soprano. Twentieth-century mezzos who have sung Adalgisa include Bruna Castagna, Gladys Swarthout, Fedora Barbieri, Ebe Stignani, Giulietta Simionato, Fiorenza Cossotto, Marilyn Horne, Agnes Baltsa and Grace Bumbry (who has also sung Norma).

Romani's libretto, based not only on Alexandre Soumet but on his own libretto for Pacini's 1820 opera *La Sacerdotessa d'Irminsul*, differs from Soumet's *Norma* in a number of details. For instance, in the play Oroveso is not Norma's father but simply a Gallic warrior. Soumet's Norma kills her children, while Romani's Norma contemplates doing so but recoils from the act. The opera is set in Gaul at the time of the Roman occupation. Norma, a Druid priestess and the daughter of the Archdruid Oroveso, is in love with the Roman Proconsul, Pollione, by whom she has had two children. Pollione, however, has transferred his affections to another priestess, Adalgisa, who confesses to Norma that she loves a Roman. Remembering her own situation, Norma is disposed to pardon Adalgisa until she learns that Pollione is the man in question. In a state of despair and mental anguish, Norma resolves to kill her two children. However, maternal love triumphs, and she urges Adalgisa to flee to Rome with Pollione, taking the children with them. Adalgisa refuses. She will go to Pollione, she tells Norma, but only to remind him of his duty to the mother of his children.

When she discovers that Adalgisa's plea to Pollione has been unsuccessful, Norma calls the warriors of Gaul together, declaring that the time has come to drive out the Roman invaders. Pollione, who has broken into the Druids' temple in search of Adalgisa, is captured and brought before Norma for judgement. She offers to save his life if he agrees to forsake Adalgisa. When he refuses, she confesses her guilt to her father and her fellow-Druids, and is condemned to death by fire. Moved by her courage, Pollione mounts the funeral pyre with her.

The overture is masterly in its evocation of the mood of the opera. It was to a theme first heard in the orchestral introduction to Oroveso's cavatina, 'Ite sul colle', that Verdi was referring when he wrote that no one had ever created a phrase 'more beautiful and heavenly'. Both the grave cavatina and its martial cabaletta, 'Dell' aura tua profetica', in which Oroveso is joined by the male chorus of Druids, are majestic in stature. Throughout the opera, the confidence, variety and sheer beauty of Bellini's melody are amazing. In his aria, 'Meco all' altar di Venere', Pollione uses a moderate tempo to describe to his colleague Flavio his dream of a vengeful Norma. Interrupted by the sound of the Druids' sacred gong, he launches into a cabaletta, 'Me protegge, me difende', which is the only indifferent number in the entire score.

A chorus of Druids ('Norma viene') in march rhythm precedes Norma's commanding recitative, 'Sediziose voci', its first phrases sung unaccompanied, and her great *andante* aria, 'Casta diva', the long, gently undulating line of its enchanting melody first heard on a solo flute. Delicate *fioriture* decorate the second strophe of the aria which has been compared to (and indeed is considered to have influenced) the nocturnes of Chopin. Written in G major in Bellini's autograph score, the aria and its cabaletta were transposed down a tone at the première by Giuditta Pasta to F, the key in which they are now usually performed. (Pasta had at first refused to sing 'Casta diva', finding it unsuited to her style, but Bellini persuaded her to study it for a week, after which, if she still disliked it, he promised to write her a new aria. By the end of the week Pasta had succumbed to the fascination of the aria, and sent the composer two gifts, a parchment lampshade and a bouquet of cloth flowers, accompanied by a note of apology in which she modestly described herself as 'little equipped to perform your sublime harmonies'.) The delightful *allegro* cabaletta, 'Ah! bello, a me ritorna', is an adaptation of Bianca's 'Contenta appien quest' alma' from *Bianca e Fernando*.

Adalgisa is introduced in a solo scene of highly expressive recitative, which is followed by her intense *allegro* duet with Pollione, 'Va, crudele', part of which makes use of an arietta, 'Bella Nice che d'amore', which Bellini had published two years previously. The moving Norma–Adalgisa duet, 'Sola, furtiva, al tempio', begins with one of the composer's most elegiacally melancholy tunes, continues with a more animated second section, 'Ah sì, fa core, abbracciami', in which the two women's voices blend in thirds, and concludes with a cadenza, again with the voices in thirds. Act I ends with the superb trio, 'Oh! di qual sei tu vittima', in which Norma, Adalgisa and Pollione confront their guilt and one another, its taut opening theme shared by all three characters. (Bellini took the tune from an incomplete duet intended for *Hernani*.)

After a brooding orchestral prelude, Act II begins with a scene of expressive recitative in which Norma contemplates killing her children. It broadens into a moving arioso, 'Teneri figli', using a theme heard in the prelude. The following scene for Norma and Adalgisa contains the moving *andante* duet, 'Mira, o Norma', for Norma and Adalgisa, with its equally affecting cabaletta, 'Sì, fino all' ore', in which the two women swear eternal friendship, their voices again blending sympathetically in thirds. (A melodic phrase in the cabaletta was taken from a passage in the cabaletta of the Salvini–Bonifacio duet in Act I of *Adelson e Salvini*.)

The chorus of Gallic warriors, 'Non partì', with its Beethovenian echoes, had already been heard twice before, in *Bianca e Fernando* and *Zaira*, and the melody of Oroveso's fierce yet noble aria with chorus, 'Ah! del Tebro al giogo indegno', was taken from a duet intended for the abandoned *Hernani*. A vigorous chorus, 'Guerra, guerra!', in which the warriors, incited by Norma, prepare for battle, proves, if any further proof were needed, that Bellini was not just a composer of languorous melodies. The chorus melts away at its conclusion into a mood of religious awe.

The climax of the opera is reached with the great duet, 'In mia man alfin tu sei', in which Bellini rises to positively Verdian heights in the skill with which he weaves the tense dialogue into a melodic whole. When she has summoned the Druids and confessed her sin, Norma launches the finale with the intensely moving melody of 'Qual cor tradisti, qual cor perdesti', in which, gradually, she is joined by Pollione, then Oroveso and the Druids. After Norma's last anguished solo, 'Deh! non volerli vittime', the swelling ensemble continues most movingly as Norma and Pollione are led to the funeral pyre and the opera ends on a crashing chord from the orchestra. 'The conclusion,' wrote Théophile Gautier in an essay on the opera, 'from the moment when Norma confesses her guilt, is one of the finest things in all musico-dramatic literature. The thought is sublime, and the layout for voice and orchestra equally admirable. Its restrained and masterly writing has not been surpassed by any other composer.'

Bellini knew the worth of his *Norma*. 'If I were shipwrecked,' he wrote, 'I would leave all of my other operas and try to save *Norma*.' And nearly sixty years later the aged Verdi told Camille Bellaigue, 'Even in Bellini's lesser-known operas, *La Straniera* and *Il Pirata*, there are long, long melodies such as no one before him had ever written. What truth and power there is in his declamation, in for example the duet between Norma and Pollione. What loftiness of thought in the first phrase of the introduction to *Norma*, and another, no less sublime, a few bars later. Badly orchestrated perhaps, but beautiful, heavenly, beyond the reach of any other mortal.'

Bellini's orchestration, in *Norma* as in his other operas, is hardly complex, but it is always appropriate. Asked by a French publisher to re-orchestrate the score of *Norma*, Bizet discovered that the task was neither possible nor necessary. Even Wagner, no friend of Italian opera, wrote of *Norma* that he admired 'the rich melodic vein expressing the most intimate passions with a sense of profound reality: a great score that speaks to the heart, and a work of genius'.

Beatrice di Tenda

opera seria in two acts

Principal characters:

Filippo Maria Visconti, Duke of Milan   (baritone)
Beatrice di Tenda, his wife   (soprano)
Agnese del Maino   (mezzo-soprano)
Orombello, Lord of Ventimiglia   (tenor)
Anichino, friend of Orombello   (tenor)
Rizzardo del Maino, brother of Agnese   (tenor)

LIBRETTO by Felice Romani

TIME: 1418
PLACE: The Castle of Binasco, near Milan

FIRST PERFORMED at the Teatro La Fenice, Venice, 16 March 1833, with Giuditta Pasta (Beatrice); Anna del Serre (Agnese); Alberico Curioni (Orombello); Orazio Cartagenova (Filippo); Alessandro Giacchini (Anichino)

Bellini and Giuditta Turina left Milan after the last performance of *Norma* to travel south to Naples, where they attended a performance of *I Capuleti e i Montecchi*. Bellini then continued on to his home town of Catania in Sicily with his friend Francesco Florimo. After a reunion with members of his family, the composer went to Palermo, the Sicilian capital, where *I Capuleti* was performed in his honour.

A one-act scenic cantata entitled *Il Fu ed il sará* (What was and what will be) with music by Bellini and text by Jacopo Ferretti is thought to have been performed privately at a wedding in Rome in February 1832. However, no score has been found, and the piece was most probably a pastiche put together by other hands.

By the autumn of 1832 Bellini had signed a contract to compose a new opera for Venice, its première to be preceded by a production of *Norma* at the beginning of the season. As a subject, his librettist Romani had suggested *Christine, ou Stockholme, Fontainebleau et Rome*, a play by Alexandre Dumas about Queen Cristina of Sweden, which had been staged in Paris in 1830, but Bellini was not enthusiastic. Early in November he wrote to the soprano Giuditta Pasta, 'The subject has been changed, and we shall write *Beatrice di Tenda*. It was difficult for me to persuade Romani, but I succeeded.' Bellini and Pasta had apparently seen a ballet, *Beatrice di Tenda*, at La Scala in September, and Pasta had expressed her interest in it as a possible subject for opera. (She was, some months later, to sing the role of Beatrice in the première of Bellini's opera.)

Perhaps because the subject he suggested had been discarded, but also because, as usual, he had over-committed himself and was attempting to write libretti simultaneously for Coccia, Majocchi, Mercadante and Donizetti as well as Bellini, Romani was more than usually dilatory. When Bellini left for Venice early in December, he had not received a single line of verse from his librettist. The management of the Teatro La Fenice brought it to the attention of the Governor of Venice that Romani was failing to fulfil his contract, and the problem was passed on to the Governor of Milan with the result that Romani received a summons from the Milanese police. Reluctantly and indignantly he made his way to Venice, and proceeded slowly to produce a scene or two of *Beatrice di Tenda*.

Bellini complained to a friend that his health was deteriorating because of his having to compose at great speed, for which he blamed 'my usual and original poet, the God of Sloth!' He was also apprehensive because he thought the company of singers assembled at the Fenice for the season was a poor one. His *Norma* had succeeded on the opening night of the season only because of Pasta. The rest of the cast had been mediocre.

On 17 February Bellini wrote that he despaired of finishing the opera, and that his morale was afflicted because of that 'sluggard of a poet'. The libretto continued to be squeezed out of Romani, piece by piece, and eventually, one month late, *Beatrice di Tenda* was given its première at the Teatro La Fenice on 16 March 1833. It was not well received. During Pasta's entrance aria some members of the audience thought they recognised a phrase from Bellini's most recent opera, and there were shouts of '*Norma!*' Pasta responded by turning to them in her Act I duet, instead of to Orazio Cartagenova, the baritone singing the role of Filippo, as she uttered the phrase, 'Se amar non puoi, rispettami!' (If you cannot love me, respect me!).

The five subsequent performances of *Beatrice di Tenda* were received more amiably. After the final one, Bellini wrote to a friend, 'I have been waiting for the journals to appear so that, hearing some opinion expressed, I could tell you about the reception of my new opera which, through a series of unhappy circumstances, has been as unfortunate as that of *I Capuleti e i Montecchi*. I am being blamed for the postponement of the première until the sixteenth of this month, whereas it was all the fault of the poet. Also, a powerful and noisy faction opposed to Pasta joined forces with one opposed to me, and so on the first night there was a huge noise of shouting, whistling, laughing and so on.' Although the audience called for the composer after four or five numbers which they liked, his Sicilian haughtiness, as he put it, caused him to remain in his seat 'as though nailed there'.

The situation was not eased in any way by Romani, who had appended to his printed libretto, available in the theatre, a note describing it as a 'fragment' whose plot, style and characters had been altered by circumstances beyond his control. 'It requires', he wrote, 'the full indulgence of the reader.' Shortly after the final performance of the opera, Romani published a letter in the *Gazzetta privilegiata di Venezia*, unfairly placing, in extremely flowery language, the blame on Bellini for the delayed première. The result of this was, not surprisingly, the end of the friendship between Bellini and Romani. They did not collaborate again, nor did they ever meet, although they did eventually make peace with each other by correspondence.

Despite the cool reception it was accorded at its first performance, *Beatrice di Tenda* was by no means a failure. When, a year after the Venice première, it was staged in Palermo, Bellini wrote from Paris to a friend in Palermo, 'So my *Beatrice* was well received ... I was convinced that some outside reason had induced the Venice audience to disapprove of it. I admit that the subject is horrible, but by colouring the music at times forcefully and at times sorrowfully I tried to correct and get rid of the disgust that the character of Filippo arouses.' There were performances at two theatres in Naples in 1834, at La Scala, Milan, in 1835, and in several other cities in Italy and abroad before the end of the decade. The first London performance was on 22 March 1836, and the first American production was staged in New Orleans on 21 March 1842. New York heard the opera for the first time on 18 March 1844.

Beatrice di Tenda disappeared from the repertory for the first third of the twentieth century, but it was revived in Catania in 1935 as part of the centennial commemoration of its composer's death, with

Giannina Arangi-Lombardi as Beatrice. The opera was staged at
the Teatro Massimo, Palermo, in January 1959 with Consuelo
Rubio as Beatrice, and in 1961 at La Scala, Milan, with Joan
Sutherland, who earlier in the year had appeared in three concert
performances of the work in New York, when the role of Agnese was
sung by Marilyn Horne. Other notable twentieth-century Beatrices
have included Leyla Gencer (at the Teatro La Fenice, Venice, in
1964), Mirella Freni (Bologna, 1976), Cecilia Gasdia (Barcelona,
1987), and June Anderson (Venice, 1987, and in a concert performance at Carnegie Hall, New York, 1988). The first and, so far, only
twentieth-century production in Great Britain was staged at the
Barber Institute of Fine Arts, University of Birmingham, on 16 May
1975.

Apart from the scenario of the ballet which Bellini and his
soprano, Giuditta Pasta, saw together at La Scala in the autumn of
1832, the principal source of Romani's libretto for *Beatrice di Tenda*
was a play of the same title by Carlo Tebaldi Flores, performed in
Milan in 1825. The plot is based on historical fact, details of which
Romani could also have found in volumes of mediaeval Italian
history, or in the novel *Il Castello di Binasco* by Diodata Saluzzo-
Roero, published in 1819. The historical Beatrice di Tenda (1370–
1418), widow of Facino Cane (the leader of a band of mercenaries),
married Filippo Visconti, Duke of Milan, who accused her of
intrigue and adultery, and had her beheaded.

The action of the opera takes place in the castle of Binasco, near
Milan. Agnese, one of Beatrice's ladies-in-waiting, is in in love with
Orombello, Lord of Ventimiglia, but is loved by Filippo, Duke of
Milan. She helps Filippo to be rid of his wife, Beatrice, of whom he
has tired, by falsely accusing Beatrice of being the lover of
Orombello. Under torture, Orombello, who does in fact love
Beatrice, makes a false confession which he later retracts. The Duke
orders the execution of Beatrice and Orombello, but hesitates to sign
Beatrice's death warrant after a plea for mercy from a now repentant
Agnese. However, his spirit hardened by the arrival of Beatrice's
armed supporters demanding her release, Filippo finally signs the
warrant, and the opera ends as Beatrice is led away to her death.

After a short *allegro* prelude whose opening theme will be heard
again in Act II, whose slower second theme becomes that of
Beatrice's prayer, 'Deh! se mi amasti un giorno', in Act I, and whose
third theme will also occur in Act I, the curtain rises on an opening

scene in which Filippo complains to his courtiers of the boredom of
being married to Beatrice. Structurally, and even musically, it
curiously anticipates the opening scene of Verdi's *Rigoletto*. The
courtiers' chorus is interrupted by the sound of a harp off-stage,
accompanying Agnese's delicately beautiful *andante* romanza, 'Ah!
non pensar che pieno'. Filippo's cavatina, 'Oh! divina Agnese',
begun in what the score describes as an *andante amoroso* and sung *con
abbandono*, is both ardent and graceful, surprisingly so for such a
deeply unattractive character. He is enthusiastically supported by
the chorus, who play a major role throughout the opera.

Agnese's duet with Orombello, 'Sì, rivale', from its *allegro moderato*
beginning to its *allegro giusto* stretta carries the action excitingly
forward. The female chorus ('Come, ah come') which precedes
Beatrice's aria is vapid, but the aria itself, 'Ma la sola, ohime, son io',
is one of Bellini's most exquisitely melancholy tunes, and its
cabaletta, 'Ah! la pena in lor piombò', splendidly conveys Beatrice's
growing agitation. The dramatically effective *allegro moderato* duet,
'Duolo d'un cor piagato', for Beatrice and Filippo is positively
Verdian in its urgency, though perhaps not in its prevalence of
fioriture. Its accompaniment contains an oboe melody which comes
from Act II of *Zaira* (where it was heard on clarinet).

The chorus of men-at-arms ('Lo vedeste') begins at a moderate
tempo and continues in an *allegro* which, at the words 'e nè seguir lo
ovunque vano', bears more than a passing resemblance to the
chorus of courtiers ('Scorrendo uniti remota via') in Act II of Verdi's
Rigoletto, composed eighteen years later. Beatrice's prayer, 'Deh! se
mi amasti un giorno', its theme already heard in the prelude to the
opera and again in the orchestral introduction to the prayer itself, is
admirably direct and devoid of ornament, though perhaps somewhat lacking in the necessary *gravitas*. Her brief and not very
effective duet with Orombello ('A ciascun fidar vorrei') leads
without a pause into the imposing and fiercely energetic finale to
Act I.

Act II opens with Beatrice's unhappy situation being discussed in
an oddly brisk yet melancholy chorus. In her trial scene, the moving
and melodically generous *larghetto* quintet, 'Al tuo fallo', begun by
Beatrice is developed into a huge ensemble as the other characters
and the chorus join in. Its stretta, 'Ite entrambi', launched by
Filippo's baritone voice fascinatingly anticipates Di Luna's 'Per me
ora fatale' in Act II of *Il Trovatore*. The solemn beauty of Filippo's

largo aria, 'Qui m'accolse', which he sings as he hesitates before signing the warrant for Beatrice's execution, is deeply moving, and its cabaletta, 'Non son io', with the support of the chorus, brings the scene to an exciting conclusion.

The chorus of grieving servants and friends of Beatrice which begins the opera's final scene is followed by a short but ravishingly beautiful trio, 'Angiol di pace', whose quintessentially Bellinian melody had already been heard as Orosmane's 'Deh! se tu m'ami, o barbara' in Act II of *Zaira*. Beatrice's poignant *andante* aria, 'Ah! se un' urna', with its brilliant and dramatically apt cabaletta, 'Ah! la morte a cui m'appresso', brings the opera to an end, the cabaletta an adaptation of Fernando's 'Odo il tuo pianto' in *Bianca e Fernando*.

Beatrice di Tenda is surely the most unjustly neglected of Bellini's less frequently performed operas, a dramatically vigorous and well constructed work containing some of its composer's finest and most characteristic melodies.

I Puritani
(The Puritans)

opera seria in three acts

Principal characters:

Arturo (Lord Arthur Talbot), a Royalist	(tenor)
Gualtiero (Lord Walton), Governor of a Puritan fortress	(bass)
Giorgio (Sir George Walton), his brother	(bass)
Riccardo (Sir Richard Forth), a Puritan	(baritone)
Elvira, daughter of Gualtiero	(soprano)
Enrichetta (Henrietta, widow of Charles I)	(soprano)

LIBRETTO by Count Carlo Pepoli

TIME: 1649
PLACE: In and around Plymouth

FIRST PERFORMED at the Théâtre-Italien, Paris, 24 January 1835, with Giulia Grisi (Elvira); Giovanni Battista Rubini (Arturo); Antonio Tamburini (Riccardo); Luigi Lablache (Giorgio)

Towards the end of March 1833, shortly after the last performance of *Beatrice di Tenda*, Bellini left Venice for London by way of Paris, arriving towards the end of April with Giuditta Pasta who was to introduce *Norma* to London in June. Taking rooms in Old Burlington Street, Mayfair, Bellini led an active social life, attending operas and concerts and being entertained at numerous dinner parties and musical soirées. *Norma* was not the only Bellini opera performed in London during the season, for *La Sonnambula* was given in English at the Theatre Royal, Drury Lane, and *Il Pirata* and *I Capuleti e i Montecchi* in Italian at the King's Theatre. The English music critics for the most part wrote disparagingly of them. *The Morning Chronicle* described Bellini as a mere imitator of Rossini, while *The Examiner* thought him out of his element in *Norma*, in which, 'endeavouring to be sublime, he is too apt to become merely noisy'.

In mid-August Bellini left London for Paris, where he was to keep an apartment in the Boulevard des Italiens for the remaining two years of his life. His relationship with Giuditta Turina having cooled, he felt no urge to return to Italy. Rossini was a neighbour in Paris, and Bellini also established a friendship with Chopin.

Early in 1834 Bellini agreed to compose an opera for the Théâtre-Italien in Paris. Count Pepoli, an Italian poet and patriot living in exile in Paris – he was later to become professor of Italian literature at the University of London – was chosen to write the libretto, and the subject decided upon, after several others had been considered and rejected, was the play, *Têtes Rondes et Cavaliers*, by Jacques-Arsène Ancelot and Joseph-Xavier-Boniface Saintine, which had been staged in Paris in 1833.

Bellini wrote most of his opera in Puteaux, on the outskirts of Paris, at the house of an English Jewish friend, Samuel Levys. Though he had difficulty in extracting his libretto from Count Pepoli who had no previous experience of writing for the stage, Bellini completed the opera by the end of November. Rehearsals began in mid-December, and *I Puritani e i Cavalieri* (The Puritans and the Cavaliers) was given its première at the Théâtre-Italien on 24 January 1835. Later it was sometimes staged as *I Puritani di Scozia* (The Puritans of Scotland) although its action takes place entirely in England. It is now known simply as *I Puritani*.

The opera was received with immense enthusiasm at its première in Paris. Rossini, who was present, wrote to a friend, 'The composer and the singers were twice called on to the stage, and I can tell you that in Paris such demonstrations are rare, and occur only if they are well deserved ... *I Puritani* is the most accomplished score [Bellini] has yet composed.' Much of the opera's success was due to its four leading singers, Grisi, Rubini, Tamburini and Lablache, who were among the most famous of their time and who were to become known as 'the *Puritani* quartet' because of their performances in the opera, not only at its première but also in revivals in Paris and London.

I Puritani was soon being staged all over Europe. The first London performance took place only a few weeks after the Paris première, on 21 May at His Majesty's Theatre. A production at La Scala, Milan, followed in December, with performances in Palermo, Berlin, Vienna, Rome, Madrid, Brünn (Brno), and Budapest during 1836. The opera did not reach New York, however, until 3 February 1844. *I Puritani* never completely disappeared from the repertory during those years in which productions of bel canto operas tended to be rare events. Notable performances in the second half of the twentieth century have included those of Maria Callas in Venice in 1949; Joan Sutherland, who first sang Elvira at Glyndebourne in 1960, who went on to perform the role with enormous success in London and in several American cities, and who sang it to tremendous applause at the Metropolitan Opera as late as 1986; Mirella Freni at the Wexford Festival in 1962; Beverly Sills in Los Angeles in 1973 and New York the following year; Edita Gruberova in Bregenz in 1985; June Anderson in Paris in 1987; Luciana Serra in Florence in 1989; and Mariella Devia in Rome in 1990.

When Joan Sutherland and Nicolai Gedda sang Elvira and Arturo in New York and Philadelphia in 1963, the critic of *Opera* wrote, 'She has never been so free, so radiant, so transcendent; and when Nicolai Gedda soared to a high D in their duet in the last act and Miss Sutherland disappeared into the tonal stratosphere, the audience could scarcely be blamed for becoming hysterical.' The performances at the Royal Opera House, Covent Garden, in 1964 with Joan Sutherland were the first in that theatre since 1887, though an Italian touring company had presented *I Puritani* in London at the Coronet Theatre, Notting Hill Gate, in 1909.

It is sometimes claimed that the title *I Puritani di Scozia* was given to Bellini's opera because its libretto was based on Sir Walter Scott's novel, *Old Mortality*, which deals with the struggle between the Covenanters and the Cavaliers in 1679. (It was published in France as *Les Puritains d'Écosse*). This is incorrect. The plot of Ancelot and Saintine's play, *Têtes Rondes et Cavaliers* (which is followed reasonably closely by Pepoli's libretto) has nothing in common with that of Scott's novel.

Bellini's *I Puritani* is set in and around Plymouth at the end of the English civil wars, shortly after the execution of Charles I in 1649. Arturo (Lord Arthur Talbot), a Stuart partisan or Cavalier, is about to marry Elvira, daughter of the Puritan Giorgio (Lord Walton), although her father had intended her to be the bride of a Puritan, Riccardo (Sir Richard Forth). However, when Arturo discovers that Queen Henrietta, Charles I's widow, is being held prisoner in the fortress commanded by Walton, he helps her to escape. Thinking that her bridegroom has deserted her for another woman, Elvira loses her reason. She recovers only when she is reunited with Arturo who is pardoned by Oliver Cromwell.

In a letter to Pepoli as he was about to begin work on *I Puritani*, Bellini thought it expedient to offer his new librettist some advice. 'If my music proves beautiful', he wrote, 'and the opera is successful, you may write a million letters demonstrating how composers maltreat poetry and so on, but you will have proved nothing. Engrave upon your mind in indelible letters: "In opera it is the singing that must move people to tears, must make them shudder and die" ... Poetry and music, to be effective, demand naturalness and nothing else ... Do you know why I said that a good drama is one that has no good sense in it? Because I know full well what intractable animals literary people are, and how absurd their general rules of good sense.'

The orchestral prelude to the opera, based on sketches which Bellini had made for *Hernani*, the opera he had begun and abandoned five years earlier, leads without a break to an impressive opening chorus which, beginning as a poetic evocation of the first glimmerings of dawn ('All' erta!'), develops into a splendidly martial *allegro* ('Quando la tromba squilla') as the Puritan soldiers threaten to annihilate the Stuart forces. The mood of the soldiers turns pious when they listen to the off-stage prayer ('La luna, il sol, le stelle') sung by Elvira, Arturo, Riccardo and Giorgio, but becomes festive as they are joined by the women of the castle in the joyous stretta, 'A festa!'.

In *I Puritani* Bellini's melody has acquired an even more distinctly emotive quality, and his instrumentation has certainly become more flexible and imaginative. The beautiful vocal line of Riccardo's *larghetto* aria, 'Ah! per sempre', is a fine example of Bellini's maturing style, and its *allegro* cabaletta, 'Bel sogno beato', excitingly combines romantic ardour with suave vocal agility. Elvira, heard briefly in the off stage prayer, now makes her appearance, not with an entrance aria but in a fine duet ('Sai com' arde in petto mio') with her uncle, Giorgio, who has persuaded her father to allow her to marry Arturo. A chorus of welcome to Arturo ('Ad Arturo onore') leads into the *largo* quartet with chorus (marked to be sung *con grande espressione*), 'A te, o cara', its long, gracefully beguiling melody announced by Arturo who, in its reprise, varies it to soar to a top C sharp, giving, as it were, notice that his will be a high-lying role, as befits one written for Rubini.

The Act I finale begins with a duet for Arturo and Enrichetta, its mood of desperation broken by Elvira's entrance with her ostensibly light-hearted but portentously febrile polonaise, 'Son vergin vezzosa', its highly decorated vocal line conveying something of the mental fragility underlying the bride's frenetic air of joyous anticipation. The finale gathers momentum when Riccardo challenges Arturo to a duel, using a melody borrowed from Fernando's cabaletta, 'Ascolta, o padre', in Act I of *Bianca e Fernando*. After the departure of Arturo with Enrichetta, Elvira promptly loses her mind and launches the great *larghetto* ensemble, 'Oh vieni al tempio', with one of Bellini's most heart-rending melodies. An *allegro* stretta ('Ahi, dura sciagura') of less musical interest ends the act briskly.

Act II opens with a sorrowful *andante moderato* chorus, 'Ahi! dolor', as the inhabitants of the fortress contemplate Elvira's sad condition. The sorrowfully flowing melody of Giorgio's *andante* aria, 'Cinta di fiori', is followed by Elvira's 'Qui la voce', one of the most beautiful and most affecting of all those mad scenes for heroines of nineteenth-century opera. The final bars of the aria are the first to be heard as Elvira sings off-stage in the distance, as though she were wandering the corridors repeating her pathetic refrain over and over again. When she appears, singing her melancholy aria, Giorgio and Riccardo comment sympathetically and attempt to comfort her, but she is beyond their help. The aria is based on a song, 'La ricordanza' (its words also by Pepoli), which Bellini had composed some months earlier.

Elvira's cabaletta, 'Vien, diletto', is breathtaking in its feverish brilliance and, when properly sung by a soprano with dramatic intelligence as well as vocal agility, extremely moving in its depiction of Elvira's delusion. The theme of the affecting *lento* duet, 'Il rival salvar tu dei', for Giorgio and Riccardo, is strongly reminiscent of Norma's 'In mia man alfin tu sei'. Its splendidly martial cabaletta, 'Suoni la tromba', makes an exciting, though musically somewhat crude end to the act.

Storm music begins Act III. As it dies away, Arturo enters. Hearing the off-stage voice of Elvira singing part of a tune from their days of happiness, he repeats the melody in full in his melancholy *andante* aria, 'A una fonte'. One of the highlights of the opera is his duet of reunion with Elvira, 'Nel mirarti un solo istante'. Its ecstatic *più moderato* section, 'Vieni, vieni fra queste braccia', takes him twice to a high D, the second of which the soprano usually insists on singing with him, though the score asks her to stay on the A above middle C.

The huge ensemble, 'Credeasi misera', is begun by Arturo who is asked this time to produce a top D flat followed a few bars later by a top F, which very few tenors since Rubini in 1835 have attempted. Rubini's note was, of course, not sung from the chest but in the *voix mixte* in which he excelled. (Most tenors of today merely repeat the earlier phrase's D flat. However, on one modern recording of *I Puritani* Nicolai Gedda demonstrates how to produce a high F à la Rubini, while, on another, Luciano Pavarotti demonstrates how not to, by employing a poorly supported falsetto.)

The arrival of a messenger bearing news of Cromwell's general amnesty leads to a brief joyous ensemble which ends the opera. At least, that is how it ended in Paris in January 1835. For a version of the opera that he prepared for Maria Malibran to sing in Naples, Bellini added a short cabaletta, 'Ah! sento, mio bell' Angelo', for the prima donna. Malibran did not, in fact, appear in the Naples production, but most sopranos nowadays cheerfully appropriate her cabaletta to bring the curtain down on Bellini's last and, in many ways, most enjoyable opera.

A mere eight months after the première of *I Puritani*, and a few weeks before his thirty-fourth birthday, Bellini died at the house of his friend Samuel Levys in Puteaux. His death was caused by an acute inflammation of the large intestine, exacerbated by an abscess of the liver. Had he lived a normal span of years, probably all of his operas up to and including *I Puritani* would now be thought of as his juvenilia. But they are all we have of Bellini, and at least three of them – *La Sonnambula*, *Norma* and *I Puritani* – seem genuinely mature works of genius. Bellini wrote less hastily and prolifically than either Donizetti or Rossini, composing at the rate of about one opera per year throughout his brief career. Those ten operas stand as testament to Bellini's unique melodic gift and to his artistic conscience which, rare in the Italian operatic world of his time, helped to pave the way for his great successor, Giuseppe Verdi, whose earliest operas, in particular *Oberto* and *Nabucco*, were to reveal a strong Bellinian influence. The bel canto style as practised by Rossini, Donizetti and Bellini was to linger on until Verdi bade it an affectionate farewell in *Luisa Miller* with the tenor aria, 'Quando le sere al placido'.

SELECTIVE BIBLIOGRAPHY

ROSSINI

Stendhal: *Vie de Rossini* (Paris, 1824; Eng. trans. *Life of Rossini* 1970)
M. and L. Escudier: *Rossini: sa vie et ses oevures* (Paris, 1854)
H. S. Edwards: *The Life of Rossini* (London, 1869)
F. Toye: *Rossini* (London, 1934)
L. Rognoni: *Rossini* (Parma, 1956)
H. Weinstock: *Rossini* (New York, 1968)
A. Kendall: *Gioacchino Rossini* (London, 1992)

DONIZETTI

G. Zavadini: *Donizetti: vita, musiche, epistolario* (Bergamo, 1948)
H. Weinstock: *Donizetti* (London, 1964)
W. Ashbrook: *Donizetti* (London, 1965)
J. Allitt: *Donizetti* (London, 1975)

BELLINI

A. Pougin: *Bellini, sa vie, ses oeuvres* (Paris, 1868)
F. Florimo: *Bellini, memorie e lettere* (Florence, 1882)
W. A. C. Lloyd: *Vincenzo Bellini* (London, 1909)
F. Pastura: *Bellini secondo la storia* (Parma, 1959)
L. Orrey: *Bellini* (London, 1969)
H. Weinstock: *Vincenzo Bellini* (New York, 1971)

SELECTIVE DISCOGRAPHY

(Compact Discs, except for those marked (LP)
which are 33 rpm long-playing records.
NR = not recorded.)

ROSSINI

Demetrio e Polibio: Giandomenico Bisi (Demetrio); Aldo Bramante
(Polibio) Cecilia Valdenassi (Lisinga); c. Bruno Rigacci.
Bongiovanni GB 2001–2 (LP)

La Cambiale di matrimonio: Alessandra Rossi (Fanny); Maurizio
Comencini (Edoardo); Bruno Pratico (Tobia); c. Marcello
Viotti. Claves CD50-9101

L'Equivoco stravagante: CD of the Wexford 1968 production in
preparation

L'Inganno felice: Emilia Gundari (Isabella); Ferdinando Jacopucci
(Bertrando); Paolo Montarsolo (Batone); Giorgio Tadeo
(Tarabotto); c. Carlo Franci. Notes PGP 21001

Ciro in Babilonia: Ernesto Palacio (Baldassare); Caterina Calvi
(Ciro); Daniela Dessy Ceriani (Amira); c. Carlo Rizzi.
Akademia 2CDAK 105

La Scala di seta: Luciana Serra (Giulia); Cecilia Bartoli (Lucilla);
William Matteuzzi (Dorvil); Roberto Coviello (Germano);
Natale De Carolis (Blansac); c. Gabriele Ferro. Ricordi RFCD
2003

La Pietra del paragone: Maria Costanza Nocentini (Fulvia);
Antonella Trovarelli (Aspasia); Helga Müller Molinari
(Clarice); Paolo Barbacini (Giocondo); Roberto Scaltriti
(Asdrubale); c. Claudio Desderi. Nuova Era 7132–33

L'Occasione fa il ladro: Maria Bayo (Berenice); Iorio Zennaro
(Alberto); Natale De Carolis (Parmenione); Fulvio Massa
(Eusebio); Fabio Previati (Martino); c. Marcello Viotti. Claves
CD50-9208–9

Il Signor Bruschino: Enzo Dara (Gaudenzio); Mariella Devia

(Sofia); Alberto Rinaldi (Bruschino Senior); Eugenio Favano
(Bruschino Junior); Dalmacio Gonzalez (Florville); c. Donato
Renzetti. Fonit-Cetra 2002

Tancredi: Marilyn Horne (Tancredi); Lella Cuberli (Amenaide);
Ernesto Palacio (Argirio); Nicola Zaccaria (Orbazzano); c. Ralf
Weikert. CBS CD39073

L'Italiana in Algeri: Agnes Baltsa (Isabella); Frank Lopardo
(Lindoro); Ruggero Raimondi (Mustafà); Enzo Dara (Taddeo);
c. Claudio Abbado. Deutsche Grammophon 427 331-2GH2

Aureliano in Palmira: Ezio di Cesare (Aureliano); Denia Mazzola
(Zenobia); Luciana d'Intino (Arsace); Nicoletta Cilento
(Publia) c. Giacomo Zani. Nuova Era 7069-70

Il Turco in Italia: (1) Nicola Rossi-Lemeni (Selim); Maria Callas
(Fiorilla); Nicolai Gedda (Narciso); Franco Calabrese
(Geronio); Mariano Stabile (Prosdocimo); c. Gianandrea
Gavazzeni. EMI CDS 7 49344-2

    (2) Samuel Ramey (Selim); Montserrat Caballé (Fiorilla);
Ernesto Palacio (Narciso); Enzo Dara (Geronio); Leo Nucci
(Prosdocimo); c. Riccardo Chailly. CBS CD37859

Sigismondo: CD of the 1992 Savona production in preparation

Elisabetta, regina d'Inghilterra: Montserrat Caballé (Elisabetta); José
Carreras (Leicester); Valerie Masterson (Matilde); Ugo Benelli
(Norfolk); c. Gianfranco Masini. Philips 432 453–2

Torvaldo e Dorliska: Pietro Bottazzo (Torvaldo); Lella Cuberli
(Dorliska); Siegmund Nimsgern (Il Duca d'Ordow); Enzo Dara
(Giorgio); Lucia Valentini-Terrani (Carlotta); c. Alberto
Zedda. Voce VOCE-25 (LP)

Il Barbiere di Siviglia: (1) Tito Gobbi (Figaro); Maria Callas
(Rosina); Luigi Alva (Almaviva); Fritz Ollendorff (Bartolo);
Nicola Zaccaria (Basilio); c. Alceo Galliera. EMI CDS 7
47634-8

    (2) Leo Nucci (Figaro); Cecilia Bartoli (Rosina); William
Matteuzzi (Almaviva); Enrico Fissore (Bartolo); Paata
Burchuladze (Basilio); c. Giuseppe Patanè. Decca 425 520-
2DH3

La Gazzetta: Gabriella Morigi (Lisetta); Franco Federici (Filippo);
Adriana Cicogna (Doralice); Paolo Barbacini (Alberto); c.
Fabio Luisi. Bongiovanni GB 2071-2-2

Otello: José Carreras (Otello); Frederica von Stade (Desdemona);
Gianfranco Pastine (Iago); Salvatore Fisichella (Rodrigo);
Nucci Condò (Emilia); Samuel Ramey (Elmiro); c. Jesús López
Cobos. Philips 432 457–2

La Cenerentola: Agnes Baltsa (Angiolina); Ruggero Raimondi (Don

Magnifico); Francisco Araiza (Don Ramiro); Simone Alaimo
(Dandini); Carol Malone (Clorinda); Felicity Palmer (Tisbe); c.
Neville Marriner. Philips 420 468-2PH3

La Gazza ladra: Katia Ricciarelli (Ninetta); William Matteuzzi
(Giannetto); Samuel Ramey (Gottardo); Bernadette Manca di
Nissa (Pippo); c. Gianluigi Gelmetti. Sony CD45850

Armida: Cecilia Gasdia (Armida); Chris Merritt (Rinaldo);
William Matteuzzi (Carlo and Goffredo); Bruce Ford
(Gernando and Ubaldo); Ferrucio Furlanetto (Idraote and
Astarotte); c. Claudio Scimone. Europa 350-211

Adelaide di Borgogna: Martine Dupuy (Ottone); Mariella Devia
(Adelaide); Aldo Bertolo (Adalberto); Armando Caforio
(Berengario); c. Alberto Zedda. Fonit Cetra CDC 64

Mosè in Egitto: Ruggero Raimondi (Mosè); Salvatore Fisichella
(Aronne); Siegmund Nimsgern (Faraone); Ernesto Palacio
(Osiride); June Anderson (Elcia); c. Claudio Scimone. Philips
420 109-2

Adina: Mariella Adani (Adina); Mario Spina (Selimo); Giorgio
Tadeo (Caliph); Florindo Andreoli (Ali); Paolo Pedani
(Mustafà); c. Bruno Rigacci. Voce VOCE-32 (LP: coupled
with *Il Signor Bruschino*: Sesto Bruscantini (Gaudenzio); Alda
Noni (Sofia); Afro Poli (Bruschino Senior), c. Carlo Maria
Giulini)

Ricciardo e Zoraide: NR

Ermione: Cecilia Gasdia (Ermione); Margarita Zimmermann
(Andromaca); Ernesto Palacio (Pirro); Chris Merritt (Oreste);
William Matteuzzi (Pilade); Simone Alaimo (Fenicio); c.
Claudio Scimone. Erato ECD 75336

Eduardo e Cristina: NR

La Donna del lago: Katia Ricciarelli (Elena); Lucia Valentini
Terrani (Malcolm); Dalmacio Gonzalez (Giacomo); Samuel
Ramey (Douglas); c. Maurizio Pollini. CBS CD 39311

Bianca e Falliero: Katia Ricciarelli (Bianca); Marilyn Horne
(Falliero); Chris Merritt (Contareno); Georgio Surjan
(Capellio); c. Donato Renzetti. Fonit Cetra RFCD 2008

Maometto II: June Anderson (Anna); Margarita Zimmermann
(Calbo); Ernesto Palacio (Erisso); Samuel Ramey (Maometto);
c. Claudio Scimone. Philips 412 148-2PH3

Matilde di Shabran: Cecilia Valdenassi (Matilde); Pietro Bottazzo
(Corradino); Agostino Ferrin (Raimondo); Maria Casula
(Edoardo); Rolando Panerai (Isidoro); c. Bruno Martinotti.
MRF Records MRF 108 (LP)

Zelmira: Cecilia Gasdia (Zelmira); William Matteuzzi (Ilo); Chris

Merritt (Antenore); José Garcia (Polidoro); Boaz Senator
(Leucippo); c. Claudio Scimone. Erato 2292-45419-2

Semiramide: Joan Sutherland (Semiramide); Marilyn Horne
(Arsace); John Serge (Idreno); Joseph Rouleau (Assur); Spiro
Malas (Oroe); c. Richard Bonynge. Decca 425 481-2DM3

Il Viaggio a Reims: Cecilia Gasdia (Corinna); Katia Ricciarelli
(Madama Cortese); Lella Cuberli (Contessa di Folleville);
Lucia Valentini Terrani (Melibea); Edoardo Gimenez
(Belfiore); Francisco Araiza (Libenskof); Samuel Ramey (Lord
Sidney); Ruggero Raimondi (Don Profondo); Enzo Dara
(Baron Trombonok); Leo Nucci (Don Alvaro); c. Claudio
Abbado. Deutsche Grammophon 415 498-2GH2

Le Siège de Corinthe: (1) Luciana Serra (Pamyre); Maurizio
Comencini (Néocles); Marcello Lippi (Maometto); Dano
Raffanti (Cléomène); Armando Caforo (Hiéros); c. Paolo Olmi.
Nuova Era 7140-2

(2: in Italian) Beverly Sills (Pamyre); Shirley Verrett
(Néocles); Justino Diaz (Maometto); Harry Theyard
(Cléomène); Gwynne Howell (Hiéros); Robert Lloyd (Omar);
c. Thomas Schippers. EMI CMS 7 64335 2

Moïse et Pharaon: József Gregor (Moïse); András Molnár (Eliézer);
Sándor Sólyom-Nagy (Pharaon); János B. Nagy (Aménophis);
Eszter Póka (Marie); Magda Kalmár (Anaï); Júlia Hamari
(Sinaïde); c. Lamberto Gardelli. Hungaroton HCD 12290-92-2

Le Comte Ory: John Aler (Ory); Sumi Jo (Countess Adèle); Diana
Montague (Isolier); Gino Quilico (Rimbaud); c. John Eliot
Gardiner. Philips 422 406-2PH2

Guillaume Tell: Gabriel Bacquier (Tell); Montserrat Caballé
(Mathilde); Nicolai Gedda (Arnold); Mady Mesplé (Jemmy); c.
Lamberto Gardelli. EMI CMS 7 69951-2

DONIZETTI

Il Pigmalione: Paolo Pellegrini (Pigmalione); Susanna Rigacci
(Galatea); c. Fabio Maestri. Bongiovanni GB 2109-10 (coupled
with *Rita* and other Donizetti excerpts)

Enrico di Borgogna: NR

Il Falegname di Livonia: NR

Le Nozze in villa: NR

Zoraida di Granata: Opera Rara CD in preparation

La Zingara: NR

La Lettera anonima: Rosanna Pecchioli (Rosina); Rosa Laghezza

360   THE BEL CANTO OPERAS

(Melita); Pietro Bottazzo (Filinto); Rolando Panerai (Macario); c. Franco Caracciolo. Unique Opera Records UORG 146 (LP)

Chiara e Serafina: NR

Alfredo il Grande: NR

Il Fortunato inganno: NR

L'Ajo nell'imbarazzo: Silvia Baleani (Gilda); Johanna Peters (Leonarda); Suso Mariategui (Enrico); Manuel Gonzalez (Don Giulio); Richard McKee (Don Gregorio); Bernard Dickerson (Pipetto); c. Kenneth Montgomery. MRF Records MRF-149-S (LP)

Emilia di Liverpool: Yvonne Kenny (Emilia); Chris Merritt (Federico); Geoffrey Dolton (Claudio); Sesto Bruscantini (Don Romualdo); c. David Parry. Opera Rara ORCD8

Alahor in Granata: Opera Rara CD in preparation

Elvida: NR

Gabriella di Vergy: Milla Andrew (Gabriella); Christian du Plessis (Fayel); Maurice Arthur (Raoul); John Tomlinson (Filippo II); c. Alun Francis. Opera Rara ORCD3

Olivo e Pasquale: John del Carlo (Olivo); Gastone Sarti (Pasquale); Estelle Maria Gibbs (Isabella); Sabrina Bizzo (Camillo); c. Bruno Rigacci. Bongiovanni GB 2005-7 (LP)

Otto mesi in due ore: NR

Il Borgomastro di Saardam: Ans Philippo (Marietta); Pieter van den Berg (Tsar Pietro); Philip Langridge (Pietro Flimann); Renato Capecchi (Wambett); c. Jan Schaap. MRF Records MRF-190-S (LP)

Le Convenienze ed inconvenienze teatrali: Daniela Dessi (Corilla); Franco Sioli (Procolo); Simone Alaimo (Mamma Agata); William Matteuzzi (Guglielmo); Giuseppe Lamazza (Biscroma); Armando Ariostini (Prospero); c. Antonello Allemandi. Ars Nova ACDAN 2165

L'Esule di Roma: Cecilia Gasdia (Argelia); Ernesto Palacio (Settimio); Simone Alaimo (Murena); Armando Ariostini (Publio); c. Massimo de Bernart. Bongiovanni GB 2045-46-2

Alina, regina di Golconda: Daniela Dessi (Alina); Rockwell Blake (Seide); Paolo Coni (Volmar); c. Antonello Allemandi. Nuova Era 033 6701

Gianni di Calais: NR

Il Giovedì grasso: Federico Davià (Colonel); Jill Gomez (Nina); Malcolm Williams (Teodoro); Elfego Esparza (Sigismondo); Johanna Peters (Camilla); Ugo Benelli (Ernesto); c. David Atherton. Memories HR 4482

Il Paria: NR

Il Castello di Kenilworth: Maria Devia (Elisabetta); Denia Mazzola
(Amelia); Barry Anderson (Warney); c. Jan Latham-Koenig.
Fonit-Centra 2006
I Pazzi per progetto: Leonardo Monreale (Darlemont); Susanna
Rigacci (Norina); Graziano Polidori (Blinval); Adriana Cicogna
(Cristina); Enrico Fissore (Eustachio); Vito Maria Brunetti
(Venanzio); c. Bruno Rigacci. Bongiovanni GB 2070-2
Il Diluvio universale: Bonaldo Giaotti (Noè); Yasuko Hayashi
(Sela); Martine Dupuy (Ada); Ottavio Garaventa (Cadmo);
Bruno Dal Monte (Iafet); Aldo Bottion (Sem); Nicola Pigliucci
(Cam); c. Jan Latham-Koenig. Voce VOCE-100 (LP)
Imelda de' Lambertazzi: Floriana Sovilla (Imelda); Diego D'Auria
(Lamberto); Fausto Tenzi (Orlando); Andrea Martin
(Bonifacio); c. Marc Andrae. Nuova Era 6778-79
Anna Bolena: Joan Sutherland (Anna Bolena); Susanne Mentzer
(Giovanna Seymour); Bernadette Manca Di Nissa (Smeton);
Jerry Hadley (Riccardo Percy); Samuel Ramey (Enrico VIII);
c. Richard Bonynge. Decca 421 096-2DH3
Gianni di Parigi: Giuseppe Morino (Gianni); Luciana Serra (La
Principessa di Navarra); Elena Zilio (Oliviero); Enrico Fissore
(Pedrigo); c. Carlo Felice Cillario. Nuova Era 6752-53
Francesca di Foix: NR
La Romanziera e l'uomo nero: NR
Fausta: Raina Kabaivanska (Fausta); Renato Bruson
(Costantino); Giuseppe Giacomini (Crispo); Luigi Roni
(Massimiano); Giuseppina Dalle Molle (Irella); c. Daniel Oren.
HRE Records HRE 381–3 (LP)
Ugo, Conte di Parigi: Maurice Arthur (Ugo); Janet Price (Bianca);
Yvonne Kenny (Adelia); Della Jones (Luigi V); Christian du
Plessis (Folco di Angiò); c. Alun Francis. Opera Rara ORC 1
L'Elisir d'amore: (1) Mirella Freni (Adina); Nicolai Gedda
(Nemorino); Mario Sereni (Belcore); Renato Capecchi
(Dulcamara); c. Francesco Molinari-Pradelli. EMI CMS 7
69897-2
　　　(2) Joan Sutherland (Adina); Luciano Pavarotti
(Nemorino); Dominic Cossa (Belcore); Spiro Malas
(Dulcamara); c. Richard Bonynge. Decca 414 461-2DH2
Sancia di Castiglia: Antonella Bandelli (Sancia); Adriana Cicogna
(Garcia); Franco De Grandis (Ircano); Giuseppe Costanzo
(Rodrigo); c. Roberto Abbado. Voce VOCE-103 (LP)
Il Furioso all'isola di San Domingo: Luciana Serra (Eleonora);
Stefano Antonucci (Cardenio); Luca Canonici (Fernando);

Maurizio Picconi (Bartolomeo); c. Carlo Rizzi. Bongiovanni
BG 2056-8-2

Parisina: Montserrat Caballé (Parisina); Jerome Pruett (Ugo);
Louis Quilico (Azzo); James Morris (Ernesto); c. Eve Queler.
Legato Classics SRO-836-2

Torquato Tasso: Simone Alaimo (Torquato Tasso); Luciana Serra
(Eleonora d'Este); Nicoletta Cilento (Eleonora di Scandiano);
Ernesto Palacio (Roberto); Roberto Corviello (Don Gherardo);
c. Massimo de Bernart. Bongiovanni BG 2028-30

Lucrezia Borgia: (1) Joan Sutherland (Lucrezia); Marilyn Horne
(Orsini); Giacomo Aragall (Gennaro); Ingvar Wixell (Alfonso);
c. Richard Bonynge. Decca 421 497-2DM2

　　　(2) Montserrat Caballé (Lucrezia); Shirley Verrett
(Orsini); Alfredo Kraus (Gennaro); Ezio Flagello (Alfonso); c.
Jonel Perlea. RCA GD86642

Rosmonda d'Inghilterra: Yvonne Kenny (Rosmonda); Milla Andrew
(Leonora); Enid Hartle (Arturo); Richard Graeger (Enrico II);
Christian du Plessis (Clifford); c. Alun Francis. MRF Records
MRF-127-S (LP)

Maria Stuarda: Joan Sutherland (Maria Stuarda); Huguette
Tourangeau (Elisabetta); Luciano Pavarotti (Leicester); James
Morris (Cecil); Roger Soyer (Talbot); c. Richard Bonynge.
Decca 425 410-2DM2

Gemma di Vergy: Montserrat Caballé (Gemma); Luis Lima
(Tamas); Louis Quilico (Count Vergy); Paul Plishka (Guido);
c. Eve Queler. CBS 793303 (LP)

Marino Faliero: Agostino Ferrin (Marino Faliero); Margherita
Roberti (Elena); Angelo Mori (Fernando); Carlo Meliciani
(Israele Bertucci); Virgilio Carbonari (Michele Steno); c.
Adolfo Camozzo. Melodram MEL-27030

Lucia di Lammermoor: (1) Joan Sutherland (Lucia); Luciano
Pavarotti (Edgardo); Sherrill Milnes (Enrico); Nicolai
Ghiaurov (Raimondo); c. Richard Bonynge. Decca 410 193-
2DH3

　　　(2) Maria Callas (Lucia); Giuseppe di Stefano (Edgardo);
Rolando Panerai (Enrico); Nicola Zaccaria (Raimondo); c.
Herbert von Karajan. EMI CMS 7 63631-2

Belisario: Giuseppe Taddei (Belisario); Leyla Gencer (Antonina);
Umberto Grilli (Almiro); c. Gianandrea Gavazzeni. Verona 27048-9

Il Campanello di notte: Agnes Baltsa (Serafina); Enzo Dara (Don
Annibale); Angelo Romero (Enrico); Biancamaria Casoni
(Madama Rosa); Carlo Gaifa (Spiridione); c. Gary Bertini.
CBS MK 38450

Betly: Susanna Rigacci (Betly); Maurizio Comencini (Daniele); Roberto Scaltriti (Max); c. Bruno Rigacci. Bongiovanni BG 2091-92-2 (coupled with *Le Convenienze teatrali*)

L'Assedio di Calais: Christian du Plessis (Eustachio); Della Jones (Aurelio); Nuccia Focile (Eleonora); Russell Smythe (Edoardo III); Eiddwen Harrhy (Isabella); c. David Parry. Opera Rara ORCD9

Pia de' Tolomei: Jolanda Meneguzzer (Pia); Aldo Bottion (Ghino); Walter Alberti (Nello); Franco Ventriglia (Piero); c. Bruno Rigacci. Melodram 37012-3 (coupled with *Maria di Rohan*)

Roberto Devereux: Beverly Sills (Elisabetta); Robert Ilosfalvy (Roberto Devereux); Peter Glossop (Duke of Nottingham); Beverly Wolff (Sara, Duchess of Nottingham); c. Charles Mackerras. EMI SLS 787-3 (LP)

Maria de Rudenz: Katia Ricciarelli (Maria de Rudenz); Silvia Baleani (Matilde); Leo Nucci (Corrado); Alberto Cupido (Enrico); c. Eliahu Inbal. CBS 79345 (LP)

Poliuto: José Carreras (Poliuto); Katia Ricciarelli (Paolina); Juan Pons (Severo); Paolo Gavanelli (Nearco); c. Oleg Caetani. CBS CD44821

Les Martyrs: Ottavio Garaventa (Polyeucte); Leyla Gencer (Pauline); Renato Bruson (Sévère); Ferrucio Furlanetto (Félix); Iscar di Credico (Néarque); c. Gianluigi Gelmetti. Voce VOCE-16 (LP)

Le Duc d'Albe (in Italian as *Il Duca d'Alba*): Louis Quilico (Il Duca d'Albá); Iva Tosini (Amelia); Renato Cioni (Marcello); c. Thomas Schippers. Melodram 001

La Fille du régiment: Joan Sutherland (Marie); Luciano Pavarotti (Tonio); Spiro Malas (Sulpice); Monica Sinclair (La Marquise); c. Richard Bonynge. Decca 414 520-2DH2

La Favorite (in Italian as *La Favorita*): Fiorenza Cossotto (Leonora); Luciano Pavarotti (Fernando); Gabriel Bacquier (Alfonso); Nicolai Ghiaurov (Baldassare); Ileana Cotrubas (Inès); c. Richard Bonynge. Decca 430 038-2DM3

Adelia: NR

Rita: Adelina Scarabelli (Rita); Pietro Ballo (Beppe); Alessandro Corbelli (Gaspar); c. Federico Amendola. Nuova Era 7045

Maria Padilla: Lois McDonall (Maria Padilla); Della Jones (Ines); Graham Clark (Don Ruiz); Christian du Plessis (Don Pedro); Roderick Earle (Don Ramiro); c. Alun Francis. Opera Rara ORC 6

Linda di Chamounix: Margherita Rinaldi (Linda); Elena Zilio (Pierotto); Alfredo Kraus (Carlo); Renato Bruson (Antonio);

Enzo Dara (Marchese di Boisfleury); c. Gianandrea Gavazzeni. Foyer 2CF 2045

Don Pasquale: (1) Ernesto Badini (Don Pasquale); Adelaide Saraceni (Norina); Tito Schipa (Ernesto); Afro Poli (Malatesta); c. Carlo Sabajno. EMI CHS7 63241-2
    (2) Sesto Bruscantini (Don Pasquale); Mirella Freni (Norina); Gösta Winbergh (Ernesto); Leo Nucci (Malatesta); c. Riccardo Muti. EMI CDS 7 47068-2

Maria di Rohan: Virginia Zeani (Maria di Rohan); Enzo Tei (Riccardo); Mario Zanasi (Enrico); c. Fernando Previtali. Melodram 37012-3 (coupled with *Pia de' Tolomei*)

Dom Sébastien, Roi du Portugal (in Italian as *Don Sebastiano*): Fedora Barbieri (Zaida); Gianni Poggi (Don Sebastiano); Enzo Mascherini (Camoëns); Giulio Neri (Don Giovanni da Silva); Doni Dondi (Abaialdo); Raniero Rossi (Don Enrico); c. Carlo Maria Giulini. MRF Records MRF-113 (LP)

Caterina Cornaro: Montserrat Caballé (Caterina Cornaro); Giacomo Aragall (Gerardo); Claude Meloni (Andrea Cornaro); Ryan Edwards (Lusignano); Gwynne Howell (Mocenigo); c. Gian-Franco Masini. Rodolphe RPC 32474-75

Ne m'oubliez pas: Margreta Elkins (Henriette); Alexander Oliver (André); Christian du Plessis (Franz); c. James Judd. Opera Rara OR 4 (LP)

BELLINI

Adelson e Salvini: Alicia Nafè (Nelly); Eleonora Jankovic (Madama Rivers); Lucia Rizzi (Fanny); Bradley Williams (Salvini); Fabio Previati (Adelson); Aurio Tomicich (Bonifacio); Roberto Coviello (Struley); c. Andrea Licata. Nuova Era 7154-55

Bianca e Fernando: Young Ok Shin (Bianca); Gregory Kunde (Fernando); Haijing Fu (Filippo); Aurio Tomicich (Carlo); c. Andrea Licata. Nuova Era 7076–77

Il Pirata: Montserrat Caballé (Imogene); Bernabé Marti (Gualtiero); Piero Cappuccilli (Ernesto); c. Gianandrea Gavazzeni. EMI CMS 7 64169 2

La Straniera: Lucia Aliberti (Alaide); Vincenzo Bello (Arturo); Roberto Frontali (Valdeburgo); c. Gianfranco Masini. Fonit Cetra RFCD 2010

Zaira: Katia Ricciarelli (Zaira); Alexandra Papadjakou (Nerestano); Ramon Vergas (Corasmino); Simone Alaimo

(Orosmane); Luigi Roni (Lusignano); c. Paolo Olmi. Nuova
Era 6982-3

I Capuleti e i Montecchi: Katia Ricciarelli (Giulietta); Diana
Montague (Romeo); Dano Raffanti (Tebaldo); Marcello Lippi
(Capellio); Antonio Salvadori (Lorenzo); c. Bruno Campanella.
Nuova Era 7020-21

La Sonnambula: (1) Joan Sutherland (Amina); Luciano Pavarotti
(Elvino); Nicolai Ghiaurov (Rodolfo); c. Richard Bonynge.
Decca 417 424-2DH2

 (2) Maria Callas (Amina); Nicola Monti (Elvino); Nicola
Zaccaria (Rodolfo); c. Antonino Votto. EMI CDS 7 47378-8

Norma: (1) Joan Sutherland (Norma); Montserrat Caballé
(Adalgisa); Luciano Pavarotti (Pollione); Samuel Ramey
(Oroveso); c. Richard Bonynge. Decca 414 476-2DH3

 (2) Maria Callas (Norma); Christa Ludwig (Adalgisa);
Franco Corelli (Pollione); Nicola Zaccaria (Oroveso); c. Tullio
Serafin. EMI CMS 7 63000-2

Beatrice di Tenda: Joan Sutherland (Beatrice); Josephine Veasey
(Agnese); Luciano Pavarotti (Orombello); Cornelius Opthof
(Filippo); c. Richard Bonynge. Decca SET 320-2 (LP)

I Puritani: (1) Joan Sutherland (Elvira); Nicolai Gedda (Arturo);
Ernest Blanc (Riccardo); Justino Diaz (Giorgio); c. Richard
Bonynge. Legato Classics SRO 838-2

 (2) Joan Sutherland (Elvira); Luciano Pavarotti (Arturo);
Piero Cappuccilli (Riccardo); Nicolai Ghiaurov (Giorgio); c.
Richard Bonynge. Decca 4717 588-2DH3

 (3) Montserrat Caballé (Elvira); Alfredo Kraus (Arturo);
Matteo Manuguerra (Riccardo); Agostino Ferrin (Giorgio); c.
Riccardo Muti. EMI CMS 7 69663-2

APPENDIX

The Works of Rossini, Donizetti and Bellini in Order of Composition

Rossini's works (between pages 3 and 136)

Demetrio e Polibio (composed 1806; performed 1812)
La Cambiale di matrimonio (1810)
L'Equivoco stravagante (1811)
L'Inganno felice (1812)
Ciro in Babilonia (1812)
La Scala di seta (1812)
La Pietra del paragone (1812)
L'Occasione fa il ladro (1812)
Il Signor Bruschino (1813)
Tancredi (1813)
L'Italiana in Algeri (1813)
Aureliano in Palmira (1813)
Il Turco in Italia (1814)
Sigismondo (1814)
Elisabetta, regina d'Inghilterra (1815)
Torvaldo e Dorliska (1815)
Il Barbiere di Siviglia (1816)
La Gazzetta (1816)
Otello (1816)

La Cenerentola (1817)
La Gazza ladra (1817)
Armida (1817)
Adelaide di Borgogna (1817)
Mosè in Egitto (1818)
Adina (composed 1818; performed 1826)
Ricciardo e Zoraide (1818)
Ermione (1819)
Eduardo e Cristina (1819)
La Donna del lago (1819)
Bianca e Falliero (1819)
Maometto II (1820)
Matilde di Shabran (1821)
Zelmira (1822)
Semiramide (1823)
Il Viaggio a Reims (1825)
Le Siège de Corinthe (1826)
Moïse et Pharaon (1827)
Le Comte Ory (1828)
Guillaume Tell (1829)

Donizetti's works (between pages 137 and 306)

Il Pigmalione (composed 1816; performed 1960)
Enrico di Borgogna (1818)
Il Falegname di Livonia (1819)
Le Nozze in villa (1820–21)

Zoraida di Granata (1822)
La Zingara (1822)
La Lettera anonima (1822)
Chiara e Serafina (1822)
Alfredo il Grande (1823)

Il Fortunato inganno (1823)
L'Ajo nell'imbarazzo (1824)
Emilia di Liverpool (1824)
Alahor in Granata (1826)
Elvida (1826)
Gabriella di Vergy (composed
    1826 and 1838; performed 1869)
Olivo e Pasquale (1827)
Otto mesi in due ore (1827)
Il Borgomastro di Saardam (1827)
Le Convenienze ed inconvenienze
    teatrali (1827 and 1831)
L'Esule di Roma (1828)
Alina, regina di Golconda (1828)
Gianni di Calais (1828)
Il Giovedì grasso (1828–29)
Il Paria (1829)
Il Castello di Kenilworth (1829)
I Pazzi per progetto (1830)
Il Diluvio universale (1830)
Imelda de' Lambertazzi (1830)
Anna Bolena (1830)
Gianni di Parigi (composed 1831;
    performed 1839)
Francesca di Foix (1831)
La Romanziera e l'uomo nero
    (1831)
Fausta (1832)
Ugo, Conte di Parigi (1832)
L'Elisir d'amore (1832)
Sancia di Castiglia (1832)
Il Furioso all'isola di San
    Domingo (1833)
Parisina (1833)

Torquato Tasso (1833)
Lucrezia Borgia (1833)
Rosmonda d'Inghilterra (1834)
Maria Stuarda (1834)
Gemma di Vergy (1834)
Marino Faliero (1835)
Lucia di Lammermoor (1835)
Belisario (1836)
Il Campanello di notte (1836)
Betly (1836)
L'Assedio di Calais (1836)
Pia de' Tolomei (1837)
Roberto Devereux (1837)
Maria de Rudenz (1838)
Poliuto (composed 1838;
    performed 1848)
Les Martyrs (composed 1839;
    performed 1840)
Le Duc d'Albe (composed 1839;
    performed 1882)
La Fille du régiment (1840)
La Favorite (1840)
Adelia (1841)
Rita (composed 1841; performed
    1860)
Maria Padilla (1841)
Linda di Chamounix (1842)
Don Pasquale (1843)
Maria di Rohan (1843)
Dom Sébastien, Roi de Portugal
    (1843)
Caterina Cornaro (1844)
Ne m'oubliez pas (begun 1843;
    unfinished and unstaged)

Bellini's works (between pages 307 and 354)

Adelson e Salvini (1825)
Bianca e Fernando (1826)
Il Pirata (1827)
La Straniera (1829)
Zaira (1829)

I Capuleti e i Montecchi (1830)
La Sonnambula (1831)
Norma (1831)
Beatrice di Tenda (1833)
I Puritani (1835)

INDEX

Abbadia, Luigia, 283
Abbado, Claudio, 329, 331
Accursi, Michaele, 290
Adam, Adolphe Charles, 94, 237, 275; *Le Chalet*, 251
Adelaide (Donizetti), 276
Adelaide di Borgogna (Rossini), 79–81, 82, 84, 92; Overture, 80–1
Adelia (Donizetti), 164, 279–81, 294
Adelson e Salvini (Bellini), 309–12, 314, 317, 318, 322, 330, 340; Overture, 311, 317
Adina or Il Califfo di Bagdad (Rossini), 85–7
Aix-en-Provence, 31, 48, 77
L'Ajo nell'imbarazzo (*The Tutor Embarrassed*: Donizetti), 155–7, 158, 161
Alahor in Granata (Donizetti), 159, 160–2, 212
Aldighieri, Gottardo, 164
Alexander I, Tsar of Russia, 112
Alexandria, 210, 216, 263
Alfonso, Duca di Ferrara (Donizetti), 225
Alfredo il Grande (*Alfred the Great*: Donizetti), 152–3, 185
Algiers, 210, 235
Alina, regina di Golconda (*Alina, Queen of Golconda*: Donizetti), 176–80; Overture, 179
Allemandi, Antonello, 178
Amati, Caterina, 143
Ambrosi, Antonio, 73, 80, 105
Ambrosini, Gennero, 185, 190, 201
American Opera Society, 64
Amsterdam, 74, 94
Ancelot, François, *Élisabeth d'Angleterre*, 259–60; *Maria Padilla*, 284
Ancelot, Jacques-Arsène, 348, 350
Anderson, June, 64, 77, 334, 345, 349
Androclès, ou Le Lion reconnaissant, 175
Anelli, Angelo, 34, 35–6, 290, 291
L'Ange de Nisida (*The Angel of Nisida*: Donizetti), 276, 277, 278, 279
Anna Bolena (*Anne Boleyn*: Donizetti), 143, 164, 184, 193–7, 198, 200, 201, 205, 209, 228, 333; Overture, 196
Annibaldi, Luttgard, 34
Antoldi, Gaetano, 328
Antonacci, Anna Caterina, 48
Antonioli, Doro, 139
Appiani, Andrea and Giuseppina, 286
Aragall, Giacomo, 329
Arati, Marco, 164, 265, 301
aria di sorbetto (short aria), 17
Armida (Rossini), 76–9, 80, 126
Arnault, Antoine-Vincent, *Blanche et Montcassin*, 99
Arrigotti, Giovanni, 181, 190
L'Assedio di Calais (*The Siege of Calais*: Donizetti), 252–6
L'Assedio di Calais (ballet), 254

L'Assedio di Corinto (Rossini), 123, 124, 177, 178, 319–20
Auber, Daniel François, 94; *Le Philtre*, 211
Aumer, Jean-Pierre, 334
Aureliano in Palmira (*Aurelianus in Palmyra*: Rossini), 13, 33, 38–40, 41, 55, 58, 66; Overture, 39, 48, 58
Aventi, Count Francesco, 16
Azevedo, Alexis-Jacob, 27, 44
azione pastorale (pastoral cantata), 152
azione tragica, 89–92
azione tragico-sacra (oratorio), 81–4, 188, 189–92

Bach, Johann Sebastian, 13
Baculard d'Arnaud, François-Thomas, 310; *Le Comte de Comminges*, 277
Bagioli, Nicola, 116
Baillou Hillaret, Felicità, 198, 234
Balducci, Giuseppe, 234
Balocchi, Luigi, 115, 118, 122, 123, 125
Baltsa, Agnes, 329, 338
Bandini, Signor, impresario, 325
Barbaja, Domenico, 47, 62, 108, 168, 175, 313, 316
Barber Institute of Fine Arts, Birmingham University, 345
Il Barbiere di Siviglia (*The Barber of Seville*: Rossini), 2, 11, 22, 24–5, 33, 39, 40, 44, 51, 52–61, 62, 63, 69–70, 87, 89, 111, 130, 135, 171, 177, 291; Overture, 13, 48, 58
Barbieri, Fedora, 338
Barbieri, Gaetano, *Elisabetta al castello di Kenilworth*, 185
Barblan, Guglielmo, 163
Barcelona, 9, 14, 19, 21, 24, 31, 38, 51, 71, 94, 99, 108, 123, 156, 170, 178, 195, 225, 249, 257, 260, 263, 271, 287, 295, 314, 316, 328, 345; Gran Teatre del Liceu, 235
Bardari, Giuseppe, 229, 230, 232
Barga, 8, 140; Teatro dei Differenti, 166, 188
Barielle, 281
Barili-Patti, Caterina, 253
Barroilhet, Paul, 253, 259, 276, 297
Bartoli, Domenico, 43
Basadonna, Giovanni, 192, 202, 214, 259
Basili, Francesco, *Il Califfo e la schiava*, 86
Bassi, Calisto, 83, 123, 125, 274
Bassi, Carolina, 98
Bastianelli, Cristoforo, 50
Batignano, 156
Battistini, Mattia, 223, 295
Baucardé, Carlo, 265
Bayard, Jean-François-Alfred, 273
Beatrice di Tenda (Bellini), 326, 342–7, 348
Beatrice di Tenda (ballet), 343
Beaumarchais, Pierre-Augustin Caron de, 57; *Le Barbier*

de Séville, 54, 55, 57, 58, 59; *Le Mariage de Figaro*, 57, 59;
  La Mère Coupable, 57
Beethoven, Ludwig van, 111, 112; *Fidelio*, 261; Ninth
  Symphony, 111
Begnis, Giuseppe de, 69, 70
Belisario (Donizetti), 245–8, 300
La Bella prigioniera (*The Beautiful Prisoner*: Donizetti), 162
Bellaigue, Camille, 61, 341
Bellini, Vincenzo (1801–35), 1, 2, 41, 49, 107, 123, 148,
  168, 171, 177, 178, 195, 197, 198, 237, 245, 285, 307–
  53; birth in Catania (1801), 310; studies at Real
  Conservatorio di Musica, Naples, 310; love affair with
  Giuditta Turina, 319, 337, 348; Giuditta Pasta's
  friendship with, 332–3; death of (1835), 245, 352
Belloy, Dormont de, *Gabriella di Vergy*, 164; *Zelmire*, 108–9
Benedetti, Michele, 64, 76, 81, 88, 89, 94, 152, 180
Benelli, Giovanni Battista, 111
Berg, Pieter van den 170
Bergamo, 139–40, 160, 161, 182, 194, 195, 203, 219, 225,
  245, 246, 251, 260, 266, 271, 276, 277, 295; burial of
  Donizetti in Santa Maria Maggiore, 271; Donizetti
  Festival, 199, 203, 235, 253; Donizetti Museum, 162;
  Musical Institute, 140; Teatro Donizetti, 139, 140, 156,
  214, 232, 235, 238, 253; Teatro Riccardi, 175
Berio, *Bianca e Fernando*, 313
Berio di Salsa, Marchese Francesco Maria, 63, 64–5, 67,
  87, 88
Berlin, 14, 26, 170, 216, 249, 260, 295, 320, 349
Berlioz, Hector, 130, 133, 210, 269, 273, 322
Bernardis, Raffaela de, 88, 89, 149
Bernstein, Leonard, 334
Berry, Duc et Duchesse de, 62
Berthold, G., 66
Berti, Tommaso, 12, 23, 26
Bertini, *Una Visita in Bedlam*, 188
Berton, Henri-Montan, *Françoise de Foix*, 200
Bertozzi, Angela, 143
Betly, o La Capanna Svizzera (*Betly, or The Swiss Chalet*:
  Donizetti), 249, 250–2
Bevilacqua-Aldobrandini, Gherardo, 85, 86, 92, 143, 144
Biagelli, Paolo, 53
Bianca di Castiglia (ballet), 214
Bianca e Falliero (Rossini), 98–100, 101, 124, 126, 129
Bianca e Fernando (Bellini), 177, 312–15, 319, 327, 340, 351;
  Overture, 313, 314
Bianca e Gernando (Bellini), 168, 177, 312, 313, 316
Bianchi, Eliodoro, 16, 92
Bianchi, Luciano, 29, 43, 92
Bianco, Giacinto, *Pia de' Tolomei*, 257
Bidera, Emanuele, 234, 235, 236, 237
Bis, Hippolyte-Louis-Florent, 131
Biscottini, Francesco, 73
Bishop, Sir Henry, 74, 94, 133; *Clari, or The Maid of
  Milan*, 197
Bizet, Georges, 341
Blake, Rockwell, 64, 178
Boccabadati-Gazzuoli, Luigia, 185, 187, 190, 200, 201
Boieldieu, François Adrien, *Le Calife de Bagdad*, 86; *Jean de
  Paris*, 199
Bologna, 6, 7, 10, 12, 14, 16, 21, 31, 47, 56, 85–6, 116,
  128, 144, 156, 194, 219, 257, 260, 286, 329; Accademia
  dei Concordi, 12; Liceo Filarmonico, 140; Liceo
  Musicale, 6, 9; Teatro del Corso, 12
Bombaci, *Historia dei fatti d'Antonio Lambertazzi*, 192
Bonel, M., 122, 125
Bonfigli, Lorenzo, 200, 328
Bonini, Emilia, 166
Bonoldi, Claudio, 21, 43, 76, 98
Bonynge, Richard, 44, 169, 232, 260
Bordogni, Marco, 115
Il Borgomastro di Saardam (*The Burgomaster of Saardam*:
  Donizetti), 169–71, 172
Boston, 265–6, 287, 329
Bottesi, Luisa, 80
Botticelli, Bartolomeo, 53
Botticelli, Giovanni, 152
Botticelli, Vincenzo, 38, 73, 143
Boufflers, Stanislas-Jean de, *La Reine de Golconde*, 178
Bouilly, Jean-Nicolas, 200
Boulanger, Marie-Julienne, 273

Bourgeois, Juliette, 273
Le Bourgmestre de Sardam (Mélesville, Merle and Boirie),
  170
Brambilla, Marietta, 224, 286, 295, 296
Bregenz, 77, 249, 260, 349
Brewer, Bruce, 175
Brighton Royal Pavilion, 116
Brooke, Arthur, *The Tragical History of Romeus and Juliet*,
  329–30
Brunswick, Léon Lévy, 168, 248
Bruschi-Chiatti, Abigaille, 270
Bruson, Renato, 203, 246
Brussels, 26, 195, 216, 260, 282, 291, 295; Théâtre-Royale
  de la Monnaie, 271
Buades, Aurora, 329
Bucharest, 216, 295
Budapest, 51, 77, 94, 170, 218, 295, 320, 349
Budden, Julian, 45
Buenos Aires, 27, 39, 216, 221, 235, 246, 263, 291, 295;
  Teatro Colón, 302
Bumbry, Grace, 338
Bunn, Alfred, 133
Buondelmonte (Donizetti), 229, 230–1, 232, 234, 245; *see also
  Maria Stuarda*
Busti, Alessandro, 147
Buxton Festival, 24, 140, 221
Byron, Lord, 93, 123; *Childe Harold*, 65; *Heaven and Earth*,
  190; *The Lament of Tasso*, 221; *Marino Faliero*, 238;
  Parisina, 219

Caballé, Montserrat, 2, 48, 90, 204, 219, 225, 232, 235,
  260, 302, 316, 320, 338
Cagliari, 99, 178
Caigniez, Louis-Charles, *Jean de Calais*, 180; *La petite
  bohémienne*, 148; *La pie voleuse*, 73
Caldara, Antonio, 141
Callas, Maria, 2, 41, 77, 195, 266, 316, 334, 338, 349
La Cambiale di matrimonio (*The Bill of Marriage*: Rossini), 8–
  11, 12, 14, 18, 30, 58; Overture, 10, 80–1
Cammarano, Salvatore, 240, 241, 242, 245, 246, 252, 253,
  254, 256, 257, 259, 260, 262, 265, 268, 293, 294, 295
Camozzo, Adolfo, 156
Il Campanello di notte (*The Night Bell*: Donizetti), 248–50,
  251
Campagnoli, Giovanni, 174, 181, 183, 200, 202
Campiuti, *Bianca e Fernando*, 312
Camporesi, Violante, 98
Caniglia, Maria, 266
Canonici, Giacinta, 23, 147
cantata scenica (for the stage), 118
Capecchi, Renato, 170
I Capuleti e i Montecchi (*The Capulets and the Montagues*:
  Bellini), 311, 312, 325, 326, 327–31, 332, 338, 342, 344,
  348; Overture, 330
Caradori-Allan, Rosalbina, 328
Carafa, Michele, 1, 81, 82; *Adele di Lusignano*, 279;
  Gabriella di Vergy, 164; *Il Paria*, 184
Cardini, Francesca, 61
Carlo il Temerario (Rossini), 132; *see also Guillaume Tell*
Carocci, Angiolina, 220
Carpani, Giuseppe, 111
Carpano, Adelaide, 40
Carraro, Maria, 180, 181, 182, 187, 190
Cartagenova, Giovanni Orazio, 85, 234, 342, 343
Carteri, Rosanna, 329
Cartoni, Pietro, 70
Casaccia, Carlo, 61, 147, 153, 155, 158
Casaccia, Raffaele, 170, 248
Cassago, Adelaide, 142
Castagna, Bruna, 338
Il Castello degli invalidi (*The Castle of Invalids*: Donizetti),
  162
Il Castello di Kenilworth (*Kenilworth Castle*: Donizetti), 169,
  184–7, 204, 207
Castenaso, 116
Castiglioni, Marietta, 73
castrati, 39
Catalani, Adelaide, 142

Catania, 310, 314, 316, 329, 342, 344; Teatro Massimo Bellini, 309, 310, 320, 325; Teatro Metropolitan, 310
Caterina Cornaro (Donizetti), 290, 293, 294, 300–4
Cavalieri, Rainieri Pocchini, 328
Cavalli, Marchese, 9
Cecconi, Teresa, 149, 323
Ceci, Domenico, 265
Celli, (composer), 156
La Cenerentola (Cinderella: Rossini), 54, 60, 63, 69–72, 73, 74, 78, 97, 105, 112, 117, 122; Overture, 63, 71
Cera, Venice impresario, 20, 24, 27
Certone, Carolina, 164
Cervantes, Miguel, *Don Quixote*, 216
Chabrand, Margherita, 61
Charles X, King of France, 117, 118, 120, 121
Charleston, South Carolina, 216, 320
La Chastelaine de Couci (14th-century romance), 164
Chazet, Alisan de, 26
Checcherini, Francesca, 158
Checcherini, Giuseppe, 157, 158
Chelli, Annunziata Berni, 34
Chénier, Marie-Joseph de, *Henri VIII*, 195
Cherubini, Maria Luigi, 1; *Les Abencérages*, 161
Chiara e Serafina, o I Pirati (Chiara and Serafina, or The Pirates: Donizetti), 150–1, 152, 177
Chiaromonte, Francesco, 234
Chicago, 31, 195
Chies, Angiola, 12
Chigi-Albani, Prince, 80
Chinzani, Adelaide, 98
Chirico, Giorgio de, 64
Chizzola, Gaetano, 46, 81, 89, 94, 174
Chopin, Frédéric, 348
Chorley, Henry, 175, 237–8
Ciccimarra, Giuseppe, 64, 76, 81, 88, 89, 101
Cimadoro, Giambattista, *Pimmalione*, 139, 140–1
Cimarosa, Domenico, 8, 15, 28, 37, 39, 141; *Il Matrimonio segreto*, 19
Cinti-Damoreau, Laure, 115, 122, 125, 128, 131
Ciro in Babilonia (Cyrus in Babylon: Rossini), 15–18, 49, 84, 356; Overture, 17
Coccia, Carlo, 228, 234, 323, 342; *La Figlia dell'arciere*, 279–80
Colbran, Isabella, 46, 47, 49, 62, 64, 76, 77, 81, 88, 89, 90, 93, 94, 101, 108, 111, 112, 116; Rossini's marriage to, 108, 111
Coletti, Filippo, 301, 302
Colini, Filippo, 265
Colman, George and Garrick, David, *The Clandestine Marriage*, 19
Columbus, Christopher, 177
Comelli-Rubini, Adelaide, 101, 180, 182
Como, Lake, 332–3, 337
Le Comte Ory (Count Ory; Il Conte Ory: Rossini), 117, 120, 128–30, 131, 323
Coni, Paolo, 178
Constantinople (now Istanbul), 216, 295
Conti, Carlo, 148
Le Convenienze ed inconvenienze teatrali (Theatrical Seemliness and Unseemliness: Donizetti), 172–4, 251
Corelli, Franco, 266
Corfu, 38, 175, 260, 263, 283, 295
Corini, Gaetana, 146
Corneille, Pierre, *Don Sanche d'Aragon*, 6; *Polyeucte*, 265, 268
Corradi-Pantanelli, Clorinda, 206
Correa, Lorenza, 38
Corri-Paltoni, Fanny, 172
Cortesi, Carolina, 92
Cosenza, Giovanni Carlo di, 319; *I Pazzi per progetto*, 188
Cosselli, Domenico, 166, 218, 240
Cossotto, Fiorenza, 338
Cottin, Sophie, *Élisabeth, ou Les exilés de Sibérie*, 168
Coviello, Roberto, 309
crescendo, Rossini's 15, 20, 36, 42, 44, 49, 60, 67, 71, 72, 74, 75, 87, 114, 121
Crespi, Federico, 229
Crutchfield, Will, 168–9
Cuberli, Lella, 48
Curioni, Alberico, 61, 342

Dabadie, Henri-Bernard, 125, 128, 131, 209, 211
Dabadie, Louise-Zulme, 125, 131
Dalrymple, Janet, 241
D'Annunzio, Gabriele, 219
Dante Alighieri, *Inferno*, 67, 244; *Purgatorio*, 257
Dardanelli, Girolama, 46
D'Arlincourt, Victor-Charles Prévôt, Vicomte, *L'Etrangère*, 319; *Le Solitaire*, 319
d'Aubigny, T. Badouin, *La pie voleuse*, 73
D'Auria, 153
David, Giovanni, 40, 64, 88, 89, 94, 185, 312, 313
De Angeli, Alessandro, 98
De Franchi, 149
De Grecis, Nicola, 18, 26
De Vincenti, 177
Del Monte, Gaetano, 18, 23, 26
Delavigne, Casimir, 334; *Marino Faliero*, 238; *Le Paria*, 184
Delestre-Poirson, Charles-Gaspard, 128, 182, 188
Demetrio e Polibio (Rossini), 5–8, 13, 16, 17, 21, 28
D'Ennery, Adolphe-Philippe, 287
Dérivis, Prosper, 268, 286
Dessi, Daniela, 178
Deutekom, Cristina, 77, 314
Devia, Mariella, 349
Il Diluvio universale (The Great Flood: Donizetti), 188, 189–92, 275
Dom Sébastien, Roi de Portugal (Donizetti), 294, 297–300, 301, 305
Don Gregorio (Donizetti), 156; *see also L'Ajo nell'imbarazzo*
Don Pasquale (Donizetti), 19, 157, 179, 199, 237, 289–93, 294
Donizetti, Gaetano (1797–1848), 1, 2, 19, 24, 41, 54, 57–8, 137–306, 310, 313, 316, 333, 343, 353; birth in Bergamo (1797), 139; music studies, 140; engagement to Virginia Vasselli, 170; and marriage (1828), 180; Professor at Royal College of Music, Naples, 230; death of father, 245; death of mother, 248; and death of his wife, Virginia, 259; appointed Composer to Austrian Court (1842), 286, 301; illness (syphilis), 185, 259, 297, 301, 306; death (1848), 306
Donizetti, 'Pasha' Giuseppe (brother), 139
Donizetti, Sra *see* Vasselli
La Donna del lago (The Lady of the Lake: Rossini), 93–7, 98, 99, 100, 107, 117
Donzelli, Domenico, 50, 115, 118, 146, 206, 283, 337
Dorset Opera, 165, 283
Dorus-Gras, Julie, 268
dramma buffo see opera buffa
dramma giocoso, 11–13, 34–7, 69–72, 115–21
dramma semiserio see opera semiseria
dramma serio see opera seria
Dresden, 8, 14, 41, 94, 108, 156, 218, 263, 316, 320, 328; Italian Opera, 177
Dryden, John, *Don Sebastian*, 298
Le Duc d'Albe/Il Duca d'Alba (Donizetti), 184, 233, 268, 270–2, 273, 279, 288
Dumas *père*, Alexandre, *Charles VII chez ses Grands Vassaux*, 235; *Christine*, 342
Dupin, Jean-Henri, 201
Duponchel, Director of Paris Opéra, 132
Dupont, Alexis, 125
Duprez, Gilbert-Louis, 132, 218, 227, 240, 256, 268, 269, 276, 297
Duval, Alexandre, 221; *Le Menuisier de Livonie*, 144
Duvéyrier, Charles, 270, 271
Dvořák, Antonin, *Armida*, 77

Eckerlin, Fanny, 110, 142, 145
Eda-Pierre, Christiane, 316
Edinburgh, Edinburgh Festival, 129, 320
Eduardo e Cristina (Rossini), 92–3, 94, 99, 106
Egle ed Irene (Rossini), cantata, 58
Elder, Mark, 90
Eleanora di Gujenna (Donizetti), 228
Elisa da Fosco (Donizetti), 225
Élisabeth ou La Fille du Proscrit (Donizetti), 168; *see also Otto mesi in due ore*
Elisabeth of Bavaria, Empress, 117
Elisabetta (Donizetti), 168, 169; *see also Otto mesi in due ore*
Elisabetta al castello di Kenilworth (Elizabeth at Kenilworth

Castle: Donizetti), 169, 185–6, 188; *see also Il Castello di Kenilworth*

Elisabetta, regina d'Inghilterra (*Elizabeth, Queen of England*: Rossini), 13, 39, 46–9, 52, 58, 62, 76, 112; Overture, 48, 58

L'Elisir d'amore (*The Love Potion*: Donizetti), 157, 161, 179, 180, 209–13, 214, 222, 228, 251, 252, 282, 289, 291

Elizabeth II, Queen, 48

Elkins, Margreta, 305

Elvida (Donizetti), 162–3, 164

Emilia di Liverpool (Donizetti), 157–60, 161

English National Opera, 74

Enrico di Borgogna (Donizetti), 141–3

L'Equivoco stravagante (*The Absurd Misunderstanding*: Rossini), 11–13, 14, 15, 66; Overture, 13

L'Eremitaggio di Liverpool (*The Hermitage of Liverpool*: Donizetti), 158; *see also Emilia di Liverpool*

Ermione (Rossini), 89–92, 93; Overture, 90–1

Escudier, Léon, 301

L'Esule di Roma, or Il Proscritto (*The Roman Exile, or The Outlaw*: Donizetti), 164, 174–6, 177, 276

Etienne, Charles-Guillaume, 70

Étienne-Dérivis, Henri, 122

Euripides, *Andromache*, 90; *The Trojan Women*, 90

Eustorgia da Romano (Donizetti), 225

Fabbri, Flora, 149

Fabbrica, Isabella, 150

Fabritiis, Oliviero de, 232

Il Falegname di Livonia (*The Livonian Carpenter*: Donizetti), 143–4, 170

Farinelli, *Non precipitare i giudizi*, 9

farsa giocosa, 25–8

farse (one-act comic operas), 9, 13–15, 18–20, 25–8, 85–7, 149, 162, 172–4, 181–2, 187–9, 190, 200, 248–52

Fausta (Donizetti), 202–5, 208, 227; Overture, 203

La Favorite (*The Favourite*: Donizetti), 272, 276–9; Overture, 278

Federici, Camillo, *Matrimonio per lettere di cambio*, 9

Federici, Carlo, 47

Federici, Francesco, 1, 323

Fei, Orsola, 21

Ferdinand I, King, 102

Ferrara, 7, 30, 33, 34, 206, 225; Teatro Comunale, 16, 17

Ferrari, Benedetto, *Armida*, 77

Ferretti, Jacopo, 54, 69, 70, 105, 146, 152, 153, 156, 157, 166, 167, 216, 220–1, 222, 230, 231, 342

Ferro, Gabrielle, 314

Ferron, Elisabetta, 152, 160, 161

La Figlia del regimento see La Fille du régiment

La Fille du régiment (*The Daughter of the Regiment*: Donizetti), 181, 191, 269, 270, 273–5, 276, 290, 305; Overture, 274

Le Fils par hazard (Chazet and Ourry), 26

Fioravanti, Giuseppe, 1, 98, 105, 142, 147, 153, 158, 167, 251

Fioravanti, Valentino, 310

fioriture, 20, 75

Fissore, Enrico, 314

Florence, 19, 21, 88, 94, 106, 123, 225, 257, 271, 300, 310, 316, 329, 349; Maggio Musicale, 31, 77, 113, 129, 132, 298; Teatro Alfieri, 238; Teatro della Pergola, 214, 218, 219, 227–8, 325

Flores, Carlo Tebaldi, 345; *Beatrice di Tenda*, 345

Florian, Jean-Pierre-Claris, *Gonzalve de Cordove*, 146, 161

Florimo, Francesco, 313, 319, 323, 337, 342

Flotow, Friedrich von, 94

Una follia (Donizetti), 143

Fontana, Uranio, 168

Foppa, Giuseppe Maria, 14, 18, 26, 43, 44, 329

Forteguerri, Niccolò, *Ricciardetto*, 88

Il Fortunato inganno (*The Happy Deception*: Donizetti), 153–4, 155

Fracalini, Vincenzo, 92

Francesca di Foix (Donizetti), 200–1, 202, 207, 209

Franceschini, Marianna, 216

Francis I, Austrian Emperor, 112

Francis, Alun, 165, 186

Franz Josef, Emperor, 117

Fraschi, Giovanni, 16

Fraschini, Gaetano, 301, 302

Frazzi, Vito, 13

Frémont, Mlle, 122

Freni, Mirella, 345, 349

Frezzolini, Giuseppe, 166, 172, 177, 209

Il Fu ed il sarà (*What was and what will be*: Bellini), scenic cantata, 342

Funk, Friderike, 81

Il Furioso all'isola di San Domingo (*The Madman on the Island of San Domingo*: Donizetti), 207, 208, 214, 215–17, 218, 224

Fusconi, Giuseppe, 105, 142

Gabriella (Donizetti), 164–5

Gabriella di Vergy (Donizetti), 163–6, 280

Galli, Filippo, 14, 21, 34, 40, 50, 73, 101, 102, 194

Galli, Vincenzo, 167

Gallianis, Teresa, 73

Galli-Curci, Amelita, 334

Galzerani, Antonietta, 192

Garcia, Manuel, 46, 52, 55, 56; *Il Califfo di Bagdad*, 86

Garofolo, Luigi, 166

Gasdia, Cecilia, 175, 329, 345

Gasparri, Gaetano, 11, 12

Gavazzeni, Gianandrea, 195, 246

Gaveaux, Pierre, *L'Échelle de soie*, 18

Gayarré, Julian, 270

La Gazza ladra (*The Thieving Magpie*: Rossini), 37, 73–6, 84, 85, 112, 122; Overture, 74

La Gazzetta (*The Gazette*: Rossini), 22, 61–3, 64, 71, 82; Overture, 62–3, 71

Gedda, Nicolai, 2, 132, 334, 349, 352

Gemma di Vergy (Donizetti), 164, 231, 234–6, 237

Gencer, Leyla, 2, 48, 195, 204, 225, 232, 246, 260, 302, 338, 345

Generali, Pietro (composer), 323

Genero, Giambattista, 209

Genoa, 39, 106, 123, 124, 145, 178, 180, 227, 257, 287, 313, 314, 319; Teatro Carlo Felice, 177, 178, 190, 312, 313; Teatro Margherita, 190

Genoino, Giulio, 149

Gentili, Serafino, 34

George IV, King of England, 116

Ghent Royal Opera, 271

Gherardini, Giovanni, 73

Giacchini, Alessandro, 256, 342

Giacomini, Giuseppe, 203

Giaiotti, Bonaldo, 190

Gianni di Calais (Donizetti), 180–1, 182, 183, 275

Gianni di Parigi (Donizetti), 197–9, 209, 228

Gilardoni, Domenico, 167, 168, 169, 172, 174, 175, 177, 180, 181, 182, 183, 184, 187, 188, 190, 200, 201, 202, 203, 204, 312

Gioia-Tamburini, Marietta, 160, 161, 200

Giordani, Giuseppe, 78

Giordano, Giuseppe, 172

Giorgi-Belloc, Teresa, 14, 73

Giovanna I di Napoli (Donizetti), 225

Il Giovedì grasso (*Carnival Thursday*: Donizetti), 181–2

Giraldoni, Leone, 270

Giraud, Giovanni, *L'Ajo nell'imbarazzo*, 156

Giulini, Carlo Maria, 298

Gli Esiliati in Siberia (*The Exiles in Siberia*: Donizetti), 168; *see also Otto mesi in due ore*

Gluck, Christoph Willibald von, 91; *Armida*, 77; *Orfeo ed Euridice*, 33; *La rencontre imprévue*, 86

Glyndebourne Opera, 22, 129, 195, 349

Goethe, Johann Wolfgang von, 222; *Jerry und Bätely*, 251; *Tasso*, 221

Goldberg, Fanny, 301, 302

Goldoni, Carlo, *Il Matrimonio per concorso*, 62; *Tasso*, 221

Gossett, Philip, 91–2, 117–18

La Grâce de Dieu (D'Ennery and Lemoine), 287

Granchi, Almerinda, 259

grand opéra, 124, 125–7, 131–5, 267–72, 276–9, 297–300

Grassi, Cecilia, 181

Graz, 51, 94, 175, 295, 320

Graziani, Francesco, 116

Greater Miami Opera, 99

Grecis, Nicola de, 9

Grétry, André, 275

Grisi, Giuditta, 328, 338
Grisi, Giulia, 206, 237, 290, 337, 338, 347, 349
Grove's *Dictionary*, 30, 246
Gruberova, Edita, 260, 329, 349
Guarnaccia, 156
Guasco, Carlo, 293
Guerrini, Adriana, 320
Guglielmi, Giacomo, 69
Guglielmini, Giuseppe, 143
Guglielmo Vallace (Rossini), 132; *see also Guillaume Tell*
Gui, Vittorio, 35
Guillaume Tell (*William Tell*: Rossini), 10, 37, 54, 97, 101, 124, 128, 131–5, 195; Overture, 133

Halévy, Jacques, *La Reine de Chypre*, 294, 303
Handel, George Frideric, 13; *Israel in Egypt* (oratorio), 126; *Rinaldo*, 77
Harrow Opera Workshop, 173
Hartford College of Music, 21
Hasse, Johann, 141
Havana (Cuba), 203, 216, 235, 260
Hayashi, Yasuko, 190, 314
Haydn, Joseph, 121; *Armida*, 77; *The Seasons*, 12, 58
Heinefetter, Sabina, 209
Henry, Luigi, 254
Henry, M., 273
Hernani (Bellini's abandoned opera), 333, 335, 340, 350
Herodotus, 16
Hérold, Ferdinand, 88–9, 334
Hiller, Ferdinand, 7, 16, 17, 33
Hobhouse, John, 93
Hofer, or The Tell of the Tyrol (Rossini), 133; *see also Guillaume Tell*
Hoffmann, François Benoit, 105
Homer, *Iliad*, 90
Horne, Marilyn, 2, 31, 35, 95, 99, 124, 338, 345
Houston, 31, 195, 225; Grand Opera, 94–5
Hugo, Victor, *Hernani*, 333; *Lucrèce Borgia*, 224–5

Imelda de' Lambertazzi (Donizetti), 192–3, 194, 207
L'Inganno felice (*The Happy Stratagem*: Rossini), 13–15, 16, 17, 18, 26, 143
Inno reale (Royal Hymn: Donzinetti), 178
L'Ira d'Achille (*The Anger of Achilles*: Donizetti), 141, 142
Isabella Maria, Queen of Naples, 185–6
Isouard, Nicolas, *Cendrillon*, 70
The Israelites in Egypt or The Passage of the Red Sea (Rossini), 126
L'Italiana in Algeria (*The Italian Girl in Algiers*: Rossini), 34–7, 39, 41, 43; Overture, 36
Ivanhoe (Rossini), 122
Ivanoff, Nicola (singer), 238

Jawureck, Constance, 128
Jommelli, Niccolo, 62, 77, 320
Jonson, Ben, *Epicoene, or The Silent Woman*, 291
Jouy, Victor-Joseph-Etienne de, 125, 131, 161
Joyce, James, 132

Kabaivanska, Raina, 203
Karl der Kühne (Rossini), 132; *see also Guillaume Tell*
Kean, Edmund, 317
Kelston, Lucy, 316
Kenny, Yvonne, 186, 228
Kentish Opera Group (amateur), Orpington, 27
Kiri Te Kanawa, 94
Kobbé's *Complete Opera Book*, 113, 336
Kotzebue, August von, 148; *Die Deutschen Kleinstädter*, 145; *Emilia*, 157; *Der Graf von Burgund*, 142
Kraus, Alfredo, 2
Kurz, Selma, 241

Lablache, Federico, 253
Lablache, Luigi, 162, 163, 174, 181, 183, 188, 190, 214, 237, 290, 312, 313, 323, 347, 349
Lachner, Franz, *Catharina Cornaro, Königin von Cypern*, 294
Lacy, Michael Rophino, 126
Lanari, Alessandro, 210, 214, 218, 328
Lanari, Clementina, 9
Langridge, Philip, 170

Laroche, Enrichetta, 194
Latham-Koenig, Jan, 190
Lauretti, Ferdinando, 216, 220
Lauri-Volpi, Giacomo, 266
Lavigna, Vincenzo, 43
Layner, Giovanni, 16
Lazzari, Agostino, 64
Lee, Sophia, *The Recess, or A Tale of Other Times*, 47
Lefebvre-Faure, Caroline, 281
Lemoine, Gustave, 287
Leonora di Guzman (Donizetti), 277
Leopardi, Giacomo, 97
La Lettera anonima (*The Anonymous Letter*: Donizetti), 149–50
Leuven, Adolphe de, 168
Levasseur, Nicholas-Prosper, 116, 118, 125, 128, 131, 276, 297
Levys, Samuel, 348, 352
Lewis, Matthew G., *The Monk*, 262
Lhérie, Victor, 248
Die Liebesprobe (*The Love Test*: adaptation of Rossini's *La Pietra del paragone*), 22
Lillo, *Il Conte di Calais*, 293, 294
Lima (Peru), 283, 291, 295
Lind, Jenny, 274
Linda di Chamounix (Donizetti), 233, 285–9, 290, 294; Overture, 287
Lipparini, Caterina, 105, 167
Lisbon, 14, 19, 21, 24, 38, 51, 88, 94, 99, 102, 108, 146, 178, 203, 206, 231, 257, 260, 263, 280, 287, 295, 298, 320, 328, 329; Teatro Sao Carlos, 85, 86
Liverpool, 158
Livorno, 168, 195, 228
Lockroy, Edouard, *Un Duel sous le Cardinal de Richelieu*, 293, 294
Loewe, Sophie, 283
Loewenberg, Alfred, *Annals of Opera*, 30, 117
London, 14, 30, 35, 39, 116–17, 121, 166, 174, 203, 206, 216, 218, 221, 225, 235, 237, 246, 253, 260, 280, 295, 316, 333, 344, 348; Camden Festival, 94, 186; Camden Town Hall, 238; Collegiate Theatre, 173, 186, 200, 221; Coronet Theatre, Notting Hill Gate, 349; Covent Garden, Royal Opera House, 74, 83, 95, 118, 126, 133, 158, 169, 195, 241, 265, 277, 295, 329, 331, 334, 338, 349; Guildhall School of Music, 118, 253; Henry Wood Hall, 305; Her Majesty's Theatre, 74, 94, 106, 124, 133, 156, 168, 169, 195, 225, 241, 274, 287, 291, 316; His Majesty's Theatre, 35, 41, 56, 64, 113, 129, 320, 338, 349; King's Theatre, 48, 71, 83, 88, 108, 348; Little Theatre (marionettes), 24; Lyceum Theatre, 211, 216, 249, 251; Opera Club, 282; Princess's Theatre, 64; Queen Elizabeth Hall, 80, 90, 124, 175, 228, 257, 263, 283, 295, 314; Rossini's apartment at, 90 Regent Street, 116; Royal Academy of Music, 246; Royal Festival Hall, 302; Sadler's Wells Theatre, 9, 19, 246; St James's Theatre, 129; St Pancras Town Hall, 21, 64, 232, 287; Scala Theatre, 277; Surrey Theatre, 274; Theatre Royal, Drury Lane, 16, 41, 94, 133, 277, 317, 334, 348
Long Island Opera Society, 283
Lorenzani, Brigida, 162
Lortzing, Gustav Albert, *Zar und Zimmermann*, 170
Los Angeles, 31, 349
Lotti della Santa, Marcellina, 164
Loyselet, Agnese, 50, 155
Loyselet, Elisabetta, 52
Luca, Giuseppe de, 27
Lucia di Lammermoor (Donizetti), 2, 94, 148, 158, 179, 196, 197, 229, 231, 240–5, 245, 246, 247, 254, 256, 260, 288
Lucrezia Borgia (Donizetti), 197, 223–7, 228, 296
Lugano, 192, 251, 260
Lugo di Romagna, 173, 188
Lully, Giovanni Battista, *Armida*, 77
Lumley, Benjamin, 168
Luzio, Gennaro, 172, 188, 201

McCormack, John, 334
Macerata, 24, 27
Madrid, 14, 26, 51, 88, 90, 175, 178, 186, 203, 206, 218, 263, 277, 280, 314, 316, 320, 349
Maffei, Andrea, 230

Maffei-Festa, Francesca, 40
The Maid of Judah (Rossini), 126
Malanotte-Montresor, Adelaide, 29, 32
Malaperta, Silvio, *Il filtro*, 211
Malibran, Maria, 229, 231, 352
Malta, 94, 257, 260, 263, 280, 283, 295
Manfredini-Guarmani, Elisabetta, 16, 29, 43, 80
Mantua, Teatro Vecchio, 145
Manzi, Antonio, 309
Manzi, Maria, 46, 61, 64, 81, 88, 89, 94
Manzocchi, Almerinda, 253
Maometto II (Rossini), 100–4, 105, 112, 122, 123, 124, 177; *see also La Siège de Corinthe*
Marcello, Benedetto, 320; 'Estro poetico-armonico', 124
Marchesi, Teresa, 29
Marchionni, Luigi, 246; *Edoardo III, ossia L'Assedio di Calais*, 254; *La Figlia dell'esiliato*, 168; *Il Proscritto romano, ossia Il Leone del Caucaso*, 174–5
Marcionni, Stanislao, 319
Marcolini, Marietta, 12, 16, 21, 34, 43
Marenco, Carlo, *Pia de' Tolomei*, 257
Margherita, Queen, 271
Mari, Luigi, 38
Maria Carolina, Duchesse de Berry, 62
Maria Carolina, Empress of Austria, 286
Maria Clementina, Queen, 163
Maria Cristina, Queen of Naples, 230
Maria de Rudenz (Donizetti), 262–4, 265, 267
Maria di Rohan (Donizetti), 293–7, 298, 301
Maria Padilla (Donizetti), 281, 283–5, 286
Maria Stuarda (Donizetti), 195, 229–34, 245, 288; Overture, 232
Maria Theresa, 286
Mariani, Luciano, 224, 332
Mariani, Teresa, 69
Marini, Girolamo, 280
Marini, Ignazio, 198, 229, 234, 279
Marie-Louise, Grand Duchess, 324
Marié de l'Isle, Mécène, 273
Marino Faliero (Donizetti), 231, 234, 236–9, 240, 250, 261
Marmontel, Jean-François, *Bélisaire*, 246
Marras, Giacinto, 309
Marrast, Armand, 131, 132
Marschner, Heinrich August, 94
Marseilles, 225, 283
Martina Franca, 8, 295
Martinelli, Gaspare, 85
Martinelli, Luigi, 143
Martini, Padre, 6
I Martiri (Donizetti), 265; *see also Poliuto*
Les Martyrs (*The Martyrs*: Donizetti), 265, 266, 267–9, 270, 273, 276; *see also Poliuto*
Mascagni, Pietro, *Parisina*, 219
Massol, Jean-Étienne, 268, 297
Mathilde de Morwel (French play), 105
Matilde di Shabran (Rossini), 101, 104–7, 108, 112; Overture, 106
Mattei, Padre Stanislao, 6, 140
Maturin, Charles Robert, *Bertram*, 316–17
Mayr, Giovanni Simone (Johann Simon), 1, 140, 144, 146, 151, 160–1, 163, 164, 170, 177, 185, 186, 210, 221, 268, 276; *Alfredo il Grande*, 152; *Alonso e Cora*, 140; *Atalia*, 124; *Che originali!*, 161; *Ginevra di Scozia*, 140; *Saffo*, 140
Mazzanti, 146
Mazzarelli, Rosina, 256
Mazzolà, Caterino, 41
Mazzucato, Alberto, *Luigi V, Re di Francia*, 206
Méhul, Etienne Nicolas, *Euphrosine et Coradin*, 105
Melas, Teresa, 153, 158
Melba, Nellie, 241
Melbourne, 211, 287, 291
Mélesville, Anne-Honoré-Joseph, 170, 251
Meloni, Alessandro, 256
Mendelssohn, Felix, 202–3
Mercadante, Saverio, 1, 224, 302, 316, 323, 343; *Il Conte d'Essex*, 260; *Il Montanaro*, 316
Mercier-Dupaty, Emanuel, 200
Merelli, Bartolomeo, 141, 142, 143, 144, 145, 152, 161, 198, 281, 286, 313, 319; *Cenni biografici*, 145

Méric-Lalande, Henriette, 162, 163, 224, 226–7, 312, 313, 316, 319, 323
Merle, Jean-Toussaint, 170
Merola, Giuseppina, 227
Merritt, Chris, 64, 99
Messa di Gloria (Rossini), 101, 124
Metastasio, Pietro, *Demetrio*, 6; *Olimpiade*, 141
Metternich, Prince, 112, 286
Mexico City, 216, 235, 260, 295
Meyerbeer, Giacomo, 99, 237, 316; *L'Esule di Granata*, 161
Miami, Dade County Auditorium, 99
Migliorucci, *Paolo e Virginia*, 50
Milan, 19, 21, 26, 39, 70, 102, 132, 144, 168, 171, 180, 225, 230, 231, 245, 249, 257, 287, 291, 313, 328; Piccola Scala, 22, 182; Teatro alla Scala, 21, 23, 32, 38, 40, 41, 43, 73, 74, 76, 86, 88, 95, 98–9, 100, 113, 118, 124, 132, 142, 150–1, 156, 161, 170, 175, 195, 198, 199, 203, 205, 206, 210, 214, 224, 226, 229, 231, 234–5, 237, 238, 266, 277, 281, 283, 284, 286, 287, 293, 313, 316, 319, 328, 329, 334, 337, 338, 343, 344, 345, 349; Teatro Canobbiana, 172, 209, 210; Teatro Carcano, 194–5, 332, 333; Teatro Santa Radegonda, 168
Milanov, Zinka, 338
Miles, Bernard, 158
Miller, Jonathan, 90
Milnes, Sherrill, 243
Minnesota Opera, 77
Modena, 22
Moïse et Pharaon (*Moses and Pharaoh*: Rossini), 83, 125–7, 128, 131; *see also Mosè in Egitto*
Molière (Jean-Baptiste Poquelin), *École des femmes*, 57; *Monsieur de Pourceaugnac*, 182
Mombelli, Domenico, 5, 6, 7
Mombelli, Ester, 5, 6, 115, 118, 146, 155
Mombelli, Marianna, 5, 6
Mombelli, Vincenza Viganò, 5, 6–7
Moncada, Carlo, 105, 147
Monelli, Raffaele, 14, 18
Monelli, Savino, 73, 80, 150, 155
Monsigny, Pierre-Alexandre, *Aline, reine de Golconde*, 177
Monte, Toti dal, 241, 287, 334
Monte Carlo, 260
Monteverdi, Claudio, *Il Combattimento di Tancredi e Clorinda*, 30
Monticelli, 147
Moore, Thomas, *Loves of the Angels*, 190
Morandi, Giovanni, 9
Morandi, Rosa, 9, 93, 150
Morgan, Lady Sydney, 64–5
Mori, Mlle, 125, 128, 131
Moriani, Napoleone, 262, 286
Morlacchi, Francesco, 1, 177; *Il Colombo*, 177; *Gianni di Parigi*, 199
Mosca, Luigi, 156; *L'Italiana in Algeri*, 35
Mosè e Faraone see Moïse et Pharaon
Mosè in Egitto (*Moses in Egypt*: Rossini), 17, 81–4, 85, 88, 122, 125, 126, 127, 191; *see also Moïse et Pharaon*
Il Mosè nuovo (Rossini), 83
Mozart, Wolfgang Amadeus, 6, 8, 15, 28, 37; *La Clemenza di Tito*, 109; *Don Giovanni*, 114, 226; *Die Entführung aus dem Serail*, 86; Jupiter Symphony, 42; *Le Nozze di Figaro* (*The Marriage of Figaro*), 57, 59, 130
Munich, 8, 14, 16, 21, 35, 51, 74, 88, 94, 173, 246
Muratori, Anna Maria, 80
Murray, Doreen, 158
Mussorgsky, Modeste Petrovich, *Boris Godunov*, 75
Muti, Riccardo, 95
Mysliveček, Josef, 77

Nagher, Carolina, 18, 23, 26
Naples, 14, 21, 39, 47, 48, 61, 82, 88, 92, 101–2, 106, 123, 124, 156, 161, 170, 175, 188, 199, 225, 228, 231, 246, 248, 249, 254, 257, 271, 287, 295, 313, 328, 342, 344; cholera epidemic (1836–7), 248, 253, 257, 259; Conservatorium, 184, 240, 259; Palazzo Cassano, 282; Real Collegio di Musica, 230, 309, 310; Teatro dei Fiorentini, 61, 62; Teatro del Fondo, 47, 62, 64, 149, 164, 168, 170, 180, 181, 182, 187, 188, 189, 200, 201; Teatro Nuovo, 147, 148, 149, 153–4, 158, 159, 166, 167, 168, 169, 172, 248, 249, 251; Teatro San Carlo, 46, 47,

48, 61, 76, 81, 82, 83, 88, 89, 90, 93, 94, 101, 108, 148, 152, 153, 162–3, 164, 165, 168, 174, 175, 180, 183, 184, 185, 190, 192, 198, 200, 202, 203, 214, 229, 230, 234, 235, 240–1, 253, 259, 260, 265, 301–2, 310, 312, 316
Nasolini, Sebastiano, 323
Naumann, Johann Gottlieb, 77
Ne m'oubliez pas (*Do Not Forget Me*: Donizetti), 304–6
Neblett, Carol, 320
Negrini, Vincenzo, 206, 337
New Brunswick, New Jersey, Rutgers University, 246
New Orleans, 108, 195, 225, 241, 274, 277, 291, 344; St Charles Theatre, 113, 218
New York, 9, 14, 30, 35, 41, 56, 64, 74, 83, 93, 94, 106, 113, 129, 133, 195, 211, 216, 218, 225, 232, 235, 238, 241, 246, 249, 251, 260, 265, 274, 277, 291, 295, 298, 316, 329, 333–4, 338, 344, 345, 349; Carnegie Hall, 219, 235, 260, 271, 302, 320, 329, 345; City Opera, 195, 260; Helen Carey Playhouse, Brooklyn Academy of Music, 216; Italian Opera House, 124; Mannes College, 188; Masonic Hall, 83; Metropolitan Opera, 27, 274, 287, 334, 349; Palmo's Opera House, 287; Park Theatre, 71, 320; Town Hall, 64; Vineyard Opera Shop, 199
Niccola III of Ferrara, 219
Nicelli, 156
Nicolai, Karl Otto, 94
Nicolini, Giuseppe, *Abenamet e Zoraide* 146
Ninetta, or The Maid of Palaiseau (Rossini), 74; *see also La Gazza ladra*
Nizza de Grenade (Donizetti), 225
Noja, Duke of, 310
La Nonne Sanglante (Anicet-Bourgeois, Cuvelier and Mallian), 262
Norma (Bellini), 2, 123, 197, 285, 312, 315, 326, 327, 333, 336–41, 342, 343, 348, 353; Overture, 339
Notti d'estate a Posilippo (Donizetti), 250
Nourrit, Adolphe, 122, 125, 128, 131, 132, 265
Nourrit, Louis, 122
Novaro, Michele, 293
Nozzari, Andrea, 46, 64, 76, 81, 88, 89, 94, 101, 152
Le Nozze in villa (*The Wedding in the Villa*: Donizetti), 144–5, 169

L'Occasione fa il ladro (*Opportunity Makes the Thief*: Rossini), 23–5, 29, 58
Odessa, 260, 283
Offenbach, Jacques, 26–7, 130, 275
L'Olimpiade (Donizetti), 142
Oliver, Alexander, 305
Olivieri, Lodovico, 5, 6
Olivo e Pasquale (Donizetti), 166–7, 168
Omaha (Nebraska), 90; Joslyn Arts Museum, 284
Ongaro, Federico dall', 293
opera buffa, or *dramma buffo*, 8–11, 20, 21, 22, 27, 40–3, 52–63, 86, 111, 143–5, 153–7, 166–7, 169–71, 201–2, 274, 275, 289–93
opéra comique, 128–30, 197–9, 209–13, 273–5, 281–2, 304–6
opera giocosa, 250–2
Opera North, 74
Opera Omaha, 284
Opera Rara, 173, 186, 200, 206, 221, 228, 238, 253, 263, 283
opera romantica, 167–9
opera semiseria, or *dramma semiserio*, 50–2, 74, 141–3, 150–1, 157–60, 176–8, 200–1, 215–17, 220–3, 285–9, 309–12, 332–6
opera seria, or *dramma serio*, 5–8, 15–18, 26, 29–34, 38–40, 43–5, 76–81, 87–92, 100–4, 111, 145–8, 152–3, 160–5, 174–6, 183–7, 192–7, 202–8, 213–15, 218–20, 223–48, 252–67, 279–81, 283–5, 293–7, 300–4, 315–27, 336–53
Oporto, 21, 231
Orlandi, Elisa, 194, 216
Orlandini, Antonio, 152
O'Sullivan, John, 132
Otello (Rossini), 42, 52, 54, 63–8, 116, 117, 231
Otter, Anne Sofie von, 329, 331
Otto mese in due ore (*Eight Months in Two Hours*: Donizetti), 164, 167–9, 170, 196
Ourry, E.-T. Maurice, 26
Ovid, *Metamorphoses*, 140, 141
Oxford Festival, Holywell Music Room, 86

Pace, Giovanni, 61
Pacini, Antonio, 122
Pacini, Giovanni, 1, 105, 122–3, 323, 328, 338; *Cesare in Egitto*, 146; *Il Corsaro*, 338; *Il Falegname di Livonia*, 144; *La Gioventù di Enrico V*, 105; *Ivanhoe*, 123; *La Sacerdotessa d'Irminsul*, 338
Pacini, Luigi, 23, 40, 100
Padua, 9, 90, 144
Paganini, Niccolò, 106
Pagliughi, Lina, 48
Paisiello, Giovanni, 1, 15; *Il Barbiere di Siviglia*, 54–5, 57; *L'Inganno felice*, 14
Palacio, Ernesto, 175
Palermo, 48, 64, 161, 200, 235–6, 251, 287, 316, 328, 342, 344, 349; Conservatorium, 160; Teatro Carolino, 160, 162; Teatro Massimo, 329, 345
Pallavicino, Carlo, 77
Palomba, Giuseppe, 14, 61, 62, 82
Pannain, Guido, 15
Paolina e Poliuto (Donizetti), 266
Paolina e Severo (Donizetti), 265; *see also Poliuto*
Il Paria (*The Outcast*: Donizetti), 164, 183–4, 186, 233, 239, 272
Paris, 14, 21, 24, 26, 27, 35, 51, 88, 94, 101, 102, 105, 116, 117, 123, 126, 128, 144, 146, 148, 164, 168, 170, 184, 188, 190, 195, 199, 200, 201, 218, 224, 225, 231, 240, 244, 256, 260, 262, 265, 280, 303, 305, 316; Bellini's apartment in Boulevard des Italiens, 348; Comédie-Française, 57; Conservatoire, 117, 145; Opéra, 83, 122, 123, 125, 126, 128, 129, 131, 132, 135, 161, 211, 265, 268–9, 270–1, 276–7, 294, 297, 298, 301, 334; Opéra-Comique, 57, 70, 251, 269, 270, 273–4, 281–2, 305; Salle Pleyel, 302; Théâtre de l'Odéon, 122, 337; Théâtre de la Renaissance, 276; Théâtre Favart, 317; Théâtre-Italien, 115, 117, 118, 119, 121, 122, 123, 180, 230, 237, 268, 289, 290, 294, 298, 347, 348
Parisina (Donizetti), 207, 218–20, 263; Overture, 219
Parlamagni, Annetta, 105
Parlamagni, Antonio, 21, 105
Parma, 123, 219, 295, 302, 304, 324–5; Teatro Ducale (now Teatro Regio), 323, 325
Pasini, Ignazio, 245
Pasta, Giuditta, 115, 118, 194, 206, 332–3, 337, 339–40, 342–3, 344, 345, 348
Pavarotti, Luciano, 132, 329, 334, 352
Pavesi, Stefano, *Agatina, o La virtù premiata*, 70; *Edoardo e Cristina*, 92; *Ser Marcantonio*, 12, 19, 290, 291
I Pazzi per progetto (*Lunatics by Design*: Donizetti), 157, 187–9, 190
Péchés de vieillesse (*Sins of Old Age*: Rossini), 135
Pedrazzi, Francesco, 224, 229
Pellegrini, Felice, 61, 116, 118
Pepoli, Alessandro, *Anna Bolena*, 195
Pepoli, Count Carlo, 347, 348, 350
Pergolesi, Giovanni Battista, 141, 320
Perrault, Charles, *Les contes de ma Mère l'Oye* (*Mother Goose Tales*), 70, 71
Persiani, Giuseppe, *Costantino in Arles*, 328
Perucchini, Giovanni Battista, 333
Perugia, 125, 126
Pesaro, 5, 6, 22, 24, 64, 85, 94; Fondazione Rossini, 119; Liceo, 118; Rossini Festival, 14, 88, 90, 99, 102, 113, 118
Petite Messe Solennelle (Rossini), 135
Petrosellini, Giuseppe, *Il Barbiere di Siviglia*, 54
Philadelphia, 64, 74, 216, 225, 246, 249, 251, 316, 329, 338, 349; Grand Opera, 329
Philippo, Ans, 170
Philopera Circle, 64
Pia de' Tolomei (Donizetti), 248, 253, 256–8, 259, 265, 278
I Piccioli virtuosi ambulante (assembled Mayr), 144
La Pietra del paragone (*The Touchstone*: Rossini), 13, 20–23, 24, 32, 38, 58, 63
Pietro l'Eremita (*Peter the Hermit*: Rossini), 83; see also *Mosè in Egitto*
Il Pigmalione (Donizetti), 24, 139–41, 142, 188
Pilotti, 156
Pindemonte, Ippolito, *Enrico VIII*, 195
Pinotti, Elisabetta, 80
Pinza, Ezio, 27

Il Pirata (*The Pirate*: Bellini), 312, 313, 315–18, 319, 320, 322, 328, 337, 341, 348; Overture, 317

Pisaroni, Rosmunda, 88, 89, 93–4

Pixérécourt, René-Charles-Guilbert de, *La Cisterne*, 151; *La Fille de l'exile, ou Huit mois en deux heures*, 168

Pizzochero, Carlo, 150

Place, Antoine de la, 128

Planard, François-Antoine-Eugène de, *L'Échelle de soie*, 18

Planché, James Robinson, 133

Plessis, Christian de, 305

Poggi, Antonio, 220, 256

Poggioli, Carlo, 150

Poliuto (Donizetti), 164, 264–7, 268, 269, 273; Overture, 266

Pons, Lily, 241, 274, 287, 334

Ponselle, Rosa, 338

Pontiggia, Teodolinda, 26

Porto, Carlo, 218, 227, 240

Portogallo, *L'Oro non compra amore*, 12

Porugini, Leonardo, 309

Pozzi, Gaetano, 40

Prague, 51, 77, 108, 206, 295, 320

Préviati, Fabio, 309

Prévost, Alex, 122

Prévost, Ferdinand, 122, 125, 131, 297

Price, Janet, 186

Pritchard, John, 158

Prividalli, Luigi, 23, 24

I Provinciali, ossia Le Nozze in villa (Donizetti), 145

Puglieschi, Giovanni, 80, 155

I Puritani (*The Puritans*: Bellini), 237, 318, 347–53

Pushkin, Aleksandr, *Boris Godunov*, 75

Puzone, Giuseppe, 165

Puzzi-Tosi, Giacinta, 229

Racine, Jean, *Andromaque*, 90, 91

Radiciotti, biography of Rossini by, 37, 50, 77, 80

Raffanelli, Luigi, 9, 14, 26

Raffi, Adelaide, 143

Raineri-Marini, Antonietta, 198

Rambaldi, Gaetano, 105, 146

Ravaglia, Luigi, 85

Ravenna, 178, 266

recitativo secco, 10, 20, 42, 83, 171, 189, 222, 250, 274, 310, 314

La Regina di Cipro (*The Queen of Cyprus*: Donizetti), 294, 301; *see also Caterina Cornaro*

Reina, Domenico, 229, 234, 319

Remolini, Domenico, 9

Remorini, Raniero, 50, 81

Rennert, Gunther, 22

Revival Opera Company, 277

Ricci, Edvige, 174

Ricci, Federico, 1; *Un Duello sotto Richelieu*, 293, 294

Ricci, Luigi, 1

Ricci, Tommaso, 9

Ricciardo e Zoraide (Rossini), 87–9, 90, 92, 99, 106, 107, 112; Overture, 88

Ricciarelli, Katia, 99, 175, 225, 260, 263, 325, 329

Ricordi, Giovanni, publisher, 13, 241, 245, 253, 290

Righetti-Giorgi, Geltrude, 51, 52, 69

Rinaudo, Mario, 323

Ringhieri, Padre Francesco, *L'Osiride*, 82

Ringhini, Francesco, *Il Diluvio*, 190

La Rinnegata (Donizetti), 225

Rio de Janeiro, 156, 218, 221, 249, 263, 283, 291

Rita (Donizetti), 281–2, 283

Roberto Devereux (Donizetti), 195, 259–62, 268; Overture, 261

Rodolfo di Sterlinga (Rossini), 133; *see also Guillaume Tell*

Romanelli, Gian Francesco, 38

Romanelli, Luigi, 21, 22, 146

Romani, Felice, 38, 40, 41, 86, 98, 99, 144, 150, 151, 161, 177–8, 194, 197, 199, 205, 206, 209, 210, 211, 213, 218, 219, 224, 227, 228, 230, 234, 260, 279, 280, 312, 313, 315, 316–17, 319, 320, 322, 323, 324, 325, 328, 329, 332, 333, 334, 336, 337, 338, 342, 343, 344, 345

Romani, Pietro, 60

La Romanziera e l'uomo nero (*The Lady Novelist and The Man in Black*: Donizetti), 184, 200, 201–2, 209

Rome, 7, 14, 19, 21, 31, 35, 39, 41, 47, 63, 64, 69–70, 73, 86, 126, 133, 147, 170, 178, 188, 199, 225, 249, 260, 265, 266, 295, 316, 320, 349; Piccolo Teatro dell' Opera Comica, 19; Santa Cecilia Library, 117; Teatro Apollo, 105, 106, 270, 271, 279, 280, 294; Teatro Argentina, 52, 53, 54, 56, 70, 80, 97, 145, 146, 155, 160, 257; Teatro dell' Opera, 90, 108, 203; Teatro Valle, 5, 7, 8, 50, 53, 69, 70, 71, 155, 156, 157, 166, 214, 216, 220, 221, 222, 314; Terme di Caracalla, 266

Ronconi, Giorgio, 216, 220, 248, 256, 262, 283, 293

Ronzi de Begnis, Giuseppina, 202, 214, 229, 230, 231, 234, 259

Roocroft, Amanda, 329

Rosich, Paolo, 12, 34

Rosini, Giovanni, 221

Rosmonda d'Inghilterra (Donizetti), 227–9, 243

Rossi, Anafesto, 265

Rossi, Caterina, 69

Rossi, Gaetano, 8, 9, 10, 29–30, 111, 112, 184, 283, 284, 285, 286, 287, 319

Rossi, Marianna, 43

Rossignoli, Paolo, 21

Rossi-Lemeni, Nicola, 195

Rossini, Anna (*née* Guidarini: mother), 5–6

Rossini, Gioachino (1792–1868), 1, 2, 3–135, 143, 148, 153, 159, 171, 175, 177, 178, 198, 230, 284, 285, 286, 290, 291, 310, 311, 316, 319–20, 323, 337, 348, 353; birth in Pesaro (1792), 5–6; studies at Liceo Musicale, Bologna, 6; musical directorship in Naples (1815), 47; directorship of Théâtre-Italien, Paris (1824), 117, 122; death of mother (1827), 128; retirement from opera-writing, 135

Rossini, Giuseppe Antonio (father), 5–6

Rota, Anna Maria, 329

Roti, Carlo, *Biana e Fernando alla tomba di Carlo IV*, 312

Rotellini, Luigi, 309

Rousseau, Jean-Jacques, *Pygmalion*, 139, 140

Rovere, Agostino, 198, 286

Royal Mancester College of Music, 329

Royer, Alphonse, 276, 277

Rubini, Giovanni Battista, 149,162, 163, 180, 181, 182, 183, 194, 198, 237, 238, 312, 313, 316, 332, 333, 347, 349, 352

Rubini, Serafina, 177

Rubio, Consuelo, 345

Ruffini, Agostino, 236, 237

Ruffini, Giovanni, 237, 289, 290, 291

Sacchèro, Giacomo, 294, 301, 303

Sacchini, Antonio Maria Gasparo, 77

Saint-Just, Claude Godard d'Aucour de, 86

St Louis, Missouri, Opera Theatre, 118

St Petersburg, 24, 54, 70, 74, 94, 132, 178, 195, 216, 295; Imperial Opera, 70

Saintine, Joseph-Xavier-Boniface, 348, 350

Sala, Adelaide, 50

Salatino, Pietro, 213, 214, 231

Salernitano, Masuccio, 329

Salieri, Antonio, *Angiolina*, 291; *Armida*, 77

Salins-les-Bains, 117

Salsa *see* Berio di Salsa

Saluzzo-Roero, Diodata, *Il Castello di Binasco*, 345

Salvatori, Celestino, 170, 245

Salvi, Lorenzo, 190, 198, 216, 251, 279

Salvi, Matteo, 271, 272

Salzburg Festival (1992), 31

Samoiloff, Countess, 338

San Francisco, 31, 195; Opera House, 102, 232; Opera Theater, 173; War Memorial Opera House, 90

Sancia di Castiglia (Donizetti), 213–15, 216, 228, 231

Santley, Sir Charles, 223

Santolini, Diomilla, 214

Santunione, Orianna, 139

Savastano, Antonio, 314

Savinelli, Anna, 16, 17

Savinelli, Francesco, 16

Savona, 16, 44, 45, 216, 221

Sbigoli, Americo, 146

La Scala di seta (*The Silken Ladder*: Rossini), 18–20, 26, 27; Overture, 19

Scatizzi, Stefano, *Emilia di Laverpaut*, 157
Schaap, Jan, 170
Schenk, Eduard von, *Belisarius*, 246
Schiassetti, Adelaide, 115
Schiller, Friedrich, *Maria Stuart*, 230, 232; *Wilhelm Tell*, 131–2
Schipa, Tito, 334
Schippers, Thomas, 124, 271
Schmidt, Giovanni Federico, 46, 47, 76, 80, 92, 152, 162–3
Schütz-Oldosi, Amalia, 248
Scimone, Claudio, 108, 109
Scott, Sir Walter, *The Bride of Lammermoor*, 241–2; *Ivanhoe*, 122, 126; *Kenilworth*, 47, 185; *The Lady of the Lake*, 94, 95, 97; *Old Mortality*, 349–50
Scotto, Renata, 195, 295, 320, 329, 334, 338
Scribe, Eugène, 128, 211, 251, 268, 270, 271, 277, 297, 298, 334; *L'Homme noir*, 201; *Leicester, ou Le Château de Kenilworth*, 185; *Le Nouveau Pourceaugnac*, 182; *La Sonnambule*, 334; *Une Visite à Bedlam*, 188
Scudellari-Cosselli, Anna, 166
Sedaine, Michel-Jean, 177–8
Semiramide (Rossini), 85, 86, 110–14, 116, 122, 126, 189, 284; Overture, 113
Serafin, Tullio, 27, 31, 334
Serassi, Antonio, 221
Serda, Émile, 268
Serra, Luciana, 349
Serrao, Paolo, 165
Serre, Anna del, 227, 229, 230, 231, 342
Servoli, 167
Sestini, Bartolomeo, *Pia de 'Tolomei*, 257
Seydelmann, Franz, *Il Turco in Italia*, 41
Sgricci, *Imelda*, 192
Shakespeare, William, 329; *Henry V*, 105; *Othello*, 64, 65, 324
Shaw, George Bernard, *Major Barbara*, 243
Shelley, Patrick, 165
Sherborne School, Dorset, 165, 283
Le Siège de Corinthe (*The Siege of Corinth*: Rossini), 102, 122–5, 126, 131, 320, 337; Overture, 124; *see also Maometto II*
Siena, 13, 86, 90, 173, 182; Teatro dei Rinnovati, 216, 218, 257
Sigismondo (Rossini), 42, 43–5, 46, 51, 58, 65, 87
Il Signor Bruschino (*Mr Bruschino*: Rossini), 25–8, 42, 58
Sills, Beverly, 2, 124, 195, 225, 232, 260, 329, 349
Silvestri, Alessandro, 270
Simionato, Giulietta, 2, 31, 35, 113, 195, 329, 338
Sinigaglia, 19, 257, 328
Sivelli, Carolina, 29
Slorach, Marie, 165
Sografi, Antonio Simone, 139, 140; *Le Convenienze teatrali*, 172; *Le Inconvenienze teatrali*, 173; *Olivo e Pasquale*, 166; *Il più bel giorno della Westfalia*, 166
sonate a quattro (Rossini), 6
La Sonnambula (*The Sleepwalker*: Bellini), 332–6, 337, 348, 353
La Sonnambule (ballet), 334
La Sonnette de Nuit (Brunswick, Troin and Lhérie), 248
Sorrentini, Luigia, 38
Soumet, Alexandre, 122, 123; *Norma, ou L'Infanticide*, 123, 337, 338
Spada, Filippo, 85
Spada, Luigi, 23
Sparano, Francesco, 61
Spech, Adelina, 220
Sperduti, Gabriele, *Imelda*, 192
Spiaggi, Domenico, 234
Spiegl, Fritz, 158
Spoleto, 144, 216; Teatro Nuovo (Spoleto Festival), 271
Spontini, Gasparo Luigi Pacifico, 1; *Fernando Cortez*, 101; *La Vestale*, 58
Stabat Mater (Rossini), 135, 286, 290
Stade, Frederica von, 94–5
Staël, Mme de, *Corinne, ou l'Italie*, 118
Steibelt, Daniel, *Cendrillon*, 70
Stendhal (Henri Beyle), *Life of Rossini*, 7, 8, 12, 20, 22, 30–1, 34, 39, 64, 78, 80, 82–3, 91, 98, 100, 104, 107, 109, 113, 131
Sterbini, Cesare, 50–1, 52, 54

Stich-Randall, Teresa, 31
Stignani, Ebe, 338
Stolz, Rosina, 276, 297
Stony Brook, NY, 283
La Straniera (*The Stranger*: Bellini), 312, 318–22, 323, 337, 341
Strauss, Richard, 35, 107; *Elektra*, 27; *Die schweigsame Frau*, 291
Strepponi, Giuseppina (later Sra Verdi), 257, 279, 280
Sullivan, Sir Arthur, *Trial by Jury*, 336
Supervia, Conchita, 35
Sutherland, Joan, 2, 113, 158, 195, 204, 225, 227, 232, 241, 243, 274, 334, 338, 345, 349
Swarthout, Gladys, 338
Sydney, 225, 274

Taccani, Elisa, 332
Tacchinardi-Persiani, Fanny, 227, 240, 243, 256, 288
Tacci, Nicola, 18
Taddei, Giuseppe, 246
Tadolini, Eugenia, 265, 286, 293
Tamburini, Antonio, 150, 155, 160, 177, 180, 192, 200, 201, 202, 237, 290, 312, 313, 316, 319, 347, 349
Tancredi (Rossini), 26, 29–34, 39, 62, 122, 284
Tarantini, Leopoldo, 250
Tasso, Torquato, 221–2; *Gerusalemme liberata*, 30, 76, 221–2, 223
Tati, Filippo, 180
Teatro Comunale Chiabrera, 44
Tebaldi, Renata, 123–4
Tellini, Ines Alfani, 329
terzettone, 103
Têtes Rondes et Cavaliers (Ancelot and Saintine), 348, 350
Tetrazzini, Luisa, 241, 334
Todràn, Pietro, 29
Toldi, Adelaide, 251
Tokatyan, Armand, 27
Tomicich, Aurio, 309
Torquato Tasso (Donizetti), 184, 197, 220–3, 224
Torri, Alberto, 146
Torrigiani, Luigi, *Cesare in Egitto*, 323
Torvaldo e Dorliska (Rossini), 50–2, 53, 54, 63, 67; Overture, 52
Tosi, Adelaide, 174, 183, 185, 312, 313
Tottola, Andrea Leone, 61, 62, 81, 82, 86, 89, 90, 92, 93, 94, 95, 108, 109, 125, 147, 148, 152, 153, 154, 157, 163, 182, 185, 192, 203, 309, 310
Toye, Francis, *Rossini*, 51, 77, 78, 86, 91, 124
travesti roles, 99, 123, 124, 164, 166, 206, 288, 295, 329
Treviso, 44, 313
Trezzini, Carlo, 323
Trieste, 9, 13, 24, 206, 216, 225, 287, 328
Troin, Mathieu-Barthélemy, 248
Troupenas, publisher, 129
Troyanos, Tatiana, 329
Tulsa, 77
Il Turco in Italia (*The Turk in Italy*: Rossini), 20, 40–3, 50, 63, 65, 73; Overture, 42
Turin, 24, 35, 48, 156, 195, 203, 227, 271, 287; RAI auditorium, 314
Turina, Giuditta, 319, 337, 342, 348

Ugo, Conte di Parigi (Donizetti), 205–8, 209–10, 214, 215, 217, 219; Overture, 207
Ugo, Re d'Italia (Rossini), 116
Unger, Caroline, 170, 218, 245, 262, 319
Upstage and Downstage (Donizetti), 173; *see also Le Convenienze ed inconvenienze teatrali*

Vaccai, Nicola, *Bianca di Messina*, 313; *Giulietta e Romeo*, 328, 329, 331
Vaccani, Domenico, 12
Vaccari, Antonio, 256
Vaëz, Gustave, 276, 277, 281, 282
Valentini, Filippo, 216
Valesi, Luigia, 85
Valle, Cesare della, Duke of Ventignano, 100, 101; *Anna Erizo*, 101; *Maometto II*, 123
Valle d'Itria Festival, 80, 141, 260, 295
Varesi, Felice, 286

Vasoli, Pietro, 21, 40
Vasselli, Antonio, 214, 259, 262
Vasselli, Virginia (later Sra Donizetti), 170, 180, 188, 194, 216, 248, 259
Velluti, Giovanni Battista (castrato), 38. 39
Venice, 7, 16, 21, 31, 32, 35, 38, 47, 51, 64, 77, 86, 94, 116, 123, 156, 166, 172, 184, 190, 192, 203, 228, 249, 253, 260, 295, 312, 320, 332, 349; Teatro Apollo, 256, 257; Teatro La Fenice, 9, 26, 27, 29, 30, 43, 93, 102, 108, 109, 111, 112, 123, 214, 245, 246, 248, 257, 262–3, 283, 328, 342, 343, 344, 345; Teatro San Benedetto, 34, 92, 93, 144; Teatro San Luca, 142, 143; Teatro San Moise, 9, 14, 18, 19, 21, 23–4, 26, 27–8; Teatro San Samuele, 143, 144
Venier, Marco, 147, 153
Verdi, Giuseppe, 1, 20, 31, 43, 49, 53, 54, 59, 60–1, 78, 134, 142, 193, 225–6, 235, 241, 242, 254, 266, 289, 339, 341; Aida, 267; Alzira, 241; Un Ballo in maschera, 261; La Battaglia di Legnano, 241; Don Carlos, 298; La Forza del destino, 275, 278; Luisa Miller, 241, 353; Macbeth, 114; marriage to Giuseppina Strepponi, 257, 280; Nabucco, 127, 286, 294, 296, 353; Oberto, 353; Otello, 64, 67, 68, 317; Rigoletto, 67, 226, 261, 346; La Traviata, 258; Il Trovatore, 114, 193, 233, 241, 346; Les Vêpres Siciliennes, 272
Verger, Giovanni Battista, 143, 166, 177
verismo (realismo), 1, 195
Verni, Andrea, 69, 70, 142
Vernoy de Saint-Georges, Jules-Henri, 273, 290, 294, 303, 304, 305
Verona, 144; international congress in (1822), 112
Il Viaggio a Reims (The Journey to Rheims: Rossini), 115–21, 122, 123, 128, 129, 130, 131; Grand pezzo concertato a quattordici voci, 120–1, 130; Overture, 118–19
Il Viaggio a Vienna (Rossini), 117
Vial, Antonietta, 245
Vicenza, 38, 41
Vienna, 8, 14, 16, 21, 24, 39, 41, 48, 51, 57, 64, 77, 88, 94, 99, 102, 105, 108, 111–12, 117, 142, 145, 156, 170, 175, 178, 203, 216, 218, 249, 266, 283, 291, 294, 297, 298, 300, 301, 316, 320, 349; Kärntnertor Theater, 64, 108, 286, 288, 293, 295; Rossini Festival, 108, 111–12; Theater an der Wien, 64; Wiener Kammeroper, 51, 62, 282
Villani, Giuseppe, 164
Vineyard Opera Shop, New York, 199

Visconti, Duke Carlo, 198, 224
Visconti, Luchino, 271, 334
Viva la Mamma, (Donizetti), 173; see also Le Convenienze ed inconvenienze teatrali
Vitarelli, Zenobio, 53, 56, 69
Vivaldi, Antonio, 141
Voltaire, 105; Mahomet, ou Le Fanatisme, 101; Sémiramis, 112; Tancrède, 30; Zaïre, 323–4

Wagner, Richard, 1, 111, 134, 277, 341; Der fliegende Holländer, 119; Die Meistersinger, 32; Rheingold, 119
Warot, 281
Warsaw, 14, 132; Chamber Opera, 141
Wartel, Pierre-François, 268
Washington DC, 216
Weber, Carl Maria von, Der Frieschütz, 79, 109, 111
Weimar, 16, 131
Weinstock, Herbert, 47
Wellington, Duke of, 112
Welsh National Opera, 277
Wexford Festival (Theatre Royal), 13, 14, 64, 156, 182, 253, 287, 316, 349
Wiklund, Anders, 198
Williams, Bradley, 309
Williams, La Verne, 165
Winter, Berardo Calvari, 160, 170, 174, 185, 190, 192
Winter, Peter, 323

Xenophon, Cyropedia, 16

Zaira (Bellini), 315, 322–7, 330, 331, 346
Zamboni, Luigi, 52, 53
Zampieri, Mara, 246, 316
Zanardini, Angelo, 270
Zancla, Paolo, 142
Zavadini, Guido, Donizetti, 161–2
Zeani, Virginia, 64, 108
Zelmira (Rossini), 107–10, 111, 122, 148
Zerbini, Carolina, 21
Zilioli, Domenico, 158
La Zingara (The Gypsy Maiden: Donizetti), 147–8, 149, 154
Zingarelli, Nicola, 310; Giulietta e Romeo, 329
Zora (Rossini), 126; see also Moise et Pharaon
Zoraida di Granata (Donizetti), 145–7, 155, 161
Zucchelli, Carlo, 116
Zweig, Stefan, 291